Surveyor III visited by Apollo 12 Astronaut Charles "Pete" Conrad in 1969.

Call Me Pat

Dedicated to
Mrs. L. A. (Muriel) Hyland
and Ginger Hyland.

Call Me Pat

The Autobiography of the Man Howard Hughes Chose to Lead Hughes Aircraft

by L. A. "Pat" Hyland
edited by W. A. Schoneberger

The Donning Company/Publishers
184 Business Park Drive, Suite 106
Virginia Beach, VA 23462

Steve Mull, General Manager
Tony Lillis, In-house Editor
Eliza Midgett, Designer
Barbara Bolton, Project Director

Library of Congress Cataloging in Publication Data:
Hyland, L. A., 1897–
Call me Pat : the autobiography of the man Howard Hughes chose to lead Hughes Aircraft / by L. A. (Pat) Hyland.
p. cm.
Includes index.
ISBN 0-89865-871-3 ($19.95. — ISBN 0-89865-873-X (pbk.) : $12.95
1. Hyland, L. A., 1897– . 2. Businessmen—United States—Biography. 3. Executives—United States—Biography. 4. Hughes Aircraft Company—History. 5. Bendix Corporations—History.
LD3500.R46 1993 93-29631
378.778'72—dc20 CIP
Printed in the United States of America

Contents

Foreword

Pat Hyland was a remarkable individual. He was one of the finest advisors I had when I was intimately involved with the General Motors purchase and operation of Hughes Aircraft. Because of his long heritage in corporate America, including his years with both Hughes and Bendix, Pat Hyland had a unique perspective on business. This enabled him to achieve keen insight into the automotive business, despite the fact his years of experience were primarily in aviation and aerospace.

I had the great pleasure of knowing Pat Hyland for many years. However, I *really* came to know him during and after the General Motors purchase of Hughes Aircraft from the Howard Hughes Medical Institute. I came to recognize Pat's keen insight into dealing with people, his steadying influence on the sometimes complicated GM and Hughes relationship and his forward-looking perception of the future. All this was the case despite the fact that Pat Hyland was in his eighties. He was truly an amazing man!

Readers of this book will be treated to Pat's particular view of the business world and his personal insight into what we need to do to make it better. This from a man who came to this country from Canada in the early 1900s, and had the opportunity to serve in the United States Army, United States Navy, and the Naval Research Laboratory. He was an entrepreneur, starting his own company, and subsequently was a manager with Bendix and Hughes Aircraft. Readers of *Call Me Pat* have the opportunity to live with Pat during the uniquely American odyssey—from the beginnings of the industrial revolution right up to the space age.

Moreover, Pat Hyland played a key role in American advances in high technology through his service on a host of government committees and advisory boards, ranging from the CIA to the Guided

Missile Committee that effectively set the post-World War II course for this country in the missile age. A true patriot, Pat's duties are chronicled in Chapter 11—his "other" jobs.

Pat Hyland had what is perhaps an unparalleled opportunity to observe, work with and manage a wide range of disciplines. His perception and insight into the management of this broad spectrum of responsibilities provides an advanced management course for everyone. We can all learn from Pat Hyland; his teachings will live for generations to come.

Donald J. Atwood
Retired Vice Chairman of General Motors
Retired President of GM/Hughes Electronics
Former Deputy Secretary of Defense

Acknowledgments

The enthusiastic response of every person contacted regarding Pat Hyland's autobiography is reflective of the high esteem in which he was held at Hughes, at Bendix and in the aviation/aerospace industry as well as the community. Particular thanks are due Ken Richardson, Malcolm Currie, Ted Westerman, Ray Silvius, Lou Gregg and Rob Hall for getting the project underway at Hughes and for shepherding it from its conception through publication. And, of course, to Michael C. Armstrong, current chairman of Hughes Aircraft for continuation of the book project. In addition, thanks to Allen Puckett, Harold Rosen, Bob Roney, Leo Stoolman, Tom Carvey, and former Hyland secretaries, Eva Meyers and Carol Harris, for their helpful recollections and answers to questions. And, to Pat Bouley for numerous acts of assistance; to Yoko Takai for supplying copies of Hughes Aircraft photos, old and new; and to Barbara Hugh, not only for her excellent *Hughesnews* and personal files, but also for her wonderful memory and unfailing willingness to help.

Mary C. Crawford transcribed the nearly 900 pages of Pat Hyland's recollections at the Ranch. Michael Whalen provided superior legal counsel to the Hyland family. And, of course, thanks to Don Atwood for his counsel and for providing the Foreword to this book.

Thanks also to former Bendix employees Pete Leatherwood, Cramer Bacque and Bill Hilliard who supplied valuable Bendix material and information. And thanks to Jack Real for his always invaluable insight and counsel as well as to Dr. Chaffin, both of whose close associations with Howard Hughes are documented in the book. In addition, thanks to Bill Winberg, former historian for the *Queen Mary* and *Spruce Goose*, for making available the Hughes photo file and, of course, to Vern Olson, senior vice president of Summa Corporation, for permission to use the Hughes photos.

Finally, thanks to Pat Schoneberger, consummate reader, for pouring over several "final" edited versions of the manuscript, checking for readability, continuity and consistency.

Introduction

Confronted by a staggering 875+ pages of personal recollections representing nearly 90 years of an exciting, diversified life, we recognized that, in addition to his achievements over a lifetime, Pat Hyland had a remarkable memory and ability to recall. After going over the pages, we flippantly observed: "Pat Hyland began his career in the artillery in World War I and remembered and recorded every shot fired by his unit!"

Pat Hyland's personal recollections provide an unparalleled perspective on World War I, on the peacetime Navy following the Great War, on the Naval Research Laboratory, on entrepreneurmanship, on Bendix, on the U.S. government, on Hughes Aircraft and of interest to many readers, on the mysterious Howard Hughes. As a top level participant in at least two corporations and "the man Howard Hughes chose to lead Hughes Aircraft," Pat Hyland provides insights no one else could.

These are Pat Hyland's views. A truism of every history or biography we've ever written is that each could be subtitled, "That's not the way I remember it." We perceive events past through our own eyes. Nothing wrong with that. But, the recollector may have put his own "spin" on an anecdote because that's the way he or she remembers it.

We put the recollections into logical sequence and carefully edited to eliminate much of the myriad of detail Mr. Hyland had documented. We adhered to Mr. Hyland's words/thoughts, but attempted to assure accuracy and readability. Knowledge of the aviation/aerospace industry (Editor's Notes, subheads, and chapter titles are essentially mine) has helped produce what we hope is a readable chronicle of the life of this remarkable man.

William A. Schoneberger
Malibu, California
1 August 1993

Prologue

Born in 1897 on my grandfather's farm in Nova Scotia, Canada, I was brought to America just before the restrictive immigration laws of 1900. That year marked not only the beginning of a new century, but also of a new era. Hence, my early years were spent in that great transition from agriculture to industry. The world was transformed from one era that had witnessed little change for centuries to another in which entire nations—and their people—would contribute to an evolution of technical knowledge that moved even faster than society could absorb it.

The North or South Poles had yet to be discovered. The air was still the domain of the birds. Nevertheless, a pioneering spirit was alive—and the air was already yielding to radio waves and flying machines.

The time between my early years and the present day (as I write this) has been more than ninety years. Those years have been kind to me. Of course, there have been "shadows in the valleys and sunshine on the hills."

I have been in and on the ocean, in and on the earth, and miles into space. I have even had a minor part in space exploration.

This, however, is not a "rag-to-riches" story. Instead, it is a recital of the succeeding stages through which I have passed—that ultimately led to a variety of frontiers.

The rate of progression was slow. It took two complete business lifetimes for me to go from nadir to zenith.

The first lifetime, ending in 1954, was spent in the acquisition of general technological and management knowledge. It equipped me for the challenge presented when the fabulous Howard Hughes offered me the leadership of the troubled Hughes Aircraft Company.

Although at that time Hughes Aircraft was acknowledged to be a great national technical resource, it had suffered a series of traumatic management changes that had brought the company to the edge of insolvency and dissipated top level personnel.

The subsequent transformation of Hughes Aircraft to financial stability, a place near the top of the *Fortune 500,* administrative order, continuing technical superiority, and a quarter century of accelerating growth occupied my second lifetime.

Looking back, I cannot recall making a long-time master plan for my life. Genetics from my forebears gave me the mind, physique and will. By training, example and caring, my parents instilled in me curiosity, frugality, loyalty and appreciation of the Ten Commandments.

This basic foundation was augmented by the strict secondary education of the day, Army and Navy discipline, "moonlighting," corporate participation, curiosity, and government advisory exposure. All these combined to provide the essential structure and principles of my life.

Chronicling my two lifetimes, I have carefully mapped and documented throughout this book certain principles, conclusions and actions that may be of help to future explorers.

(Editor's Note: Pat Hyland was given the nickname "Pat" when he joined the Navy. It seems at least one prior USN notable was named Hyland—and he was called "Pat" by everyone who knew him. So, when young Hyland went into the Navy in the early 1920s, he was automatically given the moniker, "Pat." Never particularly caring for Lawrence, Hyland much preferred Pat. He was known by that name until his death at age 92.)

Chapter I
Establishing a Foundation

I received an excellent New England high school education in Melrose, Massachusetts. Basics were three foreign languages (Latin, French, German), English, algebra, plane and solid geometry, plus two years each of physics and chemistry. We were also exposed to music, woodwork, art, civics, history and geography.

My extracurricular interests included debating, men's quartet, and one interest that would mean much in the future, steam engines. As a hobby, the school's maintenance supervisor collected working models of steam engines. Fortunately, he persuaded the principal to approve a non-credit class in steam engineering.

I enrolled. Most important, in addition to my classroom instruction, the chief engineer allowed me to work on the boilers and engines that powered the heating and ventilation for the school.

For two years in high school, I climbed out of bed at 4:00 a.m., walked to school, and helped the fireman stoke the fires in the furnaces, bring up the steam and start the engines that powered the blowers. Occasionally, when the fireman drank too much, I operated the school's whole heating system until the chief engineer arrived.

Concurrent with my schooling, I gained practical experience in housing renovation. When I was in fifth grade my family purchased an old house on a quarter of an acre in Melrose. From then on through my high school years, we worked at restoring that house.

My father had acquired a small construction company and worked an eight hour day plus two hours traveling time. This left him three hours a day to work on the house.

I helped my father do the job from top to bottom. It was valuable experience in complete rehabilitation of an old house. Unfortunately, the restoration was interrupted when my father became ill. Less than two years later we lost our house when the mortgage was foreclosed. We moved into a partitioned-off section of another, inferior house. My mother took over the office work at the construction company and I became "chief cook and housekeeper."

At the time, I was too young to recognize the full extent of our family disaster. I continued in school, our food was adequate, and because of the family's frugal life-style, there were few changes.

My father's health gradually improved. His small construction business began to flourish because of a Boston building boom. He managed to make the delinquent payments on our former house (which had not been sold). We moved back into our restoration home.

By the time the restoration was completed, my handyman status was established in foundations, plumbing, heating, carpentry, roofing, painting, pruning, cooking and household work. I'm proud to say I can still do any of them.

Early Telegraphy

About 1909, a series of articles on wireless telegraphy appeared in the *Boston Post.* I devoured every word.

A week later, I was walking on my way to a piano lesson when I heard strange sounds somehow related to a wire structure on the roof of a neighborhood house. The noise seemed eerie and high-pitched. Out of curiosity, I knocked at the front door. I asked the young man who opened it about the strange noise.

Inviting me in, he proudly showed me an assembly made up of an old Ford spark coil, some copper wires wound on a varnished paper cylinder and a condenser made up of a stack of old glass photographic plates with tinfoil sheets between them. He called it a transmitter.

He had another arrangement with a copper coil wound on an Edison phonograph cylinder, a tiny condenser made of tinfoil inserted between sheets of paper impregnated with candle wax, a galena crystal detector and a pair of headphones. This was his receiver.

The young man explained that in another section of Melrose there was a counterpart. He demonstrated his equipment's ability by using a telegraph key to actuate the transmitter. He then transferred part of the key mechanism to the receiver. From it, I was able to hear regular sounds. He called it Morse code.

That day in 1909 was, for me, the beginning. Over more than 75 years, I have always had some association with radio in one form or another.

Enter the Aeroplane

The following year, 1910, an announcement appeared in the *Boston Post* about an aircraft demonstration at the old racetrack near the adjacent town of Saugus. Several types of aeroplanes were to be flown, plus motorcycle and airplane races around the Saugus Fairground track. Also scheduled was a balloon ascension with a lady acrobat. A plane carrying the first air mail was to take off and land near a Boston post office. It was almost too much for a single day.

The article said admission was 50 cents, a fee beyond my meager means. But I figured no fence was high enough to obscure the sight of a flying aeroplane.

On a hot August day, I trudged the eight miles to the Saugus racetrack. Fortunately, a hill was adjacent to one side of the track. Happily I climbed it for a privileged grandstand seat to watch the show.

First, the lady acrobat performed on a trapeze attached to a tethered balloon a couple of hundred feet above the Fairground. The crowd was amazed at her daring.

Next came aeroplane and motorcycle races. The motorcycle always won because it could make turns around the track more readily than an aeroplane.

Late in the afternoon, I saw a few people entering the Fairground beneath a fence. I followed so I could get a closer look at the aeroplanes and pilots.

For a flight, the pilot was perched precariously on a seat just forward of and between the wings of the plane. They wore riding pants, shiny boots with leather leggings, tight jackets, long scarves wound around their necks, helmets and goggles. It was an impressive and romantic uniform to a boy of 13.

However, I discovered the aeroplane engines were difficult to start and the process dangerous. The propellers had to be hand-turned while the pilot manipulated the ignition switch. After a long warmup, the aeroplanes trundled onto the racetrack being used as an airstrip. One of my greatest thrills that day was seeing the legendary Lincoln Beechy take off to do his acrobatic flying.

That was the beginning of my interest in aviation. To this day, I avidly read all accounts of aviation deering-do.

Early Goals

Although they obviously changed with age, I had a series of conscious and subconscious personal goals, beginning when I was about 11. My first goal, during the fifth grade, was to organize and lead a track team of three other boys and myself. We were quite successful on the Melrose grade school circuit.

My first job was at the Melrose YMCA bowling alley, working as a pinsetter for two cents per game. I was then hired by a landscape gardener, who had two other boys working for him. One mowed lawns, the other raked; I was assigned the somewhat grubbier tasks of edging, sweeping and loading. I clearly recall setting myself a goal. I was determined to replace the kid with the lawn mower. Eventually, I did.

During my high school years, I worked at various odd jobs. I delivered the local newspaper on Fridays and the Boston paper on Sunday. For almost a year, a couple of afternoons a week, I also taught piano for 50 cents a lesson.

No doubt my goals in those days were encouraged by the Horatio Alger stories I enjoyed reading. "Do or Die!," "Sink or Swim!," and "Survive or Perish!" were all books that exerted a powerful influence on my young mind.

My first real career goal crystallized at the beginning of my junior year in high school. I decided to take college preparatory courses during my last two years. Before making that decision, however, I sought the advice of two maternal uncles, one an eminent physician in Brooklyn, New York.

The other uncle was an MIT graduate who had a doctorate in

chemistry, with high distinction, from the University of Heidelberg, Germany. The latter, upon his return to the U.S. some years before, had been appointed Assistant Director—under the controversial Dr. Harvey Wylie—of the Pure Food and Drug Laboratory of the U.S. Department of Agriculture in Washington, D.C. Within our family, this uncle was highly regarded for his learning, his important position in the government and for his wealth. I recall hearing him say that, following his appointment, he had averaged a 10 percent increase in salary each year over a period of 20 years. I thought that was noteworthy.

About this same time, wireless had become RADIO. My interest had increased. An important part of each receiver was its detector, and several varieties of radio were using the principles of both electricity and chemistry. This introduced me to a whole new technology.

My "chemistry" uncle advised me to consider a college education along technical lines. In my senior year of high school, I arranged interviews with professors of chemistry and electricity at two universities. Unfortunately, during our discussions, they showed no enthusiasm for either my scholarship or my ambitions. By the time the final interview ended, I felt so defeated that I gave up considering technical schools.

I also belonged to the high school debating society and was a member of the championship team in the suburban school debating league for smaller cities around Boston. In my senior year we won another league championship and a medal. I was so pleased with myself I decided to become a lawyer.

A family friend recommended that I enroll in the Boston University Law School. I was enthusiastically greeted by the registrar and embarked on a legal career. I soon discovered, however, that the subject of torts made little sense to me, contracts were a bore, and only the law of agency held my interest. It seemed the most logical of all the courses, so I felt no need to ponder much on the subject. I soon learned differently. When my final exams were graded, I had passed torts and contracts, but my logical analyses on agency resulted in a fat zero. From this I learned that agency was a matter of rule, precedents and the common law, as well as statutes. Logic and horse sense were secondary. Disgusted with the result of my first year's effort, I left college and never returned.

I did take with me, however, one Latin phrase etched over the portico of the law school, *"Ignoratia legus neminum excusa"* ("Ignorance of the law excuses no one"). I now make no important decisions without legal consultation.

Goals play a major role in the lives of most people. They may be subconscious and may not even be perceived by their owner; but goals are there, nonetheless. Alternatively, they may be a matter of conscious thought and decision. The usefulness of goals depends on the experience of the person setting them. Those set early in life may be only daydreams and of little value. However, goals set later in life, founded on experience and realistic perception of the possible and the practical, can serve well in guiding one to a course of action that reaps achievement, contribution and some degree of satisfaction.

On My Own

In the spring of 1915 I briefly worked for my father, but was eager to get out in the world on my own. I found a job paying $12.00 per week as a general handyman at the American Fireproofing Company.

In the autumn, as construction work slowed down, I worked briefly for the Boston and Maine Railroad as a mail clerk in the freight claims office. Although the pay was $5.35 per week, less than half the rate I had received before, the job offered a valuable compensation that more than made up the difference: I was given a railroad pass that allowed me to travel anywhere on the line during my time off. I explored the size, industry, agriculture and population of New England.

When winter set in, I went to work for the Barrett Company in Everett, Massachusetts, making tar paper and roofing materials. That lasted through the winter, but as summer approached, I decided to test my abilities by moving to New York City. In those days, as now, it was the place where many young people sought adventure.

The Barrett Company had a plant in Weehawken, New Jersey. I persuaded the Everett plant manager to give me a letter to the Weehawken plant manager. I landed a job there as a general helper or roustabout. I painted big storage tanks, made flashing for roofing out of tar products and asbestos, made demonstration roofs, and cleaned gutters and the areas around the tar stills when they boiled over. Cleaning sewers and drain pipes in winter is a miserable outdoor job. So, when I found this task was scheduled for me just as winter was setting in, I reluctantly quit and chanced finding another job across the Hudson River in New York City.

Within three days, I was hired at a plumbing supply house. The job was no world beater, however. It paid $4.00 per day and was temporary. I was to assist two men counting inventory stored in a basement. I soon learned that not only was I expected to be a good counter, but also to cheerfully fetch a tin pail full of beer twice a day to keep the two men happy. The job lasted two weeks.

An employment agency found a better one as a shipping clerk with a hotel supply house. I handled petty cash, helped pack boxes and on occasion went with a team to the New York docks to hunt shipments destined for us from various steamship companies. I found this part of the work fascinating.

On the docks the confusion of loading and unloading horse-drawn drays was exceeded only by the language of sailors of all nationalities. I quickly learned that a 25 or 50 cent coin placed correctly achieved wonders in locating a shipment.

Unexpectedly, one day at work my steam engineering experience proved useful. The steam engineers union, the organization of people who operated the boiler plants that heated the city buildings had gone on strike. Our chief shipping clerk mentioned that the owner wanted to close down the business during the strike. But, he was afraid his building would freeze up.

An idea popped into my head. I checked the boiler room and found a single, large boiler with a firebox similar to one I had worked with at Melrose High School. I told the chief shipping clerk I could keep the boiler working during the strike. He literally ran upstairs to get the big boss; the two of them came down beaming. I operated the boiler during the whole two weeks of the strike. I became the fair-haired boy around the company.

During this period, the war in Europe took a bad turn. In April 1917, the United States declared war against Germany and Austria-

Hungary. There was no doubt or hesitation in my mind. I knew I would enlist. The final impetus came when I attended a church meeting where the fabled Sir Harry Lauder and his Scottish band gave a patriotic theme performance to stimulate recruiting.

I enlisted in the Army and chose the Field Artillery as my desired branch. That choice proved fortunate in the end—but painful in the beginning.

Over There

Being tall and skinny, I had few attributes sought after in a combat soldier. I soon recognized I was just another warm body in the Army. Following basic recruit training, I was assigned to Battery A, Twelfth Regiment Field Artillery, Second Division.

In those days artillery depended on horses and horses needed skilled riders.

We were taught to ride the hard way. After being led to horses without saddles, we were instructed to mount by leaping onto the back of the horse. Along with several others, I jumped with such momentum that it hurled me clear over the horse—and flat onto the ground.

When we were finally all mounted with our feet hanging down and our hands gripping the reins, we trotted our horses around the field, bumping up and down. It wasn't long before anguish set in.

Glancing at the other men, I realized they, too, were hurting. But the drill master kept us bumping at a trot for what seemed like hours. I moved back and forth, trying to ease the pain. Others did the same. However, during that painful riding lesson, I learned something. As I watched the ludicrous contortions of others, I started to laugh. Somehow laughter made the suffering more tolerable. All through life I have used that technique during times of stress.

That night none of us sat down to eat. The following days were purgatory indeed, but somehow we survived and became skilled riders in a short time.

A few weeks later I learned the Field Artillery was the only branch of the Army that conducted its own communication. The rest of the Army used the Signal Corps. Furthermore, I heard our company commander was seeking a man to handle and maintain the telegraph and telephone communication equipment. I rushed to the first sergeant and applied for the job.

The first sergeant had always looked upon me with jaundiced eyes. But when he learned I knew something about communications, with a sigh of relief he assigned me the job.

Although I didn't realize it at the time, that assignment began my lifelong career in radio and aviation technology. It was also a fine example of Samuel Johnson's age-old maxim: "Chance favors the prepared mind".

The Second Division was one of the first from the USA to be sent to France. There, the American Expeditionary Force commander sent our unit to a French artillery training school in eastern France near the Swiss border. Our special communication detail was introduced to radio, both in aircraft spotting for artillery and for general communication within the Army.

At that time, one function of a radioman was as intermediary between airplane pilots and ground gunners. Cloth panels were used to communicate with the aviator. The aviator used radio to communicate with the ground. This access to pilots and their aircraft kept alive in me the spark of aviation interest generated years before at the Saugus Fairground.

The American Army had neither adequate telephone nor telegraph equipment. But, in the French artillery, radio played an important part in daily operations. Four times a day, there was a radio report of wind direction and velocity at ground level—and aloft at points along the front. These reports were used for artillery aiming, aircraft spotting, and for transmission of emergency instructions when wire lines were down. When a French artillery unit took up a position in the field, the radio section set up its antennas at the same time as the guns were being positioned.

All of this was new to the American Army in 1917.

It was at the French Army radio training unit that I first heard: "Le Situation Militaire sur le Front Francaise" ("The Military Situation on the French Front") during a news program prepared by the French Central Command. Every day at 11:00 a.m. a status report on Allied troops in various sectors was transmitted from the Eiffel Tower in Paris. The signal was received on equipment made by French technicians who were our instructors. With two years of high school French, I could interpret what was being said.

Shortly thereafter our regiment was transferred to an active front. We were introduced to trench warfare. Our guns were heavily camouflaged beneath trees. When they were not in service, gun crews and the rest of us in supporting sections lived underground in trenches and dugouts. The weather was awful—cold, rainy, blowing.

We radiomen had little work. Because we had no rain clothes, we stayed underground most of the time. Rumors were rampant. All bad. So, we really knew nothing about the real progress of the war.

Recalling the French equipment used to receive the 11a.m. Eiffel tower newscast, I fashioned a receiver set. It was a modified Campbell soup box, insulated telegraph wires scrounged from a trash dump, candle wax, cigarette paper, cigarette tinfoil, a detector and headphones from a real air-to-ground receiver.

The first morning after the set's completion, I tuned in at five minutes to 11. When no signal came, I kept adjusting. Faintly, I heard signals. Before long they came in strong.

My ability to receive the coded signals was limited. But my buddy, Baldy Beardsley, an experienced telegraph operator, was good at Morris code. Though he knew no French, Baldy agreed to help. Because he wasn't sure he could remember enough of what he decoded to make sense, he decided to write down each letter.

By the next day, we had rustled up paper and a pencil. At eleven o'clock we were ready. The receiver gave us a clear signal and Baldy copied down the letters. I translated the French. The first words were "Le Situation Militaire sur le Front Francaise." The report stated the French front was holding and the American First Division was advancing.

To say Baldy and I were exuberant was a vast understatement. We delivered the message to the battery commander, explaining how we'd done it. Pleased, he shook our hands. Immediately Baldy's and my status improved.

This was important to us. First of all, I was tall; Baldy was short.

We were both underweight; neither of us wore our uniforms with a soldierly manner. On the other hand, the gun crews were the cream of the crop; big, strong, well-muscled, intelligent and responsible. Communicators were looked on only as appendages to assist the military function, as a stage crew assists the actors. Baldy and I were at the bottom of the pecking order.

Our radio set raised us to the top. No other unit in the entire regiment had the capability to receive information from the outside world. Thereafter, Baldy and I were treated with respect and admiration. I felt immense satisfaction that I was now treated as one of the boys.

In retrospect, my chances of making a successful receiving set from such a conglomeration of materials had been slim indeed. Furthermore, the odds of making one sensitive enough to receive the frequency sent out by the Eiffel Tower were even more minuscule. I am now convinced that my effort was helped by the Lord, whom I call the Man Upstairs. Before and since, He has guided me through impossible situations. This was not the result of prayer nor even of belief, because a half-century would elapse before I finally recognized that the Man Upstairs was on my side.

The Second Division was foremost in ground gained, munitions and men captured, and casualties suffered. From the time we left training camp until the war was over, we were almost continually engaged in battle during bitter winters and hot summers.

Few of us survived.

On the last day before the end of the war, I was forced to drop from the ranks. I suffered from terrible dysentery caused by drinking water out of wheel ruts. I trudged towards a field hospital, but fainted en route. I was revived by a wounded soldier. Later, I rejoined my regiment in the Army of Occupation and spent another seven productive months in further training.

In that battalion, because of my high school languages, I was the only soldier who spoke some German and French. When the battalion moved, I was assigned to go ahead of the troops and choose billets for battalion personnel.

By law, every German household had to provide at least one bed for the occupation troops. No German male could have a bed if an occupation soldier needed it. But at one house, I found a young couple about to be married. The family requested that I allow the young Germans to enjoy the privilege of a bed for their wedding night. I obliged.

In the months before my discharge, I recognized several things: Radio would be part of my career; innovation, persistence and fortitude were necessary to progress; superiors and strangers were not ogres, but human beings; bits of information collected from books, experience, conversation, and sustained observation are valuable and should be stored away in one's memory against the time when they prove useful. They always do.

From then on I went forward with vigor and confidence. I received letters of commendation for other work. I was discharged in 1919 as a sergeant of artillery.

Many who have served in the military look upon those years as wasted. But to me they were vital. The Army was my second measured step in the advancement of my career. My Army experience set me on the correct course and taught me the importance of discipline, loyalty and using one's faculties to their fullest. I've followed these practices throughout life.

Back to Civilian Life

Following my discharge, I was hired as a machine operator by the New Departure Manufacturing Company, General Motors ball bearing manufacturing factory in Bristol, Connecticut. At first I found the job interesting, though repetitive. It involved learning a few skills, such as applying the right pressure on the grinding wheel, estimating time of grinding, working out the rhythm of the operation, increasing speed, working out belt tensions, and other tricks of the trade.

The rate for piece work was set at a premium over straight time. A good machinist could complete his day's allotment by the end of six and a half hours and then spend the rest of his eight-hour work day cleaning his machine, making frequent trips to the restroom, smoking, and all sorts of time-consuming motions. This procedure was common to all the old hands in the factory.

Along with the majority of other new workers, mostly World War I veterans, I chose to work the full eight hours in order to turn out more piece work and make more money. This practice irritated the older workers. Their counsel to us rookies to play the game according to their rules became more and more insistent. The shop foreman, himself an old timer, knew what was going on and added disciplinary measures to bring newer employees into line. Thus as the environment became increasingly unfriendly and my work monotonous, the challenge of my job diminished.

My living conditions weren't much better. Bristol was a small town and the big General Motors factory required hundreds of employees for which no adequate accommodations were available. I lived in a room that was mine for only 12 hours a day—seven o'clock in the evening to seven o'clock in the morning. A night shift man had the other 12 hours. I ate breakfast and dinner at a boarding house in competition with 11 other men, some of whom had long arms. I bought my lunch from a wagon parked outside the plant's gate. Under these circumstances, I accumulated a burden of aggravation and frustration.

On what turned out to be my final morning at work, I had been assigned a difficult job by the foreman. Grumbling, I was making the necessary machine adjustments to accommodate an unusually large bearing when someone opened a window. May breezes blew in; the factory oil fumes were overcome by the freshness of spring. I saw a big sign out the window. It read: "JOIN THE NAVY AND SEE THE WORLD." I shut down my machine and thumbed my nose at the foreman. We walked toward each other.

"I want my pay," I said.

"You'll get it," he replied. "You're fired."

This incident represented one of my most important steps leading towards a career centered on radio, but ultimately involving operations, engineering and management.

After being fired, I paid my room rent, put on my one decent set of clothes, and headed for the Navy recruiting station at Hartford, Connecticut. I presented my Army honorable discharge, two or three commendations and my citizenship papers to a Navy chief petty officer.

The CPO looked at them and then at me. "Would you be interested in Naval aviation?"

"I certainly would," I quickly replied.

Chapter II
The Navy Serves as Primary Training

"I can enlist you right now as an Apprentice Seaman," he explained. "That pays thirty dollars per month. But instead, I advise you to first write to the Bureau of Navigation in Washington, D.C. You should state your interest in Naval aviation and inform them that you are a citizen with an honorable discharge from the Army with commendations for radio work under active warfare conditions."

Following his advice, a few days later I wrote to the Bureau of Navigation.

The response said: "Please report to the Navy Recruiting Officer at Portland, Maine, who will enlist you. If you qualify, you will immediately be promoted to the rank of radioman first class and be transferred to the Naval Air Station, Pensacola, Florida."

I was delighted, although uneasy with the word "qualify".

Two days later I boarded the Portland train, but on the way we ran into the worst thunderstorm I had ever experienced in New England. It equalled anything I saw later in the tropics.

In Portland I walked to the Naval recruiting station. The recruiting officer was a pleasant Naval commander who greeted me formally and accepted my papers.

"I 've been expecting you," he finally said, "and now I understand why the Bureau sent me special instructions in your case. However, there is a problem. I had arranged for the chief radioman at the Portland Naval Radio Station to give you an examination over the telephone. Unfortunately, a few hours ago a thunderstorm knocked out the telephone line. My instructions were to enlist you and immediately determine if you are qualified for radioman first class before sending you to Pensacola. And in the Navy, 'immediate' means same day."

My heart sank. The last thing I wanted was to take an examination given by a chief radioman because I knew I couldn't pass a test in Morse code. An idea hit me. "Sir," I said. "I may have a solution. You can see by my papers that I have the basic military background."

He nodded.

"And in your bookcase, I noticed there is a college physics book. I'm sure I can answer any questions you choose to ask from that book. That ought to satisfy the technical requirements."

He frowned. "But what about the code examination?"

"That's easy," I replied. "Twenty words per minute is standard operational requirement. Just pick out any reading material and count out 20 words. Then place your watch on your desk and I'll tap out the words with a pencil, starting when you tell me. When I've completed the 20 words, you can see how many seconds it has taken me."

The officer thought a minute. "That sounds like a good idea." He then opened the physics book, asked me a dozen different questions, and expressed satisfaction with my answers. He placed his watch on his desk, fortunately where I could see it. He underlined 20 words, gave me a pencil and asked if I was ready.

When I replied, "Yes," he said, "Go."

I tapped away on the desk with my pencil and out of the corner of my eye I watched the second hand on his watch. When it got to 55 seconds, I said, "That's it."

"Good," he replied. "I have prepared your transportation and travel orders. Are you ready to join the Navy?"

I almost shouted, "Yes sir!"

He swore me in as an apprentice seaman, then promoted me to radioman first class. He shook my hand, wished me good luck; and I was off.

The Navy provided the foundation years of my mature life. I literally grew up in the Navy. In the Army, I was a youngster; but the Navy molded my outlook.

To Pensacola and Naval Aviation

After a succession of coaches, Pullman sleeping cars, dining cars, overnight hotels and even Jim Crow cars, I happily arrived in Pensacola about two and a half days later. During the mile walk from the railroad station to the streetcar terminal, I had my first taste of August weather in Florida. Hot and humid.

While I waited for the streetcar, a sailor came along and stood beside me. Soon another joined us. They exchanged greetings and each asked the other what he was doing in that part of the world. One said, "I'm at the Air Station and I'm heavier than air." The other sailor replied, "I'm also at the Air Station and I'm lighter than air."

They both looked normal to me. But, I soon figured out what they meant. One of them was in an aeroplane squadron, the other in a balloon and dirigible squadron. I was entering a new world.

At the main gate I was directed by a Marine to report to the Officer of the Day. After checking my papers, a sailor in the OOD's office led me to the quarantine building, where I stayed for the next two weeks.

The radio laboratory was just across from the quarantine building. The lab's function was to maintain radio equipment for aircraft, both heavier and lighter than air; to operate the Naval Air Station radio receiver and transmitter; and to conduct the radio school for pilots in training. I learned the radio officer in charge of all communication activities at the station was the famed Lieutenant Herbert Rodd, who had operated the radio equipment aboard the flying boat NC4, the first aircraft to fly across the Atlantic ocean. I was told he was a fine man, a good pilot, a nationally known radio authority and a dedicated Naval officer.

It seemed to me my course of action would be to present my Army record with its commendations to Lt. Rodd, state the unusual circumstances of my Naval enlistment, and assert that I would do my best to qualify if he gave me reasonable time to do so.

To the Radio Laboratory

Following my quarantine period I reported to the radio laboratory and to Lt. Rodd. I told him my story, emphasizing that my Army commendations were for upgrading obsolete French radio equipment by combining it with some captured German material, thus providing the regiment with workable communications from aircraft and on two occasions permitting interception of valuable German signals in tactical operations. I also stated that due to insufficient practice, my weakness was in code.

When I finished, Lt. Rodd shook his head in disbelief. "I'll be damned." After pausing to think for a moment, he added, "I should have you court-martialed and thrown out of the Navy. But in light of the fact that we need men of your demonstrated skill, ingenuity and quick action, I'll give you three months to prepare for the examination for radioman first class. I shall conduct that examination myself and will go by the book, both as to technical knowledge and the Continental code, a variant of the Morse code. You're not to go near an aeroplane," he instructed, "nor take any liberty until the examination. However, I shall give you one break. Your assignment during this three month period will be at the land radio station as a radio operator on a standard radio watch of eight hours a day. You will have day, evening and night watches successively, with ample time for study. Whenever you feel ready, I'll give you the examination."

After reporting in at the radio station, I went to work. There was little traffic. During any spare time, I studied the code and spent hours improving my speed on a small machine for code practice. Two books in the radio station were a big help. One was *Amateur Radio Handbook,* published by the Radio Relay League, and the other a manual titled, *Radio*, published by the Bureau of Standards. They contained information I had been hungry for ever since I read those *Boston Post* articles 10 years before.

At the end of two months, Lt. Rodd gave me the examination. I passed with flying colors. He congratulated me, saying I now deserved my stripes. He confirmed my assignment to the radio laboratory at the Naval Air Station. I was a qualified radioman first class.

The Radio Lab Crew

I soon became familiar with the laboratory and its personnel. It was apparent my aspirations were not the same as theirs.

Every group of people develops a personality or character. The character of this group of about 20 people was to keep a low profile, make no waves, and get by. None had technical curiosity about radio.

Navy training standards at that time did not require any significant degree of radio understanding.

Because this crew had no incentive to understand the equipment, I think it is fair to say none of them did. This included two chief radiomen, both of whom had probably made chief in the days before shipboard radio when signaling was conducted by hoisted pennants, semaphore flags and flashing spotlights.

One knew no more than half the code. He stood a watch in the receiving room where messages came from ships at sea and were recorded on paper. This chief was a master at getting one or two letters from each word and then building a whole message around them. He got away with it for years.

I was no expert in radio technology or communication operations, but it wasn't necessary there. All that was required was an inherent curiosity. I learned enough to effectively be in charge of the radio laboratory and on occasion worked at the radio station, a part of the laboratory.

There was an array of small tools, general shop supplies and radio equipment at the lab. Many of the transmitters and receivers had been made for World War I, although not delivered until after the war ended. They were equal in performance to anything else in the country. There were also many receivers, amplifiers and directional and voice equipment that could be used in different combinations. We had no instruction books for most of these, but plenty of time. It was an amateur technician's delight but there was only one other man who appreciated it: Lt. Rodd, a willing instructor and delegator.

Lt. Rodd took me under his wing. He helped me understand technical difficulties, and I continued to study those two books from the office shelf.

Soon all the radio equipment on the various aircraft was in working order, a first for the Naval Air Station.

Weekend Flying Opportunities

While stationed at Pensacola, I probably averaged 25 weekend training flights per year to New Orleans or Panama City. I became acquainted with many flight instructors and students who became captains and admirals in World War II. These associations later turned out to be helpful, in both naval and civilian life.

Because I had radio experience, I soon became a favorite crew member. In the event of one of our not-too-infrequent difficulties, I was usually able to communicate back to the station and get help on the way.

The other emergency communication gear carried on these flying boat trips was a basket of four homing pigeons. If we were forced down and unable to communicate by radio, we attached a message to the legs of two homing pigeons. One of them invariably returned to the Station with our emergency message.

Incidentally, those birds were well treated at the Naval Air Station at Pensacola. People had more faith in them than they did in radio.

Sometimes on flights when an old plane had a full load of gas and the air was warm, the pilots had a tough time taking off. They would first taxi to reach rougher waves near the shore. Then they rocked the plane back and forth to break the vacuum under the hull. If that maneuver failed, the first thing jettisoned was the radio battery. If that failed, the radio set was next. Finally, when all else failed, they would taxi close to the beach and drop off the radioman to swim ashore. They never jettisoned the pigeons.

Earning My Spurs

A beneficial factor in my early days at Pensacola was a correspondence course in electricity provided by MIT for the Navy. It helped me immediately because my knowledge of electricity was neither uniform nor organized.

An opportunity to use this knowledge came one day when there was a breakdown in power supplied to the Naval Station by the city electric system. To handle such emergencies, the Station kept a large steam-powered electric generator. However, on this day even the backup emergency generator failed. Someone suggested there was a sailor at the radio lab who had fixed electrical equipment on aircraft. By orders of the commanding officer, I was brought to the powerhouse and the OOD explained the problem.

I was bewildered. However, feeling I ought to uphold the

reputation of the radio lab, I closely examined the machine.

Fortunately, I had studied the section in the MIT course about electric generators. I checked all the connectors and rotating parts, but everything looked OK me. Then I remembered a paragraph about the failure to initiate generations. It stated that if all circuits were in a state of complete electrical balance, some generators might not function. One suggestion was to slightly rotate the fixed frame holding the brushes of the exciter.

It was a long shot, but I decided it was worth a try. I examined the circular cage that would have to be moved slightly. With more authority than I felt, I suggested we move it around about half an inch. There was skepticism; but no one had anything else to suggest.

After the adjustment was made and the bolts and nuts put back in place, the big steam engine started right up. The rotating armature increased speed, the power picked up, and the generator functioned normally.

My reputation was made; both by the success I had in radio communications for aircraft and in solving the emergency powerhouse situation.

Making Chief; Being in the Right Place at the Right Time

I had been at the Naval Station in Pensacola about two years as a radioman first class. My chances for promotion were slim. In those early post-war years, the Navy was in dire financial straits. There was little funding for Naval aviation gasoline and even less for payroll.

For a period of almost two years, there were few promotions from first class to chief. However, it turned out I was one of them.

A lieutenant commander, a senior aide to Admiral Moffett, the first chief of the Bureau of Aeronautics, came down to the Air Station for a refresher course in flight training and handling emergency communications. This included radio code practice, which most officers despised. The Air Station turned the officer over to me for code lessons. During his first lesson, the commander, a personable and likable gentleman, made a comment about anti-aircraft fire. He felt Navy gunners were getting good.

I disagreed. I told him I didn't believe Naval gunnery tactics could hit a fast moving aeroplane at any height with the equipment they had because I had seen totally ineffective ground-to-air shooting with similar guns in World War I. I explained my experience with machine guns and 75 mm guns in trying to hit aircraft in flight.

Thereafter, for the entire 30 days the commander was at Pensacola, we debated anti-aircraft problems, present and future. That left little time for code practice.

It was an enjoyable period for us both. At the end of his time, he suggested that, having received something more valuable than the "damned code," he thought it would be nice if I would certify him as having passed. I did.

About three months later, the commanding officer of the Naval Air Station received a letter from the Bureau of Navigation. It stated that Lawrence A. Hyland, radioman first class, was to be immediately promoted to chief radioman. When he called me in, the commanding officer was looking at the letter in disbelief. It was signed by the chief of the Bureau of Navigation.

"Do you know anything about this?" he asked.

I replied, "No Sir."

Early Test Flights

During these events, the officers in charge of the radio laboratory, Lieutenants Rodd and Scott, had been succeeded by Lieutenant Fred C. Dickey. From the beginning, Lt. Dickey and I got along well because by that time I was firmly established as a chief and knew my business.

We had numerous flights together. One was in a new Consolidated training plane, regarded as a step forward in Naval air training. Lt. Dickey invited me to go along on its first test flight.

After takeoff Lt. Dickey put the new plane through its paces. Climbing, he gradually raised the nose of the aircraft until it stalled and fell off on one wing. But as soon as he put the controls into neutral, the airplane recovered nicely.

Not long after, another pilot tested the same airplane. But, after putting the plane into a spin, the pilot mistakenly gave the rudder a corrective kick, which put it into a flat spin. It spun all the way down to the ground, killing the pilot on impact.

Subsequently, several pilots were killed flying the same type of aircraft until the cause was discovered and corrected. The Consolidated aircraft proved to be a fine training machine. However, I like to think my Friend Upstairs kept Lt. Dickey from kicking the rudder and getting the plane into a flat spin.

The Radio: An Afterthought in Early Naval Aviation

During one particular massive search and rescue mission I was assigned to a plane with a self-important big boat flyer who had no respect for radiomen. He believed we were all useless and only increased the plane's load.

I had installed a radio direction finder in this aircraft; that day it was working well. I was able to pick up the station near the Mobile lighthouse. I communicated with the pilot by interphone to give him bearings. When I realized we were heading for the lighthouse, I passed on that information.

The pilot didn't believe me; we almost hit it. That still didn't convince him the radio was any good, only that he was a damn good pilot.

All day we continued to search, flying back and forth about 50 feet above the ocean. Constantly I took radio bearings. As the afternoon wore on and fuel got low, I informed the pilot that I was certain his course was incorrect. He was flying away from the Air Station, not toward it. I suggested he take a new heading.

He told me what do with the information. He didn't need my help. Shortly the plane ran out of fuel. He managed to land on the water near a beach. We released the pigeons with the message that we were on the beach somewhere south of the Naval Air Station. We remained stranded overnight.

Flight Pay Through Subterfuge

For three and a half of the four years I spent at Pensacola, I had flight orders. This meant I was qualified as a radioman for duty aboard the three classes of aircraft equipped with radio at the Naval Air Station. It also meant 50 percent additional monthly pay.

The requirements for flight qualification became more rigorous as government funds became more scarce. Each month we had to accumulate either four hours in the air or 10 landings.

The 10 landings were easy. All we had to do was make one short flight. We'd bounce five times on Pensacola Bay on the way out and five times on the way back; a total of 10 landings. As gasoline became even more scarce, the big flying boats were loaded to capacity with mechanics and pilots and flown around and around at a speed barely in excess of a stall.

That didn't help the radiomen. We hit on our own solution; there was a spare balloon basket in the laboratory intended for installation of a light radio so pilots could receive weather signals during free balloon flights. We hung a block and tackle from the rafters and hooked the balloon basket onto it. The three radiomen who had flight orders climbed into the basket and it was hauled up to the ceiling. We hung there for four hours. It was certified that we had been aloft for the necessary four hours; we got our flight pay. Everybody was happy.

The First Blind Landings

Lt. Dickey was radio officer at Pensacola 18 months.His replacement, Lt. Commander Harold Dodd, was bright, efficient and a dedicated Naval officer. More formal than Lt. Dickey, he was equally appreciative when given good performance. As with his predecessor, there were several firsts during the time I served with Commander Dodd.

One of his novel ideas came after he learned of the success of the radio compass aboard the big flying boats. He asked me if similar compass equipment installed on the beach could be equally effective. I assured him it would.

A small shed was installed a half mile north of the big boat landing ramp; power and telephone lines were supplied from underground cables. A few calibrating flights were made to demonstrate the satisfactory performance of the system.

In a meeting with two pilots, a mechanic and me, Commander Dodd described the advantageous position of Pensacola Bay, which was separated from the Gulf of Mexico by a narrow strip of sand called Santa Rosa Island. The bay was more than a mile wide and several miles long, almost exactly on a north-to-south line. The water was usually calm and there were no nearby obstructions; a fine landing area.

Then he disclosed his idea: A blind landing in the bay. His plan was to use one of the big flying boats, fly due west for about 25 miles, circle around and just as he turned east, ask for a return course bearing from the radio compass station. He would then fly a reverse course, heading one degree south of the direction given. When the direction finder observed the bearing to be due south, the plane would be informed by radio. At that point a programmed left turn would commence, having a radius of about 2,000 feet or 3/8 mile. When the direction finder indicated the aircraft had a bearing due north, another signal would be given and the stopwatch time taken.

The combination of known plane speed and elapsed time would tell if the plane was correctly positioned. If all was correct, the same curve would be continued until a point due west was reached, when another stopwatch time would be taken and a signal given. If everything was still correct, the curve would be continued until the direction finder signaled due south and the time from the stopwatch taken. If all figures were within tolerance, the plane would be informed and a power glide would be undertaken with the aircraft pointed due south. The plane would gradually lose altitude until it contacted the water of Pensacola Bay.

The pilots were enthusiastic. I agreed our end could work if we practiced a few programmed turns and preset the direction finder compensators.

Permission to proceed with the experiment was granted by the Station commander and trial runs were made with full vision over a period of several days.

The predicted courses were almost entirely correct. Covers were made for the cockpit so that the pilot's view would be completely obscured, although the co-pilot would have clear vision. I trained another direction finder operator.

The test demonstration took place on a weekend afternoon when there were no other flight operations at the Station. The co-pilot's job was to be a safety observer for the aircraft and to ensure the landing area was clear during descent. Commander Dodd was aboard to observe the pilot's reactions. Everything happened as planned and tested. The smooth landing took place in mid-channel. The aircraft taxied to the runway where we two radiomen met them with congratulations.

To my knowledge this was the first blind landing ever made by an airplane. Commander Dodd never received appropriate recognition for his contribution.

A half dozen more flights were made before the experiment was concluded and at Dodd's suggestion, I was on one of them.

Over the years I have since made numerous other heavier-than-air and lighter-than-air flights and taken part in other major experiments; but that blind landing exercise was my first participation in flight research. Like one's first love, it can not be forgotten.

The Rigors of Early Aviation

The formative years for Naval aviation at Pensacola were not without danger because those fledgling flyers were the successors of Icarus, Langley and others who antedated the Wright Brothers, the first successful flyers, only 20 years before.

I experienced three plane crashes and one serious near-collision during my years in the Navy.

The first crash was in a two-place pontoon biplane. It was an N-9, a type used for preliminary flight training.

Why was I in the plane? I just happened to be around at the time and a pilot, an erratic reserve lieutenant, asked me if I wanted a ride. At full power, he taxied the plane with the pontoon almost, but not quite "on the step." As we approached the shore, I spotted a bulkhead slightly above the waterline. However, the pilot kept the engine at full power, but less than flight speed. When we were about to hit the bulkhead, he pulled the stick back and the plane jumped over the timber and headed straight for a chain link fence. But it crashed into the sandy beach before reaching the fence.

By the time the crash boats and fire engines arrived, we were clambering out of the airplane. Unquestionably the crash was caused by pilot error.

The second crash, at Hampton Roads, Virginia, was more serious. The purpose of the flight was to test the result of nearly two years of laboratory work on the reduction of aircraft ignition interference with radio reception.

On takeoff the pilots of the big flying boat rocked the aircraft back and forth, trying to get up "on the step." Finally, they "jumped" the plane into the air, but not for long. We came down with a bang. The plane's bottom sheared off; the fuselage was submerged with the lower wing just below the water's surface.

My boss and I were in the rear cockpit, the radio area. We had two new lab-built receivers aboard, but they were now under water in the submerged cockpit. Neither of us thought about the equipment. We wiggled out of the sunken plane and headed for the beach.

Later we learned the water had risen to the top wing of the old craft, but it never sank. It was fished out by a crane. Again, a case of pilot error.

My third airplane crash happened several years later at the Naval Air Station, Anacostia. During the intervening years, aircraft and engine design had improved considerably. Although the wings and fuselage of planes were then still covered with fabric, the spars and ribs of military planes were now made of duralumin, a very strong aluminum alloy. The plane we were to fly also had a new seating arrangement. The pilots sat front and back, rather than side by side; the radioman's position was behind them both.

Before the radio equipment was installed in the plane, the pilot and his mechanic had made several flights. Sitting in the rear seat, the pilot had discovered the correct angle for a good takeoff could be found by lining up a particular fin on the engine with the horizon. But on the flight I was aboard, he decided to fly the plane from the front seat. On takeoff, he lined up the same fin with the horizon; although he never realized it, the resulting angle was much steeper from the front seat. Consequently, due to the steeper angle, we got off the ground with full power and up to about 150 feet altitude before the speed decreased and the aircraft stalled. Hastily, the pilot cut the engine, the worst thing he could have done. He quickly realized his error, but too late. We crashed, hitting first on the right wing whose aluminum ribs progressively disintegrated, taking up much of the shock before the propeller and engine bored a hole in the ground.

As soon as I felt the plane shudder shortly after takeoff and the right wing dipped, I knew we might crash. Falling down and forward into the plane's interior, I hit everything in sight on the way to the back of the rear pilot seat. In addition to numerous abrasions, I received a bad cut on top of my head and a cut from knee to ankle on my left leg. I momentarily passed out. Regaining consciousness, I was horrified because I knew a crash could spew gasoline over the hot engine, causing a flash fire.

Unbuckling my parachute, I managed to climb out of the airplane just as the crash party arrived. Again, pilot error caused the crash.

My later near-tragedy episode could not be called an airplane crash because we twice landed safely and ultimately reached our destination. Our mission was to fly a large flying boat nonstop from Pensacola to Miami. After refueling, we were to pick up the Assistant Secretary of the Navy, Theodore Roosevelt Jr., son of the former President, and deliver him to Havana.

In view of the importance of the passenger, two flying boats were assigned to the mission. Both arrived in Miami without incident. The following morning we had breakfast at a cafe near the harbor. On the way out, I was accosted by a man who asked if I was interested in making $100. "That depends," I said. He told me all I had to do was pick up a package at Havana and bring it to him on my return flight. He offered to pay me $25 now and $75 more after I delivered the package.

I looked him over. He was well dressed and nice looking, but it seemed too easy. I told him I wasn't sure our flight would come back that way; we parted. That "little package" probably would have contained drugs. As early as 1922, drugs were coming into Miami!

Delivering Mr. Roosevelt to Havana as scheduled, our pilot told us we would leave Havana the morning of the third day; in the interval we should refuel the plane and make sure everything was ready to go. Then we had his permission to go ashore.

The pilots took their bags and hailed a shore boat. That was the last we saw of them until departure time.

On the third morning all hands arrived at the dock. The pilots, if anything, looked worse for wear than the crew. After we climbed aboard, our pilot taxied the plane to the open sea and took off for Miami.

Ten miles south of Key West, our luck ran out. The front four cylinders of one engine, its propeller, and part of the crankshaft broke off in a burst of smoke, fortunately falling clear of the aircraft. A few red-hot pieces of steel hit the lower wing and set the cloth afire. However, the airstream forced the cloth to burn back to the trailing edge where the fire flickered out.

Our pilot calmly landed on the rough sea and we bobbed around. In the meantime, our companion airplane circled over us. We waved; and it flew on to Key West.

During the remainder of the morning, I listened for radio signals on the communications channel. I could not send a message because our transmitter power came from a generator mounted on the upper wing of the plane. When nothing had happened by early afternoon, our pilot asked what I could do to get communications operating.

I told him I thought we could remove the generator from the wing, mount it on a strut supporting the rear end of the engine, and run the engine to create enough wind for power to transmit an SOS and some short messages. Our distress signals went out, but nothing happened.

In late afternoon, our convoy aircraft returned, circled above our flying boat, buzzed us once, and departed in the direction of Key West. I was not surprised when we received no radio signals. The radioman aboard that plane barely knew the code and had never operated an aircraft radio before.

Finally, our pilots decided to take advantage of the south wind that was causing us to drift slowly toward Key West. We tied the engine covers between the wings, using them as sails. The plane began to move through the water at a fair rate. Then the unexpected happened. A mechanic in the bow suddenly yelled, "Breakers ahead!"

The pilot shouted, "Start the engine! Pull down the sails! Hyland, take a bucket and climb out to the end of the wing on the engine side." (The remaining engine was mounted several feet to the right of the aircraft centerline, and the bucket was to be used as a sea anchor to prevent the craft from circling.)

The engine started; and I crouched on the end of the wing with the bucket trailing in the water. Slowly the aircraft eased to the left as the long line of white breakers loomed perilously close.

In the meantime, I was having a precarious ride on the wing. Standing between the struts and clinging to the forward one, I saw a wall of water high above my head coming fast toward us. As our craft rode the top of the wave, I spotted the lights of Key West in the distance.

The pilot kept the engine running, but at a slow rate in case the craft encountered more trouble. When he shouted for me to come inside, I sidled along the leading edge of the wing towards him. When I was about halfway, he shouted and waved me back. This happened two or three times. Finally, I realized that on the wing's leading edge I was going to walk into the rotating propeller. Feeling like a damned fool, I returned to the cabin along the wing's trailing edge.

The flying boat was eventually hauled up on the beach at Key West.

After a few weeks of work, we had it repaired and operating. With much tugging, pulling and improvision, we refloated the plane. The pilot taxied to the refueling dock, unaware that the tide was running swiftly in the same direction as we were going. Instead of easing into the dock, the plane struck it hard, damaging a wing spar. The pilot beached the aircraft.

After some "glue and bailing wire" fixes we were again ready to fly. This time we refueled with care. The aircraft gently took off. The pilot waggled the wings a few times to determine if the repaired spar would hold together. Nothing came apart.

My only casualty on that trip was my suitcase, which I had been so proud of. My radio officer, a careful man with money, had given me $5 with instructions to buy a box of cigars for him in Havana. I had tucked the cigars inside my bag and stored it in the bow. One night the pilot ordered us to put out an anchor and wait for daylight. In the morning, a large wave swept over the flying boat; apparently the anchor had hooked under the tip of a reef, holding down the nose of the plane. To dislodge the anchor, the mechanic and I stood on our suitcases. Mine had only a thin coating of leather over cardboard; it ended up a water-soaked, spongy mess.

When we finally made it back to the Air Station, I had no suitcase, no cigars and no money.

Seeing the World—but at Sea

At the end of my last year at the Air Station, I received orders transferring me to sea duty aboard the *USS Marblehead*, a new cruiser at the New York Navy Yard. I was disappointed. I had hoped when my transfer came I would be assigned to the *USS Wright*, the mothership for the big flying boats that accompanied the fleet; or alternatively, to the *USS Langley*, a new aircraft carrier in commission, but not yet staffed.

Aboard the *USS Marblehead* I was told to report to the navigator, whose department included radio operations. He was not impressed with my commendations or flight record. He informed me the captain wanted a battleship chief, not a landlubber.

Disgruntled, I went to the radio room. I was surprised to meet another chief radioman. Nothing he said eased my mind. He confirmed that the captain wanted a battleship chief. Despite prior service on two destroyers and on two land radio stations, all with excellent marks, he'd been reduced to radioman first class and transferred to a receiving ship for reassignment.

When I explained my background, the chief sadly shook his head and muttered, "You won't last a week."

The news soon spread among the dozen radiomen of various ratings that the ship had again received a lemon radio chief.

That night I didn't sleep well. Before sunrise, I went up on deck. When I looked up at the sky, my spirits hit bottom. Bathed in the golden glow of the rising sun, I saw a dirigible, her propellers slowly turning as she waited for the temperature to stabilize at Lakehurst, New Jersey, where she would land. I realized that was my hope for an aviation career. At sea level where I stood, my future in the Navy looked grim indeed. I almost cried in frustration.

At breakfast, I tried to absorb the high spirits of some of my peers before going topside; when I reported for duty in the radio room, I kept busy checking out radio equipment. The *USS Marblehead* with her five sister ships was intended to be a communication link for the Fleet. I discovered all equipment on the *Marblehead*, including engines, guns, bridge, and crew accommodations, was of the latest design and construction.

However, I could hardly believe my eyes when I examined the radio equipment. It belonged to the Dark Ages. The receivers had crystal detectors and obsolete tuning methods, and the one intermediate wave spark gap transmitter was also of ancient vintage. A huge 30 kilowatt (rating) arc unit, with its bulky keying system enclosed in a steel room with glass windows, occupied much of the radio room space. The arc unit had to be enclosed because the voltages required by the arc were enormous and could easily jump a foot to any conductor. The controller for that transmitter had a handle that looked as though it had come from a streetcar. Without suitable amplifiers, incoming radio signals were of such low intensity that all of the receiving equipment had to be housed in a compartment the size of a giant refrigerator.

When I checked out the communication system from the radio room to the bridge, the conning tower, and Battle Two near the mainmast, I was astonished. Communication was conducted by use of voice tubes. The ship had no telephones. Only one of the vacuum tubes was operative—an original De Forest design about the size of a pint bottle. The vacuum tubes were of pre-World War I technology.

These observations did nothing to enhance my morale. Leaning against the open doorway of the radio room, I stared glumly at the heavy traffic on the gangway. The ship was in the final stages of preparation for commissioning; there was a lot of activity. Suddenly I spotted a familiar figure. Coming aboard was Lieutenant Fred Dickey. He was being escorted to the captain, but as he passed by me, he waved. I felt better.

Lt. Dickey came to the radio room within the hour. After shaking his hand, I asked, "What in the world are you doing here?"

He smiled. "I'm the flight officer."

When I looked incredulous, he added, "Didn't you know this ship is the first to be equipped with catapults for aircraft?"

"I did not," I replied, "but I doubt it will make much difference to me. I don't expect to be here long." I unloaded my predicament and concerns about my future.

He shook his head. "I'll see the captain about that."

The following morning, the new radio officer reported to the radio room for duty and the navigator introduced him to the radiomen. In the process, the navigator mentioned that I would not only be the ship's radio chief, but also the flight radio chief. Thereafter, he treated me with tolerance and a smidgen of respect.

Lt. Dickey told me that on all future flights I would occupy the rear seat of the airplane and he'd recommended me for flight orders. That meant I would receive a 50 percent increase in pay.

When the ship was finally provided with its complement of aircraft communication gear, the *USS Marblehead* was the only ship in the Fleet so fully equipped.

The Radio Days Get Better

One day a real break came for me. The radio sets for our aircraft arrived. There were modern vacuum tubes, transmitter-receivers with spare parts, and all the paraphernalia necessary to install the radio equipment.

I must admit that at that time radio people and equipment were a headache for the skippers. There was not much technical capability on the part of either; and radio officers were low men on the totem pole.

To get our ship on the air, I disconnected the tuning sections of two spare aircraft radio sets. I connected the longwave receiver tuner to the detector of one set. I did the same for the medium wave tuner. This gave us two modern, very effective receivers. It made a tremendous difference for the radiomen. They didn't need to sit in that torture chamber with its stale air, straining their ears for the tiniest beep. Furthermore, we were occasionally in broadcast range and able to hear some music on the medium wave set. We retained that privilege for ourselves.

To Sea With the "Salt Water Navy"

We embarked for a shakedown cruise to Bermuda.

The business of the salt-water Navy is ships. Each ship is a community by itself. Throughout history, until the advent of steam-powered vessels with steel structures, the number of classes of Naval ships was small. In those days (the 1920s) when I served in the salt-water Navy, the propulsion, basic armament and skill requirements of the crew were the same from one ship to another, regardless of size.

Beginning with mechanical power, steel structures and now nuclear-power, the classes of vessels and variety of skills required to run them have steadily multiplied.

Today a ship is still a community. When lines are cast off and a ship leaves the dock, an umbilical cord is cut. The ship becomes a self-sufficient unit; subject only to the whims of nature, authority or enemy interference.

That community is a rigid autocracy headed by the captain who commands officers, crews and anyone else who happens to be aboard. This type of organization began with the first mariners and has continued to this date. The captain is the commander and the example for all officers and crew. The mission, along with the deportment and efficiency of the ship's officers and crew, is largely a reflection of the competence and leadership of the captain. Orders and assignments must be carried out without question or explanation. Each man is an intrinsic part of the whole. The safety of the ship and all aboard, including its mission, may depend on his performance.

Older hands learn almost instinctively to assess the competence of superiors. Their comments and "scuttlebutt" percolates to the younger men. No environment is better than shipboard life to teach one to distinguish followers from leaders, the skilled from the clumsy, the ambitious from the complacent, or to recognize variances of human nature.

Human characteristics are amplified on a long voyage. Tempers simmer and frustrations are magnified. Even a two-year tour of duty in the salt-water Navy provides experiences that would take a lifetime to accumulate under other circumstances.

We soon discovered why the ship needed a shakedown cruise to

Bermuda. First we had to lower the top portion of the *Marblehead's* masts and wait for low tide to make it under the Brooklyn Bridge. The Captain pulled the cord to blow the horn. The only sound that came out was a gurgle with a burst of water.

Inside the radio room plenty of corrective work was also needed. We discovered the radio transmitter was useless because its power generator was undersized; the instruction book was inaccurate as well.

When we arrived off Hamilton, Bermuda, protocol required the *USS Marblehead* to fire a 21-gun salute as we passed the fortress at the harbor entrance. We had aboard ship a two-inch saluting gun operated by a gunners mate. He laid out 21 blank cartridges. The first one loaded properly, but when the gunner pulled the lanyard, nothing happened. Hastily, he inserted another cartridge. He yanked the lanyard; still nothing happened. He sent for more rounds. Out of 21 original cartridges, he managed to shoot off only five shots—a serious breach of Naval etiquette.

For several weeks, we cruised in the beautiful blue water off Bermuda, learning to use that marvelous assemblage of machinery, called a treaty light cruiser; the first Naval ship built since World War I.

In the radio room we had plenty to do with our portion of the ship's electrical system. No prints could be found showing the wiring of the ship. Because the ship's electricians were busy with their own problems, we had the painstaking job of searching for cables ourselves. We also had to take some radio equipment apart to find out how to use it. None of the members of the radio group had any experience with either electrical or radio equipment. The job became my responsibility.

We again entered Hamilton Harbor, this time making a proper salute. The captain gave liberty to half the crew. I was one of those who stayed aboard ship.

The Rigors of Liberty for American Sailors

A small entertainment steamer had been hired to transport the crew ashore and return them. On their return voyage, the liberty-ites literally tore apart the interior of the steamer's cabin, its piano, and most of the furniture. When the steamer finally returned to the *Marblehead*, most revelers were able to stagger up the gang plank; but a cargo net was provided for those who couldn't. Some men were unceremoniously dumped into the net by a couple of husky boatswain's mates.

The day following this sorry incident, the captain informed the officers that pay for all hands was to be equally docked to cover the $13,000 repair bill for the steamboat. Thereafter, sailors were transported between ship and shore on our own motor sailers under military control.

When the *USS Marblehead* returned to the Navy Yard from our shakedown cruise, we had a maintenance stay of about a month.

Two fundamental changes were made on the *Marblehead.*—both of extreme importance to me.

One was installation of a sonic depth finder. Controls were placed inside the radio room and actuators installed within the ship's double bottoms with the diaphragm penetrating the hull.

Aviation—and "Seeing the World" —Comes to the Marblehead

The second was even more intriguing: A catapult on the after deck for launching a reconnaissance seaplane. A separate platform with a crane was installed. The crane's long arm could pick up the aircraft from the sea and replace it on the catapult.

Both the depth finder and the aircraft catapult were the first operational units of their kind on a Naval fighting ship.

Regretfully, Lt. Dickey contracted a severe case of jaundice and was transferred ashore to the hospital. I never saw him again. Though Lt. Dickey never got his first catapult shot on the *Marblehead*, he had been my salvation. I have been grateful ever since.

His replacement reported aboard a few days later. Shortly after, the *Marblehead* left on a second shakedown cruise. Stops were scheduled at Liverpool, Marseilles, Gibraltar, Naples, Algiers, Madeira, and finally back to the Norfolk Navy Yard.

In mid-Atlantic on our way to Liverpool a number of the crew were sitting on the fantail. Without warning, a huge wave caught us and engulfed the deck almost up to midship. Those men topside struggled for their lives; two crewmen were swept overboard.

We had probably experienced a Tsunami—a wave caused by a sea-bottom earthquake or volcanic eruption at the mid-Atlantic ridge. These waves travel at astonishing speeds, sometimes estimated to be as high as 400 miles an hour over the deep ocean. When they hit the shore, or a surface obstruction such as a ship, the results can be devastating.

In Liverpool harbor, the great ship *Leviathan* passed by not 100 yards away. This was her first voyage as a cruise ship after refitting from troop carrier service. I had returned on her from France to New York in 1919. Passengers lined the rails; a band played the Star Spangled Banner. The *Leviathan* gave three blasts from her horn; we were thrilled and proud to be Americans.

As *Marblehead* approached the Mediterranean through the Straits of Gibraltar on its way from Liverpool to Marseilles, the captain decided this would be an opportunity to show off his new ship to the British observers on Gibraltar. Just before entering the Straits, *Marblehead* brought up steam in all four boiler rooms and came up to a full 34 knots. Battle flags were hoisted to the masts as well as fore and aft. An impressive bow wave formed and a tremendous wake was generated. We steamed by the fortress with flags flying, guns pointed fore and aft, and sailors in whites on the portside rails as they snapped pictures of the rock.

We stopped in Marseilles for three or four days. I took my first shore leave.

Because we had anchored in the outer harbor, the liberty boat had to go a long way to a wharf named Place d' Africa,. From there it was a fair walk to the center of the city. After a round of sightseeing and cafes, I headed back. Although I had earlier checked landmarks on my way from the dock, it was now dark and I missed most of them. Soon I was thoroughly lost amid the great warehouses of Marseilles' seaport area which had a reputation of being a hangout for thieves and ruffians living off sailors. At a street crossing I saw a man purposefully striding along. Intercepting him, I said, "Bon'jour, Monsieur" and he replied likewise. I then said in my sparse French,

"Ou est le Place d' Africa?" He replied in unintelligible French.

Falling into the trap of most embryonic foreign language speakers, I repeated the same question, this time a little louder. He replied even more loudly. Soon we were shouting at each other. Finally, in English I said, "I can't understand a damn word you're saying!"

"I speak English," he replied. "I am from a Dutch ship anchored not far from yours." We laughed, shook hands and walked together to the dock for my return trip to the *Marblehead*.

A Mediterranean Cruise—Courtesy of Uncle Sam

Leaving Marseilles, we headed towards Naples, about 50 miles away. The sea was calm with only a few ripples and a light wind. Using a winch and derrick, the skipper put the airplane over the side with the pilot and me aboard. We flew back and forth over that magnificent coastline, enjoying the blue Mediterranean in late afternoon.

The pilot was eager to go ashore at Naples. He radioed a request to the ship to fly directly there. It was not granted. Circling above the ship, he again asked permission to land at Naples to make a "needed repair." No reply. This time the captain was on the wing of the bridge with his hands over his head, bringing them down. The pilot got the message and landed.

Of course I never heard what the captain had to say; but I did notice the pilot remained in his cabin during our stay in Naples.

From Naples we headed for Algiers. About five miles from our destination, the airplane was again lowered over the side. We flew over that fabled country with its white-washed buildings. It was a beautiful sight and reminded me of biblical pictures I had seen. We landed in the harbor, taxied up to the ship and were hoisted aboard.

As I recall, this was in early 1925. Algiers was a cosmopolitan city with people of all religions and all colors liberally represented.

During the few days the ship stayed at Algiers I made two trips to the city. The first, in daytime, I mingled with the people. I spotted a peddler with an attractive display of Persian rugs. Wanting a souvenir, I bartered with him, purchasing a small rug at a reasonable price. After returning to the U.S., I discovered a tiny label in one corner of the rug: "Made in Patterson, New Jersey, U.S.A."

My second trip came the night before our departure, scheduled for the early morning tide. Doing a muster, I realized one of my radiomen was missing. He was well known for his inability to hold his liquor and his penchant for women. I was responsible for all my men, so I reported the missing radioman to the OOD. He suggested I go ashore to find and bring him back. I promptly headed for the red-light district.

The district was notorious in Algiers—occupied by hookers, pimps, thieves, and cutthroats. A white foreigner, alone, was fair game. Fortunately, I wore an American uniform with belt and leggings, meaning I was on official duty. Anyone who interfered with my mission would suffer unpleasant diplomatic consequences. Americans then were loved, respected and admired for their help to France in World War I.

The natives seemed to know my job was to find an errant sailor. As I approached the brothels, some actually pointed to a certain house. When I entered, the madam pointed upstairs. After a brief search, I hauled my quarry out from under a bed. Luckily, he was not too drunk. We made our way back to the ship without trouble.

Today, it is impossible to imagine trying to do that same task.

In the morning we left Algiers for the voyage back to Gibraltar.

The ship's pilot and I had a marvelous sight-seeing opportunity. The airplane was again put afloat. We had no trouble with the takeoff and circled above the Rock a few times.

During our stay at the base of that great Rock, I remember I felt a strange sense of security. There were emanations from that massive fortress of the British Empire that seemed to calm the mind and the spirit.

Into the Stormy Atlantic

We left Gibraltar and headed southwest toward the Portuguese island of Madeira in the Atlantic Ocean, a convenient stop en route to the Navy Yard at Portsmouth, Virginia.

Up to this point, the weather had been excellent. But the farther we proceeded, the more the Atlantic lived up to its reputation. Winds were vigorous. By the time we arrived at Madeira, the waves must have been six or eight feet from trough to peak.

There was no harbor at Madeira, only an anchorage in the open sea several hundred yards from shore. One gangway was let down and shore boats lowered. The small boats pitched up, down, and sideways. One needed to be a circus stuntman to climb into a boat; nevertheless, 12-hour passes were granted and many of us went ashore.

Madeira was famous for lace, wine and hospitality. Americans were greeted with smiles. Food and music in the cafes were excellent. The famous resort was much appreciated by Europeans. Portugese, English and French phrases and songs provided a happy atmosphere.

After leaving Madeira, as we reached mid-ocean, the wind was fierce and the sea rough. In the radio room, we received an SOS from a cargo ship requesting our help. The day before a seaman had fallen and broken his leg and it was becoming inflamed. What should they do?

The message was relayed to our ship's doctor. But an old-time boatswain's mate, who happened to be in the radio room, voiced his opinion of what to do, based on an era of no doctors and two remedies—Epson salts and iodine.

When the doctor's message came back, the radiomen were hilarious. I glanced at the message and spotted the words "Epson salts."

The wind steadily increased during the next couple of days. Before long we were in a full-scale hurricane. *Marblehead* slowed down, heading into the wind to face the mountainous seas which occasionally engulfed the ships' bow. Life lines were rigged and everything possible tied down. Our great antenna, perhaps 250 feet long and consisting of six wires held apart by hoops, snapped off in the powerful wind. That left no way to communicate our situation. Below decks was a shambles. The men were seasick; attempts to serve meals were fruitless. Sleep was impossible. Water sloshed in many places. The chiefs' quarters at the stern were especially miserable because the propellers frequently would come out of the water, race and then strike the water with tremendous vibration.

After more than a day of this struggle, the wind abated and the seas calmed. The *Marblehead* resumed speed on course to Portsmouth. The ship was put into dry dock there.

My first job after we arrived at the Navy Yard was to reconstruct the antenna—strung between the main and foremast. I ordered a husky first class radioman to engage the hook on the mainmast; I elected to do the job on the foremast myself, chiefly because I was afraid of heights and felt I needed the discipline. Although slender, I was wiry and sure I could engage the hook.

Slowly, I started the long climb up that 200-foot challenge. There were only rungs on the mast and no safety belts. Afraid to look down, I concentrated on just reaching the top of the mast. With the mainmast hook already in place, I had to pull my hook an extra inch to engage the eye. Wrapping my legs and my left arm around the mast, I gave a one, two, three pull. All my adrenalin pumps were working and with a final heave, I managed to engage the hook.

To "Gitmo" and Life in the "Old" Navy

The *Marblehead* was refloated and got under way for a rendezvous with other Naval units at Guantanamo Bay, Cuba.

We proceeded south against the Gulf Stream; the climate was warm and clear. After we arrived at Guantanamo Bay, the only ship action required was a full power run in the warm water of the Gulf over a measured course between the Bay and Santiago de Cuba. When we returned to our anchorage the primary mission was to give the crew rifle and pistol practice, qualify the men as first class swimmers and train boat crews for rowing contests between ships, scheduled for later in the month. I did very well with the rifle and pistol, making "expert" in both categories. I even became a rifle instructor.

On the other hand, I fared poorly as a swimmer. The rules required the crew to dive off a gangway and swim around the ship. Most of the men easily qualified as swimmers, but about a half dozen of us had problems. As an incentive, we were awakened at 0500, loaded into a ship's boat without breakfast and made to row to shore under the eyes of a coxswain.

At the beach we were given swimming lessons. After a couple of weeks of this, two or three of the group qualified, but no amount of instruction helped the rest of us.

As the deadline for swimmer qualification came nearer, the rules were changed. It was now only necessary that we jump off the top of the gangway and swim or float the length of the ship to a target boat well aft of the stern. The time for this exercise was set when the tide was running out, giving us some help from the current—in addition to our feeble attempts at swimming and floating.

When my time arrived, I walked to the gangway, held my nose and jumped. After hitting the water 16 feet below, it seemed to me I must have plummeted 50 feet below the surface before beginning to rise. Probably it was only three or four feet at most. When my head finally broke above water, I quickly turned onto my back in float position and gently kicked and half-swam toward the stern of the ship. Everything went great; the ship slipped by at a fair speed. I felt sure I would pass the test. However, when I was only a few feet away from the target boat, the captain's gig (a motor boat that traveled 10 miles an hour) went by; the wash from its bow wave rolled over me. I almost drowned. Both my nose and mouth took doses of water. Frantically, I paddled hard and just managed to reach the target boat. I was hauled aboard coughing and sputtering.

When we returned to the ship, the OOD met us at the top of the gangway. He signed my first class swimmers certificate, but his face grimaced with pain as if he was doing something distasteful. I can't say I blamed him. It was apparent I would never make a Channel swimmer.

Many U.S. Navy ships were anchored in Guantanamo Bay, ranging from battleships, cruisers, destroyers, and supply ships to tugs, all under the command of a vice admiral. The days were filled with work parties, both ashore and afloat. In the evenings, movies were shown on the larger ships with crews from the smaller craft occasionally being invited aboard. At precisely nine o'clock, quiet would settle over the entire Fleet. Buglers on each ship sounded Taps. Since the anchorage covered more than a mile, bugle calls from the closest ships were loud and immediate, but calls became fainter and fainter as distant ships were heard last. My memory is still stirred by those bugle calls in the peace of the night from ships of war.

Opportunity Comes Knocking

My life for the next year was predictable. Or so I thought, until one day I received a letter from my old radio officer at Pensacola, Lieutenant Herbert Rodd. I read his letter over and over before really comprehending the message. Lt. Rodd was now radio officer of the Bureau of Aeronautics in the Navy Department in Washington. He provided much of the funds for the aircraft radio section of the Naval Research Laboratory (NRL) at Anacostia, District of Columbia.

I knew about the Laboratory because I'd read their quarterly news bulletins, both at Pensacola and on shipboard. The bulletins supplied information about the ongoing work at NRL and progress of radio in general. The great scientific staff at the Lab represent-ed Valhalla to me. I will never forget the names of some of its gods: Dr. A. Hoyt Taylor, Leo Young, Louis Gebhard, Dr. Hayes, Carlos Mirick.

Lt. Rodd's letter informed me he was anxious to have a radio engineer with both naval aviation and ship experience on staff at NRL. He asked if I would accept such a job at a salary of $2,200 per year. He assured me I could receive a special discharge under honorable conditions and be immediately transferred from my ship to the nearest American Naval station. There I would be officially discharged from the Navy and given transportation to Washington, D.C. where I was to report to Lieutenant Rodd.

"Wow!"

"Would I accept a job in Valhalla?"

"You bet!"

I lost no time mailing a letter of acceptance and thanks to Lt. Rodd. But awaiting a reply, doubts plagued me. It couldn't be true. I still had a year to serve on my present enlistment and had been trying to decide what I should do with my life when my service ended. I certainly never dreamed of an opportunity to work at the Naval Research Laboratory—and at such an increase over my present pay.

The six years I had spent in the Navy as an enlisted man were an invaluable growth experience. My obligation to the Navy for the formative years at Pensacola and the following two years at sea on the *Marblehead* can hardly be overemphasized. They prepared me well for higher educational experiences during my civilian years at the Naval Research Laboratory.

Today, 60 years later, I can better evaluate the things I learned during those years in the Navy.

First and foremost is the maturation provided by the 24-hour-a-day association with hundreds of men of all ranks, ratings, skills, talents, and forefathers. I gave respect to rank, but assessed competence. I learned the difference between intellectual honesty and published platitudes, the difference between shallow vanity and proud humility and the meaning of individuality. I also discovered that morality and climate vary with geography. On my lonely night watches, I observed that nature's radio waves gave the same priority to a happy report of a baby's birth as they did to a frantic SOS.

I reported to Pensacola with previous experience as an Army sergeant with aviation, radio and field communication service under active wartime conditions. I left with an up-to-date education in electronics, firsthand experience with aircraft, a defined career, and confidence from diverse achievements.

I had indeed entered a new frontier.

Ships are the business of the Navy and instant readiness its objective. I enjoyed my contribution and thrilled at the fleet exercises. Viewing them from an aeroplane, I was awestruck at the complex maneuvers of an entire fleet. Keeping radio silence, the ships moved with the precision of a fine machine over a thousand square miles of ocean controlled only by flags, whistles and semaphores.

Many thousands of men directed the immense power of the mighty Fleet, each confident that the other men on the various ships were also performing in accordance with their training, doctrine and the Articles for the Government of the Navy. I was proud to be a part of such an organization.

During my last month in the Navy, I mulled over many things. I faced the fact that I probably would not receive another promotion for at least several years, if at all, because I lacked sufficient sea duty and because the size of the Navy was being reduced to that of a peacetime force. I also realized that if I left without a specific job, finding work in the civilian labor force could prove difficult. I didn't even have an idea of where in the U.S. I wanted to live.

Only then did I appreciate the true measure of Lt. Rodd's intervention in my life by providing a job opportunity which so exactly fitted my needs.

My first four years in the Navy had been a special kind of college; my two years at sea a finishing school. I was now prepared to face my idols at the Naval Research Laboratory with humility and hope.

CHAPTER III
From USN to NRL

The Captain of the *Marblehead* received a radiogram from the Bureau of Navigation directing that I be transferred to the closest U.S. port to receive an honorable discharge and transportation to my home port.

The next day I reported to the *USS Richmond*, another light cruiser, scheduled to leave the next day for Philadelphia. I was on my way.

At the Philadelphia Navy yard I was given an honorable discharge, my pay, and fare to Boston.

But, I headed for Washington D.C., reporting immediately to Lt. Rodd's office. He told me a problem had developed.

To prevent educational deficiency, the Naval Research Laboratory had made a rule that no applicant could be considered for a job on the technical staff without having an engineering degree from an acceptable college, or in its absence, passing an equivalent examination from the Civil Service Commission.

But, in my case NRL officials made an exception. They told Lt. Rodd even passing the Civil Service examination would *not* satisfy them; the Laboratory already had too many non-degreed people.

However, Lt. Rodd had persisted—agreeing to create a second position at the Laboratory, to be occupied by an applicant with a degree, provided the officials would accept me if I passed the Civil Service examination. They consented reluctantly, on the proviso that I serve for six months on a trial basis.

The decision was a blow to my hopes. I had no idea how difficult the examination would be, nor did I feel confident of surmounting such a formidable hurdle. But, I assured Lt. Rodd I would go to the Civil Service Commission and do my best.

That evening I went to see my uncle, the assistant director of the

Pure Food and Drug Laboratory of the Department of Agriculture. I explained my problem.

"I believe you might be able to pass the examination," he said. "On the experience side you stand to have very high marks, although you may have a deficiency in mathematics." He assured me I had an important factor in my favor—the veteran's bonus of five percentage points over the examination grade. Certification required a mark no lower than 75 percent, including the veteran's bonus.

I also learned my uncle was a member of the Civil Service Commission. He promised to help me through the procedures.

When I reported back to Lt. Rodd and told him of my forthcoming examination, I also mentioned my experience with the direction finder aboard ship and its successful application in winning the Fleet radio competition. Extremely interested, he arranged for me to talk to a senior scientist of the Bureau of Ships.

First Exposure to Bureaucracy

The scientist was affable, polished, self-assured, and initially interested. However, after detailed questioning, he concluded that what I had accomplished by calibration phenomena (which he did not understand) was purely chance. It probably could not be duplicated in any other ship or aircraft; in fact it might be dangerous, he said.

No rebuttal was accepted. He said he admired my good work, but the idea was not anything the Navy would consider. (Within 10 years, the reason for the phenomena had been determined, proving my contention correct.)

The BuShips scientist didn't have all the right answers, nor did he have enough curiosity or respect for the experiences of others to learn that his own education was incomplete. That experience helped me deal more wisely with people in later years.

When I took the Civil Service examination I felt comfortable with my answers based on experience. I thought I did reasonably well in chemistry and physics (both subjects I had liked in high school); got by in algebra; floundered a bit in trigonometry; and missed out completely in calculus.

A week later I got the results. My grade was 70 percent. With the five-point veteran's preference my total score was 75 percent. I had just squeaked by.

NRL officials were satisfied, hiring me with the understanding that my record would be reviewed in six months and a final determination of my employment made.

History of NRL

In 1915 at the direction of Secretary of the Navy, Josephus Daniels, a special Navy Consulting Board was established, with Thomas Edison as chairman, to advise on " . . . the imperative needs of the Navy . . . machinery and facilities for utilizing the natural inventive genius of Americans to meet the new conditions of warfare. . . ."

At the direction of the then-Secretary of the Navy, the Naval Research Laboratory was established in March 1922 initially to study physics, physical chemistry, electronics, and underwater acoustics. It was to be built on a site near the Potomac River below the town of Anacostia in the District of Columbia.

When completed, the new and attractive buildings would be separated by broad lawns. The offices and laboratories would be furnished with suitable equipment for productive work far superior to any then in place.

The core of the staff was to be drawn from engineering groups already in place at the Washington Navy yard, but new hires from the scientific community (located and qualified with help from the Civil Service Commission) would also be added.

The Laboratory began functioning in 1923 with surprisingly little start-up confusion.

My employment started three years after it opened. The shakedown period was completed; about 75 percent of the intended personnel were in place. The organization was operating smoothly and effectively under Captain E. G. Oberlin.

It was a new organization with a new mission, so no lengthy procedures or precedents had to be overcome. Captain Oberlin encouraged innovation. He didn't create new routines to interfere with the freedom of department heads.

For personal development, I could not have chosen a more fortunate atmosphere. On Friday afternoons all engineers and scientists were required to attend seminars, not only to update their education but also to ensure synergism in the evolution of their projects. Considerable performance incentives were offered, including cash bonuses for exceptional work, the right to commercial ownership of patents, encouragement to join professional societies, leaves to participate in projects of interest to the Navy and, most important, the stimulation of intellectual growth in the humanities as well as the sciences.

My family situation also benefited. When I had appeared at my relatives' homes in my Navy uniform, they had not been overjoyed with my CPO position. However, when I appeared in civilian clothes, explaining I had been hired to work at the Naval Research Laboratory with the title of engineer, my status improved.

Indoctrination at NRL

When I reported for duty, I first met with Dr. A. Hoyt Taylor, superintendent of the Radio Division. Perhaps in his late forties, he was impressive. Though a mite crusty in his speech, he was obviously a man of competence and integrity. Smiling as we shook hands, he said I had presented a problem both to him and to NRL. But, he said, I had successfully hurdled the first barrier and would receive a fair shake and be accorded the same treatment as any other promising candidate. Wishing me well, he instructed me to report to the chief of the Aircraft Radio Section.

The section chief, Carlos B. Mirick, greeted me warmly. I was the ideal addition to the Aircraft Section, he said.

Mr. Mirick was working on a remote-controlled airplane project. Coincidentally, I had worked on a remote-controlled airplane at Pensacola.

At NRL Mr. Mirick developed an ingenious scheme by which he could fly an airplane with radio control. He had done it. The experimental airplane was of the same design I had flown with Lt. Dickey at Pensacola. It was primarily a training craft and therefore had plenty of control margin, but not much speed. The controlling aircraft was an HS-2 flying boat, a pusher with the pilot and copilot side-by-side in a double cockpit just forward of the wings. The pilot was in the left seat and Mr. Mirick with his controls in the copilot seat. The control equipment was mounted behind the pilot.

I was the safety man in a nose cockpit usually provided for a gunner. My equipment consisted of about a dozen ordinary bricks. In the event that control of the test plane was lost, my job was to throw bricks at its propeller, thus causing a crash before a dangerous course was set. (When I think of the complex destruct systems used today in connection with guided missile and satellite launches, I laugh at our primitive scheme; fortunately, we never had to use it.)

Mr. Mirick's control system worked well. We could take off the test aircraft, fly around in a normal fashion and successfully land it. However, the test plane had to be in sight all the time and piloted constantly. Aircraft in those days did not have the inherent stability of present-day aircraft, nor were there autopilots able to fly an assigned course, speed and altitude. The pilot was the stabilizer, flying by the seat of his pants, the feel of the wind on his cheek and his ability to see the horizon. An automatic stabilizer was needed. Mr. Mirick determined that a gyro was the only device that could provide a stabilizing effect. He deferred further work on the remote control system until a gyro stabilizer could be developed.

Coincidentally, a few officers at the Bureau of Aeronautics had reached the conclusion that for better bombing accuracy a gyro stabilizer was needed.

Native Curiosity and the Byrd Flight

The environment at NRL was highly stimulating for my learning, individual growth and forward thinking.

I had a strong curiosity about all the facilities at the Laboratory, most of which had equipment unfamiliar to me. The shops and woodworking plants were more diversified than anything I had seen before. On one pretext or another, I got to know the doers and movers: the Laboratory director, department heads, engineers and lead technicians. I wanted to know these people who were preeminent in their fields.

Several of the department heads, many of my engineering associates, and even the director invited me into their homes. The resulting synergism helped whenever I needed assistance on a project.

When my six month probationary period ended, I was called in by the head of my department and welcomed as a permanent employee. I had entered a new frontier. I was becoming familiar with its dimensions and accepted by its pioneers.

One such pioneer was Malcolm Hanson, who, while on leave from NRL, had been radioman on then-Commander Richard E. Byrd's first attempt to reach the North Pole by air. Hanson had been granted leave from NRL. When Byrd's expedition failed, Hanson returned to the Laboratory, continuing his job as assistant chief of the Aircraft Radio Section.

Malcolm Hanson was a genius. He was also unpretentious, helpful, cheerful and friendly; a truly nice guy. He kept in regular contact with Commander Byrd, an ambitious explorer with new ideas.

Less than a year after Hanson's return to NRL, the Navy Department again requested he be allowed to assist Byrd on a new project.

Raymond Orteig of New York City had offered a $25,000 prize to the first aviator who could fly nonstop from New York to Paris. Although there had already been several tragic attempts to win the prize, Byrd was confident he could complete the flight in the right airplane. For its part, the Navy was interested in the long distance radio operation that would take place during the flight and in the solution to many problems with aviation radio communications.

The Wanamaker family of Philadelphia, operators of department stores in Philadelphia and New York, agreed to finance the Byrd project. Byrd told Hanson that as soon as he could locate a suitable airplane, he wanted Hanson's assistance with the radio equipment.

Hanson, in turn, asked me to help on the project. We made a good team. Hanson was the better engineer, but he knew I could provide shop know-how and flight experience.

Hanson and I were granted leave by NRL (without pay) to assist Commander Byrd with his radio work. Byrd's project agreed to pay us $25 per day, plus expenses and equipment costs.

Our first job was to obtain the equipment. From my Pensacola experience, I knew the type of generator that should be used on the flight. Driven by a small controllable-pitch propeller, it could be mounted on the wing. I found one in a salvage yard, and although sure of its characteristics, I decided to test it in a wind tunnel. The wind tunnel was in New Jersey; I had to catch a train from Pennsylvania Station in New York. The generator, a streamlined unit, resembled a bomb. As I walked through the station with it on my shoulder, I created a furor. People hastily gave me a wide berth.

The generator's test was satisfactory. Thus, perhaps the highest-cost item of radio equipment was obtained at a fraction of its original price. The savings on that item alone had justified my appointment as Hanson's assistant.

The receiver was also easy because we found a discarded USN experimental unit in the same salvage yard. Although its limited band range had been unsatisfactory for the Navy, it was ideal for Byrd's flight.

The transmitter required larger vacuum tubes, more efficient use of power, and much lighter weight than any then used on aircraft. We used every trick of the trade in component design to reduce weight and literally hung the transmitter in space, supporting it by elastic cords. The scheme saved several pounds of cabinet weight and assured maximum cooling.

Byrd's aircraft was newly designed by Anthony Fokker, perhaps the greatest aeronautical engineer of his time. Made of wood, fabric and wire, it featured a single wing with wooden spars, ribs, and thin plywood skin. Byrd and Fokker collaborated on three important factors: crew, fuel tanks and engines. However, even with the bare minimum of space allocated for these elements, no room was left for radio equipment. Consequently, quite a hassle ensued about each unit to be installed.

The receiver, generator and antenna reel were finally accommodated, but no solution could be found for the transmitter. At last, Mr. Fokker called for a keyhole saw and drill. He cut open the leading edge of the wing just above the pilot's seat, displaying a space that could house the transmitter. He ordered a suitably shaped cover for the hole. The problem was solved.

There is no substitute for the firsthand knowledge and experience of a good engineer in solving critical problems.

Byrd chose Floyd Bennett, a former chief aviation mechanic, as his copilot. Bennett had a great reputation in the Navy, particularly with flying boats.

The first test flight was made from the Teterboro, New Jersey, airport. The plane took to the air like a graceful bird. Several hours later it returned, made a picture book approach and touched down. But, as the plane rolled down the runway, its tail slowly lifted higher and higher. The nose hit the ground; the plane flipped over, coming to rest flat but upside down. The engine and nose fatally crushed Bennett. (As his memorial, the Navy named Floyd Bennett Field on Long Island in his honor.)

Neither Byrd nor the Wanamakers were deterred by the tragedy, however. After reviewing the situation, they decided to use a proven airplane, the Ford trimotor, an all-metal aircraft designed for passenger use. Almost an exact image of the Fokker airplane except for a slightly larger tail surface, the trimotor had proven itself on many flights.

Operations were transferred to Roosevelt Field in Garden City, Long Island. Byrd's original lead of more than a year had been lost. By this time both Charles Lindbergh and Clarence Chamberlin were getting ready for their flights. All three, Lindbergh, Chamberlin and Byrd, were at Garden City at the same time.

Although Byrd recognized the competition, he wouldn't be hurried. He insisted on extensive flight tests, including a full load test over long distances to calibrate engines and fuel consumption.

All three competing aircraft were flying gas tanks. Lindbergh had to use a periscope because one of his gas tanks was immediately in front of the pilot's seat. Chamberlin and his sponsor, Charles Levine, were jammed up in front of a huge gas tank.

The Ford aircraft, originally designed for passengers, had a longer cabin. Byrd installed a huge tank between the pilots and the compartment where the navigators would ride. Communication between them and the pilots was by interphone; emergency crawl space was available under the fuel tanks.

Byrd, Lindbergh and Chamberlin all recognized the danger in taking off from the short field at Garden City. But Byrd contrived a solution: a 20-foot ramp at the beginning of the runway, equivalent to several hundred feet of level runway. Although the three pilots were highly competitive in their ambition to win the big prize, they exchanged information regarding flight plans, maps and routes. Byrd also allowed Chamberlin and Lindbergh to use the ramp for takeoff.

All three calculated the amount of fuel load, probably praying their calculations were correct.

Lindbergh spoke to me about installing a small radio for his flight. But when I explained that nothing could be done for less than 20 pounds, he regretfully gave up the notion because he had no weight margin whatever.

Chamberlin also wanted a radio. He invited me to ride in the copilot seat of his novel and efficient Bellanca airplane on two test flights. However, when I told him the weight of radio and battery, he, too, mournfully shook his head.

Lindbergh was ready first. On a cloudy and misty morning his Ryan monoplane was positioned at the top of the ramp. With the engine and gravity working together, the overburdened plane had a good start by the end of the ramp. The takeoff was straight and the aircraft slowly picked up speed. But could Lindbergh make it over the telephone wires at the end of the runway?

A small crowd of us watched during the interminable takeoff, until at the last possible second his plane's wheels lifted and cleared the wires by inches. A shout went up and Lindy was on his way. The positive help of Byrd's ramp, minus the 20 pound weight of a radio, were the difference between life and death in those last few seconds of his takeoff.

Commander Byrd was as excited and proud as the rest of us when the report came in that Lindbergh had passed the last checkpoint off the coast of Nova Scotia.

It's a matter of record that Lindbergh almost ran into a lighthouse on the Irish coast. Parenthetically, it is also a matter of record that his inductor compass later proved to be unreliable because errors were introduced by pendulum and gyro effects due to the erratic action of the aircraft in rough air. Fortunately, the random plus and minus errors canceled each other out. This was one reason behind the nickname "Lucky Lindy."

Lindbergh landed at Le Bourget in Paris without incident, trundled up to a receiving group, stepped out of his aircraft and said, "I am Charles Lindbergh," as if the whole world didn't know.

Byrd Presses Onward

In the meantime, Byrd was persevering with calibration flights and watching the weather. The spring of 1927 had continuously bad weather, particularly from New York to Paris; the only break that season came during the Lindbergh flight.

Byrd was delighted when he heard Lindbergh had landed at Paris. Although disappointed that his own efforts were not in time, as a true aviation pioneer, he looked on the flight as the beginning of a new era for aviation. The $25,000 prize had been won. But the prize was unimportant in the total scale of values of that venture.

Evaluating the proposed Byrd flight, the Navy continued to evidence interest in many aspects, especially the use of a larger aircraft. The Wanamakers agreed to continue to finance the project, now close to readiness.

After the Fokker aircraft had crashed and in view of rising costs and unexpected complexities, the Wanamakers decided to assign an influential executive to manage the project with particular emphasis on public relations. They chose Grover Whalen, president of their New York City store. Whalen was an impressive man: figure, voice, gestures, and dress. His every public appearance—at our hangar, at press conferences or just getting in and out of an automobile—was an imposing event. As he strode along, accompanied by his staff, even the air was changed by the scent he wore.

This is not criticism, because Whalen was truly a great and productive man. Under his direction, there was no letup in our efforts to continue Byrd's flight tests and perfect every detail.

During this time Hanson was busy with his job at the Laboratory and in negotiation with a new company that planned to exploit intercity radio communication. Thus, I was delegated most of the work on design and installation of the Byrd radio equipment, together with flight tests and crew indoctrination.

The public had great interest in the contest, an interest enhanced by crashes, fatalities and plane disappearances. Notable political, aviation and media figures often visited the hangars at the Teterboro and Garden City airfields. Because we were such a small community, I formed attachments with many of them that lasted for years. That was my first introduction to what I call "the big time."

Among the media figures was Ernie Pyle, a small man who could have easily been lost in a crowd. At that time Ernie was employed by the North American Press Association which specialized in big event stories. I learned much from him about people and practices of the news media.

The original composition of Byrd's crew was to have been Floyd Bennett as pilot-radio operator, a copilot, and Byrd as navigator. After the death of Bennett, a new pilot was selected; a copilot-radio operator was later appointed. Byrd remained as navigator.

During the extended flight tests, there seemed to be tension present in the cockpit. I was along on several flights and was not satisfied with the cockpit atmosphere, or the radio capability. Though I made tentative comments, they were not well received. I did not pursue the subject.

With only a few test flights remaining, Bernt Balchen, a famous Norwegian pilot, was added to the crew. He was to be in the navigator's cabin along with Commander Byrd. He was young, cheerful and competent; a real pleasure to work with.

About that same time, because of my concern about radio operation, I installed another piece of radio equipment: an automatic signaling device attached to the radio transmitter. It would be in operation during Byrd's entire flight except when there was need to receive signals.

Takeoff of the Byrd flight was made in front of officials and an ample supply of newsmen. The big plane with its three engines roaring and proven takeoff performance had more margin over the telephone wires than did Lindbergh's plane.

Unfortunately, shortly after *America* left Garden City, the weather went from bad to worse for the remainder of the flight. However, the automatic radio signals continued to be heard for 1,800 miles before they gradually faded out.

Nearing the Irish coast, Byrd noticed the interphone responses from the cockpit seemed garbled and ordered Balchen to take over the controls. After some persuasion, Balchen crawled up front. Byrd's navigation was nearly perfect and after a momentary glimpse of the French coast, he estimated the final distance to Paris.

As *America* neared Le Bourget, the bright lights of Paris illuminated the dense fog. Byrd tried to communicate by radio with no success. It was later found that the trailing wire antenna had been reeled in shortly after passing the French sea coast to keep the heavy lead weight at its end from hitting houses or power lines below. The people at the airport heard the plane's engine overhead, but were unable to help.

After a few passes over the airport, Byrd decided to return to the coast to attempt a landing in the water near the beach. Landing successfully, it was a tribute to the performance of the aircraft, pilot and navigator.

I gained an unexpected dividend from my association with Byrd's flight. The *New York Times* and many other newspapers carried a North American Press story about the remarkable performance of the radio designed by Lawrence Hyland and Malcolm Hanson. A few papers even carried my picture. My newfound friend, Ernie Pyle, had given me worldwide publicity for the long distant radio communication from aircraft to ground.

The Lindbergh-Byrd-Chamberlin efforts at Teterboro and Garden City had an important influence on my career. It reignited my interest in radio work during my off-hours. I had first engaged in extra work during my Pensacola days for my own satisfaction and to increase my earnings. Ships in port called me whenever they were in need of radio service work. Though calls had sometimes been frequent, they never interfered with Navy duties.

Back to NRL and Continuing Research

When I returned to NRL I was assigned to assist another engineer who was trying to solve the problem of ignition interference with radio operations on aircraft. I had worked on engine ignition interference suppression—with little progress and not much hope.

In those days aircraft communication from air to ground was excellent, but from ground to air it was not. Each engine spark plug was a little radio transmitter. The resulting ignition interference caused a continuing roar in the pilot's headphones, overriding anything but the strongest radio signal,.

Two groups at the Laboratory were trying to cure the problem. One was experimenting with filters inside the receivers. The other, the Mirick group, was attempting to discover a source of electrical suppression.

I didn't agree with either approach, particularly the second. I had spent too many years in aircraft trying to detect useful signals through the roar of ignition interference. Throwing precaution aside, I expressed my dissatisfaction with the project's progress to my section head, Carlos Mirick.

A few days later, to my surprise, he canceled former suppression directives and issued a new one, placing me in charge of the new project.

After researching all domestic and foreign literature to find what was going on around the world on this important subject, I realized there were at least 10 laboratories in the U.S. alone working on the problem.

Unraveling Aircraft Radio Communications

One day I needed information about a particular kind of receiver. I walked next door to the Ship Receiver group. Over a period of time, I had managed to strike up a speaking relationship with the stern-looking, rawboned Scandinavian senior engineer who ran it.

When I found his office vacant, I went to his laboratory. There was a large cage made of two layers of fine copper mesh. All the seams were overlapped and soldered; the doors were of radiation-proof construction so that there could be no electromagnetic signal leakage. This was a true Faraday cage, named for the English experimenter.

The image of that cage continued to rattle my mind. An idea hit me. I remembered the radio compartment on the *Marblehead*. It had a Faraday shield against electrical noise in addition to a cork shield against acoustic noise.

I concluded the Faraday shield principle might be helpful to my assignment. I had a small, battery operated, aircraft radio receiver and a magneto and spark plug combination rig which I had used to test several varieties of interference suppressors intended to deaden the noise.

A few days later, I got up enough nerve to ask my next door neighbor if I could use his cage for an hour or so. Because he was taking leave the next day and there was no test equipment in the cage, he agreed.

Next morning I took my receiver, ignition simulation rig, and a helper to the next door Laboratory. Leaving the ignition rig outside with my assistant, I entered the cage and set up the receiver. With the door shut, I put on earphones and had him turn the magneto crank. I heard nothing. But as soon as I cracked open the cage door, a familiar roar was in the earphones. I shut the door and there was silence. I reversed the procedure, putting the ignition rig inside the cage and the receiver outside, reasonably close to the cage. I signaled for my helper to turn the crank. Listening to my receiver, I heard nothing. I opened the door a crack and the roar resumed.

Removing my earphones, I returned to my own workroom. Shutting my door, I leaned back in my chair and grinned happily. I knew I had the answer.

Several attempts at shielding spark plugs and radio equipment had been among experiments listed in literature I had studied. In some cases the magneto, switch and wires had been shielded, but no improvement noticed. No attempt had been made to shield the entire spark plug because high tension voltage would cause the spark to jump to any grounded conductor within an inch of the spark plug terminal.

The answer was to devise a spark plug and connector that would allow for complete shielding. This seemingly simple solution was difficult. But, within a few months I found what I thought was a satisfactory arrangement.

For a field test, I prepared clean, new, braided copper tubing to go over all ignition wires and mechanisms of an airplane, with special end fittings and spark plug covers to assure no electrical leakage. I took the assembly to the Anacostia Air Station. in Washington. With the help of Lieutenant George DeBaun we installed the test arrangement on a two-seater biplane. We crossed our fingers.

The engine started normally and was given a lengthy warm up. I sat in the rear seat and listened in on the receiver. It sounded suspiciously good. We started the engine several times to validate our shielding installation and confirm proper operation of the engine and radio receiver.

I was ready to go. Lieutenant DeBaun got his goggles; we climbed in the airplane and took off. I tuned to WRC, one of our local radio stations, blissfully listening to music and the announcer. I passed the headphones to DeBaun. He listened, made an "O" with his fingers, shook his fist in triumph, and passed back the headphones. We landed at the test field.

A new era of aircraft radio communications had arrived.

That test aircraft made many demonstration flights. But the idea of a completely shielded ignition system was not warmly received by other test pilots at the Naval Air Station. The engine ignition system was the holiest of holies. Anything that could be a hazard, or was even just new or "different," was regarded with suspicion. The pilots also felt a pound of added weight was an unnecessary addition.

However, DeBaun's and my enthusiasm wouldn't be dampened. DeBaun continued his missionary work with pilots at the Air Station. I made patent disclosures for the shielded spark plug.

The First Bendix Connection

The Eclipse Aviation Division of the Bendix Corporation heard of the new invention. I was invited to meet with two executives at their plant in East Orange, New Jersey. That evening during an excellent dinner, they evidenced some interest in the spark plug invention and asked to see my disclosure. I readily agreed.

A few weeks later we met again; they said the systems disclosures were of no value to the company. However, they did offer to pay me $10,000 for my spark plug invention. Today, that would be equivalent to more than $100,000. In 1928, to me it was all the money in the world. I needed no counsel or advice to accept the offer.

Within a few months of my disclosure, at least eight other inventors came forward, claiming priority. Lawyers jumped in with both feet.

The subsequent hearings and lawsuits lasted for nearly 15 years.

Under Navy regulations, to which I had gladly agreed, I received commercial rights, but the government had the remaining rights to all inventions. The handling of disclosures and patent applications was by Bendix lawyers, but the name appearing on the patent was a Navy lawyer. However, litigation in subsequent years was handled by Bendix lawyers.

The main issue was structure of the spark plug. The grounded conductive shielding on the plug had to cover and surround it completely. There could not be even a tiny hole or crack, or the electromagnetic signature of the ignition system would escape, interfering with radio reception.

Litigation continued for years. At one point, Bendix Aviation Corporation, the general manager of the Eclipse-Pioneer Division, and I were collectively being sued for $21 million. The Department of Justice intervened twice as appeals by each side were carried up to the U.S. Supreme Court on two separate occasions.

Litigation on my behalf was always successful, and apart from lawyers (who always seem to make out), I was the only person who made any money on the invention—the $10,000 originally paid me by Bendix.

The final adjudication of the Supreme Court was in our favor.

(The ultimate disposition: Shortly after the final adjudication in July 1943, the subject was brought before Bendix Corporation's board of directors. Legal advice to the board was that there had been thousands of infringers of the patent throughout the world; it would be tremendously costly to try to recover damages from them. Moreover, many infringers were good customers of Bendix. The recommendation was to give the patent rights to the public and close out the case. The Bendix board so decided.)

The benefits to the U.S. government and its citizens because of free use of this patent have been immense—perhaps in the billions of dollars.

However, in the written histories of the Naval Research Laboratory, there has never been any mention of this invention. The reason: immediately after the successful demonstration, the project was closed out by NRL. Its job was done.

In the 1980s I visited the Naval Research Laboratory and was shown the exhibit of NRL accomplishments. I found only a sentence or two regarding the spark plug invention. Notwithstanding the minimal return in public recognition and lack of royalty payments, I am more than satisfied about my contribution to aircraft and other mobile communication throughout the world.

However, I want to make it clear that the spark plug invention did not derive from a great intellect nor from a great laboratory. It came about by application of curiosity, observation and action—the true Yankee inventor syndrome.

No matter its origin, that invention had an enormous impact on my career.

The Beginning of Radar

Upon completion of the ignition interference investigation in November 1928, I received my next NRL assignment. It was to devise a method of effective radio direction finding better fashioned for small aircraft. The project was relatively simple from a radioman's point of view, but somewhat more difficult for pilots.

Pilots of that era were not concerned about radio communication or radio direction finding.

Work on the project started about the same time as higher radio frequencies began to be used. We decided to try direction finding at higher frequencies. It required new antenna, receiver, and transmitter.

After considerable work on these components, I finally had a package that was a good approximation of what was needed. We began our first trial of high frequency direction finding.

The transmitter was installed on the second floor of the Laboratory, facing the Naval Air Station at Anacostia; the receiver was in the cockpit of the demonstration aircraft just beneath the antenna. We placed the airplane on the Air Station's compass rose (about two miles from the transmitter) and rotated it to a position that should give maximum signal reception.

A telephone call to the Lab put the transmitter into operation; I sat in front of the receiver, probing for what I hoped would be a good signal. Within minutes I found it. I instructed my assistant, Chief

Radioman Hines, to gradually rotate the airplane in order to see if I could find the zero point. Sure enough, it was there and the superregenerator really worked. The airplane was slowly inched around; the superregenerator performed; an unbelievably sharp point was found where the sensitive meter needle was at zero.

After a short lunch break, I decided to begin calibration and had the airplane positioned at a point about 10 degrees away from the zero signal. Just then a small plane landed. I recognized it as the personal aircraft of Chance Vought, the great designer of Naval reconnaissance aircraft of that period. I was naturally in awe and went to get a better view of Mr. Vought and his airplane.

I remembered that I had mentioned to members of our car pool that Chance Vought occassionally gave rides in his plane to the Station staff. One young lady had practically demanded that I get her a ride on his next visit. So, I headed for the hangar to ask Mr. Vought if he would give a ride to a nice young lady. He agreed.

I quickly phoned the Lab to tell my friend that Chance Vought had agreed to take her up, provided she got to the Station in a hurry. She made the trip in short order; Chance Vought immediately took her up. Not only a good aircraft designer, he was also a good showman, performing Immelmanns (Editor's note: named for the famed German WWI aviator, the Immelmann turn is a half loop with a half roll on top.), loop-the-loops, and falling leaves—all within half an hour. After landing, the excited girl told everyone she'd had the time of her life. (That young lady, incidentally, was later to become my wife.)

When I returned, I found Chief Hines in the state of a frustrated experimenter. He said the receiver performance was erratic. Just about the time he approached a zero position, the needle would waver back and forth as though there was a loose connection. I assured him I would find the trouble.

Replacing him in the cockpit, I checked all circuits. The receiver seemed to be performing properly; I was about to proudly announce I had located the trouble when suddenly the meter needle wavered. Using earphones, I heard peculiar noises. They did not sound as if they came from ordinary bad connections. I made a few adjustments and felt things were under control; but, the disturbances suddenly returned.

I sat on the edge of the cockpit and stared down at the equipment in frustration. Idly I looked around and spotted a medium-sized aircraft as it taxied to the runway and took off. Shortly after it was airborne I glanced down. The meter needle was wavering back and forth. Before I could climb back into the cockpit and readjust it, the wavering stopped.

Another airplane started down the runway and was airborne. Again by accident I glanced down and spotted the meter wavering in much the same manner as before. A small high performance fighter plane rolled up to the starting point on the runway. Of course, I observed the spectacular takeoff. The plane used only half the runway before it was airborne. Out of the corner of my eye, I noticed the meter needle frantically moving much faster than it had before.

I finally began to tie things together. I suspected some sort of reradiation from the neighboring airplane's flight.

I hoped for a validation takeoff and flight with the meter positioned so I could watch it and the aircraft at the same time. Fortunately, it happened. The Air Station had a new Ford all-metal Trimotor passenger aircraft. At that moment, it was at the end of the runway, running up its engines in preparation for takeoff. As the plane moved ponderously down the runway, the needle on the meter never moved. But shortly after takeoff, the needle began to register with slow but full-scale wavering. I knew we had something.

We shut off the equipment and parked our test aircraft in the hangar. I rushed back to the Laboratory to meet with Taylor, Young and Mirick. I explained everything that had happened and what I believed had taken place. Frankly, it had all started when Chance Vought took the young lady for her exciting ride.

Leo Young accepted my explanation, but Taylor and Mirick requested more data. At the end of our meeting, I wrote a memorandum outlining what had happened, and put it in the section files.

Next day Carlos Mirick decided to temporarily suspend the high frequency direction finding project, stating that the test aircraft with its fancy antenna should be used for initial experiments on the new phenomenon.

The test aircraft was positioned on the compass rose (Editor's note: used for calibration of an aircraft's compass), pointed the same direction as before. A series of flights were programmed to overfly the compass rose on paths spaced at 30 degree intervals for the entire 360 degrees around the rose.

The flights confirmed the original assessment of the phenomena. However, the observed signal patterns exhibited two other interesting characteristics. First, the Doppler effect (Editor's note: change in frequency when two sources are in rapid motion) differentiated between approaching and receding flights. Second, as the target plane approached the compass rose, the rate of signal slowed, passed through zero, and as the plane receded, resumed a rate slightly slower than the approach rate .

After these flights were completed, we held another conference, agreeing that an important basic discovery had been made. We felt the preliminary analysis was correct. It could now be reported to Commander Almy, director of the Laboratory, with a recommendation that he apply to the Radio Division of the Bureau of Ships for an appropriation to carry on further definition and possible application of the discovery.

The Next Brush with Bureaucracy

Commander Almy was enthusiastic and promised to go to the Bureau. He felt our discovery might be the most important one of his tour of duty at the Laboratory. He pointed out, however, that it would take time to process a new authorization by the Bureau; meantime he would fund the project out of a $100,000 discretionary allotment made to the Laboratory each year.

We began a new series of experiments with two overflights, approaching and receding as before about five miles in either direction. A proposal was made that we determine if the phenomena would occur at even higher frequencies. Future tests would be made, depending on the results of each series.

We equipped a small van with a rotatable high frequency antenna array and the necessary instrumentation.

Because we knew some kind of visual record would be needed, I was instructed to make careful hand drawings of the meter readings showing signal strength as a function of time. The data recording of the two flights was extremely successful. The noticeable difference between the approaching and receding interferences. showed up as beautiful sine waves, except for a flattening out when the target plane was in the immediate vacinity of our receiver.

A month or more after these first tests, we revised and improved our instrumentation. We felt we were really on to something important. Each extrapolation was working; we were increasingly confident of our work's future value to the Navy.

Then Commander Almy called us into his office. He had received a letter from the Bureau of Ships stating the project had been disapproved and funding denied.

Of course, we were astounded.

The following day, Commander Almy made a special trip to the Radio Division of the Bureau of Ships. He described our discovery, the subsequent proof and extensions, and explained the future possibilities. He added his opinion that our discovery would turn out to be worth a division of battleships to the Navy. (This statement later proved to be true at Pearl Harbor.) In spite of his arguments, an official at the Bureau of Ships was adamant, stating that the work was to be discontinued.

Concurrent with Almy's visit to the Bureau, I was carrying out some double frequency tests that had been scheduled.

There were extra dividends from those tests.

One afternoon a line squall approached, increasing static from one low frequency broadcast receiver used on the test.

Inside a test van I intended to shut off another, high frequency, receiver; but, I heard no sound and turned away, thinking I had turned it off. But, the receiver was on. I put on headphones and heard only the normal low noise level of the test signal from the station. Inside the field station the static was still roaring from the broadcast receiver. Almost unbelievably, I realized that at higher frequency, there was much less static effect in the reception.

To my knowledge this was the first time it was noted that high frequency radio is not bothered by ordinary static nearly as much as the low and medium frequency radio.

I reported the results of the tests to Carlos Mirick, who was interested, noting the project was really indicative of many things.

Word came that Commander Almy again wanted to see us in his office. Because of the results of the double frequency tests, we went in a sort of euphoria. Our balloon was broken when Commander Almy reported the results of a second visit to the Bureau of Ships. He told us that once again the project had been disapproved. He had no alternative but to terminate it. We were instructed to complete detailed reports, make necessary patent applications and resume work on the high frequency direction finder. He ended by expressing his appreciation for our work, assuring us he still felt it had great potential value for the Navy.

When I told Dr. Taylor of the termination of the project, he exploded. When exercised, his voice went up two octaves and his expletives were awesome.

After he calmed down we agreed to somehow find a way around this obstacle; our other assigned projects were intertwined with technology needed to explore radio detection phenomena.

This bureaucratic barrier placed against further development of radio detection of aircraft was an aberration—but of enormous proportions—from normally sound Navy management policy for its Laboratories.

The worst, however, was yet to come.

The Beginning of Private Enterprise

Leo Young and I had become well known in radio technical circles for our work in transmitter frequency control and stability. We were often consulted by commercial industry. Since we had evenings, Saturday afternoons and Sundays at our disposal—and because there was a continuing demand for our products and advice—we set up a small company to formalize our "moonlighting." We named it the Radio Research Company. We employed a very capable technician, installing a shop in his cellar. Ultimately, we expanded into a 400-square foot shop.

Although radio was in its infancy, advertising was becoming

important. Stations wanted to demonstrate to potential advertisers the effective area of their transmitters. To meet this need, we bought a Ford Model A van, installed radio field-strength measuring equipment, connecting it to a rotatable coil antenna in a boxlike structure on the van's roof. With not more than a half-dozen comparable mobile field-strength devices in the country, we had a profitable part-time business.

Though not officially recognized, NRL was aware of our work. We supplied the Lab, gratis, with considerable information about wave propagation and antenna patterns, particularly those of multiple-tuned antenna arrays.

Since World War I, the Navy had been experimenting with rigid dirigibles, which had been demonstrated effectively in Germany. One of Germany's great airships, renamed the *USS Los Angeles*, had been delivered to the Naval hangar at Lakehurst, New Jersey as partial German WWI reparation. A "shakedown flight" for training American crews was scheduled to Washington, D.C.

When I heard of this flight, it occurred to me the occasion might offer an opportunity to determine if aircraft detection phenomena would happen at low frequencies. The mammoth metal structure of the *Los Angeles* was about a wavelength longer and corresponded to the same frequency used by a radio station in Washington. My field-strength van was ideal for such an experiment at any broadcast frequency. All I needed was the proposed course of the dirigible so I could select an appropriate site for my equipment.

The probable flight path would be from the Capitol, heading toward Mt. Vernon (the George Washington home). Using road maps and automobile reconnaissance, I picked a field near Four Corners, Virginia, as ideal. It was on a direct line to the antenna of radio station WMAL and had neither buildings nor trees to interfere with my vision of the approaching dirigible.

A couple of days later I drove my van to my field test site. However, I had failed to notice that the green in the nice flat field was corn about a foot high. Paying no attention to the corn, I positioned my van in the middle of the field. I tuned in WMAL, rotated my roof-mounted search coil, got suitable maxima and minima of signal strength and went outside to wait for the dirigible.

It appeared over the horizon right on schedule. I jumped inside the van to listen for the signal. Sure enough, the meter needle began to slowly move, first to the top end of the scale and then down to zero. Back and forth at a uniform rate. Then as the airship came closer, the rate finally slowed to zero. When the dirigible began its turn to retrace a course toward the Capitol, the slow needle movement resumed. At that moment I heard a shout. I stepped outside to find what the noise was about.

It came from an irate farmer, standing with his dog. When he began with a few well-chosen expletives, I held up my hand, explaining that I was checking the radio transmission from the dirigible, now playing music. Praying that there would be no announcement of call letters, I offered to let him listen. He was impressed. I told him ours was a secret Government project and very important. Thus mollified, he said, "You can work here anytime," and turned away. With a mixture of relief—and satisfaction with the experiment—I climbed in the van and drove away.

Next day I reported the results (and the incident) to Carlos Mirick. He said I should summarize the wavelength experiments and conclusions in a report to the director.

This report was forwarded from the director's office to the Bureau of Ships.

The Bureau's reaction was immediate. An official made a personal visit to the Laboratory, instructing Commander Almy to call me in. The Bureau official told me my work was completely unauthorized; as an employee of the Naval Research Laboratory, my interest should be Navy interest 24-hours a day. He pointed out that my technical work should be solely that authorized by the Navy.

My response was also immediate. I replied that under such circumstances, I could not continue my work at the Laboratory. I resigned on the spot, ending my direct Navy association.

Those six years as an engineer at the Naval Research Laboratory had nourished my nascent objective for a career in aviation radio. Also, the patent policy of the Laboratory and its industrial suppliers made it possible for me to step into civilian life with both social and business relationships firmly established.

From that day forward, I became a full-time employee of the Radio Research Company. My partner, Leo Young, remained at the Naval Research Laboratory with Taylor and Mirick. All three had long and useful careers.

Further Developments in Radar

Young and I frequently discussed unclassified work at the Laboratory. I knew that he and Taylor would continue their investigation of the reflection phenomena by associating it with their primary project on the propagation of high frequency radio waves. They were excited by the possibility that techniques learned in a purely scientific investigation, when applied to this new discovery, could result in something that might have an important military use.

Putting all the Laboratory experiments together, Young described a system that contained all the elements of what today is called radar— although at that time the name had not yet been invented.

Later he informed me that two U.S. patents, No. #1,979,297 and No. #1,981,884, had been issued in 1934 in the names of Taylor, Hyland, and Young, relating to the discoveries of aircraft detection and signal reflection and refraction (Editor's note: basic radar technology).

After patents were issued, copies were routinely acquired by embassy attaches from many countries and forwarded to their own experts at home.

Usually such a process takes several months. Thus, it seems more than coincidence that in 1935 almost every major foreign country duplicated the experiments described in those two patents, then initiated their own radar developments.

Detection, signal reflection and refraction work in the United States was carried on chiefly by the Naval Research Laboratory and the Army's Ft. Monmouth Signal Corps Laboratory. Emphasis was on detection of aircraft by radar located on the ground or on ships. Pulse radar was decided upon by most investigators. It was determined that transmitted energy should be concentrated in beams. But narrow beams at the frequencies then possible could only be achieved by use of very large antenna dishes or reflectors.

In Great Britain, the foresight of Lord Swinton and Air Marshal Henry Tizard encouraged development of a remarkable device invented by Dr. Bowen, called a magnetron, that made possible use of much higher frequencies for radar, thus permitting a smaller antenna reflector. The magnetron was the key device in development of airborne radar. The tactics developed by Sir Robert Watson-Watt after his visits to the United States and his utilization of British technical developments proved to be the salvation of England from relentless attacks by German bombers during World War II.

Radar and Politics

As a result of the initial success of German submarines against allied ships in the Atlantic, Winston Churchill's plea to President Franklin D. Roosevelt was finally answered by transfer of 50 American destroyers to Great Britain. This raised an uproar in Congress and with some of the populace. Charges of misuse of government property and the breaking of neutrality placed Roosevelt in a difficult position.

At the height of the controversy, Lord Swinton and Air Marshal Tizard made another important decision. They foresaw the probable fall of France and the possible fact that Britain might have to face the German armies alone without essential military supplies and food. They recognized that their progress in radar technology, particularly the magnetron tube and tactical applications of both ground-based and airborne radar for air defense—all much accelerated by the war—should be of extreme interest to the United States. Despite the then unfavorable U.S. political climate, they foresaw the possibility of American involvement.

A high level British committee, headed by Air Marshal Tizard and Dr. Bowen, was charged with the responsibility for gathering every scrap of information about British radar and its uses. The information was transported by the committee to the United States and presented as an offering for whatever American assistance might be granted.

American military authorities greeted Air Marshal Tizard with open arms, quickly alerting President Roosevelt to the value of the proposed contribution. The President understood its military value, and also, with his usual appreciation of political opportunity, saw the solution to the destroyer problem. He ordered that extensive publicity be released to show the value of the British information to the American public. At the same time, the President froze any release of information regarding American radar work. He personally assured Congress that not only was the British information important, it was the price he had exacted in return for the 50 destroyers. The Roosevelt ploy was amazingly successful. Congress and the public were convinced of the value of the British radar contribution, unaware of the prior American work that had initiated the technology.

Newspaper articles and radio reports on radar continued without any mention of American participation. Finally, I was motivated to write to Commander Lavender, head of the Navy Patent Department, saying I was unable to understand why there had been no publicity about American detection devices.

A few days later a visitor, an American Naval officer, showed up at my Bendix office in Washington (where I was then stationed). He established credibility by mentioning names of other officers known to me, then brought up my letter to Commander Lavender. He explained the President's predicament—the 50 destroyers and the use of the Tizard revelations as offset—emphasizing the importance of public acceptance of partnership with Great Britain if later hostilities involved the United States. He assured me a suitable announcement of American work would be made at a later date.

I accepted the explanation, assuring him of my cooperation and understanding.

Actually, I went further. A few days later I learned that my former associate, Malcolm Hanson, now a Naval officer, had fatally crashed into an Aleutian mountain. As a tribute to him, and as a contribution to the war effort, I again wrote Commander Lavender, this time stating that I wished to contribute to the public whatever radar rights I had.

The letter was never acknowledged, nor did I expect it to be. Moreover, until recently, I never disclosed the facts of this incident.

The progress accomplished between the mid-1930s and now is incredible. Today, thousands of eyes look at radar displays, in effect extending human vision and judgment to great distances. Air Traffic

Control centers for multiple airport regions cover the nation, making a huge contribution to flight safety. Radar is used in aircraft blind landing systems, where elevations from thousands of feet down to a few feet are measured. The current world airline system could not operate without radar. In the military, airborne radar detects other aircraft at long ranges; radar guides air-to-air, air-to-ground, and ground-to-air armaments with high precision. More exotic are the uses of radar for tracking and control of objects in space hundreds of thousands of miles from earth.

Radar is today knit into the fabric of society.

During my lifetime, it has been my privilege to see radar flower, bloom and spread all over Earth and into space. Radar and computers grew up together. Their prolific marriage produced, through ingenious minds, many creations giving incredible performance.

I am sure there is credit enough to satisfy all who have participated in the evolution of this fascinating technology.

Chapter IV
The Budding Entrepreneur

My departure from NRL—and from my protected income environment during the years in the Army and Navy—was a traumatic change. I hadn't properly anticipated the impact.

I now had responsibility to meet the weekly payroll of Radio Research Company. In normal times, with orders on the books, it would have been easy. But this was 1932—the height of the Depression.

Fortunately, a Buffalo organization was formed to establish a city-to-city radio business. They contacted NRL to ask if an engineer could provide a source of equipment for frequency stabilization.

The inquiry came to Dr. Taylor, then to Leo Young. Leo and I talked it over and thought that if the two of us worked together, our Radio Research Company could devise equipment using crystal frequency control circuits operated in a nearly constant temperature environment.

Leo and I met with the managing partner of the Buffalo organization and his consulting engineer. We proposed a working model on a time and material basis, including $25 per day for each of us. We got the job.

The crystal circuit was routine, but a suitable temperature control was something else. A local instrument manufacturer, who had begun production of a super sensitive, adjustable mercury temperature control, met our requirements.

In a few weeks we had the model ready to demonstrate to our customers. They were pleased with the results. They required five finished units with frequency separation and suitable packaging. Each of the units would represent a radio station and be located in a room at a warehouse leased by the group. Their objective was to demonstrate to the newly-formed Federal Radio Commission that such an arrangement would make efficient use of frequency spectrum just above the broadcast band for telegraph use only.

The Radio Commission's deadline was six months from time of application. Three months had already passed. The Buffalo manager insisted we undertake the work, promising a bonus if we completed the project on time.

Leo and I looked at each other. Leo said we'd have to discuss it and would give him our answer the next day.

We were in a quandary; the job looked too big for us. Our garage spaces were small; and neither of us had time to do all the work ourselves. We would need a full-time workman. Moreover, special heat insulated metal cabinets would be needed. It meant an outlay of several thousand dollars.

Leo and I knew a young mechanic who was interested in radio and aviation. In the past we had used him on small jobs. We decided to ask if he wanted to make these five units for us. He did.

The next day we told our prospective customers we would do the job on a time and material basis, but needed an advance of $2,000, plus prompt weekly payments of salaries and material bills. They agreed. We were in business.

Our new employee, Ruel Colvin, started work the following morning. It proved to be a lifetime association for him.

It was long days for Colvin and short nights for us. We even put a penny behind the fuses in Colvin's cellar to supply necessary power for our electric tools.

Suprisingly, all completed units tested well in Colvin's cellar and were delivered to the leased warehouse the day before the Federal Radio Commissioners were due to witness a demonstration.

The demonstration was successful. The Commissioners were ready to give our customers a license. However, competitor interests intervened. An extended legal battle ensued with an adverse settlement. Fortunately, Radio Research Company was not involved. We were paid for the job, including bonus.

Pioneering in the Early Days of Radio

Leo and I realized that the precise frequency control of quartz crystals in our constant temperature ovens could also cure a problem of concern to radio listeners at the time.

Listeners could have programs frequently interrupted as frequencies shifted because of changes in temperatures, tuning or other local conditions.

Young and I heard radio station WJSV in Washington was experiencing poor frequency control, drifting up and down by as much as several hundred cycles. This drift caused intolerable noises in home radio receivers. WJSV had been warned to improve its control.

We visited the proprietor of WJSV, convincing him we could solve his problem. He gave us an order for one of our frequency controls systems; when installed, it provided WJSV with a more stable signal than any other station in the Washington area.

Other orders followed. Radio Research Company soon had five employees, all working in a cellar with primitive tools. One proved to be a good supervisor; two were competent craftsmen. They worked during the day, and my partner, Leo, and I continued to work at night. Our products were innovative and accepted by the industry. Radio broadcasting, an important part of our market, was growing rapidly.

During this period Leo was studying transmitter frequency separation and stability at his regular job at NRL. Ultimately he concluded there should be a frequency separation of about 10,000 cycles per second (10 kilocycles; or 10 Kc) between frequencies of stations in the same area. Thus, even if the frequency should drift back and forth a few cycles per second, stations would not interfere with each other.

At the same time, I had completed development and patenting of a holder with electrodes and adjusting screw for a quartz crystal. The frequency of any broadcast-band transmitter could be controlled by use of an appropriately cut crystal.

We made two or three small transmitters, demonstrating to our own satisfaction that frequency stability, along with the 10 Kc channel separation, was what we needed. We had already developed frequency stability equal to a few cycles per second. We were sure the combination of this stability and the 10 Kc channel separation would solve the radio interference problem.

The Federal Radio Commission was being bedeviled by many in the industry to devise a method of frequency control. One Commissioner happened to be a former Navy lieutenant commander whom Leo and I both knew. We explained to him our scheme to separate frequency allocations by 10 Kc, stabilizing them with quartz crystal control. We invited the Commission to visit our shop to view a demonstration of our frequency control and channel separation system.

They accepted and set a date. We had a bear by the tail. We cleared as much space as possible in the shop, rented a couple of dozen undertaker's chairs and prepared for the demonstration.

When the Commissioners arrived, they were accompanied by the distinguished counsel for the Institute of Radio Engineers. Fortunately, the demonstration went smoothly; our visitors expressed satisfaction that we had discovered a valid solution for a difficult problem.

The Government Mandates the Requirement

At a meeting two weeks later, the Commissioners announced that broadcast frequencies would be allocated with 10 Kc separations; also, stations would be required to have appropriate frequency controls installed by a specific date. (That 10 Kc standard channel separation survives to this day.)

Stations had to rush to comply. Western Electric had done some work along the same line and announced it would furnish radio transmitters in full compliance with the Federal Radio Commission's order at prices in the range of several hundred thousand dollars. Some big-city radio networks took advantage of the offer. However, smaller stations didn't have that kind of money; they called us for prices. We said we could supply our frequency control and crystals cut to their frequency assignment for about $950 per unit. We would also furnish schematic diagrams and information for intermediate amplifiers to connect our unit into their existing equipment.

After WJSV's successful modification of its old transmitter with our frequency control system, James S. Vance (the initials provided the call letters WJSV) asked if we could build a more powerful transmitter, strong enough to serve the entire Washington area from his present transmitter, several miles south of Alexandria, Virginia.

Leo and I decided to undertake the job, even though we knew we would need more money to finance the operation. With some trepidation, I went to our local bank and showed the manager our audit book and statement roster. I also invited him to visit our shop. Though he never accepted the invitation, he did grant the Radio Research Company a $500 line of credit.

I arranged a similar line of credit with the local General Electric distributor, knowing their shop could do work we were unable to do in our small shop.

We hired two more men and were on our way. But after the first radio station equipment was installed, I ran into trouble. I couldn't get the correct amount of power out of the final transmitter amplifiers. I resorted to all kinds of tuning schemes and couplings to solve the problem.

The situation was even more difficult because WJSV's owner was engaged in an attack on Governor Al Smith in his candidacy for the Presidency. The bitterness ultimately got to the Federal Radio Commission. They notified the Radio Research Company that we had to meet the construction completion date for the new transmitter and pass the Radio Commission's approval—or the WJSV license would be revoked.

I was frantic. The date was drawing closer and I knew we could not pass the test for the appropriate amount of modulation. I suspected the problem was in the coupling between the transmitter and antenna, but could find no way to adjust it. On the way home after a frustrating night working on the problem, I suddenly recalled an old formula: The matching of the coupling from transmitter to antenna was a sqaure root relationship. I had been working on a linear one. Tired as I was, I turned my car around and returned to the radio station. I applied the formula to my work; immediately the power transfer and general performance met the Commission's requirements. Not bothering to go home, I spent the rest of the night sleeping peacefully in my car.

Next day the Federal Radio Commission engineer showed up. He examined the equipment, was complimentary, and asked for a demonstration. I proudly adjusted the controls, turned on a modulation tester; the meters responded to the satisfaction of the inspector. WJSV received its license. It was the first radio station with a transmitter of its size and class fully in accord with the Commission's new specification.

First Impact of the Defense Business

Government business from the Navy and to a lesser degree from the Coast Guard was very profitable for Radio Research Company. But we discovered that, though these government orders were fairly large, we were often in a feast or famine situation. We were either overloaded or had no work.

At times it was necessary to ask our employees to work extra hours at no pay. But they recognized the depressed employment situation and had a certain amount of inherent loyalty and dedication, which all good employees have. All this allowed us to get away with what today would be unfair labor practices.

Due to a shortage of income, we were once forced to make a 10 percent reduction in employee pay; but we promised to make up the deficiency as soon as we received our overdue funds. Though a few grumbled, the men went along with the reduction; within a month the 10 percent deficiency was returned.

Later on we attempted to do the same thing. This time we received some rather plain spoken words from the men about our employment practices. For the first time we realized employees are not willing to take the risks an employer must take to ride out bad periods, even though we had tried to keep them working full time.

Thereafter, we cut down overtime and never again tried to put into effect an employee pay cut, even temporarily.

Radio Research Company received fill-in jobs from commercial aviation. For example, at one time we received an order from the Peruvian government to install radio equipment in a flying boat and on a converted yacht. The yacht was to be the tender for the flying boat and both were scheduled to go up the Amazon River to deliver a surprise attack on Colombia.

We also received an order to equip a big flying boat with high-powered radio and ground equipment, all to be used in an expedition into the interior of New Guinea.

The Peruvian and New Guinea jobs were handicapped by the fact that the aircraft's radios were subject to ignition interference. We knew how to cure radio interference, but the pilots had no knowledge on the subject; they wouldn't allow us to make changes to their regular ignition systems. Consequently, we faced an almost impossible job meeting minimum specifications. But in each case, the need was so great we were able to get by with what we, frankly, regarded as poor performance.

Then one day the Argentine government sent a representative, a captain in their Air Force, to not only give us an order for special radio equipment, but also to stay with us during its manufacture and until the equipment was delivered. There was no equipment available at that time to meet the Argentine requirements, which involved new frequency ranges and intricate receiver performance. They had come to us. Their embassy attache had obtained our name from his military acquaintances who told him our company could meet new needs.

The order was of a considerable size and represented not only a large amount of engineering work, but also several months of manufacturing. The development was a major undertaking. But Leo and I felt we knew how to approach the job, meeting its challenges one by one. Unfortunately, we looked at the reward without assessing the risks. A paramount error. Completing the job would mean enough profit to buy a lot and build our own building that would be equipped to do our special work. A second paramount error for a rapidly growing, newborn firm.

Nevertheless, we thought of ourselves as shrewd businessmen and took the precaution of stating in the Argentine contract that the job was to be paid on a time and material basis. However, when our initial estimate and quoted price had been exceeded, we were compelled to agree on a fixed amount for the project's completion.

While all this was going on, the size of the Argentine order and its future potential had given us visions of grandeur; before we had profit in hand from the job, we bought a lot and ordered construction of a new building to our specifications. Full of optimism, we felt comfortable with the expenditure because costs were well within the bounds we had projected for our available capital. The consequence of this premature decision, combined with a further cost overrun on the Argentine job, was a disastrous loss of capital. Ultimately, we completed the job to the satisfaction of the Argentine government, but we lost our shirt in the process.

The need to raise more money became an immediate necessity. We decided to mortgage our new building. Our construction contractor recommended an insurance man who could arrange mortgages. After inspecting the building and us, he decided it was a good risk and gave us a 60 percent mortgage at five percent interest, a little above the market at that time.

Radio Research Expands

From the original cellar, we had progressed to a 400-square-foot store, then doubled that floor space by acquiring the store next door. Now we had a brand new building with 3,200 square feet of usable floor space. We felt sure it would last the Radio Research Company a long time.

Leo agreed I should purchase the machinery because of my past shop experience. Happily I went to Baltimore and shopped around. At that time everyone was buying new machinery because there was an economic recovery trend in the country; but I was hunting for secondhand items.

Machinery dealers were loaded with inventory. I bought good used machines—lathe, milling machine, shaper, drill press, punch press, and power shear along with an assemblage of tools.

Although we didn't recognize it, we also acquired something besides a new building and machinery: OVERHEAD. Prior to this time, there had been none. Leo and I did engineering without charge. We were our own purchasing agents, employment office, tax preparers, bookkeepers and janitors. Not only did we not charge the company for these services, we never billed them to the customer. As owners, we also contributed the taxes and paid the insurance.

When we finally recognized that our prices included only materials, labor and profit, and did not take into account all of these other administrative costs, we raised them and made allowance for our own efforts. However, it never seemed to make much difference to our unit cost because our prices were still below the market.

Impact of the Depression

Leo and I had both been at NRL in 1929 when the stock market collapsed; it had been something we read about but never participated in. It had no effect on our products either, because broadcasting requirements remained good even during the Depression.

I had bought my first house, complete with mortgage. But when Washington real estate began to show signs of trouble, I decided to question our real estate man. While assuring me that everything was OK, he did ask me what bank I was doing business with. When I told him, he said, "If I were you, I wouldn't keep too much money on deposit in that bank."

I wasn't particularly worried because we did not have much money in our account. Just to be sure, the next day I went to the bank president, whom I knew. I told him I had heard rumors his bank was in difficulty because of bad real estate loans.

The president, a fine looking man of impressive means and a loud baritone voice, acted horrified to hear of such rumors, assuring me my fears were unfounded and insisted his bank was as sound as the United States Treasury.

I went away happy.

A few days later, two men came into my little office at Radio Research, presenting their credentials as Secret Service agents. They said it was a function of the Secret Service to investigate any adverse allegations regarding national banks. They said they knew I had made charges at our bank that were groundless. By spreading the rumor the bank was in trouble, I had committed a criminal act. They leaned on me pretty hard. As they continued, my temper rose until I finally had enough.

I told them I had not spread any rumors, but had heard some. I also told them I had taken the rumors immediately to the president of the bank and was assured his bank was in good condition. I told them I felt they should be complimenting instead of criticizing. Apparently they got the message; they left shortly with assurances that my action appeared justified.

Nevertheless I felt uneasy.

Then came the Roosevelt election. Our new building was at the edge of the Baltimore & Ohio Railroad yard and the day and night before the inauguration Pullman cars began to arrive from the Middle West. The election campaign had shaken the whole country; there was a tremendous influx of people who wanted to see Roosevelt.

I didn't go to the inauguration, but instead went to our plant. I remember standing at the window overlooking the railroad yard and the Capitol beyond it, wistfully wondering if the time ahead would really be as bad as many had predicted.

I found out in a hurry. Roosevelt's first important action was to close the banks. Riding a bus downtown, I went to my bank. On its door was a sign: "Closed by order of the conservator." I couldn't believe it. I had spent my last dime on bus fare, planning to withdraw money from the bank. Dejected, I walked home, then drove the family car to the office.

There wasn't much money there. It dawned on me that in a few days there would be a payday—and no funds. Something had to be done and quick.

Leo, startled as I by our bank's closure, at least received his pay from NRL. I had the responsibility of keeping the show on the road at Radio Research, figuring a way to do it without money.

I spent all afternoon on a financial statement and balance sheet. Making several copies, I inserted each in separate envelopes. I was determined to call on the two banks still open in Washington to see if I could raise funds.

First thing the next morning I visited the National Metropolitan Bank. Its president was a crusty, plain speaking old gentleman who was not very robust and had no charisma; but, he knew his business. I had met him once before; he seemed to vaguely recognize me. He stood up, shook my hand and invited me to sit down.

I told him my purpose was to secure a loan for our company. His face crinkled a bit as if in a smile and he said, "You're the first and there will be many more. I suppose you have a financial statement?"

I gave him the envelope containing our statement. After studying it, he said, "Well, you do have some assets. Equity in the building, some machinery, work in process and receivables. Not much cash and most of that is in your regular bank. You are up to date in payables and have a net worth suitable to your growing business. I see why you need the loan to meet your payroll, but, young man, this bank never establishes a new account with a loan. One of your best assets was the credit you had with your own bank. When it failed to open, they robbed you of a very important business asset and you are now in a predicament not of your own making. Now, I am sure the conservator of your bank will attempt to have you pay off that loan. Don't you do it, not until they have given you full credit for the amount of your deposit. He will use every threat and means to make you pay, but tell him to go to hell. He has done you great damage. Even after he gives you credit for your deposit, only agree to pay the remainder of your loan in small installments over a long period of time."

"As for your payroll problem," he added, "the Riggs Bank, which as you know is one of the largest in Washington, may be able to help you. I have reason to believe they are willing to take care of legitimate small business requirements and suggest you see them right away."

I thanked him for his counsel and headed for Riggs. Although there was a line, it wasn't long before a loan officer heard my story. Essentially he made the same observations as the National Metropolitan president about my business statement, but agreed to make us a loan equivalent to about a month's requirements for the company. I left with the assurance we could stay in business at least another month.

Pay day arrived. With our bank loan I was able to meet most of the payroll. In anticipation of a shortage of payroll funds, I had gone to several neighborhood stores, arranging for them to accept chits which I would issue to our employees. They would also be able to cash Riggs Bank checks at collaborating stores.

Of course, I called other important customers, asking that they make prepayments. I was told in each case, but one, that they were in the same boat. All assured me they would do their best to pay their bills as soon as the banks reopened.

Desperate Need for Cash

After the bank moratorium was declared by President Roosevelt, I telephoned a very important customer in New Jersey with whom I had an excellent relationship. He owed us just over $3,000. I told him the importance of that amount.

"I will wire you the money at once," he said—and did.

The following day I was notified by Western Union they were unable to pay me the $3,000 because their bank was closed and they didn't know when it would open.

So there I was with a wired authorization for $3,000 and an acknowledgment by Western Union of their obligation—but a total inability to fulfill it.

That customer who agreed to help us was the president of the DeForest Radio Company, who had wired us the $3,000. When I received the bad news from Western Union, I called him again, explaining our predicament. He assured me he would pay in cash if I could pick it up.

My 4:00 a.m. departure the next morning became a nightmare. I ran into an ice storm that lasted all the way to New Jersey. I slithered along on the icy road for a short distance and then stopped to put on tire chains, but they didn't help. The vertical windshield of that era was a big help. On the inside of its surface I had a newfangled coiled wire heater about a quarter of an inch in diameter and a foot long. It gave me a horizontal half inch slit through which I could see the road.

That day I drove nearly 400 miles round trip peering through that slit. My eyes felt as big as golf balls and my lids as rough as sandpaper. Nevertheless, I reached the plant near Jersey City and received the money. Arriving back in Washington after midnight with my life-preserving cash in hand, I went to bed happy, knowing the Radio Research Company would survive.

During the remainder of the Depression the broadcast station business remained good. But whenever we received an order, I immediately called the customer and requested a cash payment before delivery. There were a few mild protests, but in most cases the customers agreed.

Radio Research continued to grow and was soon besieged by people seeking employment. Though we were running a tight shop and had been managing with our existing small staff, we felt we *could* use two of the applicants profitably.

One was a young German, a skilled machinist, who had become a U.S. citizen. Laid off by the Washington Navy Yard, he desperately needed a job; and we needed him. Although we had managed to operate our new lathe, we were no experts.

We offered him a job, explaining we could only pay him $15 a week, about a third of the going rate. He accepted and came to work at once.

The other man was an experienced draftsman who had been without a job for two weeks, having been laid off without notice by his company.

We offered him a job at the same pay rate as the other man, but added that we would have to make work for him at first until we had use for his expertise. He jumped at the opportunity. Those two fine employees were with us for years.

The National Emergency Procurement Agency

Early in the Roosevelt administration an unexpected situation presented a bonanza for Radio Research. The President and Congress established a new procurement agency with the power and funds to purchase equipment and services on an accelerated basis. Red tape was slashed and orders given out across the board for supplies of every sort—in particular for military purposes.

Under the Coolidge and Hoover administrations military services had been starved for men and equipment. Roosevelt, a former Under Secretary of the Navy and raised in an environment which led him to be well versed in foreign affairs, realized that the United States had not kept up its defense readiness.

With these newly available funds, the Navy in particular was anxious to replace outdated equipment on ships and aircraft. Among their urgent requirements were those for aircraft direction finders and frequency meters to improve both reliability of communication and flight safety.

Bureau of Ships and Bureau of Air rushed to get out specifications for their requirements.

For Radio Research the orders were big business. On the other hand, for larger companies, Navy requirements were too small, highly specialized and represented high tooling costs and shorter delivery times.

Therefore, we operated virtually in a noncompetitive field. New orders rolled in first from the Navy, then the Coast Guard and later the Army. Our requirements for people and space increased rapidly.

Growing Pains of Radio Research

As Radio Research outgrew the cellar, the little store and finally our 3,200-square-foot building, Leo and I made our first major mistake. We invested in a new building.

Investing in a building is a mistake made by nearly all new and small businesses. There is a mania to get one's own building with a nice entrance. However, that decision chews up a lot of capital, as we soon learned. In those early days the mortgage amount was usually less than half the value of the structure, let alone the added cost of machinery and equipment.

Radio Research would have been much better off had we conserved our operating capital by renting vacant space—plentiful on the market then.

We made a second major mistake when we received new orders from the National Emergency Procurement Agency. Instead of renting additional space for assembly operations and utilizing our own building for machine operations, we decided to build a second floor on top of our existing brick structure. Furthermore, we neglected another simple rule. In general, if orders double, the number of people and amount of space to produce the new volume should also double.

Of course, there is an economy of scale, particularly with respect to tooling, but generally the lack of efficiency in a growing organization means that such economics are not immediately realized. The volume of our orders had more than doubled and was increasing. That was why we had decided to add the second floor. Unfortunately it soon proved completely inadequate. We compounded our problem by acquiring not only that second floor, but by adding a two-room addition to the first floor. Looking back today I can't understand how we managed to stay in business amidst the confusion and dirt.

We were increasingly aware of the need for more working capital. Buildings and machinery are tangible items, but working capital, consisting as it does of paper and services, is intangible and generally underestimated. In our planning we provided for fixed capital but almost neglected the working capital of overhead or general expenses or both. Another unproductive item we overlooked was construction time and expense.

In spite of new volume and contemplated profits we were always in need of additional financing. However, what we lacked in business acumen, we made up for with enthusiasm, innovation and being on the ground floor of what is now called electronics.

We also had a high degree of self-confidence that must be an example of the old adage, "Fools go in where angels fear to tread."

One of the weakest features of our business operation was our total lack of concern for legal and accounting responsibilities. We kept a simple set of single-entry account books, if you could dignify them by that title, and from time to time we presented our idea of a financial statement to the banks. We saw no reason for seeking any legal advice. As a matter of fact decades passed before I fully appreciated the value of both legal and accounting professionals. Some predicaments I became embroiled in from time to time approached catastrophic risks, but I was blissfully unaware and managed to survive. I do not think it is overstating the case to say that my neglect of appropriate legal and financial advice probably cost me millions of dollars during those times and later.

Roosevelt Fireside Connection

A notable peak in our market acceptance was achieved when we performed a chore for the new President of the United States. President Roosevelt was preparing to make his first speech after his inauguration, the famous one in which he said, "The only thing we have to fear is fear itself." He wanted to sit at his desk but his staff couldn't locate a suitable desk microphone. At that time the only microphones available at the White House were stand-up or hand-held types. They desperately called around and learned there was nothing commercially available. A staff member recalled our small company. He brought us a hand microphone, explaining what the President needed. We designed and lacquered a small wooden base and a couple of shaped pieces to accommodate the mike.

President Roosevelt made his first Fireside radio speech using a desk microphone stand fabricated by Radio Research Company.

Continuing Navy Business

One of Radio Research's more important products was a frequency indicator for the Radio Division of Bureau of Air. This frequency indicator needed a very wide scale and the design required use of half a dozen crystals. The first model we made and submitted to the Navy for approval did a remarkable job maintaining stability over a wide set of conditions. Based on its acceptance, we went into what we called quantity production—maybe half a dozen units per day. Because of increased numbers we made a few simple tools at the instigation of our German machinist. However, when we put together the first of the production models, the accuracy of the unit was unsatisfactory. We ended up with 10 units with the same unstable characteristic. The problem was getting serious; all of our own capital and most of what we could borrow was tied up in that procurement.

We were doing our best to find the deficiency in our production crystal frequency indicator. Finally, in desperation, I told our men, "I'm going to take that prototype unit apart piece by piece, examine every detail, and find out why it works so well and our others don't."

I laid out a clean sheet of paper and began to take the model apart. Everything appeared identical to our own production units with the exception of a loose adjusting screw in the back bearing of the variable condenser. I paid no attention to it because it did not seem important. When I could find no differences between the sample model and our units I was thoroughly discouraged. I put the prototype back together, tightened the loose screw on the condenser and retested it. Much to my amazement this prototype was now as bad as the production units. I did the only thing I could think of: I loosened the adjusting screw on the back bearing of the model. Lo and behold, the unit worked as well as it had originally. I did the same on each of our production units. All then tested within specifications. I'd never been in a situation where a loose screw solved a problem.

Later we had competitors for that job. Two were successful bidders, but unsuccessful performers. They had copied our crystal frequency indicator unit, item for item, but never did find out about the loose screw. Unable to get their units to work, they finally defaulted on the job. That loose screw turned out to be a well-kept company secret; we had a tight grip on that market for years.

Another problem in connection with the frequency indicator business came when a truly large procurement was made by the Navy. Bids were received from our company and Radio Corporation of America. Our bid was lowest; but RCA insisted we had infringed on its patents.

The matter was submitted to the Navy patent office for a clarifying opinion. It was headed by Lt. Commander Harold Dodd, radio officer at Naval Air Station, Pensacola, and moving spirit of that first blind landing experiment.

I went to Commander Dodd and related the story of my patent dilemma. It was not new to him. RCA had made a powerful protest on the basis of patent rights.

Commander Dodd told me he could not yet commit himself one way or another. I left disheartened; we badly needed that business.

A week later the Navy awarded the contract to Radio Research. In an opinion prepared by Commander Dodd, he pointed out to the procurement officer that our price was more than 15 percent below RCA's and that in any lawsuit, the only damages that could be recovered would be triple damages on the basic royalty rate of 5 percent—or a total of 15 percent.

That was justification enough for the procurement officer; we got the business. I would now guess that RCA decided the loss of that little contract was not enough to warrant the expense of a lawsuit. We proceeded on what was to be the first increment of perhaps 100,000 of those frequency indicators.

The Coast Guard required a different type of frequency indicator.

Radio Research was almost out of new orders. The Coast Guard procurement became important. It seemed unlikely we would have any competitive bidders. On the other hand the procurement was vital to our company to keep our people at work. Therefore, I decided to cut our price to the bone. I figured in minimum profit, counting on good luck to help us finish the work at or under the price I was going to quote.

However, after submitting my bid, the more I thought about it the more certain I was that there could be no possible competition. I decided to withdraw my original bid, submitting a new one at double the price.

I hurried to the procurement office to ask the chief clerk to return my bid because I needed to make a change. He took out two envelopes. As he handed me my bid I got a look at the other envelope—from General Radio Company, a fine institution that was tops in the frequency measuring business.

Another decision. With my bid in my pocket I walked around the block a few times, thinking about General Radio. They were good manufacturers; and I felt they would be in with a low price. I concluded it was too risky to submit an inflated bid. I removed my original bid from its envelope and without making any changes, put it in a new envelope. Returning to the procurement office, I resubmitted our original bid.

The bids were opened three days later. Mine was first. But I waited with baited breath for the bid from General Radio. The officer tore open the envelope, took out the bid and read aloud the message it contained: "No bid."

I had outsmarted myself. Most important, I'd done our company out of several thousand dollars. That loss, however, was ultimately a good cause. Our people remained on the job; subsequently we made many more units for the Coast Guard. The product helped our business over a low point. Without it I would have had to terminate several employees.

Shortly after this incident we were again in financial trouble. We decided to go after business from the Radio Division of BuShips, even though that organization was still headed by the same individual whose decisions had caused me to resign from NRL. But BuShips had much larger procurements of radio equipment than did BuAir. One major procurement was for a frequency meter made by General Radio.

General Radio had already completed one order of the meters, which were larger and covered a wider frequency than those we made for BuAir. However, I had seen the equipment and felt sure we could handle that class of work. Thus, when the next procurement came out, I submitted a low bid and won the award.

We made an almost exact copy of the General Radio product. But since that firm had used some of its own parts, which it would not sell to us. I had to use parts from alternative manufacturers. When our first unit was assembled I discovered we could not maintain its calibration within the specifications agreed upon with the Navy.

I had an excellent engineer working on that job. For a month he did everything he could think of to correct the performance of our unit. Knowing that too much concentration for too long a period of time often prevents the ability to separate the "trees from the woods," I reluctantly told him to take a week off while I undertook the job.

The primary deficiency was poor frequency stability with temperature changes. Any corrective action could be evaluated only by changing room temperatures and making observations over a period of about three hours. I finally set up a cot in the test room, located an alarm clock and found a solution within four or five days. Secretly I was delighted at the chance to do some responsible engineering again, establishing that I had not lost my technical competence in a sea of administration.

We made delivery and a small profit on the procurement. Unfortunately this and other overruns in time and costs strained our financial resources to the breaking point. I doubted our bank would increase our loan. I concluded my best hope lay in finding someone who would invest in our business.

Bendix Becomes a Player in the Game

Meantime we had other products to develop and produce. One of these was a new type of direction finder for BuAir.

Eclipse Instrument, a division of Bendix Corporation, had invented and was about to produce a new type of synchronizer that I knew would be ideally suited for this Navy application. I telephoned Charles Marcus at Eclipse Instrument and asked if we could purchase some of these devices.

Mr. Marcus told me he would be in Washington in a few days and would stop by. When he arrived, instead of talking about synchronizers, I unloaded my frustration about our financial problems.

Mr. Marcus was sympathetic, but remarked that frequently small companies were in that kind of financial trouble. We got down to business, talking price, performance and delivery of the synchronizers to solve our problem with the direction finders.

We reached agreement; Mr. Marcus invited me to lunch. In the more relaxing atmosphere of lunch, he suggested that perhaps a closer association with Bendix Corporation could be an advantage for both of us.

Because we desperately needed more capital I asked what he had in mind. When Mr. Marcus suggested that Bendix might want to acquire a half interest in Radio Research, I told him I would have to discuss it with my partner, Leo Young. It never occurred to me that Marcus might be even more anxious to buy than I was to sell.

That evening Leo and I talked it over. Concerned about our financial predicament, Leo thought we should conclude an arrangement with Bendix if at all possible.

In order not to appear anxious, I waited two days before phoning Mr. Marcus. He said he was pleased and had already talked to Vincent Bendix about the possibility of an association with our company. He requested a financial statement, adding that Mr. Bendix planned to be in Washington soon and would stop by our plant.

Charles Marcus and Vincent Bendix arrived at our plant about a week later. Mr. Bendix was a legendary figure because of the success he had with the Bendix starter, which was then on all automobiles. Later, of course, he formed Bendix Aviation and its varied divisions to make both aviation and automobile parts.

Mr. Bendix looked over our shop, talked with me about future product possibilities and finally offered to buy a half interest in Radio Research for $100,000. I assured him I would seriously consider his offer, but would need to consult with my partner.

That night I met with Leo and explained the offer from Mr. Bendix. Leo was delighted. Because of his concern about the scope, problems and particularly cash requirements of our expanding operation, he told me he would be relieved to have it all under the wing of a big outfit such as Bendix.

We concluded the agreement with Bendix. It not only gave them half interest in our company, but Mr. Bendix put me under contract for 15 years at a salary of not less than $5,000 per year. The year was 1935.

The day we received a check for $100,000 Leo and I were walking on cloud nine.

However, we descended to reality within a few days. We had obtained financial security, but also an obligation to deliver the products and profits we had predicted. Other factors would have horrified any lawyer or accountant. The $100,000 was invested in our company. Since Bendix now owned one half, his cost of acquisition was only $50,000. My salary provision of not less than $5,000 per year was ridiculous, although it proved amazingly beneficial at a later date. The old adage, "One does not know when he is ignorant," certainly applied in our case.

Although Leo Young and I were business partners, and in a sense remained so for life, our interests diverged. Most of his work was in a classified area. I was busy trying to learn how to run a business. In 1936 we sold the remainder of Radio Research to Bendix Aviation Corporation, splitting the proceeds. Leo stayed at NRL. I went along to Bendix.

Chapter V
First Exposure to the Corporate Syndrome

The association with Bendix began in time to take advantage of new business created by President Roosevelt's efforts to lead the country out of the Depression.

Our business steadily increased beyond the capacity of our plants. No space was available in Washington nor was there time for new construction. A vacant plant, suiting our requirement, was located in Baltimore. A decision was made to move the office, engineering, and manufacturing to Baltimore, retaining marketing and special fabrication in Washington. Before long our thriving business filled facilities in both cities.

Bendix had at the same time acquired two other small radio companies: W.P. Hilliard Company in Chicago and Dayton Radio Products Company in Dayton, Ohio.

Vincent Bendix and Charlie Marcus consulted with me about personnel, products and locations, pointing out that Bendix Corporation had recently vacated a large factory building in Chicago formally occupied by Stromberg Carburetor Company. I was directed to visit the two companies and make a recommendation regarding their absorption—along with Radio Research—into what would be the Radio Division of Bendix.

Hectic Days of Startup

Things were really happening. Orders were flowing in, but a reported breakthrough in radio direction finders threatened our preeminence in that field. There were the usual mixups coincident with moving together with increased inspection visits to the various plants. The solutions—taking several months and never easy—involved negotiation, compromise and patience. I seemed to have a shorter and shorter supply of patience as time passed. And, there were frequent demands to confer with Mr. Bendix, wherever he might be.

The influx of orders was unreal. The military agencies, ready with projects of various degrees of priority, gave us more business. We had to hire more engineers and draftsmen. As development and designs were completed, machinists and assemblers were added.

Moving more than half our activities from Washington to Baltimore was simple for equipment, but troublesome for people. The basic one man show in Washington had to be divided into two sections. I had made no preparation for supervision. Bill Hilliard provided a partial answer when he was transferred from Chicago to Washington. He took over completion of a transmitter project and by force of personality ran the Washington operation as well. I undertook sales, personnel relocation and equipment assignments in the Baltimore plant.

Personnel relocation was difficult because families were not eager to move. However, jobs were still scarce; living quarters in Baltimore were more economically attractive. Ultimately, nearly all employees agreed to transfer.

Dealing with the direction finder breakthrough was a more complicated challenge. However, one of our employees, Wilbur Webb, had been vigorously carrying out unidirectional radio direction finder research in the Washington-Baltimore area. He had demonstrated remarkably good results in both aircraft and ground mobile testing, proving the product to be technically effective and capable of economic manufacture and installation.

The Air Corps had been aware of the importance of this major development and issued the largest single radio procurement up to that time. We were successful bidder for these new unidirectional devices and decided to produce the new equipment in the old Bendix Stromberg plant in Chicago.

We borrowed a master mechanic from Bendix Eclipse. He helped us select and install new machinery and assisted in the hiring of a competent manufacturing man.

The Baltimore radio direction finder group was reassigned to the Chicago plant with Wilbur Webb as chief engineer. Bill Hilliard as manager had the job of blending the Baltimore group with the new employees and establishing an independent, self-sufficient organization.

Vincent Bendix and Charlie Marcus appointed me general manager over the entire Bendix Radio Division. My time was to be divided between the Baltimore and Chicago plants and ultimately I was to dispose of the plant in Washington.

I had a secretary in both Chicago and Baltimore, but the actual Radio Division headquarters was in my briefcase. I carried it on trains, airplanes and automobiles between Baltimore, Chicago, New York and Washington as well as to places in between.

I appointed a manager for the Baltimore plant, giving him full responsibility for its operation. The Radio Division now had two plants widely separated with two plant managers and a total of several hundred employees.

The View from Vincent Bendix

From time to time Vincent Bendix commanded my presence at his office, a large suite on the 36th floor of the Waldorf Astoria Tower in New York. He and Charlie Marcus were intensely interested in the latest radio activities.

An office adjacent to the entry was occupied by Henry Gossner, corporate secretary and majordomo of New York operations. A room next to Gossner's office accommodated employees and visitors waiting for an audience with Mr. Bendix.

At lunchtime waiters and an assistant maitre d' set up tables, handed each visitor and employee a menu and sent one in to Mr. Bendix. We would pull chairs up to the tables, awaiting the arrival of Mr. Bendix, the great man, who appeared right after the food arrived. The first plate was always served to Mr. Bendix. In addition, he received smaller empty plates. When others were served their lunch he would send a small plate for a sample of any food that attracted him. The result of this and other meals served Bendix was a huge belly on a small frame; it could only be called corpulent.

Johnny Walker Red Label was served at will to employees. More expensive Black Label was served to visitors.

During the morning Bendix conducted his business from his bedroom, frequently calling in his employees for consultations. I was then really a fair-haired boy; if present I was called in first. Invariably VB was lying on his bed, partially covered by a sheet being vigorously worked over by a masseur.

After questions, answers and speculation as to the future of aircraft and electronics, Bendix would instruct me to wait in an outer reception room in case he needed additional information. I waited for what was left of the morning, had lunch and then waited all afternoon. After a few days I discovered Bendix did no business in the afternoon. He left early, using the back door. He never reappeared.

During the long afternoons we Bendix confidants buttered up to each other, convinced ourselves of our importance and began to believe we were big shots. I, at least, began to degenerate.

Time spent in that Waldorf Astoria compound, plus constant travel, used up an inordinate amount of time and didn't improve my disposition. I began to give hasty answers, make snap judgments and lose touch with reality. Occasionally I checked with Henry Gossner to make sure Bendix had departed in the afternoon. I'd then go over to Mr. Marcus' office at the Grand Central Building where we'd have lengthy discussions about engineering, international sales, patents and corporate administration. Those occasions gave me an insight not only to the vagaries of Vincent Bendix (and later Howard Hughes), but also to the workings, finances and customs of a large corporation. To say I was amazed with my introduction to big business would be an understatement.

Unprepared for Management Responsibilities

I had entered a new frontier for which I was totally unprepared. After two or three months of living in such a super-heated environment, I suddenly realized that both finances and time necessary for my responsibilities as division general manager were being dissipated.

Finally I decided to sidestep invitations to the Waldorf Astoria and Bendix headquarters in South Bend. Instead, I concentrated on our Chicago and Baltimore plant. But, I was a little late. I found that production in Chicago was on schedule, but working capital was negative. Work in process and inventory had increased, but cash was running out and there were unpaid bills. Unfortunately, I also discovered Baltimore was behind in deliveries; they, too, were beset by cash problems that could only be satisfied by a contribution from corporate funds. Also, the lifeblood of our Radio Division—innovation, ingenuity and that magic compatibility with the customer—had dwindled.

At the time affairs of Bendix Corporation were in disarray. The cause of these problems was a huge increase in orders as rearmament of France, England and the United States accelerated. Military demands were almost insatiable. New plants and equipment were required. Startup costs associated with rapidly increasing production imposed severe strains on corporate finances. Cash reserves of the parent company were shrinking.

Soon I discovered General Motors owned 23 percent of Bendix Aviation, giving GM effective control. Presently three GM executives descended on us. One was a manufacturing man, another an accounting executive and a third, Ernie Breech, a major corporate GM executive. These GM people knew their business. Our executives, from Mr. Bendix through corporate staff and down through division management, all went through the wringer.

I distinctly remember a scene with the GM financial executive in a room at the Statler Hotel in Chicago. I was on the frying pan. I didn't make a good showing; near the end, I protested that the aviation radio business was a special business.

He came right back, saying, "Pat, one thing you must understand is that there are *no* special businesses. All have to be conducted on a sound business basis with planning, efficiency and profit in mind. You folks seem to have forgotten all three of those requirements."

After these and other critical comments, I was furious. But, by the time I got back to my hotel, I recognized the validity of some comments. Though I did not fully agree, it was a fact that the financial performance of Bendix Radio Division had not been satisfactory. Over the years I've concluded that the GM financial executive had been correct; there are no special businesses. The fundamental rules are the same for all. When we deviate from those rules, we invite trouble.

Breech Takes Over Bendix

The upshot was that we wound up with Ernie Breech managing Bendix; new finance and manufacturing vice presidents—Edwin P. Palmer and Dave Thomas—were appointed. In carefully orchestrated maneuvers Vincent Bendix was "encouraged" to take an office in the Grand Central Building from which he managed some of his other interests.

A new, experienced manager was appointed for the Baltimore plant. I was retained as a general manager, but didn't realize the title was in name only. I was "encouraged" to expand the marketing operation in Washington and product development in Baltimore.

We all came back to earth with a bang and began to again run our business.

Then Hitler partitioned Czechoslovakia after Mr. Chamberlain had compromised to achieve "peace for our time." French and British military buyers descended on us; orders rolled in for advanced equipment. As the political situation heated up in Europe, there were requirements for rifles and bullets, airplanes, engines and radios. The aircraft receiver-transmitters on which we had lost money in supplying the Argentine government were now in great demand by the British. Our volume rose, and with it, the disposition of our executives.

Several months later Charlie Marcus visited me in Baltimore. He said he felt the new plant manager was doing an excellent job and could handle increased responsibility. He explained that government procurement and financial opportunities now justified an experienced full-time Washington representative. He pointed out my unique qualifications for this assignment and my success in the complex expansion during the prewar period. He concluded by saying he hoped I would accept such an important and special position.

Charlie Marcus buttered me up pretty well. Of course, I realized what was really happening. I had *not* done a good job as division general manager and was being eased out. Nevertheless, I felt I could make a contribution because of my Washington associations.

In retrospect, I now see what my problems had been as an inexperienced general manager. First, I had not learned to delegate authority. I wanted to make all decisions, big or small, technical or administrative. This was not always possible. Second, at that time I had no broad management knowledge beyond my ability as an innovator, technician and salesman. I had no experience with inventory control, production control and subcontracting. These and other things were to be learned as my business education evolved during the next 10 years.

However, my mistakes at Bendix Radio Division were never repeated.

Coping with the Prewar Surge

Back again in Washington, I started a new phase in my life. I made the rounds of Army, Army Air Corps, Navy and Coast Guard offices. Occasionally I would drop in at Commerce, Treasury and the Federal Radio Commission. My salary remained the same, but I had a secretary and an expense account.

With Poland under attack by Hitler, war was declared by several European nations; foreign military business surged upward from that time on.

Mr. Roosevelt saw the shape of things to come. He began to strengthen the American military machine. New manufacturing facilities were required. The Reconstruction Finance Corporation, formed to help during the Depression, was now used to finance an industrial foundation for our military forces.

Red tape was cut. Old and trusted manufacturers were given authority to proceed with jobs on the basis of a handshake; paperwork was held to a minimum. With Bendix both in aviation and automotive as well as in ground and aircraft radio equipment manufacturing, demands for our products spiraled upwards.

With it came a need for more working capital.

Our corporate treasurer phoned and revealed he was facing a financial calamity. My relationship with him had never been the best. He didn't understand radio, he didn't like our highly volatile financial operations and he didn't particularly like me. That feeling was reciprocal. However, he did know I had done a good job getting advance payments from the military on certain projects.

Knowing his problem had to be urgent for him to call me, I asked what I could do to help. He said the company was running out of money; he would be unable to meet the next payroll, 10 days away. He explained the banks couldn't help because he'd already exhausted his credit limit. Due to our rapid growth, "things had gotten away from him a little." He knew it would take him several weeks to establish expanded lines of credit. He asked if I could get for the company a $2 million advance payment within that 10-day period. I offered no assurances, but agreed to try.

I called the colonel in charge of disbursements in the regional office at the Bush Terminal in Brooklyn. While arranging some advance procurement payments with the Army, I had become acquainted with him. Making an appointment for the next day, I caught a train to New York and located the Bush Terminal, an enormous structure on the Brooklyn waterfront.

I explained the company's problem to the colonel; he offered to look into it quickly. He promised to call me in a day or two. I reminded him of the urgency and the need to meet the next payroll; he completely understood.

I returned to Washington to wait. He phoned the next day to say he had talked with his superiors. In view of the almost total dedication by Bendix Corporation to government work, they felt it would be proper to handle the situation. The colonel required certain information not only from my office, but also from the central Bendix office in Detroit.

However, he was concerned there might be a problem. The following day was Rosh Hashana, the important Jewish holiday. Even if he received the information the next day, the holiday could be an obstacle to immediate processing; nearly all of his staff, including the two officials who had the disbursement warrants, were Jewish and would have the day off.

I thanked him, assuring him we would take things one step at a time. First, I would get the information he needed delivered to him.

For a long while I stared out my office window, concentrating on how to overcome the impediment that could prevent the smooth operation of a great corporation in its essential government work. As I pondered, my secretary brought in my afternoon cup of coffee. An idea flashed through my mind. My secretary was an attractive girl. She was also a hard worker, extremely bright and, shall we say, a free thinker, fond of men. I asked her if she would like to take the Congressional, a fast, through train to New York, and deliver papers to the Bush Terminal in Brooklyn. Without hesitation she agreed. I instructed her to phone the Detroit and Baltimore offices to gather the required information.

When my secretary brought me the last piece of paper for signature, I said, "I suggest you take these to New York and sweet talk those two disbursement guys. Somehow get them to come in for a few hours tomorrow with a couple of stenographers and write that $2 million check."

She smiled. "Leave it to me." She didn't take time to go home and change, but she did have a cosmetic bag. I hustled her to the train, gave her money and wished her well.

As it turned out she didn't need much money—only cab fare and her overnight stay at a Brooklyn hotel. She allowed a man on the train to buy her dinner in the diner and immediately took a taxi to Bush Terminal.

The colonel introduced her to the two disbursement officers. After looking at her papers, they laid out plans for needed documentation in the morning. They arranged for stenographic help. By this time it was late. My secretary invited the two men out for a drink and supper at company expense. They accepted with pleasure, had a good time and after supper walked her to a nearby hotel.

Early the next morning she returned to Bush Terminal to supply any further information in order to process the check. When it was issued, one of the officials even gave her a ride to Pennsylvania Station where she caught the Congressional to Baltimore. En route, she again allowed a passenger to buy her dinner.

Before leaving the disbursement office she called to tell me she had the check. I instructed her to meet me at Baltimore station where she could turn it over to me, then go on to Washington.

She was waiting for me on the observation car platform when the train stopped in Baltimore. I took the check; she went on to Washington.

I rushed to Union Bank; arrangements had already been made for the check. The next morning in Detroit the Bendix treasurer was notified by his bank that $2 million had been wired from Baltimore. Bendix people were paid on time.

My secretary told me she was delighted at the opportunity to ride the Congressional and had enjoyed her dinners. She was certainly a whiz.

So it was that a fascinating charmer preserved the financial integrity of a great corporation in a critical situation.

Although the Bendix treasurer *never* acknowledged my assistance, at least he no longer looked the other way when we passed in the hall.

Bendix Joins the Big Time

During these late prewar years, there were nationwide rules, regulations and priorities regarding materials, people and equipment. Congress broke many of its own rules by ramming through legislation authorizing new defense expenditures. In spite of every good intention, red tape still got in the way. My job was to find ways of cutting through or going around it.

Following the "Day of Infamy," Pearl Harbor, December 7, 1941 the President, with Congress concurring, issued a Declaration of War. U.S. manufacturing went into high gear.

The military had been preparing for months for such an eventuality; they were ready with logistic plans. Within a few days of the Declaration I received a call from the office of the chief signal officer of the Army to be present at a briefing—and to bring a senior officer of Bendix with me.

Charlie Marcus and I attended the briefing. The Chief Signal Officer made some preliminary remarks to the relatively small group about the urgency of the situation. Then he stated the Signal Corps had chosen five major contractors to be the core of its communication procurement. He pulled open a curtain, revealing a long blackboard with a chalked list of tables. The five contractors listed on the blackboard were Western Electric, General Electric, Westinghouse Electric, RCA and Bendix.

Charlie Marcus and I were startled that Bendix was included in such august company.

Using a long pointer, the General said, "I will read off the allocations of volume in the order of the dollar amounts involved." The first was Western Electric with a volume of $420 million. Next was General Electric with $360 million. Third was Bendix with $320 million. I nearly passed out. The entire volume of Bendix Aviation with automotive products, aircraft products and radio products had totaled only $30 million the preceding year.

I couldn't believe my ears. Worse, I couldn't even confirm what I heard because I couldn't see the damn figures on the blackboard. Here I was at one of the most important events of my life and I couldn't read the figures because I was not wearing my glasses.

The General said the allocation for Westinghouse was just under $200 million. RCA was another unbelievable figure—only $20 million. RCA was the major factory in radio. Their total capacity was in the hundreds of millions of dollars, but their products were for the home market and not initially useful to the Signal Corps.

I fidgeted and sweated during the rest of the briefing. The General detailed the kinds of equipment the Signal Corps expected each of the five suppliers to produce.

Charlie leaned over and whispered to me that not only was he surprised at the amount, but wondered how in the world we could ever produce that kind of volume.

Charlie and I stayed after the briefing. Up close at the blackboard, I squinted to make sure I had heard the figures correctly. After reading the list of products, I knew we could handle the technical part of the job. But I was in the same quandary as Charlie on how we could produce the volume. We had neither the plants nor the capital.

The next day I went to the Chief Signal Corps procurement officer. A week before he had been a colonel and a good friend of mine. Now he was a general and worthy of the job. As soon as I started to talk, he held up his hand. "I know," he said. "You wonder how Bendix is going to produce the equipment we need. We know you don't have plant space, but we believe we have time to arrange for Reconstruction Finance Corporation to provide financing for a plant to your specifications that will enable you to do the job. We will see that you get the necessary priorities and shall expect you to be in production within a year."

"Pat," he continued, "we are taking a long shot here. Before I agree to this action, I want your assurance that your company has the will and patriotism to carry out this assignment. We'll provide the support if you assure me of your belief that Bendix can do it. I know you'll want to consult with your officers, but I need to get on with the job. If you'll shake hands and give me your assurance, I'll issue orders right now."

Again I was in a quandary. Charlie had returned to New York to phone Ernie Breech, the president, in Detroit to give him details on what had happened at the briefing. I did not know Ernie Breech well and couldn't be 100 percent positive how he would respond. I felt he was aware of my successful operation of the Washington office, but was sure he also knew of my inadequate performance as general manager of the Radio Division. Would he trust my judgment on this?

But, I was also sure now was the time to make a commitment for the company. If I later had the disapproval of the president and board of directors, we could back out with grace, but if I delayed the decision now, we might not get a second chance. I hesitated for what seemed hours, though actually only a few seconds. I held out my hand, saying, "We'll take it on and thanks for your confidence." We shook hands and both kept our commitments.

Within a few days Detroit approved the commitment and the rush started. The resources of the corporation were placed at the disposal of the Radio Division. Calculating the size of the building, its design, selection of architects and the paperwork for a major plant was accomplished in record time. Financing through the Reconstruction Finance Corporation took longer because it was a large project.

Bendix already owned a large plot of land north of Baltimore in the town of Towson, Maryland; the site was ideal for the size of plant we needed, about 300,000 square feet. Knowing the product line (frequency indicators at first), I insisted the plant should be air-conditioned. When the design was complete the architect announced it would be the first large plant in the country to have complete air conditioning.

The manager who had succeeded me at the Radio Division left. He was replaced by a new man with no experience whatsoever in the radio business. This new manager made it plain he wanted no part of me. He was courteous, but firm.

However, I was instrumental in finding a good manufacturing man in Buffalo to serve as manufacturing manager in the new Towson facility. The engineering talents of both Bill Hilliard and Wilbur Webb were also accomodated.

The profits from the new operation were so large it was frightening. Our president, Ernie Breech, decided we should make an immediate gesture to show we were not profiteering during a wartime situation. He ordered that a check for $12 million payable to our primary customer, the Chief Signal Officer of the Army, be hand carried to that gentleman in Washington.

The general was pleased and complimentary, both of our performance and financial responsibility.

New Plants are Hell

About a year after the Towson plant reached full operation it was noticed that many workers were scratching themselves. This quickly led to the discovery that the plant was infested with fleas. They were multiplying so fast we had to shut down operations. We sent the workers home and called in exterminators. At their first check they found no apparent breeding places. But since all ventilation was supplied by the air conditioning system, a detailed examination was made of all ducts. Experts found temperature and humidity within the system were ideal for propagation of fleas.

The air conditioning equipment and factory were treated and arrangements made for permanent protection. Production was resumed. All subsequent air conditioning systems benefited from this experience in the nation's pioneering installation.

On the Fourth of July of our first year the road in front of the plant was crammed with vehicles; a lot of public interest was focused on the big new plant on the Towson road. On Independence Day the traffic was unusually heavy, but it suddenly came to a screeching halt. In front of the security house at the main gate, one of the guards, stark naked except for a gun belt, boots and a cap pistol, was in the middle of the road directing traffic. His direction consisted of throwing out his arms and stopping traffic in both directions. Cars were backed up for miles. Other guards were mustered from the plant to chase the offender. They caught him and hustled the naked man behind the factory gates. No one ever really determined the cause of this display of naked justice.

Friez Instruments Flamboyance

Another Baltimore Bendix Division was expanding as wartime demand for weather information increased. The Air Corps, in particular, wanted more and better weather instruments available for domestic and foreign operations. The Friez Instrument Division, acquired by Bendix, was one of the two major suppliers of weather equipment in the United States. However, the plant, too small and completely inadequate for the production needed by the Army Air Force, went through somewhat the same building process as had the Radio Division.

Because I was engaged in other projects and did not see the Friez plant until it was completed, Mr. Marcus suggested I visit the plant while preparations were being made for its dedication. I arrived at the plant, was shown the factory, engineering and administrative quarters. I was pleased with what I saw. Then I was taken to the general manager's office. It was in a penthouse. I almost passed out. The office was large and beautiful; sliding glass floor-to-ceiling windows faced an attractive scene of trees, fields and hills. Outside was a covered patio.

The office's focal point was a kidney-shaped desk with a high backed chair for the general manager within the curve, but with the drawers on the outside. They were decorative, but completely useless. On top was a bronze replica of the great statue in Washington honoring the Navy. There were expensive drapes, mahogany furniture and a tea table. A tasteful sofa and several chairs completed the furnishings.

Adjacent to this office was a richly-furnished dining room with mahogany table and chairs. A beautiful rug was on the floor, shining silverware on a buffet. An elegant chandelier completed the arrangement.

Next to the dining room was a kitchen equipped with up-to-date appliances. On the other side of the dining room a door led to a large bedroom with a mahogany four-poster bed. A period writing desk, an upholstered lounge chair and lamps completed the luxurious setting. It was apparent the whole penthouse had been designed by the cultured general manager, whose father, after leaving France, had established Friez Instrument Company in downtown Baltimore many years before.

I phoned Charlie Marcus to tell him the executive offices looked to me like a cross between a custom-made Cord automobile and the ladies room at Radio City Music Hall. I suggested we squelch any idea of a grand opening. I emphasized that any congressman coming into the penthouse built with government money during wartime would raise a howl certain to hit newspapers and radio.

A decision to dismantle the whole office penthouse and store the furnishings for disposal at a later time, almost broke the general manager's heart. But, Charlie Marcus and I made it stick. An austere set of office furniture was moved into the penthouse along with staff and stenographic desks; it was a respectable layout.

Bendix and Truman

Near the end of the war the Bendix machine was operating with steady, high quality production at decreasing costs; many of our plants had been cited for exceptional performance. However, a small order at the Radio Division for about $1,000 caused an uproar that brought public notice to a senator and probably helped his subsequent election to the Presidency.

The Navy Department requested we make a small special fitting for a particular airplane. I didn't want to accept the job, but I also didn't want to appear uncooperative. When asked the price, I said, "Well, we have a minimum price of $1,000, because this is a model shop job. I have no idea of what it will cost. I expect the paperwork will cost more than the device itself."

The Navy approved the price and gave me a short order form for the device. We had to have an order for the small fitting because it was illegal to donate something like that to the Navy without going through even more red tape.

The model shop at Baltimore made the device; a cost ticket for about $600 for machine time was reported to the accounting office. Other charges—assembly, inspection and tests—were *not.* The amount of $1,000 was billed on the short form order, but our records showed only $600 was spent to make the device.

Sometime later the Truman committee was established to investigate pricing and profits of defense contractors. Of all of the hundreds of millions of dollars of Bendix production and careful pricing to assure a reasonable profit, that item—showing $600 in costs and $1,000 in payment—was singled out by the staff of the committee as an example of excess profits made by a government contractor. I am sure Senator Truman was never in possession of the true facts, but was given profit margin only. He made it the central point of his committee recommendations. The media jumped in with his name and findings. The whole mess received countrywide attention.

The name of Harry Truman stuck; his work remembered.

After President Roosevelt's death, Mr. Truman became President of the United States, much to my disgust at the time. President Truman went on to wind up the war and saw the country through phases of an overheated economy and a scarcity syndrome to a cooling-off process and restoration to peaceful economic and social normalcy. Mr. Truman was reelected and became, in my opinion, one of the great Presidents of the Twentieth century.

Learning Corporate Politics

At Bendix in the early '40s I became acquainted with Roy Hurley, a tireless worker with considerable manufacturing experience. He was also a creative thinker and interested in aviation. Hurley was climbing up in Bendix via manufacturing the same way I was climbing via engineering. But every now and then our paths crossed. We discovered we had similar views about the company and the military procurement system.

After Mr. Breech and the manufacturing and financial men from

General Motors came to Bendix, Hurley ended up under Dave Thomas, the manufacturing vice president. I aligned myself with Charlie Marcus, engineering vice president. Marcus and Dave Thomas held each other in mutual disrespect; and though Hurley and I respected each other, we soon became adversaries in the palace political scene.

At General Motors, manufacturing was the dominant factor; the GM people carried this preference over to Bendix. There was no question that the Thomas-Hurley manufacturing team rated more highly with Ernie Breech than did the Marcus-Hyland engineering team. Fortunately, the paths of Hurley and Hyland did not cross too often.

Hurley was on manufacturing committees in the Department of Defense; I was on engineering committees. Roy Hurley did a magnificent job and won plaudits for finding ways to make shell casings out of steel to replace scarce brass, while I made a good showing in the growing radio field and kept a firm grip on the military-industrial interaction for Bendix.

Hurley soon recognized the advantage of my Washington government/military relations situation. Through Dave Thomas he sold Mr. Breech the idea that I was really needed in New York as a backup for Mr. Marcus in the engineering office. Moreover, it seemed more appropriate for the Washington office to be a function of manufacturing.

Mr. Breech acquiesced, but not until he came to Washington and interviewed me. We exchanged views for nearly a full day. Ultimately, he came to the same conclusion as Hurley, but for a different reason. I had apparently convinced him of the importance of engineering in the new era of aviation and high technology. Mr. Breech decided I should go to New York in a corporate engineering capacity, take over operating responsibility under Marcus and make decisions whenever he was abroad for the company.

The change was immediate. I was assigned to New York, while Roy Hurley took over the Washington office. He had really won that round. The opposition was in full control.

Strangely, I won a round, too. The most important committee of

Bendix under the board was called the Administration Committee; it was chaired by the president. This committee was composed of two vice presidents, plus the director of finance, the treasurer and secretary of the corporation as well as group executives and outside general counsel. However, in order to have engineering continuity, I was invited to be an associate member with full status whenever Mr. Marcus was absent. That gave me a leg up.

Roy Hurley and I remained on the same level as long as he was with Bendix. After the war he left to become president of Curtiss-Wright.

Harriet Hyland, mother of Pat.

Pat Hyland's mother and father, George and Harriet, with young Pat.

Lawrence A. Hyland, Melrose (Mass.) High School (class of 1915).

Lawrence A. Hyland with brother Alexander, c. 1905.

Grade school class, Melrose, Massachusetts, c. 1908, Hyland is seated, second row, second from right.

Hyland's WWI Artillery friend, "Baldy."

Chief Radioman Hyland when he served aboard USS Marblehead.

USS Marblehead *(first post-WWI ship launched) with Hyland's own statistics and identification.*

BUILDERS OF BYRD'S RADIO ARE GRATIFIED BY SENDING RECORD

Malcolm P. Hanson and L. A. Hyland, of Naval Laboratory, Designed Set.

MESSAGE FROM PLANE IS HEARD 3,000 MILES

Device for Broadcasting of Call Letters Is an Outstanding Feature.

By **ROBERT D. HEINL.**

The first time in history that an airplane on a journey of such length has been able to so continuously keep in touch with its base, the operation of the radio installation on Commander Byrd's America brought particular gratification to its designers and builders, Malcolm P. Hanson and L. A. Hyland, at the Naval Research Laboratory in Washington Modestly enough, these young radio engineers, the former of whom is 32 years old, and the latter only 29, never held any promise

BUILDERS OF RADIO ON AMERICA

Hugh Miller, Post Staff Photographer.

Left to right—Lawrence A. Hyland and Malcolm P. Hanson, radio engineers attached to the Naval Research Laboratory here, who designed and built the radio receiving and sending sets that kept the America in touch with the world.

Newspapers across the United States headlined the role of Hyland in the Byrd transatlantic flight, c. 1927.

Bendix Vice President Pat Hyland received U.S. Distinguished Public Service Award for contribution to development of radar. Hyland is shown with scope unit of Bendix airport search radar used for international air traffic control.

Bendix Flight Research team at USN Technical Training Center, Gainesville, Georgia, 1945. Hyland is in center of group.

U.P. Radio story of Hyland as "Unsung Hero" in radar development.

UPRA

Serviced by U.P.
1300 Radio Stations
throughout the

NAMES IN THE NEWS
(REG.U.S.PAT.OFF.)

-0-

NAMES IN THE NEWS. THE PERSONALITIES BEHIND TODAY'S HEADLINES AND THOSE WHO WILL MAKE TOMORROW'S. STATION (- - - -) PRESENTS ANOTHER IN THE SERIES "NAMES IN THE NEWS," AS PREPARED BY THE UNITED PRESS RADIO FEATURE STAFF. NOW.....

THE UNSUNG HERO

ONE OF AMERICA'S UNSUNG HEROES---A FORMER ENLISTED MAN WHO DID MORE THAN MOST GENERALS TO WIN THE WAR---WILL RECEIVED BELATED HONORS TODAY.

THE UNITED STATES NAVY WILL BESTOW IN DETROIT ITS HIGHEST CIVILIAN HONOR, THE DISTINGUISHED PUBLIC SERVICE AWARD, ON LAWRENCE A. HYLAND WHO MADE THE FIRST PRACTICAL APPLICATION OF RADAR TO THE DETECTION OF AIRCRAFT.

HYLAND'S DISCOVERY, MADE IN 1931, IS LIKELY TO RANK WITH THE GREAT SCIENTIFIC DEVELOPMENTS OF ALL TIME. WHAT HE FOUND OUT WAS SIMPLY THIS---THAT RADIO WAVES CAN BE BOUNCED OFF PLANES IN FLIGHT, NOT ONLY REVEALING THEIR PRESENCE BUT ALSO, TO SOME EXTENT, THEIR POSITION. A LONG LIST OF IMPORTANT DEVELOPMENTS RESULTED FROM HYLAND'S DISCOVERY.

FOR ONE THING, WE LEARNED HOW AIRCRAFT COULD BOMB TARGETS SHIELDED BY FOG OR CLOUDS. WE LEARNED HOW TO THROW A RADAR RING AROUND THE NATION, TO PROTECT IT FROM HOSTILE AIRCRAFT. WE LEARNED HOW TO POINT BATTLESHIP GUNS AT HARGETS INVISIBLE EXCEPT BY RADAR.

HYLAND'S DISCOVERY ALSO HAS SAVED CIVILIAN LIVES. BECAUSE OF IT, WE NOW HAVE THE GROUND APPROACH CONTROL SYSTEM---COMMONLY REFERRED TO AS G-C-A---WHICH PERMITS A GROUND STATION TO LOCATE AND "TALK DOWN" AN AIRLINER CAUGHT IN THE FOG. IT WAS THIS SAME G-C-A WHICH ENABLED THE BERLIN AIRLIFT TO OPERATE IN SPITE OF THE WORST WEATHER GERMANY HAD HAD IN MANY YEARS.

THE MAN WHO MADE THIS IMPORTANT DISCOVERY NEVER GRADUATED FROM COLLEGE. IRONICALLY, HE SERVED IN BOTH THE ARMY AND NAVY, BUT NEVER ROSE ABOVE ENLISTED RANKS. NOW, HE IS VICE PRESIDENT OF THE BENDIX AVIATION CORPORATION AND RANKS AS ONE OF THE NATION'S TOP PRACTICAL SCIENTISTS.

HYLAND WAS BORN 52 YEARS AGO IN WOODLAWN, NOVA SCOTIA, BUT ... WENT TO BOSTON, WHERE HE BECAME A NATURALIZED CITIZEN AT THE AGE OF 22.

IN HIGH SCHOOL, HE WAS POPULAR ENOUGH TO BECOME PRESIDENT OF ... SENIOR CLASS, AND DEVOTED ALL HIS EXTRA-CURRICULAR ENGERIES TO THE DEBATING TEAM. PERHAPS IT WAS THIS DEBATING EXPERIENCE THAT PROMPTED HYLAND TO ENTER THE BOSTON UNIVERSITY LAW SCHOOL.

BUT HE STAYED ONLY A YEAR AND, WHEN WAR BROKE OUT, ENLISTED IN THE ARMY AS A PRIVATE. IN A YEAR OF FIGHTING HE ROSE TO SERGEANT AND SAW PLENTY OF ACTION AT CHATEAU THIERRY (SHAT-OH TEE-REH), SOISSONS (SWAH-SAHN), ST. MEHIEL (SAN MEE-EL) AND THE ARGONNE. AFTER THE WAR, HE STAYED ON IN GERMANY WITH THE ARMY OF OCCUPATION, AND FINALLY WAS DISCHARGED IN AUGUST OF 1919.

HYLAND HAD HAD ENOUGH OF THE ARMY---BUT NOT ENOUGH OF THE ARMED SERVICES. SO, IN 1920, HE ENLISTED IN THE NAVY AS A RADIOMAN, FIRST CLASS. A YEAR LATER, HE PARTICIPATED IN THE FIRST "BLIND LANDING" OF A NAVY FLYING BOAT BY MEANS OF RADIO. IN 1923, HE BECAME A CHIEF RADIOMAN AND TWO YEARS LATER, WHILE STATIONED ABOARD THE U-S-S MARBLEHEAD ON AN AUSTRALIAN CRUISE, HIS VESSEL WON A FLEET RADIO CONTEST.

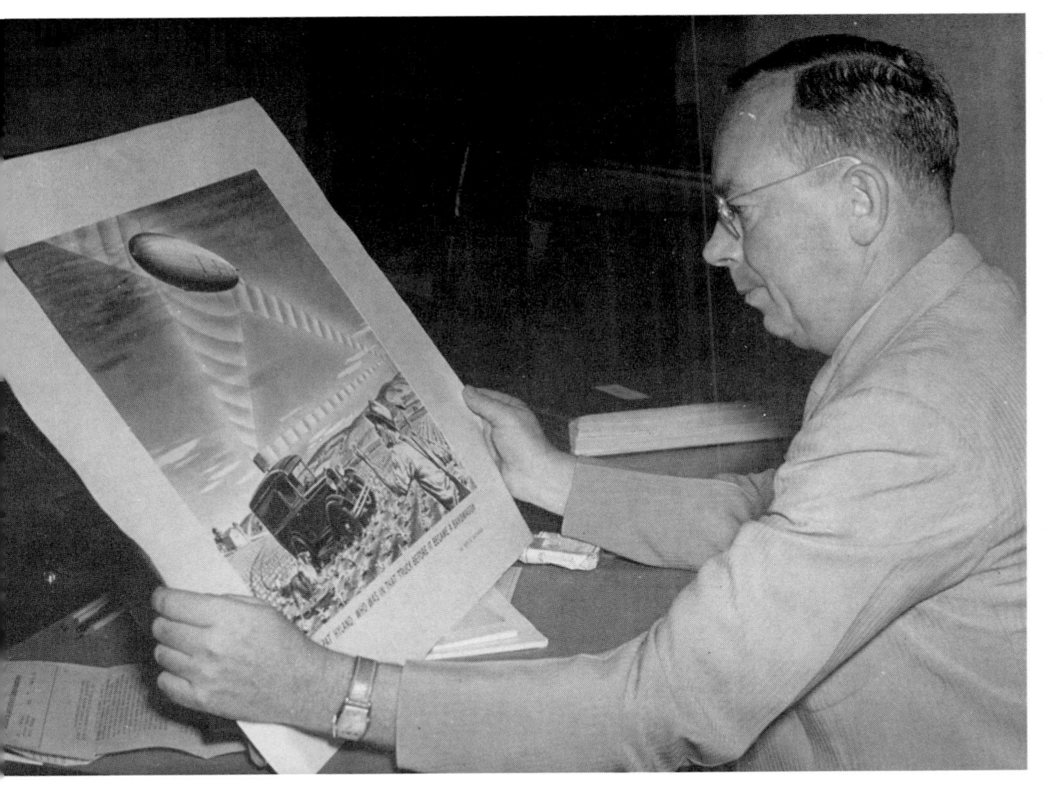

Hyland with artist's concept of 1932 field radar demonstration (done during Naval Research Laboratory days) used for Bendix advertising.

Gala costume party with famous names: Mr. and Mrs. Pat Hyland at right; Mr. and Mrs. Donald Douglas, Jr., left.

Air Force Secretary Harold Talbott's 1954 letter recognizing Hyland's key role in U.S. guided missile program. The letter begins . . . "Dear Mr. Hyland: I wish to take this occasion to extend to you my personal thanks and appreciation for the important contribution you have made to the guided missile program of the Air Force through your work on the Strategic Missiles Evaluation Committee."

[illegible] 1[illegible] 1954

Dear Mr. Hyland:

I wish to take this occasion to extend to you my personal thanks and appreciation for the important contribution you have made to the guided missile program of the Air Force through your work on the Strategic Missiles Evaluation Committee.

I have read your Committee's report and have discussed it in detail with Mr. Gardner and General Twining. Action to implement the general conclusions of the report is presently being taken.

The quality and effectiveness of our air atomic strength must depend in large measure upon a continuing close working relationship between the military and American science. In this connection, I am aware of the heavy demands being made on you by various agencies of the government and deeply appreciate the fact that you have been willing to take time from your full schedule to give the Air Force the benefit of your broad experience and judgment in this complex and critical area.

Sincerely yours,

H. E. Talbott

Mr. L. A. Hyland
Vice President - Engineering
Bendix Aviation Corporation
Fisher Building
Detroit 2, Michigan

Hughes Research and Development Laboratories staff; Hyland fourth from right; key Hughes executive John Richardson at far right.

Pat Hyland receives congratulations from President Lyndon B. Johnson for long and dedicated service to U.S. (1965).

Hyland views Hughes Canadian plant expansion model; at right is key Hughes executive Roy Wendahl.

Howard Hughes prior to flight of XF-11, 1946.

Howard Hughes revs engines of his XF-11 in preparation for first flight, 1946.

›p) XF-11 takes off from Hughes
ld, Culver City on first flight, 1946.

›ttom) Wreckage of XF-11 in Beverly
lls yard; Hughes has been taken to
›pital.

The sometimes-bombastic Vincent Bendix, 1936.

Hyland receives Distinguished Public Service Award from Rear Admiral Rico Botta; Bendix President Malcolm P. Ferguson, is at right.

Press briefing to show Hughes radar: (left to right) Hyland, BG J.W. Andrew, commander, 27th Air Division, Norton AFB, Andrew Haeff, Roy Wendahl, Nathan Hall, 1955.

With the legendary Lt. General Clarence "Bill" Irvine.

Welcoming Dr. Lee A. DuBridge, president of California Institute of Technology, who addressed HAC scientists and engineers, 1957.

Fifth anniversary at Hughes Aircraft; (left to right) Clarence Shoop, Roy Wendahl, John Richardson, John Black, Mr. Huestis, Bill Wooldridge, Joe Ferderber, Nate Hall, Hyland, Allen Puckett, Andrew Haeff, Howard Hall, L. J. Levisee, C. H. Brubaker, Paul Kempf, Edward Boykin, 1959.

Lockheed Skunk Works' Clarence L. "Kelly" Johnson, Hyland, at YF-12A bvriefing, 1964.

Vice Admiral W. F. Raborn is impressed by the middy-bloused assemblers on the Polaris missile guidance line, with J. Ferderber.

Hughes Syncom with key developers, left to right, Donald D. Williams, Thomas Hudspeth, Harold Rosen.

Historic first photo transmitted back to earth by Surveryor I, 35 minutes after landing on the Moon, June 1966.

*'V Star is Born'—The actual flight model of Syncom 3 communications satellite is depicted photo-
·aphically as it might look against a starry night sky 22,300 miles over the Pacific Ocean. Although
ncom is traveling about 7,000 miles an hour, it appears to hover in a fixed position because its orbital
eed matches the rate of the earth's rotation, much like an Olympic hammer-thrower's iron ball remains in
xed relation to his whirling body. Syncom was built for the National Aeronautics and Space
dministration by Hughes Aircraft Company.*

An Emmy to Hughes for development of the Early Bird communication satellite, accepted by Harold Rosen, 1966.

Secretary of the Navy, Paul R. Ignatius is welcomed by Hyland for Phoenix review; executive vp Roy Wendahl in center, 1967.

Hyland, Vice President Hubert Humphrey, with Robert J. Collier trophy, awarded for 1967 to team of Hughes, JPL and General Dynamics for success of Surveyor program. Hyland accepted on behalf of "tens of thousands" who took part in the program.

Vice President Humphrey with Muriel Hyland, daughter Ginger Hyland, and Hyland at Collier Trophy ceremonies.

Annual L.A. Hyland patent awards (a tradition still maintained) recognize individual creativity and inventions. Hyland jokes with engineer Web Howe at 1969 dinner.

Hughes Aircraft received the U.S. Air Force Institute of Technology's 50th Anniversary Commemorative Medal for support of the Institute's education with industry program; Hyland accepts medal from Major Donald Michel.

Dayton Ohio — April 14, 1977 Hand writ! —

Wire to Pat Hyland — via Jimmy Doolittle

Dear Pat:

Sorry I cant attend the presentation to you tonite as I am involved here at Wright Field in the "Super-Cruise" Conference. Fact is I've got to give a speech on the subject. As I have told many people, I never understood why you havent been given at least a hundred times more credit for all the wonderful things you have done for our country, than you have, but after a short study of Boolian algebra I know why! Your overall shyness, the careful thoughtfulness of others and the total lack of egotism on your part has not been recognized by others nearly as much as by Jimmy & me. We both know how great your contributions have been not only in the scientific fields of radar, electronics and national defense but in your personal relations to so many people. — God Bless you —

C.L. "Kelly" Johnson

P.S. Did you really meet my friend Howard Hughes?

"Kelly" Johnson "writ by hand" letter delivered by Jimmy Doolittle, 1977.

Hughes family of missiles, 1969. U.S. Army's wire-guided TOW anti-tank missile (Ed. note: more than 600,000 produced by Hughes by mid-1993) in foreground; background, left to right, are USAF long-range AIM-47A; AIM-4F Falcon for F-106; USN TV-guided Walleye; AIM-26A nuclear Falcon for F-102; USAF TV-guided Maverick; tactical air-to-air AIM-4D for F-4; USN long-range Phoenix for the F-14. Hughes' original Falcon was first successful air-to-air guided missile.

Then senior vice president-operations John Richardson receives 25-year service pin from Hyland, 1973.

General Jimmy Doolittle and Hughes Aircraft consultant Charlie Marcus (who had been Hyland's mentor at Bendix) renew stories after 40 years. The two often met for lunch before WWII at Lexington Hotel in New York with other aviation cronies (Marcus was then vice president at Bendix; Doolittle was director of Aviation Department of Shell Petroleum and a major in U.S. Army Air Corps reserve), 1978.

n executive vice president John Richardson, who joined ghes in 1948, was a pilot in WWII, later headed Hughes yton office, was director of military sales, director of rketing and senior vice president-operations, 1978.

State of Company reports in 1979 included Chairman of the Board Allen Puckett (left), Hyland.

Hughes Executive Office in 1978; Executive Committee, Hyland, Puckett, Richardson.

Pioneer Venus Multiprobe, foreground, and Orbiter, undergo ground testing before highly successful launch, 1979.

Charlie Marcus, who managed Hughes patent program, was honored in 1974 for his "many contributions, foresight, and inspiration."

Hyland receives Aero Club of Southern California's Howard Hughes Memorial Award from William R. Lummis, Summa Corporation chairman and first cousin of Howard Hughes, 1981.

Hyland with Hughes Clown Club members that included engineers and scienti who entertained hospitalized children, including at Spastic Children's Society.

rty-five years of company leadership: -chairman Malcolm Currie (center) Chairmen Emerti Allen Puckett and and at the 1989 State of the Company ress.

photo) Hyland with Senators John Clellan, J. W. Fulbright, and NASA's Hugh Dryden, c. 1960s.

Hyland with Japanese industrialist and president of NEC, Dr. Koji Kobayashi (center), and NACL executive Takesuki Nakamaya, 1970.

The well-traveled Hyland bids "farewell."

Viewing portrait unveiled at 90th birthday celebration at Hughes Aircraft.

Chapter VI
Bendix and the War Years

From the beginning I got along famously with Mr. Marcus, whom I had known quite well for a number of years. I settled quickly into my new assignment with Bendix. We agreed my job and title should be executive engineer. The year was 1942.

I knew the office had been established in New York because Mr. Marcus liked to live there, though the plant in that area was located in East Orange, New Jersey. That required him to take the subway to the ferry stop, cross the Hudson River on a boat, and take a commuter train to East Orange.

On those train trips that we shared he told me about the history of the company, his association with Vincent Bendix, and their struggles to become established in the aircraft electrical business.

Although we had an active office in New York, the power center of the company was in Detroit where Mr. Breech was now the focal point. Unbeknownst to us, he had definite plans for top-side organization and probably personnel.

Mr. Marcus was the vice president in New York. Engineering, patents, and foreign contracts were understood to be his responsibility. However, foreign patents and contracts were virtually dormant in these early war years. Domestic patents were largely in the hands of division patent lawyers. Nobody else was doing company-wide engineering supervision; Mr. Marcus had more or less assumed that responsibility.

We had a tight little operation with a few secretaries and no other staff. To a degree we were isolated from the rest of the corporation. I think Mr. Marcus believed he was being bypassed and was now out of the company's mainstream. That's not uncommon in corporate life, particularly when there are changes in policy as a consequence of new management.

But I assumed that with the corporation's growth, the engineering load would continue to increase; Mr. Marcus would need assistance. We discussed the engineering organization of the divisions in the East—Eclipse-Pioneer, Radio, Scintilla Magneto, and Friez Instrument.

As a director of the corporation Mr. Marcus received the monthly financial statement and detailed breakdown of corporate operations. After two or three months, it gradually sunk in to both of us that all figures on the statement were showing great increases except engineering, which remained fairly constant. Although the corporation's business had increased five fold, engineering remained constant. This meant that existing engineering staffs were probably overloaded even for current products. Nothing was left over for new product development, let alone research. This didn't bode well for the company's future.

We realized that with corporate emphasis now on manufacturing, the engineering picture would change little unless very positive actions were taken.

In talking further, there was no likelihood we could sell our assessment to Detroit. But we had sufficient latitude to bring about changes by talking to the divisions. Neither Marcus nor I was well suited to sit back and let the world go by, particularly a world embroiled in war. We knew big changes were ahead in military weapons. Demands for new, improved and different equipment were already beginnning to emerge. We decided to move ahead.

Engineering in the Hustings

Our first target was the Scintilla Magneto Division in Sydney, New York. (Editor's note: a magneto is an alternator with permanent magnets used to generate current for ignition in an internal combustion engine.)

We were taken through the plant by the manager, chief engineer, his assistant, the factory manager and his assistant, and chief accountant, all Swiss. Bendix and Marcus had discovered Scintilla Magneto in Switzerland during a trip through Europe. At first, Bendix had a license under the Scintilla Swiss patents, but shortly thereafter persuaded these managers to set up a U. S. plant. Before agreeing, the Swiss toured New England and New York, settling on the town of Sydney, New York, a sort of a junior Switzerland. They bought an abandoned silk mill, converted it into a small, beautifully-equipped manufacturing plant, and made Scintilla Magnetos. They had already built a brand new plant several times the size of the old silk mill and were in production making not only magnetos but also shielded spark plugs, a favorite at that time.

The Scintilla Magneto, a beautiful device both electrically and mechanically, like the plant itself, was perfection.

When we came to engineering we couldn't believe what we saw. There was a nice bench with a couple of chairs. There were two Leyden jars, standards of electrical measurement invented about 100 years before, a few hand tools, and a drafting table. That was all. The main drafting room was in a manufacturing department at another part of the plant.

The two engineers were concerned mainly with problems arising from production, spending most of their time in the plant. There was very little else for them to do because product design had been standardized and was highly regarded throughout the world, better even than the Bosch Magneto, a major competitor.

But we knew engine changes were coming; it was inevitable there should be new and different magneto designs in the future as engine developments took place under the pressure of the war.

By prior agreement, we made no comment to either Walter Spangler, the chief engineer, or Rudy Fry, his assistant. We congratulated Herman Henny, the manager, on his efficient, low cost, high quality production plant. Before departing, Charlie set a date for Spangler to visit Eclipse Pioneer in East Orange; I gave a separate invitation to Rudy Fry for the Bendix Radio plant in Towson. Those plants had fine engineering departments with environmental test facilities, ample instrumentation, well-calibrated measurement equipment, and electrical and mechanical specialty tools.

The inspection trips by Spangler and Fry were made. When we visited Scintilla three months later, the beginnings of change had taken place. In six months the engineering department was radically different from our original visit. Apparently the engineers got the word.

There were five other large plants that were focal points for rapidly expanding aircraft production requirements. In preparing for visits to these plants, Charlie and I talked over what we had seen at the Scintilla plant. We recognized that we faced a considerable problem bringing the engineering departments up to capability. We knew big changes were ahead in military weapons. Calls for new, improved and different equipment were beginning to emerge.

We believed it would be better to work with the plants directly because of the probable cool reception a major overhaul of corporate engineering policy would receive.

Each of the plants had roughly 200 engineers, a number that had not changed much since the beginning of the war. As we visited the plants we told the general manager and chief engineer that we believed major changes were in the offing in their activity. We then told them that they should plan to take on more engineers of high quality. As a target, we said they could reach a rate for equipment and technical people as a percentage of total sales as it was before the war. We told them, too, that we would support them in their endeavor to take on more engineers, space and equipment. We charged them with making substantial progress and improvement in the next year or so.

What followed was extremely interesting. Two divisions went from engineering forces of 200 each to about 1,000 in a comparatively short period. Another went to 750, one to 500, and the fifth changed hardly at all. It seemed the growth hormone of each of these divisions got up to a certain point but would go no further. That experience engraved on my mind the fact that some managers are capable of continuing to address expanding opportunity and others simply top out at some level.

My "Tough Guy" Reputation Backfires

In carrying on our crusade to expand engineering's presence, we expected to run into opposition from some manufacturing people, particularly since all divisional managers had manufacturing backgrounds. We devised a strategy. I would usually be the point man, berating the plant manager for his laxity in building up engineering staff. I would tend to override objections and strongly back the engineers. Then, after the plant manager was softened up, Charlie would come in and smooth things over. We accomplished our objective. Nowadays it's called the "good cop/bad cop" technique.

The resentment built up in some of these managers, however, finally got to the point where they compared notes. They banded together to go to Mr. Thomas, the manufacturing vice president. He went to Mr. Breech. He in turn talked to some of the group executives. When Mr. Breech was in New York he called Mr. Marcus to request that Marcus and I meet with him in his suite in the Waldorf Astoria.

Charlie and I found there were two major group executives with Mr. Breech.

Mr. Breech announced that he had received serious complaints about me from almost all managers around the company. He had found that while what I was attempting to accomplish was desirable, I had made myself so offensive that the consensus was there was not enough room in the corporation for them and me.

"Pat, I know your intentions were good but I am in the position where I can afford to lose you, but I cannot afford to lose all of them, so I want you to know that my decision is taken reluctantly. I want to get together with you and Mr. Marcus and arrange a suitable termination for you and also take it up with the board of directors at our next meeting."

The meeting ended; Charlie and I went back to our office.

Of course, it was a terrible shock. I thought I was doing a hell of a job for the corporation. While I had serious debates with some manufacturing people, it never occurred to me their resentment had gone so far.

I wasn't bothered about a job. I had been approached by several companies over a period of years; at one time I was encouraged by a Navy official to start a company (which the Navy would finance in order to benefit from some things I had initiated).

My concern was I wanted to continue with Bendix. I had associations with engineers and the company that had been built up over years. We were going places and doing things, expanding the company; I wanted to keep it going at the same rate.

Charlie was not as surprised as I, but he agreed the severity of the decision was excessive. He said he would try to find a way of tempering Mr. Breech's judgment, but could see no immediate hope.

Raytheon Revisited

After a weekend of uncertainty, I went into the office Monday. During the morning Mr. Marcus received a call from Mr. Breech, reminding him of a meeting with Raytheon the following Thursday. Mr. Breech suggested I come along because I had been responsible for bringing Raytheon to the company's attention as a potential acquisition; therefore, Mr. Breech felt I should be present to act as an introductory official.

This Thursday meeting was to be the second attempt I had initiated to acquire Raytheon.

The first attempt had taken place several years earlier when Lawrence Marshall was president of Raytheon. He called, suggesting a meeting in New York, noting that he had seen what I was doing at Bendix Radio and felt there might be a community of interest between the two companies. Because he was somewhat past retirement age, he was interested in disposing of his interest in Raytheon and felt he could probably find some other large stockholders willing to dispose of their shares at a suitable price.

I knew Raytheon not only had an excellent standing in general electronics, but also was one of the larger manufacturers of receiving and transmitting vacuum tubes. I told Mr. Marshall there might very possibly be an interest and requested that I go to Boston to look over his plants. Following the visit I was extremely interested in their development program which seemed to be extraordinarily productive and far sighted.

Back at Bendix I talked with Mr. Marcus and Mr. Bendix, suggesting it might be productive for them, plus the corporate secretary, to make the same visit.

At Raytheon's Walton Plant, the four of us met Mr. Marshall and his associates. I was disconcerted when Mr. Marshall took the morning telling us about the virtues of his Attleborough factory which made machinery for the jewelry industry and did special work manufacturing rolled metals for thermostats.

This discussion was of no interest to Bendix, Marcus and certainly not to me; but we managed to survive the morning without any blowups. We adjourned for lunch at the Plaza Hotel in downtown Boston. During lunch Vincent Bendix did something I'd never seen him do before. He drank glass after glass of wine. At the end of a long lunch, as we were about to return to Walton, Bendix leaned forward and fell flat on his face on the table. He spilled a glass of wine over his shirt and generally made a mess of things. Marshall, somewhat of a Puritan, was disgusted. He said it was quite apparent Mr. Bendix was not able to go back to the plant; and, unfortunately, he was not going to be available again that week. So the meeting broke up. I was put out with both Marshall and Bendix for different but quite sufficient reasons. But there was nothing I could do about it. At Bendix, we passed up a marvelous opportunity to get a real buy of what I felt was going to be a great company.

When the opportunity again arose to look at Raytheon, I jumped at the chance and told Marcus and Breech about it. They agreed to visit Raytheon. Although this meeting was scheduled after Breech informed me I was to be terminated, he nevertheless asked me to join it.

This time the meeting started extremely well. Breech and Marcus were impressed by what they saw of the Walton plant. Marshall said that in the interim they had gone out of the receiving tube business. They had reduced their position in conventional transmitting tubes but had more than compensated by the addition of magnetron production. Magnetrons are the heart of radar transmitters.

I was again impressed by the developments I saw in engineering. Privately I told Breech and Marcus this would be a great opportunity to add to the product mix at the Radio Division.

Late in the afternoon, after preliminary testing of each other, we got down to a discussion of the company's values. Raytheon presented a financial statement and sales analysis to Mr. Breech. It had already been agreed between the Raytheon comptroller and Mr. Breech that the trade would be on the basis of book value. As Breech looked over the statement he said that in his opinion Raytheon's book value would be about \$4.25 a share; the Raytheon comptroller said he made it about \$4.50. There was quite a discussion between the two of them; the longer it proceeded the more rigid each one became. Instead of compromising at \$4.375, as time wore on each became more red in the face, more adamant. By the time we had to leave the two were poles apart, with no progress toward agreement.

Once more we had blown it. That was the last opportunity we would ever get to acquire what proved to be one of the greater electronic companies in the industry.

Breech went back to Detroit, Marcus and I to New York. I suspect Breech realized he had made a monkey of himself. We were sure he had. This unfortunate experience certainly didn't brighten my prospects with either Bendix or Breech.

Hyland the Hero

The directors met the following week. I was not invited.

Mr. Marcus glumly went alone; I glumly stayed at the office, wondering what was going to happen. One of the first items on the agenda was the annual advertising presentation for the year ahead.

There were six artist renderings of various aircraft with Bendix products; the copy was a brief description of the products and their importance to airplane performance.

I'm told the artist had done a wonderful job; the renderings had a dynamic appeal extraordinary in such advertising. The presentation made a hit with the directors. Mr. Breech was very complimentary and asked who the genius was who thought up these ideas. The Bendix advertising director and advertising representative responded enthusiastically with my name. Breech grunted, the program was approved, and they went on to the next item, patents. The outside counsel reported to the directors that an important patent case, in which Bendix was the assignee, had been to the Supreme Court twice, and that a decision had been finally made in behalf of Bendix. Breech asked who was the inventor and what was the product. The counsel replied the invention was a particular type of spark plug, now in general use by the aircraft industry; the inventor was Pat Hyland.

According to Mr. Marcus, Breech had a pained look on his face, but complimented the counsel on carrying the case to a successful conclusion. The board went on to other business. Later, the advertising executive revealed a plaque covered by a sheet of opaque paper. He said, "I have a presentation I want to show to the board. It is of extraordinary importance to the corporation and one which we plan to present nationwide to newspapers. It commemorates a breakthrough made years ago. We are making the first public announcement of a most important contribution to the national defense. It is known as radar."

With that he pulled aside the opaque paper; the plaque showed a dirigible coming over the horizon with radio waves going to the dirigible and reflecting down to a van parked in a corn field. Then another series of radio waves was shown from a station to the van. He announced that this discovery had been held in great secrecy by the War Department and it was only in the last week they had released the discovery for publication.

There were lots of "oh's" and "ah's." Breech asked again the name of the inventor. Almost before the question got out of his mouth he had his head in his hands and said, "Don't tell me it was Pat Hyland." The advertising man said, "Yes, it was."

Breech had no other choice than to say, well we certainly should congratulate Mr. Hyland about these extraordinary achievements we have seen. Nothing further was said about Hyland at the meeting; no mention was made that a decision had been made to terminate me. When Charlie Marcus returned, he said a decision has been made to hold everything.

Mr. Breech again came to New York, and invited us both to meet him at the Waldorf. This time no others were in attendance. He said, "Well, Pat, after what happened at the board meeting the other day, it would certainly have been foolish for me to have tried to convince the directors you should be terminated." He continued, "I thought it over and I think it would be unwise from the standpoint of the corporation to do so, now that I have seen some of these things. I think the smart thing to do, however, is pacify these manufacturing fellows who have been so incensed at the way you handled them. I suggest it would be wise if you would continue to report to Mr. Marcus but he should interface between you and the corporation for perhaps as long as a year. In other words, you should carry on your functions in the office and do planning and engineering work as necessary through him, but stay out of touch with the manufacturing people long enough for things to quiet down."

I quickly agreed because I really did want to stay with the company and continue the work that had been so successful.

All this happened about mid-June 1943. During the next several months I thought over the matter. I decided the method of operation in which I was the bad guy was certainly not best for my reputation. It was not effective for achieving cooperation and communication among the engineering people in the corporation. That rapport was, I believed, necessary to give us a competitive edge in the future.

I decided to use charm and persuasion instead of sarcasm and irony. Of course, people from the divisions visited us in New York so I was in contact with them and yet kept within the letter of isolation stipulated by Mr. Breech. Charm and persuasion worked. At Christmas I received a letter from Mr. Breech:

"Pat, I'm very glad to tell you that your behavior during the past several months has been very impressive indeed. The people who were damning you at one time are praising you now, and I want to have my Christmas present to you be a release from the stipulation that you stay at the New York office and under the control of Mr. Marcus. You are to resume your normal function as an executive engineer.

With kindest regards, Ernie Breech."

I was indeed glad to receive that letter; furthermore, I was glad the incident had occurred the way it did. I needed the corrective action. From that day on I substituted courtesy and consideration for vinegar in my associations.

The Reorganization is Under Way

Shortly after Mr. Breech came to Bendix with two GM officials, he brought others into the corporate staff. One, a long-time close friend, was Leroy Kiley. Mr. Kiley's noteworthy background began as a World War I pilot in an Italian Air Force Group that included other Americans such as Fiorello LaGuardia, later mayor of New York. They made a noteworthy contribution to the effectiveness of the Italian Air

Force. Kiley had extensive business experience and was an established patent attorney.

In my case, a new and soon-important man was introduced to the Detroit central office: Andrew Kucher, a former associate of Mr. Breech who was at one time in charge of GM consumer products. Andy Kucher had been an assistant to Charles F. "Boss" Kettering, the great General Motors engineer. He had come up through the Frigidaire Division and, among other things, designed the compressor that enabled Frigidaire to offer the first five-year electric refrigerator guarantee.

Kucher was assigned to establish a Bendix Research Laboratory in the Detroit area.

Andy Kucher, Charlie Marcus, and I became fast friends. Roy Kiley and I also hit it off together in the New York office. During the period of my isolation, Kiley and Kucher were strong supporters of mine. I'm sure they intervened with Mr. Breech and were perhaps helpful in having my isolation shortened.

Later, another individual, Ted Zoaral, joined the New York office; he was to be manager of a newly-created International Division.

Thus, eventually the New York office was fully staffed with executives in each area of responsibility formerly carried out by Charles Marcus: Hyland, engineering; Kiley, patents; and Zoaral, foreign operations.

Mr. Marcus was surrounded by placements from Detroit. I am sure he was fully aware of what was going on; he was bright, sensitive, and perceptive. As this orchestration developed, Marcus made his visits to England longer and more frequent.

This allowed each of us to dig deeply into our specialties, although we were fully responsive to Mr. Marcus whenever he was there.

About a year after Andy Kucher joined Bendix, Mr. Breech employed another former GM executive, Lewis Crusoe, as vice president without portfolio. Mr. Breech had known and admired Mr. Crusoe at GM; when he heard of Crusoe's departure from General Motors, Breech felt that this man could take any top job in Bendix; he couldn't be allowed to run loose and perhaps go with a competitor.

It was soon apparent Mr. Crusoe was one of the best executives I had ever known. He was a better manufacturing man than any in the company, and was a better financial man than either our treasurer or comptroller. I was afraid he might be a better engineer than I was; I knew when it came to automobile design and marketing he was probably better than anyone else in the business.

Crusoe and I struck up a friendship almost at once. We had several things in common: He was a farmer with a fine spread in northern Michigan where he was training his son to be owner/operator. I was looking for a farm in Michigan; I liked that life and, while not on a scale of the Crusoe operation, I felt I needed more physical work than the Fisher Building allowed.

Further, Crusoe loved horses. As a child in the early 1900s, I spent summers on my grandfather's Nova Scotia farm, riding the plow horse to water every night. I was also in the horse artillery in World War I, living on a horse for nearly two years.

We also shared the same impatience about "plank holders" in the corporation. Plank holders are defined as people promoted to jobs beyond their capabilities with prerogatives without responsibility. They were an economic drain and impediment to corporate operations.

Bendix Research Laboratory Is Established

With enthusiasm and competence Andy Kucher carried out his mission to establish a Bendix Research Laboratory. Andy had two or three ideas in mind, so the search for projects did not take long. His experience had been with components chiefly useful in the big-ticket consumer field. But as a personal objective, he had always wanted to play a part in aircraft. He believed the configuration of aircraft used in the war was inefficient, both structure and airflow. In addition, he had been associated with the GM research laboratory which, under Boss Kettering, had done a great deal of work on a basically different type of aircraft engine. The engine, based on what was called a swash plate instead of crankshaft, was expected to be particularly suitable for smaller aircraft. Kucher decided that the combination of the new GM engine and his own ideas about aircraft structure and airflow would make a suitable project for the Bendix Research Laboratory.

A second major project was to develop technology for molding low-pressure plastics using precast molds of much lighter and less costly construction than those used for high-pressure plastic products. This project involved a new plastic materials, hence a considerable chemical laboratory.

These were each major projects; with the assistance of Mr. Breech they were reviewed by engineers from the GM laboratory and approved as long-term projects.

The lab projects involved processes and markets with which Bendix was not immediately concerned. Therefore, there was no particular liaison with engineering other than natural technical interests of the two groups.

Andy Kucher and I got along well both socially and professionally. I was particularly interested in the evolution of the model aircraft he designed and had tested at the University of Michigan wind tunnel and structures laboratory in Ann Arbor. He used some newer wing forms developed by NACA (predecessor to NASA). The shape and structure of fuselage junctions with the wings and tail surfaces were considerably different from anything then common in the industry. In particular, there was a smooth fairing from fuselage to wing and tail surfaces so that airflow was not abruptly or sharply changed, but had a smooth transition from one part of the aircraft to another.

The models made by Andy Kucher much resembled present-day high speed aircraft with smooth transition from fuselage to wings and tail. I believe Andy was ahead of his time. His vision can now be seen in current aircraft, and for that matter, in birds.

However, Mr. Breech became concerned that airplane structures were something beyond the scope of Bendix's interests; one reason was that it could compete with the business of some of our major customers. Breech had Kucher display his models to Dutch Kindelberger of North American Aviation (also a part of the GM "stable" at the time).

Kindelberger admired the models but said the additional cost to produce the aircraft would not justify the small improvements in airflow. This reaction from Kindelberger was not unexpected; he was a great seat-of-the-pants designer and, while very sound in structural matters, he nevertheless was arbitrary in his approach where cost was concerned.

The GM engine design proved to be efficient but a problem developed. The vibration associated with the four-cylinder swash plate construction was severe; after a further couple of years of investigation, there was no noticeable improvement. The cooperative approach between the Bendix aircraft design and the GM engine work was reluctantly terminated.

Meanwhile, work continued on the plastics project. I was becoming progressively more occupied with guided missile activity, and so, while my social relationship with Kucher continued, I saw less and less of him in our respective technical projects.

Bendix Moves Without Bendix; Then Without Breech

Within a year after Mr. Breech was elected president in 1942, Vincent Bendix faded out of the picture. His occupancy of the corner office was interrupted by longer and longer absences. Finally, we did not see him again.

By mid-1943 Bendix "the company" was really rolling. All divisions were in full production. The corporate staff was functioning smoothly and the economies of scale were showing up in the profit figures.

But, an unexpected event occurred: Edsel Ford died. His father, Henry Ford I, had been the autocratic head of Ford Motor Company for years. Henry had trained his son, Edsel, in autocratic management. But Edsel, a comparatively young man, didn't have the opportunity to train one of *his* sons as a likely successor. That son, Henry Ford II, was then a Navy Lieutenant. There was no leader in the then-existing management of Ford, because strong executives usually did not stay around long. However, one man, Harry Bennett, head of the Service Department and a hatchet man with a remarkable inside intelligence organization, was a force to be reckoned with.

During the war, Ford, as all other automotive companies, had converted completely to war production. Both the Ford family and government officials were concerned about the company's continued effective war production without Edsel Ford. Additionally, the family was concerned about how to manage the return of the plants to automobile manufacturing after the war.

The family agreed that Henry Ford II was the best answer to the need, provided he could be backed up with experienced management. Consequently, Henry was discharged from the Navy and in September 1945 was named president of Ford Motor Company. An immediate search began to find a suitable first lieutenant.

Ernie Breech, president of Bendix, had the qualifications required. His GM experience was outstanding. He had been handed the major job of taking over ailing Bendix, then converting it from a losing proposition with sales volume of $30 million a year to a profitable giant of nearly $1 billion in annual sales.

Ernie Breech was asked to become Ford's executive vice president, with sweeping powers. He accepted. He showed me a handwritten letter from Henry Ford II stating that he, Henry, was pleased at Breech's acceptance of the job and was looking forward to a long association.

A meeting of the Bendix Board was hastily convened. Breech's resignation was accepted; the job of finding a new president commenced. It was agreed by the Board there were several good candidates among the group executives of the corporation. They were young, had demonstrated capabilities and there was no need to go outside.

Bendix Looks Internally

The choice quickly narrowed to two men. Charlie Marcus, the most senior vice president, had been associated with automotive and aviation production. He had performed valuable and important functions on antitrust litigation, overseas operations, licensing, patents and the quality of Bendix product engineering. He had been a director for many years but had been outside the mainstream of management for the past ten years.

The other candidate was Malcolm Ferguson, whose father had headed Eclipse Machine Company when it was acquired by Vincent Bendix to manufacture his electric drive. Malcolm, brought up in the business by his father, had gone to a technical college where he had been an outstanding student. He had progressed in the company until, in his early fifties, he was named general manager of the largest plant in the company, making both automotive and aviation products. He had also arranged for spinning off several important products for manufacture in other plants. He'd done an excellent job of acquiring plant space, building new buildings, staffing them, and getting them into production to the satisfaction of the War Department and the company treasurer.

Malcolm Ferguson was interviewed by the directors. They were impressed by his presence. Unfortunately, Mr. Marcus was in Paris; but the directors decided that since he was in his early sixties, he was a little old for this responsibility. They elected Mr. Ferguson as president.

Charlie was hurt, not so much by the fact that he had been bypassed, but that he had not been consulted at all and had been informed only after the fact.

Breech at Ford

Henry Ford II got a lot more in his choice of Ernie Breech than he had bargained for. Breech took with him Lewis Crusoe, a former top official of Fisher Body Works, who became controller of Ford Motor. Next to go from Bendix was William Gossett, former senior partner of Hughes, Hubbard and Ewing, who handled the Bendix account. Gossett became Ford's general counsel.

Finally, about two years after Breech left, he hired Andrew Kucher from Bendix Research Laboratory. Andy became director of research and a corporate vice president.

The Bendix contingent arrived none too soon. After the death of Edsel, Harry Bennett had taken over and from his limited mandate was running the company with the finesse of an avalanche.

But the team of Henry Ford II, Ernie Breech, and Lewis Crusoe proved tough, competent and diligent. I continued on friendly terms with Crusoe and Kucher. I was apprised of what was going on, especially during those first two years. They quietly retired Harry Bennett. They hired the Whiz Kids—Bob McNamara, Arjay Miller, Charles "Tex" Thornton, Ed Lundy, Francis C. Reith, Wilbur Andreson, Charles Bosworth, Ben Davis Mills, George Moore, and James Wright—who in later years became heads of great corporations, the Defense Department, or great foundations. Ford was under control in just a few months and in the black within a year.

Crusoe, after herculean efforts in manufacturing, marketing and finance as president of the Ford Division, retired and spent his final years in Florida. He was my great and good friend and teacher.

Bendix Under Ferguson

Malcolm Ferguson, as group executive of the Bendix South Bend Works, had been on the Bendix administration committee for some years and was well versed on the entire company. Ferguson was not one to tip apple carts by premature or hasty decisions. Marcus was confirmed as head of engineering for the corporation; I was his deputy.

Malcolm Ferguson was to be an important factor in the continuing affairs of Bendix.

A second generation Bendix man, Ferguson's first job was at the Elmira, New York plant. That plant manufactured the Bendix drive, necessary for starting automobile engines, a standard part on every American automobile for many years.

In the late '20s the three founders of Bendix—Vincent Bendix, Henri Perrot, John Ferguson—became very wealthy men, expanding their operations into many fields. After the 1929 crash, however, the losses of these three men were as large, or perhaps larger than, their total fortunes. For example, Bendix stock which had been used as collateral for other financial transactions, reached a high of $120 during the glory years. At its low point, after 1929, it was $4.

The once-wealthy senior Ferguson declared bankruptcy and died, unfortunately before his son Malcolm finished college. Upon graduation with honors as a mechanical engineer, Malcolm returned to Elmira to take a job with the Eclipse Machine Division of Bendix. Final liquidation of the Ferguson estate was nearly complete except for an auction, attended by Malcolm, for personal effects in the Ferguson home. Years later Malcolm told me, with tears in his eyes, how he attended that auction, using what little money he had to buy his father's watch, the only memento he had of former great days.

That traumatic experience was an important factor in Malcolm's life. It resulted in a dichotomy: In matters involving capital expenditures, compensation, and equipment, Malcolm Ferguson was penurious. However, where expansiveness of vision, innovation and personnel were concerned, he was at the forefront of modern business practice. Malcolm was studious and friendly. Although not ambitious, he had vision; he wanted the firm to grow in the forefront of transportation equipment, particularly assemblies for automobiles and aircraft. He had that rare balance of humanity and activity so necessary for a productive life, whether for the individual, the corporation, or the nation. He was a hard, effective worker, interested in and comprehending of every branch of the business, whether it be legal, accounting, engineering, manufacturing, personnel relations or construction.

In my opinion, Ferguson was one of the better-equipped, more productive corporate chief executives I have known.

He had no use for the lazy or the dilettante. Unfortunately, he placed me in that latter category. In 1942 Malcolm was corporate vice president and general manager of the South Bend plant. I made my first visit after becoming executive engineer for the corporation. I was in his office at 9:00 a.m. He was hard at work as usual; his secretary told him I was there. I had telephoned ahead to make an appointment.

His secretary said he was busy, so I waited. He knew I was not a mechanical engineer and had no knowledge of the business and products of the South Bend divisions—automobile brakes and carburetors, and aviation brakes, wheels and struts. I'm sure he felt I was some wise-guy from the East elevated to a job for which he had no capability. He let me wait. I had received the cold shoulder in other Bendix divisions so I knew my future relationship depended on waiting him out. When I finally was ushered in, he brushed me off courteously, directing that I be taken to the office of the chief engineer, Victor Kliesrath.

Kliesrath, Bragg and Ethel

Victor Kliesrath had an interesting background. Born in Brooklyn, son of an immigrant, he had been brought up under very poor conditions. He'd battled his way through school. He was a natural mechanic and loved engines. He was inventor of several useful engine components. He became first a mechanic for the foremost racing boat owners and then a racing boat driver; through this association he met another racing enthusiast, Caleb Bragg.

Bragg, a quiet and unassuming character, was born with a silver spoon in his mouth; his family owned the American Bible Society. Young Bragg was interested in racing automobiles; he soon found Kliesrath. The two teamed up; Kliesrath worked with him to tune his race car engines. They were a strange pair. Caleb was quiet and unassuming, but with an explosive temper which he rarely showed. Kliesrath, on the other hand, led an explosive life, going from one tantrum to the next—but never with engines.

Kliesrath came up with the idea of using the vacuum properties of engines to actuate brakes of heavy trucks; certainly cheaper and almost as effective as pressure air brakes. An arrangement was made for Kliesrath to supply know-how and Bragg money; they formed Bragg-Kliesrath Corporation, specializing in vacuum-actuated brakes. Bendix acquired Bragg-Kliesrath in the late '20s. Kliesrath ultimately was named chief engineer of Bendix South Bend; Caleb Bragg became a consultant.

Bragg-Kliesrath started with a little factory and office in Brooklyn. Bragg had a desk on one side of the room; Kliesrath's desk was on the other side. The secretary had a desk in the middle. While they generally worked well together, they had an occasional difference of opinion. It would start slowly, but rising temperatures were usually followed by shouting. Soon one or the other would grab an ink well and throw it at the other, who would immediately return fire. The walls on either side of the desks were covered with ink. But the secretary timed her reaction to the explosions so well she was never hurt. As a matter of fact, that timing ability may have accounted for later success. The secretary was Ethel Merman.

I didn't know all this when I entered Kliesrath's office. He was seated at his desk in one corner of a large, well-lighted room. He was busy scratching his name on papers before him. But without warning he grabbed the remainder of the pile, threw it in the air and said, "The hell with it."

The papers he threw were salary increases for engineering personnel. I later learned it was Kliesrath's habit to get about a third of the way through salary increase and then blow up. There was a distinct effort by the more politically inclined to get on the good side of the secretary (by providing a box of chocolates, a flower, or other attention) so that their papers would be in the top third of the pile of salary increases.

Kliesrath apologized for his outburst, but said he got damn sick of giving raises to people who could not design their way out of the rain.

I told him Mr. Marcus was anxious to get things going now that the new engineering organization had been established. In his absence on a trip to Europe, he had asked me to meet with general managers and chief engineers to assure them his function was not to interfere with their operations, but to have me know what was going on. Marcus wanted to offer his assistance to the divisions in expansion or appropriation requests they might have.

Vic Kliesrath was glad to know why I was there; he would do his best to see we got word of problems, or of support required for what he needed to do. With that, I think we got along very well.

Anti-trust Proceedings Against Bendix

Driven by economic necessity, there was considerable Bendix reorganization after the war. Business volume decreased quickly from $900 million to about $150 million per year. Although Kucher and I had been designated co-chairmen of a long-range planning committee to determine future products of the corporation, the establishment of the committee came much too late for it to be of any immediate benefit.

Immediately after the war the Department of Justice decided that Bendix was a monopoly and instituted antitrust proceedings. One primary objective was the Bendix patent holdings in the United States and abroad. The threat to the corporation was serious. A realignment of the New York office was made. I was transferred to Detroit from where engineering would be thereafter conducted. Kiley was retained in New York as an assistant to Mr. Marcus in handling patent litigation and also to free Mr. Marcus from the load of handling foreign business. However, handling foreign licensing of Bendix patents was still to be done by Mr. Marcus.

Charlie undertook supervision of our defense against the monopoly proceedings with vigor and capability. He interrupted his established regime of frequent and extended work overseas to devote himself to the task. He realized, however, that the anti-trust proceedings would not last forever and when the suit was completed he would find himself without a well-defined job.

After the adjudication, Marcus resumed his practice of investing much time abroad, eventually establishing a Paris office from which foreign patent and contracting arrangements were conducted. His efforts had not only resulted in several hundred profitable patent license royalty streams, but also in establishing partial ownership by Bendix of several French and German companies. He always came to the United States for quarterly meetings of the board. We always got together for trading information and discussion of international political and economic affairs. Charlie was a true cosmopolitan gentleman: cultured, Chesterfieldian in dress, at home in four languages, suave, diplomatic, a top negotiator. He was both friend and mentor to me, providing a dimensional breadth over the years that was truly remarkable for me.

Preparing for the Future

I continued from South Bend, making the rounds of our various plants. I was greeted with real enthusiasm only at the Radio and Friez divisions in Baltimore. I didn't have to wait at any other offices after South Bend; there was no opposition voiced, but neither was there any stated support. Rather a "wait and see" attitude could be sensed. These divisions had accepted our corporate growth plan and, to the extent of their capability, were carrying it out. They voiced appreciation for our efforts. But it was made clear they wanted to run their own shows. While appreciating assistance, they did not want interference or direction about how they should do their own product planning, engineering, development and manufacturing.

Their quite understandable attitude put me in a peculiar position. By osmosis, through associations with forward-looking leaders in the armed services, and through occasional publicity on new technologies throughout the war, I had come to realize that a new product world had been born. This world was clearly emerging as an important field of opportunity for future business.

I knew the Navy had established a laboratory as part of the Johns Hopkins University Applied Physics Laboratory to forge ahead in certain of these new areas. This lab was a foremost factor in electronics, and in particular, guided missiles.

I considered electronics and guided missiles to be the basis of major new business opportunities; and of substantial service to the country. But when I mentioned these facts to various Bendix divisions, I found little interest. I encountered a deep-seated fear of change. I learned to believe in the existence of this fear, but I never understood it and rarely sympathized with it.

Even though the war in Europe was by then over and the Japanese outcome looked more favorable all the time, there was no letup in production. Forward planners, particularly those associated with research and development, were busy looking to what the future might be. An Army unit was formed to exploit the information people were bringing back from the German laboratories at Peenemünde. Missiles, large and small, sprouted from all the services. Word began to get through that the public wanted no more of a war in which their sons and daughters, or fathers and mothers, might again be involved. They wanted a "push-button war."

It was understandable why Bendix division people refused to recognize the potential of the guided missile field. They were still being pushed for production; their engineers were busy with existing development work for aircraft, tanks and other weapons already established. They didn't see a need for getting into a new field about which they knew nothing.

This situation didn't change much until the unexpected resignation in 1946 of Mr. Breech, and then Andy Kucher, head of Bendix Research.

The Changing Role of the Laboratory

When Andy departed, the role of the Research Laboratory was reviewed. Kucher's projects were long range and going in directions that had no immediate benefit to existing Bendix operations. There was some feeling the Research Laboratory should be closed. Marcus and I opposed that, but most of the people concerned were lukewarm; one or two actively opposed the Laboratory.

When it was discussed by the board, support for the Laboratory came from an extraordinary direction. Hugh Baker, of the brokerage firm of Baker, Hardin and Weeks, said no big corporation in this day and time could expect Wall Street support if it did not have a laboratory and research program. He said it didn't make any difference whether the research was successful, but it must be on the list of activities of the company. The board approved the continuation of the Laboratory and its appropriations. It was saved for the future of Bendix—and had a significant impact on my career.

In the years since my first meeting with Mr. Ferguson at South Bend, his estimate of me had changed somewhat. We were now well acquainted; he had learned to tolerate my advocacy of product research and engineering.

In 1947, shortly after the board's action sustaining the Research Laboratory, Mr. Ferguson called me in. He said there was nobody else in the company who wanted to be Laboratory director and he felt nobody at the Laboratory could manage the job. Therefore he was going to make me director of the Laboratory, a vice president of the company for research, and in effect, in charge of engineering and research for the company. My job title was later amended to v.p. engineering and research—the first time Bendix had formally recognized engineering and research at that level.

I had the job; the money had been appropriated; it was up to me. Mr. Ferguson didn't tell me how to do the job so I had a free hand.

I had observed laboratory operations for some time. I disagreed with Andy Kucher about basic product goals he had established. To a degree, part of my problem was solved almost immediately when a couple of the mechanical and chemical engineers left.

I gradually terminated the plastics and aircraft activity and began to move the Laboratory in the direction of missiles and electronic controls. The change came at a good time; defense missile programs were in their infancy and many of the younger engineering community were aware of these new developments. It was astonishingly easy to attract competent people. In a relatively short time, the Laboratory staff was completely reoriented to new goals and was almost in the forefront because of the wartime technical experiences of the newer people.

A basic change in U.S. defense research and development policy had also taken place. Formerly, research and development was handled by the companies, appearing as overhead items in financial statements. Department of Defense research managers now told companies they wanted a hand in company R&D programs directed towards weapons. They indicated they would finance programs that were approved by them but would disallow costs of independent research that, in their opinion, did not coincide with Defense Department objectives.

Our Laboratory landed attractive contracts in more promising areas. In fact, we were overloaded. In an effort to interest production divisions of the corporation in this new technology, I went around to try to sell their taking part in this bonanza. I had done this once before and had been rebuffed. But I thought that with now-available funds, we might have a better chance of interesting them in missiles. My guess was wrong; their full attention was directed to improving their position in existing fields.

I couldn't disagree because I had seen companies attracted by new areas, forgetting that established products were productive, who directed their attention to the new, losing profitable markets where they had good position.

Postwar Business Conditions Change the Ground Rules

When the surrender of Japan ended World War II, the government immediately canceled production orders for conventional weapons and for parts of every kind, type, and description. In the course of one day the defense industrial machine went from full load, all-out production to nearly zero production, with consequent confusion in the minds of management about to do for the future.

Some management of corporations sought to overlook that the world had changed from 1940 to 1945. They tried to take their firms back to prewar products and markets. In general that did not succeed. Others embraced the opportunity for change and new beginnings. Many of these efforts succeeded handsomely.

Before the end of the war in the Pacific I made a serious attempt to interest several Bendix divisions in taking on missile projects which would fit in well with their technical and manufacturing capabilities. All of them summarily rejected the idea; they saw no possibility for profit from that in the immediate future. To them, profit meant production; engineering and science were expense items; there was as yet no missile production work on the horizon. These divisions felt that, when the war was over, their historical markets would need all their attention.

The Research Laboratory nevertheless persisted. When the flood of postwar production cancellations came, one category of defense work was kept intact: research on missile technologies. Research Laboratory developments in several technologies were sufficiently advanced that orders would be for production quantities which could not be handled by the Laboratory's facilities. So I made another round of the divisions, this time with promising orders in hand. With noticeable reluctance, several larger Bendix divisions accepted the offer to take part in government research and development work. They provided space, but demanded (and got) assurance that if any of them should incur a loss on the work, the loss would be absorbed as a Research Laboratory expense and expunged from their performance score.

The Laboratory remained as prime contractor, subcontracting portions of the work to these divisions, taking a small percentage for sales and handling expense, and passing through to them funds to cover the cost plus remaining profit, as allowed by the government.

There was improvement in company financial statements now, because engineering was being paid for and, thus, overhead reduced. Within two years, all participating divisions came to corporate headquarters, stated that conducting business through the Research Laboratory was cumbersome and unnecessarily expensive, that our engineering and marketing were inadequate, and that they could do those jobs better themselves. We agreed; all projects were transferred over. I don't recall any acknowledgment of the part we played in getting these divisions into missiles, but certainly the corporation was now in the missile business in a big way.

Of course, we had not neglected ourselves in the work to be undertaken. We had two or three ongoing missile projects. We needed now to augment them. I needed help too, because I realized that while I was doing a fair job of administration, much more was needed in laboratory technical direction than I could ever supply.

Bendix is Blessed with Research Geniuses

By fortuitous circumstance, a remarkable man, Dr. Harner Selvidge, became interested in an industrial position. He had been in the Johns Hopkins Applied Physics Laboratory, in the development of proximity fuses and had the qualifications necessary for technical leadership of our Laboratory. By the time he became available, I had also found and interested another applicant, Dr. Charles Kimball, who had similar qualifications. I sensed that Dr. Selvidge was the kind of fellow I needed to help me out, so we made Dr. Kimball director of research at the Laboratory, and Dr. Selvidge joined me at the central office.

Between us, we interested two other remarkable men in the activities of the Laboratory. One of them, Dr. Albert Hall from the Massachusetts Institute of Technology, later became deputy secretary of the Air Force for Intelligence, and decades later was still a consultant to the USAF. The other, Beardsley Graham, later became a director of COMSAT and a consultant to many growth companies.

For a couple of years Dr. Kimball did tremendous service as director of research at the Laboratory. He left Bendix in 1950 to found the Midwest Research Institute in Kansas City, a major factor in research in the middle west.

During the year preceding the resignation of Dr. Kimball he was instrumental in preparing a proposal to the U.S. Air Force Materiel Command on electronic equipment for the so-called "1959 Interceptor." This was later designated the MX program. It was a completely new concept for a fighter, making use of the experiences of World War II pilots, and embodying the new technologies of supersonic aerodynamics, jet engines and electronics.

Bendix received an invitation to attend a briefing—background and requirements for MX—by General Seville of the office of the USAF chief of staff. The specifications, subsequently sent around by the Air

Force, presented a tremendous challenge to the industry; the number of airplanes to be purchased was estimated at more than 1,000.

The proposal was a major technical effort. It was truly blue sky. As the project definition was clarified by continuing work I became apprehensive about the extensive research and development required, time span, and cost needed to do the job.

When Bendix was not the successful bidder, I was actually relieved. Little then did I imagine that in a few years time, when I joined Hughes Aircraft Company, which *was* the successful bidder, one of my major tasks would be to see that this project was carried through to a successful conclusion.

Although Dr. Kimball left Bendix and the Research Laboratory, Dr. Selvidge, Dr. Hall and Beardsley Graham stayed. They not only led the Laboratory as it became one of the most productive in the country, but also had an impact on many larger divisions of the company and on the reputation of the company itself.

From my standpoint, they had an even greater effect on me and my life.

During this time, in addition to my Bendix job, I was involved in various governmental committees having to do with missiles, space, atomic energy, and intelligence. My associates on those committees were tops in their professions; I was a pretty good journeyman, but a long way from the top. In my technical committee assignments, my mission was to adapt science to current weapon requirements. My job as director of our Research Laboratory was to encourage product-oriented new science and its translation into the engineering of Bendix products.

Under the influence of Selvidge, Hall and Graham, I was pushed, dragged, kicked, pummeled, cajoled, threatened, and persuaded to live up to and become proficient in the requirements for the jobs I held. Under their influence I was, if not reborn, at least re-shaped. They saw that within five years computers, supersonic aerodynamics, nuclear physics, telemetering, semi-conductors, astrodynamics and a host of other pioneering applications would come from the advanced technical explorations of the past half century.

Their intent was not to make me into a practicing scientist, but rather for me to have an appreciation, perhaps even an instinct, for recognition of the environment necessary to keep ourselves, our company, and even our country abreast of the burgeoning technological world.

Progress and Serendipity

Through the exertions of these three men, that goal was at least partially achieved. Under the direction of Selvidge, Hall and Graham the Laboratory leaped forward, not only on its own developments but also on those of associated engineering departments throughout the company.

The first rocket project awarded to Bendix Research Laboratory was for a high-altitude sounding apparatus to be used for weather purposes. It was a neat little project to cut our teeth on and gave us firsthand experience of a complete job. That successful project was followed by a more important one. We were an invited bidder for the Navy's Sparrow air-to-air guided missile.

The design of the target detection and tracking device we proposed for the Sparrow missile was novel indeed. We were so taken with it we brought it also to the attention of the Air Force. The Air Force said the device would not fit into the volume allocated for its air-to-air missile; they demanded to see a model before proceeding to award. The results of that model work provided a dividend that was quite unexpected.

In pursuing the project, we inadvertently found an entree to the Sandia Laboratory of the Atomic Energy Commission. Dr. Selvidge accompanied our engineer to Wright Field. There he ran into Paul Larson, an old friend of his from the Johns Hopkins Laboratory, now general manager of Sandia Laboratory in Albuquerque. Larson invited Dr. Selvidge to come to see his laboratory. Selvidge did not mention this invitation to me; later, I sent him to Sandia for a wholly different purpose. However, that chance meeting was the root of our atomic energy project.

Although we were disappointed our guidance proposal for Sparrow did not survive the award process for either Navy or Air Force, as it turned out awards from the Atomic Energy Commission more than made up for these losses.

Among other interesting projects we were awarded was one for control of the reactors in a nuclear-energy-powered submarine. In this instance, Captain Hyman Rickover awarded two projects—one for electronic controls to Westinghouse, the other for hydraulic controls to Bendix Research Laboratories.

The method ultimately chosen by the nuclear submarine forces was the electronic controls from Westinghouse, but that did not happen before we had experienced the drive and competence of Captain Rickover.

The Bomb

I first heard rumors in the early '40s that something big was afoot in the atomic area. One day, returning from a blind flying demonstration at Cape Canaveral, the plane flew over a huge new plant in Tennessee. It looked new. For reasons I cannot define, I felt it was associated with atomic energy. Sometime later a banner headline in a paper had only two words—"ATOMIC BOMB."

The war continued; there were increasing demands for production. I really didn't associate Bendix with the atom. The uses of nuclear energy, however, triggered my curiosity. I sensed we were at the beginning stages of a great new force; Bendix was not in it, but probably should be.

Harner Selvidge had preeminent qualifications as a physicist and recent skills in advanced weaponry, including guided missiles. It seemed to me he could help satisfy my curiosity about atomic energy. I heard that the holy of holies, Los Alamos Laboratory, had an associated unit at Albuquerque that fabricated and arranged testing of the bombs. That facility seemed to be a good place to start; I asked Dr. Selvidge to visit both Los Alamos and the Albuquerque laboratories, find what was going on and, if possible, stay around until he got an order—if only for $5,000—so we might get a foot in the door.

Selvidge was gone for more than a week, then showed up at my office one morning with his briefcase full of papers. I had become well acquainted with him. I knew the length of his introductory remarks was always in proportion to the importance of what he had to say. He described in great detail where he'd been, what he'd seen, whom he met, what jobs they held, the internal politics of Los Alamos—but not a hint of what he had accomplished.

Finally I demanded, "OK, it's a big deal—so what did you get?"

He opened the bulging briefcase and took out a bunch of blueprints. He said, "These are just a few of what is available." I asked, "What is available for us?" He said it might be several million dollars. In astonishment I said, "For the love of Mike, tell me what it's all about."

Selvidge began his amazing saga. He first went to Los Alamos, managed to survive security, named the few people he knew there, said his purpose was to be a supplier, was treated courteously, shown around a few unclassified areas, then was assured they would call him if they had any requirements, and politely ushered him on his way.

It was obvious Los Alamos had its own suppliers with whom they were perfectly satisfied and had developed a pattern for handling visitors from outside the circle.

Not one who could be easily brushed off, Dr. Selvidge decided to try Albuquerque. So he drove the long miles of spectacular terrain that separates Los Alamos from Albuquerque.

The next morning he broached the one-story, wartime, wooden building with the office of the general manager of Sandia Laboratory. He gave his name to the secretary; immediately out came his old friend and associate, Paul Larson, who greeted him effusively. They went into Larson's office, shut the door, and reminisced. Larson looked harried; Selvidge commented on that; ordinarily Larson was a placid man.

Larson confided the Atomic Energy Commission had advised only the day before that an emergency would require immediate production of atomic bombs. Further information had been promised but not yet received. But he had started assembling material lists and had located a few drawings. He understood only two bombs had been made—one of the gun type, and another called Fat Boy. He presumed Fat Boy would be the preferred design.

Selvidge asked for a general description of what was required; Larson outlined the complicated nature of the bomb, most of which was mechanical or electrical and well within the capabilities of Bendix. The only items outside our scope of operations were the nuclear material and its immediate containers and the explosive materials which caused the compression needed to initiate an atomic reaction.

Selvidge explained that all of these electromechanical parts were within the scope and expertise of Bendix. He described the engineering and manufacturing capabilities of the corporation. Larson said he knew Selvidge and Hyland, and that we had been engaged in classified projects. He said it would save him a great deal of time and concern to have the Bendix facilities available when he needed them. Larson also told Dr. Selvidge he could talk to Hyland, but to no one else, and that Hyland should be instructed not to discuss the matter with anyone else.

Selvidge requested that he be given a few blueprints of some of the things required so he could take some specific items back to illustrate the kind of work, numbers, and tolerances that required. Larson agreed to assemble a few such prints. Selvidge left, walking on Cloud 9.

The next morning about a dozen drawings awaited him at Larson's office. They called for piece parts and assemblies requiring different kinds of processing. There were indications, however, that all the parts had been made in a model shop; if any quantities were required, there would be a need for tool design and industrial engineering.

Confirmation of requirements came from Washington but no statement of quantity. Extreme secrecy was cautioned, with disclosure limited solely to those with a "need-to-know." Related assemblies were to be fabricated in different plants; any plant utilized should have walled off, segregated sections with provisions for maximum security.

Selvidge was quick to point out that although Bendix had a diversity of plants, they all were calibrated and thereby capable of exchanging the production of parts and subassemblies.

Concluding the meeting, Larson said it looked as if Bendix Aviation was ideal for this assignment; if suitable arrangements could be made he saw no reason to look for an alternative manufacturer.

It sounded like a fairy tale to me. We looked over the drawings; it appeared what was shown fitted into the engineering and machinery capabilities of five different plants. This new work could keep together valuable technical people and units now being disbanded as orders were canceled.

I told Selvidge we should immediately let Malcolm Ferguson know about our good fortune. He said: "Absolutely not!"

"You're kidding," I replied. He said, "I certainly am not. You cannot tell *anyone* about this."

That was a show stopper. I decided I'd better get a little information firsthand, so I arranged for the company airplane to take the two of us back to Albuquerque. When we arrived, four days after Selvidge had left, we were greeted by Larson and the office door closed. He said, "The heat is really on. I've been instructed to go ahead, give Bendix the authority to proceed, and supply you with the necessary drawings."

I said Selvidge told me I couldn't even tell the president of the company. He said, "That's exactly right. You can't tell him. You cannot tell the divisions who the customer is, you can't tell them where to send the material when completed, and furthermore, I may not be able to give you written confirmation for two or three months."

I stared in utter disbelief. I said, "You're out of your mind." Larson grinned, looked at me and said, "It's as simple as this. Do you want the business under these terms?"

"Let me see if I have it straight," I answered. "You are giving me a verbal go-ahead. I am expected to buy perhaps millions of dollars worth of material and pay millions of dollars of wages for an unknown customer. If you got knocked off tomorrow morning, I will have no proof you had authority to do this!"

"That's it," he said. "Take it or leave it!"

My reply was, "I'll take it, but I don't know how in the world I'll get by with it."

"I believe you'll be able to do it," he replied.

Larson proposed we get the necessary blueprints and manufacturing instructions. The three of us walked out of the building and into a huge, lightly-guarded field covered with rows and rows of desks under tarpaulins. Every now and then he would stop at a desk, take off a top cover and pull out sheets of drawings—some on vellum and some just blueprints. He carefully recovered each desk. It took all three of us to carry the bundles of drawings back to the office. Many were originals with no back-up copies, unless there happened to be some at Los Alamos.

As we left, there were handshakes all around. Larson said, "I trust you guys." And we said, "We trust you."

It later turned out this first "order" was for about $15 million, an absolute godsend to Bendix.

Selvidge and I headed back to Detroit. En route, we had little to say. We were overcome with what we had heard, what we had seen, and what we had committed to. It was incredible that information and drawings of the greatest weapon the world had ever known were arranged on tables in a virtually unprotected field on the outskirts of Albuquerque. But this was no less incredible than the conditions stipulated by Mr. Larson—and the agreements to which we had committed Bendix.

The next morning I walked into Malcolm Ferguson's office.

"Good morning. I have some news for you."

"Good or bad?" he asked.

"I think that is a matter for determination," I replied.

I didn't beat around the bush. I told him I had received a commitment from a new and valued customer with whom we had done no prior business. The commitment, of a highly secret nature, was for several million dollars; it would keep several of our plants busy for an extended period of time—with more to follow.

"What's the hitch?" he asked.

"There can be no written order for perhaps several months. I am unable to tell you who the customer is, what the product is or to whom it will be delivered," I announced. I also told him work must start at once, material orders must be made at once, and we would have to take the financial risk for our commitments.

It so happened I knew we were loaded with cash; the financial burden wouldn't be beyond our capability. But, Malcolm, a Scotsman, was careful with obligations and risk. He looked at me for a moment; in fact for several moments.

"Do you recommend this?"

"Yes, sir," I replied.

"How are you going to handle it?"

I told him I would issue orders and instructions through our Research Laboratory and get the show going by personal visits. He got up, held out his hand and said, "Good luck."

That, too, was incredible.

Atomic Work in Secrecy

The project got under way with more than usual speed because of the need for more work at a crucial time, but also because of the mystique involved. In a few weeks Larson gave us another order. This time an Army colonel, a Navy captain, a Bendix manufacturing man, and I were designated a committee of four to find and equip a manufacturing plant of a million square feet for production of atomic bombs. We found the ideal location in Kansas City. Within a year, the first production Fat Boy bomb was delivered, to be followed over the years by others of different, improved designs.

Of the principals involved in on the secret from the beginning, Paul Larson (the Army colonel), Malcolm Ferguson (Bendix president), William Payne (manufacturing manager), and William Holton (Bendix treasurer), have since died. Still surviving are the Navy captain, now Admiral James Russell, Dr. Selvidge, and myself. In those days, great undertakings and commitments were made on mutual trust and faith, and sealed with a handshake. And the faith was always kept!

I resigned from Bendix in 1954. Up to that time, all American atom bombs except the first two were manufactured in that Bendix Kansas City plant.

So Much for Security

As with all serious business, there are occasional moments of surprise and comedy. With the atom bomb, there were two incidents associated with security.

Although manufactured in Kansas City, the bombs ultimately were stored in tunnels dug into desert mountains. The bombs left Kansas City in supposedly disguised freight cars. These were ordinary rail cars; every possible step was taken to make them look ordinary. There were two bombs in each, with accommodations for two guards with food, toilet facilities, lights and reading material. The guards were not allowed to smoke, or even to talk when the train was stopped. Ventilation openings were masked; a special kind of air conditioning kept the guards comfortable during the long desert trip. Even waybills were torn from a pad that appeared to have had some use. There was no reason to believe any notice would be taken of these cars as being any different from others in a long string crossing the western deserts.

At a junction of two lines near the middle of the desert, cars were exchanged; there were two side tracks for each line. One train with the bomb cars had stopped near the junction; the rear part of the train was shifted onto the side track to the other line. The bomb cars, which were in the middle, were supposed to be on the end of the remaining original cars. But some change now had to be made because of orders received en route. The guards, being very quiet, heard shouted instruction from one brakeman to another: "Ship them damn bomb cars over to Track 3."

So much for security.

The second incident happened at a Bendix plant in New Jersey. Extraordinary precautions were taken to segregate weapon parts manufacturing to comply with security regulations. Nobody up to and including the plant general manager had been told the name of the customer or the purpose of the parts they were fabricating.

One day a salesman came into the lobby of the plant and asked to see the purchasing agent. When asked what his product was, he replied, "Paint."

After a phone call to purchasing, the receptionist told the salesman no paint was needed. The salesman insisted he had a special paint and knew it was needed. The receptionist was firm, but the salesman insisted, demanding to see the general manager. This meeting was refused, but the salesman said, "Can I talk to him on the phone? I guarantee he will see me." The receptionist got the general manager's secretary on the phone; the paint salesman said, "Tell your boss I have the paint he needs for his bombs." The secretary knew nothing about bombs, but she did know there were nuts who sometimes came to the factory and had to be handled. So she told her boss, who, although not officially informed about any such products, was not oblivious about what went on in his plant. He agreed to see the man.

To be sure there was no risk, he invited in the manufacturing manager and a security guard stood outside his door. The salesman was ushered in. The manager asked him what this bomb business was all about. The salesman answered that he didn't want to be kidded, saying:

"I know you're making parts for the atom bomb because you have ordered a special kind of paint used for no other purpose by any other customer, a particular blue specified only by the Atomic Energy Commission."

The salesman was turned over to the manufacturing manager for prices and quantities; he was correct.

So much for security, part II!

Hyland as a Troubleshooter

With Bendix Research Laboratory well established and productive, I was able to turn my attention to other challenging areas.

For example, in 1947 the Radio Division was in trouble. Military volume was forecast to be sharply reduced and the two consumer products scheduled to fill in some of the gap—radio and television—were not doing well.

I had participated in initial planning for the changeover from military to commercial products, including a seminar at RCA in which full disclosure had been made about problems and prospects for the television set business. The Radio Division had not accepted our recommendations about the changing nature of engineering and production that would be required for success in the postwar commercial market.

In particular, the radical change from military to consumer equipment had not been fully comprehended, either by the division or by me. Those of us in military electronics had a somewhat low opinion of broadcast and television technology and no real conception of commercial marketing, distribution (including proper inventory management) and completely different retail distribution requirements through jobbers and dealers. We were innocent of retail financing requirements. The division had stepped up to marketing problems well, but in the transition from wartime to peacetime economy, there were shortages of materials. Moreover, despite our self-serving assumptions, the technology of audio and television receivers was as advanced as that of military equipment—but the requirements were different. The customer expected to use his or her purchase immediately, with no instruction book or training. Ease of tuning and automatic volume control were mandatory.

The commercial market was different from military equipment; the design criteria were as difficult for commercial as for military, but different. Television was an even greater engineering challenge than radio. Display tubes were in short supply; there was a vast difference in quality of items produced by independent companies and by those in the RCA group, whose quality was quite superior.

Furthermore, we were in the furniture business for the first time. We knew nothing about cabinet design and our personal preferences didn't sell.

The burden of learning the game of consumer broadcast receivers was superimposed on a group at Radio Division already burdened with ongoing production for a reborn military market and even work on new military requirements. Unfortunately, Radio Division monthly operating statements received at the central office did not separate new consumer products results from results for military production.

This situation had been overlooked by me in the central office because of my confidence in Radio Division management and my own preoccupation with new weapons technology.

The group executive for the Radio Division had not indicated any particular problems when I questioned him at administration committee meetings. But, the comptroller expressed concern with Radio Division statements, which had been deteriorating for several months. He reported the same concern to Malcolm Ferguson. I was directed to visit the Division and see what the trouble was.

When I arrived, everything looked familiar. It was springtime, the climbing roses on the security fence were beautiful. I was greeted at reception by an old friend and walked to the office of the general manager. He was an old and valued friend, but he hardly looked up as I came in the office. His desk was piled with what appeared to be production schedules. He looked tired and preoccupied. We talked for a few minutes, but it was apparent he was anxious to get back to his charts. So I excused myself and told him I wanted to walk around the plant. To my surprise, he didn't offer to go with me.

I made my way to the office of the manufacturing manager, whom I had hired into Bendix. He didn't seem his usual optimistic self. But when I asked to see the plant, he offered to show me around.

Military assembly line activity was somewhat reduced, but there was more activity on the consumer side. Several production lines had been set up, but only two were operating. The manufacturing manager told me the changeover had not been easy. The other lines had been shut down until some product changes could be made to satisfy the marketing people. I was accustomed to changes in military products, but these seemed simple in comparison. I inquired further.

He responded, "Our costs have been running so high the engineering department designed a few changes to reduce costs. But the changes have resulted in poorer performance; dealers and distributors are unhappy."

I asked about engineering, suggesting he take me to the the chief engineer. He said, "You won't find him in his office. He's out in the department, trying to get these products fixed up."

The chief engineer had been a gem with every quality necessary for a great engineering manager. He knew his business, was orderly and meticulous. He presented the solution for a problem with focused intensity. I thought I knew him. I had hired him long ago at Radio Research Company. At that time I paid him about 40 percent more than I was paying myself; it was apparent this man was what we needed and could help us build a great future. Up to this time, he had more than lived up to expectations.

When I walked into his department, I could not believe my eyes. The floor, desks and tables were dirty. Wadded papers were around the wastebaskets. There were radio and TV sets in disarray all over the place. The chief engineer was slumped over a drafting table in a corner. The other engineers seemed unproductively busy. My manufacturing guide had discreetly left as we came to the department. I was standing in the middle of the room, nonplused.

However, I knew the one thing I mustn't do was indicate either displeasure or pessimism. I walked over to the chief engineer, smiled and said, "I see you've got problems."

He responded, "Nothing but."

"Well, the easiest thing about a problem is its solution, if you can outline the problem," I advised.

We talked for a few minutes; he acted as if he were defeated, which was certainly not in character.

"I'm going to go back and talk to the marketing people. I'll see you after a while," I told him.

I went to the general manager and asked if he had an empty office.

He directed me to an office; I walked down, left the door open and sat down at an empty desk.

I swiveled the chair around to look out the window, wondering what in the world I could do. It was apparent things were in a bad way here.

Sitting by myself at that empty desk was the smartest thing I could have done. While I sat, the grapevine was working. Word had gotten around I was there. They speculated about the reason I was there. The people wanted to do something to help. Some decided to pay me a visit.

I knew many people down to the foreman level because many old timers still had important jobs at the Division. In the course of the day I talked to a half dozen of my old colleagues. The picture began to unfold. I made a few more departmental visits; as time went on I began to know the questions to ask. By the end of the second day, I was aware what the problems were and began to have a feel for what had to be done.

I telephoned the group executive that evening and discussed the picture with him, indicating what I wanted to do. He was very glad to unload the problem on me and said he would back up anything I did. As far as he was concerned, I could act without delay or interference.

The next morning I went to see the general manager. He was a good and capable man who had worked himself into a corner trying to unravel complex and inferior engineering by shuffling papers and juggling schedules. He was my friend, but I told him gently but firmly he had damaged his health by putting in long hours over frustrating problems; he should take a long rest. When his health was restored, we would talk about another job for him.

He was a proud man, but also a realist. He agreed that perhaps it was the best thing to do. I saw him leave with regret.

Then I went to the manufacturing manager to tell him he had a new job and what I expected of him as general manager. Without being critical of his friend and former boss, he told me he felt his hands were now untied and that there were many things he could do, providing he had the support of the chief engineer.

I answered, "I can guarantee you he will give you the necessary cooperation. I intend to make the engineering department my next stop."

I played it straight with the chief engineer. I told him that what I had seen and heard were completely out of character with everything I knew about him.

"You've forgotten all the fundamentals and are way off track. I know that you're capable of correcting it. First, I want you to spend the day cleaning up the joint. Get the floor and benches cleaned; put the tools and instruments in place; get an inventory by model of units on hand for test or repair. Then record all design changes you have already made and put all new changes in the configuration control book. Get a clear statement of all deficiencies remaining. I will be in here tomorrow to see that it has been done. Then I want you to get out schedules on the things that you're working on, both in design of the new equipment and correction of defects already experienced. I want a program laid out for the configurations to be built and the tests to be made, one step at a time. This business of making four or five simultaneous changes on different parts of the system and trying to cut corners by testing for several things at once is not workable. You don't know where you're going. You know that and I know that; you've got to get back to first principles."

He looked a little sheepish, but said, "I guess I had it coming. And you'll have no more trouble with me."

"Okay, let's go to see the new general manager."

We three got together, laid out a program, came into agreement and finally I said, "Look, I'm going back to Detroit in a day or two, but I'll be back for as long as necessary to get this show on the road. I want you to know I'm not here to look over your shoulder, but I am here to expedite anything you need and to back you up in case you are doubtful on any particular step you ought to take. Appropriations, I will guarantee. Performance I must insist on, but the corporation will back you at every step and I will be here to see that you get whatever you need."

Before I left at the end of the week, the plant seemed to come alive. There was an undefinable feeling any observer perceives when he enters a productive and proud organization.

There was still a long road ahead, but I felt we were going to make it. At the end of about five months, I called up the group executive and told him he now had the Radio Division back under his control.

The Radio Division experience was an important lesson in my business life. I had been in troublesome situations before, but only in smaller companies or where I had individual responsibility. To step into a very large organization (Radio Division annual volume was then $2-3 million), find it in a confused state, losing money, and with stress on top management above their capability to handle, was a challenge above anything I had ever experienced.

I knew the people—hundreds, perhaps thousands—were competent and had demonstrated that over a period of time.

Sitting in that empty office, posed with a problem and uncertain as how to approach it, the answers came walking in to me.

I learned and subsequently proved that people have the answers. They know the situation in their own area and if talked to, will offer opinions. Out of the integration of those opinions comes the basis of policies and action.

I was to find these lessons continuously useful thereafter.

Education on Radio Design

I was not in agreement with many designs chosen for cabinets for radio and television equipment. And I was not pleased with the sound that came from the loudspeakers. There was a period of time when what I called "boom-boom" sound was coming out of speakers. It seemed to captivate people all over the country. I thought it was awful. Consequently, in the fullness of my wisdom, I decided to show these people how to design one of their radio models that was due for market the following autumn.

The designers ultimately came up with a console that looked good to me; a model was made that pleased me. Simultaneously I had the acoustic people do a better job than before with the sounds that came out of the speakers. I was well satisfied with the total package.

Along with other models of the new radio line, mine was put into production; I waited confidently for reports from retailers. First reports were mediocre; later reports put my "special" at the bottom of the list. What a lesson! You do market research in the market, not in your own imagination.

The Search for Acquisitions

The Bendix Research Laboratory was functioning smoothly and had a variety of work and a comfortable backlog. It was more involved with "global war" operational concerns than any other division of the corporation. In this postwar period, there was a continuing scramble of companies that had grown during the war to find not only enough new ventures to fill the difference from earlier production rates, but even to maintain prewar directions.

Experiments we made in long-range planning, a hasty effort after the German surrender, did not prove productive.

An alternative was considered: Acquisition of companies already in business with management, product and distribution in place. Some might be small, but if enough in related fields could be found, they could make a substantial addition to our company's volume. There was also a possibility that a search might find a comparatively large company, perhaps closely held by elderly people who wanted to retire, that could be bought at a reasonable price. It was decided to look into this matter. I was charged with the job.

This interesting assignment ultimately resulted in acquisition of a small, well-managed filter company. The principals wanted to stay as operators, but wanted to get their investment out. That division proved to be a profitable operation, gradually expanded and, after two or three further acquisitions, became the Fram Filter Division of Bendix.

I looked at a dozen other prospects, but none measured up to our requirements. In most cases the trouble was management. One or more of the people who had founded the business or operated it during the war had died or left; the organization had gradually deteriorated. There were often competing companies in the same business; there was little likelihood the prospective company could be reorganized and recapture a market. So, although some product lines looked interesting, financial prospects were not attractive.

There were companies that appeared to have financial prospects, but their field of interest was so far away from anything we knew that they could not be seriously considered.

From my standpoint the process was most educational. The opportunity to examine dozens of different businesses with balance sheets disclosed, to look at engineering, factory, product, distribution and personnel from the janitor to the chief executive, and to talk with people at all levels without interference, was of great benefit to me.

In nearly all cases, an effort was made to put the plant in the best possible condition and for people to put their best foot forward, but nevertheless, some prospects were sorry indeed. In the process, I learned a great deal from talking to people, trying to discover their business problems, to learn where the "bodies were buried," and their real reason for selling.

These principles applied to evaluation of any division or business, whether within our corporation or one not under our control. The people knew the problems in their own areas. They even knew the good and bad supervisors one level above them. But generally, they had neither the exposure, nor the interest, to handle the whole picture.

Thus, the four parts of my job—research and development, engineering, fixing, and acquisition evaluation—fitted well. They made for a broad training that proved very useful in my future.

The Color Television Controversy

Picture a converted barn on the outskirts of Stamford, Connecticut. It had been shipped piece-by-piece from its original location in western Massachusetts. There was a wartime Christmas party at the house in honor of Charlie Marcus. At the time, he was vice president of engineering; I was executive engineer. The party was given by an old friend, Alan Patterson, an early aviator who had later set up business in Shanghai and Manila. He and his wife, a Thai, had fled China ahead of the oncoming Japanese. Guests included a Russian count who had been kicked out of Siberia by the communists, and his date, a lady lawyer named Frieda Hennock, a wheel in New York City politics. It was a great party.

Now, skip ahead to the postwar years. At issue were color television broadcast standards before the Federal Radio Commission. The choice was between a mechanical scanning system advocated by Columbia Broadcasting System (CBS) and an electronic scanning system advocated by Radio Corporation of America (RCA). Mechanical scanning existed. It worked. A number of sets had been made and were in use, particularly in hospitals. Mechanically-scanned color, however, could not be received in black and white by television sets then in public use.

Limited electronic scanning had been demonstrated; but it was not quite ready for production because the picture tube was still expensive. It had not been tooled up for quantity production at a reasonable price. Electronically-scanned color could, however, be received by monochrome black and white receivers as well as on color receivers.

After World War II Bendix had converted its Maryland military aircraft radio plant to production of black and white television receivers; Bendix had a stake in television. I went to Baltimore to be briefed on the color situation. Our people felt the choice of CBS's mechanical scanning would be grossly unfair to the public—and an inconvenience for the Baltimore Division. Admittedly, the system would be ready for general use sooner than the RCA electronic-scanning system.

Our Baltimore people said the Federal Radio Commission seemed to be equally divided, but the swing vote would probably be cast by an ex-Coast Guard captain, a communications expert. When I learned it was Captain Webster, an old friend, I decided to go on to Washington to chat with him.

I had first appeared before the Federal Radio Commission about 1930, shortly after it was formed, and again a few years later when I was seeking a license for a broadcast station I had built. A decade later I was astonished at the size and importance of the Commission offices.

I headed for Commissioner Webster's office. He greeted me warmly; we made pleasant small talk.

I explained my present occupation and my interest in color TV, commenting that his might be the swing vote. He said he didn't believe his vote was in doubt; he had firmly decided that mechanical scanning was the only answer and that the public would brook no further delay. He observed that it might take years before a color picture tube, so necessary in electronic scanning, would be ready for low-cost production. He did say, however, that he was not certain all other commissioners had made up their minds.

Commissioner Webster added he was sorry I disagreed with him, but at least we could agree to disagree. That was where we left it.

I left his office disheartened; my own opinion was that the proper solution was to wait for electronic scanning which would protect the large public investment in black and white receivers.

As I walked down the hall, I read the names of commissioners on doors I passed. One said: "Frieda Hennock, Commissioner." Two steps beyond I realized I knew a Frieda Hennock. I did a double take, went back, took another look, convinced myself the likelihood there might be another Frieda Hennock was remote. I went into her office. There were a half dozen others sitting in the office, apparently waiting to see Miss Hennock. I gave my name to the secretary, asking to see Miss Hennock. "These other people are ahead of you. There may not be enough time this afternoon," the secretary responded.

"My business is pretty important," I replied, "and I wish you would take my name in and at least let her know I am here."

She did. When she returned, she said, "Miss Hennock will see you at once."

I couldn't believe it, but I followed the secretary and received a cordial greeting. We recalled the delightful Christmas party and got down to business. She knew about my radio history since Charlie Marcus had kept her informed. I told her my opinion of the extreme importance of the forthcoming FRC decision. I described the essential differences between the two scanning systems and that the CBS system was not compatible with black and white. If adopted, I argued, the CBS system would exclude millions of TV sets if it was adopted for future programming. I related an incident I had overlooked talking to Captain Webster. I had visited the RCA laboratories at Princeton, New Jersey. Dr. Engstrom and General Sarnoff had described the progress made on electronic scanning; they were confident they were within weeks of production. They stated they would license all picture tube producers in the industry on extremely favorable terms, assuring an economical price and wide distribution.

Miss Hennock seemed interested; but I could see I had not lighted any fire. I finally relied on the old, tried and true use of children. I said it would be a shame to deprive the kids of the benefits of entertainment and education color TV would insure. I told her my life had changed when color comics began about 1910. I reminded her of the drabness of black and white comics and the remarkable change that accompanied the introduction of color in one Boston newspaper; then the rapid changeover of all newspapers to this new step in the printing art.

She seized on the word "education," saying she had neglected to take that into account in her consideration of the two systems. She told me good color would make all the difference in the world. It was certainly worth waiting for in order that the benefits of color and compatibility could be realized. She thanked me effusively for coming in and kissed me on the cheek as we said goodbye.

The Federal Radio Commission voted a few days later. Miss Hennock's turned out to be the swing vote. Compatible electronic scanning color television was adopted for licensing.

I never saw or spoke to Frieda Hennock again. By the time I looked her up once more, she had died. But, she performed a great service for color television, not only for this country, but for the world.

There are so many lessons to be drawn from this single incident that I can hardly enumerate them, but certainly the principal one is that *one vote can count.*

The Decision to Leave Bendix

Adjustments came at Bendix Aviation as military volume increased and internal changes took place. A detailed review was made of all products, developments and organization in order to determine present values and future possibilities.

After Ernest Breech assumed the mangement of Bendix, the composition of the board of directors had gradually changed. Under Vincent Bendix, most directors were company men or those closely associated with its products and markets. As these men retired, their replacements were people high in the financial world—brokerage partners, bank presidents, chief executives of unrelated businesses. This changing composition continued under Malcolm Ferguson. Attendance at board meetings by Charlie Marcus, an original director of Bendix, became infrequent. He was spending longer periods in our foreign offices.

The financial condition of Bendix in 1953 was superb. Profits had been good since before World War II and remained so. Reserves were ample and dividend distributions generous. Plant and equipment were all paid for; the corporation had no debt.

I was looking to the future with rose-tinted glasses. The Research Laboratory was forging ahead into new fields. I was really sitting pretty. I had not yet learned that it is wise, when everything is looking good, to turn around suddenly to try to avoid the kick that is coming.

At Mr. Ferguson's suggestion the board set aside a number of Bendix shares to award stock options to senior employees. This action was a matter of some excitement; those who expected to participate eagerly awaited the allocations.

When they were finally announced, nearly everybody was pleased except Charlie Marcus and me. Mr. Marcus, who had "unofficially" retired, received no allocation. I received a small fraction of what I had expected. I was furious at first.

But after thinking it over, I decided it was time I realized what had happened at Bendix. First, I understood the dichotomy of Malcolm Ferguson. Though trained as an engineer, he had come up through a division where manufacturing was king; engineering and marketing were distant seconds. That division made the Bendix starter absolutely necessary to the automobile but with little or no design change for years. Ferguson had been promoted up the line until, just prior to his election as president, he had been general manager of the largest automotive division in the company.

Not since Kettering at GM had there been a dominant engineering figure in the U.S. automobile world. Nor has there been another one up to the present (Editor's note: in the late 1980s). One consequence is that we lost our product superiority to the Japanese, Germans, and Swedes.

I decided it was hopeless to try to beat the combination of an "establishment" board and an otherwise great president who had long been exposed to values established by his best customers.

I was fortified in this resolution by another fact. During the first blush of enthusiasm over our atom bomb business, Mr. Ferguson had authorized me to buy a site for a new Laboratory for expanded operations of Bendix Research. But as business returned to normal, I was unable to get an appropriation for the building.

To the new suite of directors recruited from the banking-law-brokerage establishment, I was some kind of nut or maverick who talked about such heresies as reinvestment of earnings into research and new products, and who served on government committees at company expense.

Taking into account all these circumstances, I decided to resign.

I kept on with business as usual. I didn't do any job searching because I had been averaging about one job offer a month.

During the interim at Bendix I had an inquiry that led to my consideration of the job of vice president and general manager of Hughes Aircraft.

The more I looked at Hughes, the better I liked it. I didn't know it at the time, but there were three or four people I had to satisfy. The most important were Howard Hughes and, believe it or not, the Secretary of the Air Force. The USAF job of investigating me was by a Wright Field Air Force colonel whom I'd recommended for another key position at a conglomerate. In the course of the investigations, we ran into each other, found out what we were doing, had a good laugh, and made good reports. We both got the jobs we were seeking.

When I had my contract with Hughes in hand, I submitted my resignation to the secretary of the Bendix organization. Malcolm

Ferguson was in Paris. Although he had planned to spend two more weeks seeing customers in Europe, he returned to Detroit.

We met. I told him with neither embarrassment nor anger that I had been shocked by his low opinion of my past, present, and prospective contributions to the company, as evidenced by the modest stock option. I cited four or five major functions I had performed for the company, not the least of which included bringing in about a quarter of all present business with the outlook for more in the future.

He listened without comment. When I finished, he asked if I was firmly committed. I told him I was; there was no turning back. He expressed regret, as did I. I agreed to leave in a month. Finally, he asked if I had a recommendation for a successor. I had a strong recommendation—the chief engineer for one of the aircraft instrument divisions. I said he was a better man than I. When I left, he appointed that man, A.P. "Jack" Fontaine, as my successor. Jack ultimately became president of Bendix.

Another interesting thing occurred. The board of directors almost immediately gave authority for construction of a new Research Laboratory building on the site I had chosen.

So the kick landed. It hurt, but like some others, it kicked me one rung up the ladder.

Chapter VII
The Challenges of Mr. Hughes

My association with Dr. Allen E. Puckett extended far beyond our joint service on the government's Guided Missile Committee. About 1952 a group of scientists from the Massachusetts Institute of Technology and California Institute of Technology got together to sponsor an all-day New York seminar on space. Of the Guided Missile Committee, only Dr. Puckett and I showed up. The proceedings lasted all day, with speculation covering the possible, the impossible and the romantic.

Dr. Puckett and I had lunch together—and it turned out to be important. Each had a curiosity about the other and we used the time to relate our backgrounds and experiences. We began to nurture a mutual respect and admiration that developed and lasted for many years. We both were on the original von Neumann committee, formed by Trevor Gardner, then assistant secretary of the Air Force, to counsel and advise on USAF long-range missile program. Dr. Puckett and I saw each other several times a year in 1953 and 1954.

In mid-August 1954 I was at the Bendix atomic bomb plant in Kansas City; a call came from Dr. Puckett. He said officials of Hughes Aircraft Company were having difficulty finding and selecting a new general manager. This was not news to me, because it was generally known throughout the industry that there had been considerable differences of opinion between senior management and Howard Hughes over policy matters. Many of the senior management had resigned.

Dr. Puckett said he felt I could help. Hughes people would appreciate it if I could advise them and perhaps give them a few more names to consider. Although I was busy at the time, I agreed to go to Los Angeles during the long Labor Day weekend.

I was met at the airport by Dr. Puckett and his companion, Professor Harold Koontz of the School of Business Administration at the University of California at Los Angeles. Professor Koontz had been charged by Noah Dietrich, managing assistant to Howard Hughes, with responsibility of finding, interviewing and recommending to Dietrich and Hughes a candidate for the job of company general manager.

We went direct to company headquarters in Culver City, California. Puckett excused himself; Koontz introduced me to Hughes' temporary management committee.

Four of five vice presidents were present in the board room. There were two engineering vice presidents, Robert Shank and Nathan Hall; a research vice president, Andrew Haeff; and a manufacturing vice president, Ray Parkhurst. The fifth vice president, Howard Hall, general counsel, was absent.

They carried on a general conversation with me with Koontz observing. Eventually, Professor Koontz and Dr. Haeff excused themselves; Shank and Hall asked me to review a movie showing the performance of the Hughes' fire control system and some of the rockets used for air defense. At its conclusion I was turned over to Mr. Parkhurst, the manufacturing vice president, who took me to lunch and walked me through the manufacturing plant at Culver City and another production plant near Los Angeles airport.

They were excellent manufacturing facilities. An old manufacturing hand—and I qualified—can tell in a short time whether a good job is being done at a plant. The products I could see, whether completed or in process, the machinery (which was of the finest), the state of the inventory and the stockrooms, the cleanliness of the floors, and the general housekeeping were first rate throughout. Knowing the specific products, I judged that workmanship was of the best and in full compliance with military standards.

After the factory visit I was taken to dinner by Professor Koontz. In the course of the evening, he asked my opinion of what I'd seen at Hughes.

The Search Was On—For Me

By noontime of that day, I had concluded that what they were after was not advice, but rather a potential general manager.

Earlier, as a member of the Guided Missile Committee of the Department of Defense, I had visited Hughes at Culver City. I'd been impressed by the quality of the engineering department. I was, of course, aware Hughes had been successful bidder for the 1959 Interceptor electronics and knew the company's engineering capability was of the highest order. Moreover, I had already decided to leave Bendix; but neither Koontz nor anyone else knew that.

I felt there might be a good match of my background and experience with the Hughes resources of engineering, research, manufacturing, and marketing. I decided to shoot the works. I told Koontz I was pleased with what I had seen, what I knew, and what I could foresee in the turmoil of the changing defense picture. I said that under the right circumstances, I might take the job myself.

Koontz didn't act too surprised and asked what those circumstances might be.

I told him my house in Detroit had to be sold at the guaranteed going price and moving expenses paid. I would require a contract for $100,000 a year, plus a performance bonus to be arranged, plus an option to buy stock in the company.

Koontz replied that it would have to be taken up with Mr. Dietrich and Mr. Hughes. He would try to arrange for an interview with Dietrich in the morning. He suggested I prepare a list of people whom I felt would be able to describe my capabilities—in effect, references.

Returning to the hotel, I prepared a list that contained two nationally known lawyers, two prominent scientists, a USN admiral, an Army general, a USAF general, two university presidents, two prominent government bureau executives, the president of Ford, and former president of Chrysler. When I completed that list I was pleased and a little surprised at the quality of my "references."

In the morning Dr. Koontz picked me up for a 10:00 a.m. meeting with Noah Dietrich. En route I gave him the list and later found that within two days he had checked with every name on it.

Mr. Dietrich was an interesting and charming man. He talked a little about the foibles of Mr. Hughes and of Hughes' always-intense preoccupation with business affairs. He remarked also that Hughes' two other interests were ladies and airplanes. He asked about my business and professional background, noted the aircraft radio experience, and commented favorably on my long term association with Bendix and the notable innovations coming from industry in recent years.

He made specific reference to the difficulties Hughes had had with former general managers and the troubles they had had with Mr. Hughes.

Dietrich asked if I had any qualms about the confusion and uncertainties of the engineers at Hughes Aircraft. I replied that an organization in turmoil was no new experience to me. I said that I was one of the high tech group by reputation, and coupling that with my extensive business experience, I should be able to get the situation in hand in a reasonable amount of time.

Mr. Dietrich suggested I see Howard Hall, company counsel, to work out a tentative contract. Dietrich remarked that the option part of my requirements might be a hurdle, but could be included for further negotiation. He said Professor Koontz would be the point of contact until all elements could be brought together and a meeting arranged with Mr. Hughes.

Koontz took me to Howard Hall's home; we spent about an hour getting contract terms and conditions outlined. Hall agreed to have it transcribed. A copy was to be sent me and one given to Mr. Dietrich for the approval of Mr. Hughes.

The Die is Cast

I managed to get an afternoon flight to Detroit. During the trip home I felt elated and confident I had the world by the tail. Within 10 days, I heard from Koontz that matters had progressed satisfactorily; Mr. Hughes wanted to interview me in person about some details of the contract; and it was suggested I should return with Mrs. Hyland to Los Angeles where she could look for a home.

I arranged for a few days vacation so my wife Muriel and I could examine the possibilities of a major change in our lives. In Los Angeles we were met by Professor Koontz and taken to the Beverly Wilshire Hotel.

The following morning I met with Mr. Dietrich who expressed satisfaction with events and stated he would arrange a meeting with Mr. Hughes at a very early date. He introduced me to Miss Nadine Henley, secretary to Mr. Hughes. They suggested Mrs. Hyland and I should entertain ourselves at the hotel while awaiting the interview.

Our hotel suite was pleasant; TV was interesting for a day or two since there were more channels than in Detroit and quality of programs somewhat better; books and magazines kept us going for a couple of days.

But I soon became impatient. I called Dietrich, who turned me over to Miss Henley, about when I could expect the Hughes interview. Miss Henley said Mr. Hughes was very busy; he was trying to find time between important prior arrangements. I told her I was unhappy at having my movements so restricted and that I had seen enough of the hotel. Miss Henley sympathized and said that during ordinary working hours I should feel free to do what I chose because Mr. Hughes usually did his business in the evenings and nights. She ensured me I would not be called until after dinner.

To add further to the Hughes "mystique," Miss Henley stated that the fact I was negotiating with Mr. Hughes should be kept secret, and that Mrs. Hyland, in looking at houses, should use another name, and should make no reference to Mr. Hughes or to Hughes Aircraft Company.

Several more days passed. Muriel was becoming restless and I was becoming alarmed. I finally called Miss Henley to tell her I was thoroughly put out and that if Mr. Hughes didn't see me within 24 hours I would be on my way back to Detroit and would not return to Los Angeles for any Hughes purpose. By noon the next day I was ready to make flight reservations when Miss Henley called and pleaded for 24 hours more. She said Mr. Hughes was really tied up, but promised to have an interview the next evening. I told her this delay was acceptable, but I would make a Detroit reservation for the morning after the evening interview.

During our previous waiting period Miss Henley had arranged for Virginia Tremaine, a Beverly Hills real estate agent, to take Muriel around the Beverly Hills area to look over potential homes. Out of many candidates, Muriel found two potentials and on my next free afternoon, we visited them both. One I didn't like, but the other was a delight to behold. The prospective new home was so attractive it had influenced me to give Mr. Hughes the additional day.

An Interview with Mr. Hughes

Lo and behold, soon after lunch the next day Miss Henley called to say Mr. Hughes would see me at seven that evening at the Beverly Hills Hotel where he resided. His driver would pick me up at 6:45 p.m. at the Beverly Wilshire Hotel.

The driver took me to a cottage on the grounds of the Beverly Hills Hotel complex. Mr. Hughes met me at the door, shook hands, and indicated a chair. He fit the pictures I had seen in some articles. He was dressed in a conservative business suit and was a picture of courtesy, intelligence, and competence. He immediately set me at ease and we started talking. An hour passed by while we reviewed our lives. Among his many interests was the fact that he had been an amateur radio enthusiast during his high school years. He was reasonably up to date on radio understandings and, of course, we had much to talk about in aviation.

After a while I heard a female voice in the back room and Hughes excused himself. He went into the room and closed the door. He came out shortly, apologized for the delay and resumed our conversation.

Hughes agreed with all terms and conditions of the contract except that of the option. He said that there were no other options in any of the companies that he owned, that he was trying to work out an arrangement by which such options should be given, but he could not give me one without the fact becoming noted throughout his other holdings. Hughes promised to make an option agreement in due time, but could do nothing at the present. He also stated that while the contract that had been submitted had been satisfactory in most respects, nevertheless he had a practice of having his own attorney write up such undertakings; he wanted to do so in this case. Since all other conditions had been agreeable, I stated that I was satisfied with the arrangements. We shook hands on the deal.

I asked to whom I would report, Mr. Dietrich or him? He thought about it for a moment and rather reluctantly said, "I guess it would be to Mr. Dietrich."

Mr. Hughes saw me off. Back at the hotel I found a telephone message from Dr. Koontz. He said I should return to Detroit but that Mrs. Hyland should stay so that she could sign a contract for the purchase of the home which was being arranged by Mr. Hughes. While awaiting the house contract, Muriel would be taken incognito to Palm Springs by one of the secretaries at the home office and given the run of that resort until the contract was ready.

I left for Detroit and Muriel was escorted to Palm Springs where she waited for three or four days until she flatly refused to stay longer. She was lonesome for her little daughter back home and saw no reason for further delay. That fact was relayed to the Hughes office. She was promptly returned to the Beverly Wilshire Hotel; strangely enough the home contract was available for her signature. She signed it and returned to Detroit.

Another period of waiting ensued. After a week, I called Professor Koontz to enquire what was going on. He said the contract was being prepared by Mr. Hughes' lawyer and was not ready for signature. I made a few appropriate remarks and hung up.

Another week went by. I called again. This time to Miss Henley. I felt she might know a little more first hand. She said Hughes was busy. The contract was ready, but he was out of town. He was expected to return soon. Again I waited, but not for a week this time. Three days later I called Miss Henley. This time she said Mr. Hughes had returned but was very busy with a mountain of mail. However, he hoped to get to the contract soon.

I had built up a head of steam. "Well, my patience has been exhausted," I said. "This whole business now has consumed several weeks of my time, and I don't propose to wait any longer. I have another offer which I shall look into. If the Hughes contract is not in my hands by midnight Friday, the deal is canceled forever."

It was then Wednesday and I felt two days was plenty long enough. Thursday and Friday went by with no message from Hughes. So, forlornly, Muriel and I went to bed Friday evening. We were sound asleep when, at 11:30 p.m., we were awakened by the doorbell. Putting on a dressing gown and slippers, I went to the door. There was a TWA captain (TWA was then owned by Mr. Hughes) with a brown envelope. He said, "I am to deliver this before midnight by orders of Mr. Hughes."

"Thank you very much; you have done so, and I shall so report it," I noted.

He left and Muriel opened the envelope. There was the contract signed "Howard R. Hughes." I was to report for duty November 22, 1954. A month away.

The following Monday I resigned from Bendix after 16 years of service as an employee and 20 years of association. I was then 57 years of age, two years beyond the early retirement that some select. I was starting a life of fruition which was to last another 30 years, first as employee and then as consultant. Although I didn't think of it at the time, it was the remainder of my life.

Mr. Hughes and His Eccentricities

I subsequently learned that the delay with the contract signing for the new home by Muriel was occasioned by the desire of Mr. Hughes to see what kind of a house we had selected and determine if the price was suitable since he had a keen sense of values for real estate.

We already knew he looked it over. Probably the only mutual friend we had between us, Pat DiCicco, a notable jetsetter and former husband of Gloria Vanderbilt whom I had known for years, happened to drive by the house at the time Hughes came down the driveway from his inspection to his dilapidated Chevrolet. DiCicco stopped his car and asked Hughes what he was doing there. Hughes stated that a real estate agent had offered it for sale and he was checking to see if it was a good value.

DiCicco said, "Well, I have my eye on that house and you leave it alone."

Hughes agreed. But after they parted, Hughes promptly called

Virginia Tremaine and bought the house, which he then sold to me by way of the contract signed by Mrs. Hyland.

(As an aside, the salary of $100,000 [big money in those days] remained the same throughout Mr. Hughes' life. Options were never granted. In all respects, however, during Hughes' lifetime, the association was ideal. Offsetting the fixed salary situation and the refusal of options were other benefits which were consequential, although not adequate. For me, the adequacy was supplied by freedom of action and the privilege of personal fulfillment in that position. Those were priceless.)

Although I was warned by friends in industry and the Department of Defense not to risk my reputation and career where other, good people had failed, I felt that the possibilities were excellent.

I admit to some questions in my own mind in 1954. Who was this man Howard Hughes for whom I had agreed to work? And who was this associate of his, Noah Dietrich, through whom I was to report?

Personal Observations About the Enigmatic Mr. Hughes

In 1954, Howard Hughes did not have the public image his name conjures today in the minds of many people. He was not the pain-tormented recluse he became, but instead was a high visibility, much admired achiever.

Howard Hughes was the "White Knight" of that era. He was tall, handsome, talented and a fine athlete; he was a successful movie producer, a record-holding flier, and wealthy. He occasionally won an amateur golf tournament. He attracted beautiful women and his successful ventures and adventures made him a legendary figure around the world. He was widely admired for his success in battling government bureaucrats.

His associate, Noah Dietrich, had worked closely with Mr. Hughes for nearly 30 years. The combination of those two bright minds, plus their physical and mental courage, had made them remarkably effective in their business undertakings. Their outward flamboyance hid solid, major goals.

To understand Hughes and Dietrich, it is necessary to consider the men separately and then look at the combination. Howard Hughes was sired by an ingenious father, who among other things, invented the rotary cone rock drilling tool and the system for its use. Both deeper drilling and economy resulted from these and other improvement patents, which gave the Houston-based Hughes Tool Company dominance for years in gas and oil well drilling.

Howard's father died in 1924 when "Little Howard" was only 18 years old. In the settlement of the estate, a brilliant and charismatic accountant, only a few years older than young Howard, was employed. His businesslike handling of the estate, and his grasp of legal, accounting and business principles, so captivated Howard that Noah Dietrich soon became an alter ego. The two maneuvered together for many years.

Hughes did particularly well in technical subjects in high school; one teacher is reported to have said Howard had the best mind of any student he'd ever taught.

Howard was a good, licensed amateur radio operator, an interest he maintained throughout his life. He had a fine set of radio equipment. Its use perhaps helped establish his pattern of doing business late at night.

Howard's interest in girls developed rapidly as he became an eligible bachelor. He married and divorced early, and with his interest in movie production, there were continued encounters with women.

During the boom years of the '20s, Hughes Tool Company became a tremendous money-maker, supplying funds for Howard's investments in other areas. He bought but never sold land. His interest in aviation extended beyond piloting—to aircraft design and manufacture. He bought controlling interest in TWA and RKO, and even acquired the brewery adjoining the Hughes Tool Company in Houston.

There were ups and downs. Noah Dietrich once pointed out to Howard that he was overextended and that it would be necessary to curtail his expenditures. Howard agreed. At that time his living quarters in a hotel were neither extensive nor luxurious. However, he gave them up and moved into one room, pointing out to Dietrich his cooperation.

But Howard continued to buy mink coats, automobiles, and flowers for his girlfriends, much to Dietrich's disgust.

Hughes was a pioneering experimental aircraft engineer and had the funds to exploit his notions. In the mid-to-late '30s, Hughes set a host of U.S. and international aviation records that made him a hero of the people—not unlike Lucky Lindy of a decade before. The name of Howard Hughes was in the news regularly. The country loved him and was proud of him.

Hughes experimented not only with counter-rotating propellers, but also financed construction of engine pairs, where the rotation of the engine on one side of an aircraft was opposite to the rotation on the other side, thus providing a balance of torque that would slightly increase speed.

For his 1938 round-the-world, record-setting flight, Mr. Hughes' objective was to cut in half Wiley Post's then-current record of seven days, 10 hours and some minutes. Always looking for advanced thinking, ingenuity and experience, Hughes selected Igor Sikorsky as the one in whom he would confide. There were consultations regarding flight path, landing places, distances, national territories and other details that would have to be considered in the design of the flying boat that Hughes originally believed he should use for the flight—because of the enormous over water distances he'd travel. All of this was done with the highest possible secrecy, as usual.

Hughes must also have confided in his old and valued friend, Bob Gross, then chairman of Lockheed Aircraft Company. Gross made an urgent call to Clarence "Kelly" Johnson, the great Lockheed aircraft designer. Gross arranged a meeting between Johnson and Hughes. Johnson stated that any flying boat would be slow and cumbersome, difficult to maneuver in strange harbors and no safer in a forced landing at sea than an airplane with its wings filled with ping pong balls for flotation.

Johnson assured Hughes that an alternative airplane - the Lockheed Model 14 Super Electra - was available and had proven flight characteristics. It was fitted with two of the newest 1800-series Pratt & Whitney engines. Johnson felt the plane would cut overall risks in half as compared with a float plane. It would achieve a better total elapsed time because of higher speed. It would reduce the time for refueling and checkover at landing fields. Use of that existing plane would cut preparation time for the flight to a small fraction of what a new flying boat yet to be constructed would require.

Hughes respected Kelly's judgment; he knew of the performance of the Model 14. He agreed they would proceed as Kelly suggested. The next year, 1938, preparations were complete, the flight was a great success, and Hughes achieved his goal of cutting the prior record time in half. Kelly's and Hughes' projections proved correct. The public gave Hughes a hero's welcome in a ticker tape parade on Fifth Avenue.

Howard's Famous Flying Boat

The origins of the great Hughes Flying Boat, irreverently named the Spruce Goose (a name Mr. Hughes disliked immensely, in part because only a small fraction was made of spruce), stem from the first years of U.S. participation in World War II. Shipping losses to German submarines in the Atlantic were substantial. Henry Kaiser, although leading the world in ship construction, couldn't keep pace with those losses, so he came up with the idea of a "flying ship," which submarines could not touch and which, to a large degree, could be made of wood, a non-strategic material.

Kaiser persuaded a rather reluctant Howard Hughes to join the enterprise. A new company, Kaiser-Hughes Corporation, was created. The broad notion was that Howard Hughes would lead the design and engineering effort for the big new plane and Kaiser would manage putting it into quantity production. On this basis, Kaiser-Hughes Corporation was awarded a contract to develop and build a flying boat out of non-strategic materials, excepting of course the engines and propellers. *It was to be the world's largest aircraft.*

The Challenge of the Flying Boat

In all of his undertakings up to that date, Hughes had not been handicapped by lack of funds. The Hughes-Dietrich team had been extremely successful. Hughes Tool Company had always provided a sufficient and rising string of revenues to sustain Howard's activities. Howard's timing of his interests had been such, up to then, that his enterprises became producers instead of consumers of capital after a brief initial period of investment.

The huge aircraft, however, was something else. There were development problems. Howard's personal pride, and his reputation as an achiever, were at stake. Under Howard's drive to keep the schedule, which necessarily meant a disregard of cost, it became apparent to Kaiser that the contract could not be fulfilled within the allotted funds. He negotiated himself out of the picture. Hughes reluctantly concurred, but did not halt work on the airplane. After the government's initial funding was depleted, Howard continued the work on his own money, expecting eventually to be reimbursed.

It would be almost impossible to determine how much money was really spent on the Flying Boat, but the monumental task was finally completed—much over cost and time. Because of his air racing and movie exploits, Hughes was a public figure worldwide. With this in mind, Maine's U.S. Senator Owen Brewster saw the possibility of some widespread publicity for himself; as a member of the Senate Committee to Investigate the National Defense program, in August 1947 he began an inquiry into the cost, delivery delay and lack of performance of the wooden giant.

Near the end of the hearings, Hughes decided to make a flight to show that the aircraft had indeed fulfilled its requirements. The flight, on November 2, 1947, covered a little more than a mile and was about 70 feet above the water. In Mr. Hughes mind, the flight was proof the craft could perform as expected. Concurrently, Howard had investigated some of Senator Brewster's associations and a combination of that information and the flight ended both the congressional investigation and, as a side effect, Senator Brewster's career.

Little attention has been given to another forward step of this great airplane. Mr. Hughes hired a fine radio engineer, Dave Evans (who also flew in the right seat as co-pilot), to design appropriate radio equipment and on-board intercommunication equipment for the Flying Boat. A tape made at the time records the careful steps taken by Hughes the day of the flight, from the time the aircraft left the dock until it returned. This attention to detail is further evidence of Hughes' interest in aircraft technology. In addition to radio equipment, the Hughes Flying Boat encompassed many aviation technological breakthroughs that are being used in the industry today.

However, World War II had ended. The need for a troop transport with minimum use of strategic materials was ended. There was a $25 million overrun demand upon the government, which was wrangled about for more than 25 years and not settled until after Howard's death.

Mr. Hughes and Hollywood

Hughes' interest in electronics was kept alive by the beginnings of a communication system between Los Angeles and Tucson, Arizona and by development of a sports network for making live reporting of sports events available countrywide. Without deviating from his basic interests of aviation, motion pictures, electronics, women and secrecy, this restless entrepreneur had also acquired RKO film studio. Hughes, a connoisseur of women and a master of detail, ran RKO personnel ragged with new takes and reruns to get the exact impression he wanted his films to deliver. However, one minor and now famous detail was not exactly unpleasant. On the famous "Outlaw" film with Jane Russell, Hughes was dissatisfied with the effects created by existing bras, particularly those worn by Miss Russell. He applied his knowledge of structural engineering, skin stretching, and configuration design to achieve maximum appeal. His successful effort was the basis for an extremely vigorous countrywide marketing campaign.

Mr. Hughes combined his motion picture and aviation interests in the film "Hell's Angels." He almost single-handedly wrote the script and directed the performances. He employed Colonel Roscoe Turner for the stunts and high-speed maneuvers. He hired a retired Air Force general, Clarence Shoop, an organizing wizard, to advise on safety, aircraft selection and tactics, and to establish a stimulating continuity in the film.

Meanwhile, Back at the Aviation Division

After the single flight of the Flying Boat in 1947, the only substantial activity remaining at the Aircraft Division of Hughes Tool was work on three units of the XF-11 photo reconnaissance airplane. One was for static structural test, two were for flight test.

At the close of the war, the handwriting was on the wall. Hughes, a shrewd realist in those days, read it clearly. He reached two conclusions: One, there was zero probability that Hughes Tool would be awarded a production order for either the Flying Boat or the F-11. Two, there was also zero probability that Hughes Tool could win a production order for some other new plane in head-to-head competition with already-established airframe companies such as Lockheed or Boeing.

In the presence of this reality, Dave Evans persuaded Hughes that the wave of the future lay in electronics. Evans didn't pretend to predict the future in detail, but his remarkably accurate instincts told him that in some form or another, electronics was going to be big. Most importantly, the field was wide open at the time. Hughes agreed.

He instructed Dave Evans to scour the country for the best engineers and get about a half a dozen of them to collaborate in the design and fabrication of aircraft electronics. Evans found Simon Ramo and Dean Wooldridge at General Electric, as well as Bob Shank, another capable radio engineer. They went to work at the Culver City plant, initially on airborne radar for terrain avoidance in bad weather, and for night fighter weapon aiming. This small, high quality, team laid the foundation of the future Hughes Aircraft Company.

The Tragedy of Howard Hughes' Life

Hughes now had an aircraft design and manufacturing organization and a smaller radio design and manufacturing group. But a desire remained to complete another aircraft, the F-11—with outstanding performance and his own design. Before World War II he had planned the two-boom (fuselage) design, later used in the Lockheed P-38.

The primary feature of his advanced design was to be two counter-rotating propellers on each of the two big engines so that the small counter-foil needed to balance out torque of a single propeller would no longer be a factor. No single detail of that aircraft missed his attention. He was determined that he would be credited with the conception of this marvelous machine.

In 1943 the government decided to acquire the F-11 for reconaissance, awarding Hughes a $43 million contract to produce 100 airplanes. The contract was canceled at war's end. Even in the late 1940s, the complete design of an aircraft was a major undertaking. Without government support, he went ahead on his own money, free of any concern for military specifications.

I happened to be at Wright Field on a Missile Committee inspection tour when the structure was under test at the Aeronautical Laboratory. One test engineer said the structure was an extremely good one. Judging from the load of sandbags they had put on the airplane, that seemed a reasonable conclusion to me.

The day—July 7, 1946—finally came when the XF-11 had completed ground tests and was thought ready for flight. Hughes, a great pilot, was always his own test pilot on any aircraft he designed.

The XF-11 took off from Hughes airfield in Culver City without incident, circled and headed north. Hughes was speaking calmly into the transmitter microphone, but suddenly became momentarily incoherent. Shortly thereafter there was silence.

The aircraft had crashed in Beverly Hills and burned, destroying a house at 808 Whittier Drive. Hughes was pulled from the flaming structure by a heroic passing Marine. He was taken to the hospital with what turned out to be nearly 100 fractured bones.

Questioned later about what had happened, Hughes said that it suddenly felt as if a barn door were hanging on his right wing. He could not bring it up. The aircraft went into a spin and crashed. Although there were many opinions, the consensus was that the counter-rotating propeller on the right-hand engine had failed; the rear set of blades went into reverse pitch and forced the XF-11 into a flat spin.

The broken body of Howard Hughes was put back together during numerous operations over a period of months by a team of surgeons headed by Dr. Verne Mason and his associate, Dr. Lawrence Chaffin. The reassembly and healing process was, of course, accomplished with great pain to the patient. Pain-killing drugs, principally various morphine derivatives, were used to keep his discomfort tolerable. But Mr. Hughes was not a patient patient. He willed a recovery much sooner than had been expected and demanded to be released from the hospital while still needing and using those pain-killing drugs. Leaving the hospital under the care of Dr. Mason,

Hughes was put on Valium and Empirin A. These are both potentially habit-forming. Before long, Hughes was hooked.

Empirin A contains phenacetin. This ingredient, over the long term, affected Hughes' kidneys. In addition to the drugs, Hughes was "addicted" to chocolate, a food known to have an adverse action on the kidneys. Ultimately, Mr. Hughes death was caused by kidney failure.

The crash and early hospital release marked a turning point in the career of this great independent, free thinker.

Admittedly spoiled by his early wealth and independence, he was nevertheless bright, clear thinking and courageous. When he chose, he had fast reaction time and was decisive. But the new Howard Hughes was changed. The residual pain, drugs and frustrations began gradually to eat away at the abilities and associations of this remarkable man.

Even in his best days, Hughes was no treat to work for. He could charm the birds off the trees; he could be sensitive to the problems of the little guy; he could stand against the mighty; he could humor a friend; or he could outfox a magician. He and Noah had many a laugh over the shenanigans they pulled in the business world. But he was selfish and obstinate in most of his dealings with the managers of his enterprises.

Many of Mr. Hughes' conversations with me, whether initiated by me or by him, were conducted in high secrecy. I don't recall any conversation between us when I was in the office. A few conversations took place from my home, but most of them were from pay telephones at a stipulated time.

I recall one in particular: As in the case of most calls initiated by him, we did not talk about anything related to the business; instead he brought up the subject of the Medical Institute and said it was still his ambition, as it always had been, to provide for the best and largest Medical Foundation in history. He said he had founded the Aircraft company at the suggestion of his lawyers, who told him of the tax benefits associated with it. He said he had been taken in by the lawyers who thought only of the present. He said now he was in financial difficulties regarding jet airliners and needed a lot of money. But he had given away the big source of money—the Aircraft company—and there was no way he could get a dime out of this great asset. Almost in the middle of a sentence, he broke off and said, "Pat," with a kind of a groan, "did you ever have a high enema?" He continued then with his final statement, "Damn those lawyers," and hung up. Obviously, he had called for some other purpose, but had terminated the call because of pain. I had learned it was useless to speculate and it did not bother me.

Another call came a couple of weeks later. This time the call did not last long. Hughes used up all of the time himself, with only an occasional acknowledgment on my part. In substance what he said was that since Noah had left him (Noah Dietrich, in fact, was fired) his affairs had been somewhat in disorder. He said he might have a big assignment for me, but not until two or three problems were overcome. He did not ask if I was interested, nor did he make any further statement, although there were quite a few minutes taken for this much. Neither then, nor at any other subsequent time, did Hughes ever mention his thought of a role for me in his own industrial empire.

Electronic Advances at Hughes

The Radio Group at Hughes was proceeding in parallel with the aircraft operations. They were a capable and free-wheeling group, exactly suited to develop new weapons and controls to take advantage of technology developed during and after World War II. Hughes was a friend of Lt. General Ira Eaker, one of the original "round-the-world" fliers, whom Hughes had consulted in his own preparations for a much faster circumnavigation. Hughes persuaded General Eaker to associate with him and guide the development toward military requirements. He also tried to interest Colonel Bill Irvine in the Hughes enterprises. Irvine was a brilliant, forward-thinking, but controversial Air Force officer. Although Bill chose to stay in the service, which he loved, his counsel was always available. He knew where weaponry should go.

The compact and enthusiastic radio group turned out an astonishing amount of design and products. They operated effectively during the Korean War, where they were able, within a year, to produce operational equipment that filled an important requirement of the air war.

Contracts rolled in; ideas and products rolled out; earnings jumped. The radio group of the Aircraft Division of Hughes Tool was becoming a very big business. It literally jumped into the league of the *Fortune 500.*

Not only were talented engineers attracted to the radio group, but also bright managers and administrators. Tex Thornton, one of the Whiz Kids from Ford, took a top administrative job. Word got around the country that this new Hughes organization had everything. It had, almost.

It was only natural that these bright, ambitious engineers and business managers should want quick, positive decisions—as well as stock options, so that they could participate in the growth of the business. Neither was forthcoming.

Hughes was always slow in making a decision, but wanted instant action once he decided. He would procrastinate until the last moment. He would not criticize, he did not praise—and he was very hard to find.

For Hughes Tool, TWA, and RKO, Noah Dietrich was the intermediary. He could get the ear of Hughes if necessary. Dietrich would promptly make all but the very highest decisions. Noah was a great financial manipulator and businessman. He would comprehend and deal with the problems of those three business operations—but he had no warm or personal feeling for aeronautics or electronics. He regarded them chiefly as whims or headaches and losers. He was not impressed with the radio group's performance, because its rapid expansion was soaking up Tool Company earnings for its fixed and working capital—capital that was now becoming badly needed by the developing mess at TWA.

Mr. Hughes and His Perception of the Jet Age

Hughes thought the transition from propeller-driven to turbine-driven aircraft would take two steps. First, the engines would be gas turbines instead of the usual radial piston engines but still would drive large propellers (turboprops). Then the second step would be to pure jet propulsion (turbojets). Lockheed opted for the first step with the Electra; Boeing chose to skip the first step and go to a pure jet with the 707. Lockheed suffered some bad luck with its Electra; Boeing hit the jackpot with the 707.

Hughes vacillated in ordering for TWA the new jets that would succeed the piston-engined DC-6, -7, and Lockheed Constellation. Dietrich jumped up and down trying to get Hughes to get in line for the 707. But as usual Howard procrastinated, this time for too long. It appeared he would trail behind American Airlines and United by one to two years in modernizing TWA's fleet. He was on the absolute end of the line for receiving Boeing 707s.

However, Mr. Hughes had an ace up his sleeve. Because of the need for down payments in ordering engines, the airlines did a little procrastinating of their own and neglected to order spare engines. Hughes stepped in and bought out all the engine delivery slots from Pratt & Whitney, a huge financial undertaking.

Hughes did not have the money to finance the purchase. His relationships with the banks had become increasingly strained; he had called for even more help as his predicament worsened. Finally, his primary source of finances, Mellon Bank in Pittsburgh, closed him out with much bad feeling on both sides.

In the legal mess that followed the close-out of the Hughes account by Mellon Bank, antitrust proceedings were initiated against Howard Hughes and Hughes Tool Company by the financial interests behind the new management that had been installed at TWA. Hughes and Hughes Tool were charged with the conduct of maneuvers to the detriment of fair trade. The occurrence of these suits contributed to a further reluctance of financial organizations to lend money to Howard Hughes or his companies.

Hughes ultimately prevailed in the lawsuits, although it required two trips to the U.S. Supreme Court. The final argument to the Supreme Court was prepared and presented by a professor from the University of Texas Law School. He out-maneuvered a team of pin-striped smoothies.

Before the matter was altogether out of hand, Hughes tried other combinations of banks and insurance companies without success. TWA was doing poorly and had to have additional operating funds. Finally, Hughes had to give up control, but not ownership, of TWA to a group of banks and insurance companies, who installed a new president—my old Bendix boss, Ernie Breech.

As a part of the final agreement, a solution to the aircraft and engine allocation was negotiated so that TWA got a fairly decent line position on the 707 and the other airlines got some engines.

During this disturbance, which lasted two or three years, the Hughes/Dietrich relationship began to fall apart. But it was still in being when I came to Hughes Aircraft in late November 1954.

The Medical Institute and Hughes Aircraft

I never found out why, in his early twenties, Hughes decided that his lifetime goal would be to establish a great medical institute, hopefully the greatest ever set up. There is mention of this goal, here and there, through the years of Hughes' life. After his term in the hospital, following the XF-11 crash, he instructed Dr. Verne Mason to chair a committee of three with a view to establish objectives and personnel of a medical institute.

Through his remaining business, professional and personal life, Hughes maintained this committee and its objective. He looked at and discarded several different plans. It became apparent he did not want a big hospital or any kind of imposing physical monument. He wanted and insisted upon a medical institute devoted to research, perhaps in association with a hospital or hospitals, that could assist in carrying out his objectives.

As plans began to take form, additional doctors were enlisted, all having had distinguished careers. A business organization was set up, the beginnings of which were a tax attorney, a secretary, an administrator, and an accountant. Then in late 1952, what the lawyers regarded as a real opportunity began to appear.

Although the Aircraft Division of the Tool Company was losing money, it had nevertheless been appraised by several companies as being valued at $75 million because of its product lines and personnel. The lawyers recommended that the Aircraft Division be set up as a corporation and that a gift be made of that capital-hungry operation to the Medical Institute, thereby qualifying the gift as a tax deduction from the huge earnings of Hughes Tool Company. After some pulling, hauling and legal maneuvering, the plan was modified. On December 17, 1953, the Radio Group of the Aircraft Division became Hughes Aircraft Company. Its stock, along with certain intangible assets, was given to the Howard Hughes Medical Institute.

All buildings and equipment used by Hughes Aircraft were leased by Hughes Tool to the Medical Institute, which in turn leased the facilities back to Hughes Aircraft at a much higher rate. The aviation activities of the division ultimately became Hughes Helicopters, Inc. with continued ownership for many years by Hughes Tool. (Editor's note: Hughes Helicopters was sold in 1984 to McDonnell Douglas and is currently McDonnell Douglas Helicopters.)

The working capital of Hughes Aircraft Company, such as receivables, good will, work in process, etc., was given to the Medical Institute by the Tool Company in return for a note for $18 million at five percent annual interest. Those assets, in turn, were given to Hughes Aircraft Company by the Medical Institute in return for 75,000 shares. So Hughes Aircraft Company started off with nothing in the way of tangible assets, little capital, some fine products and people, but with almost a hundred vacancies in top and middle management spots. The Medical Institute, however, was established finally with a medical board, an accountant, an administrator and a secretary, but as yet no mission. It did, however, have a substantial income from the lease money paid the Institute by the Aircraft Company. On the other side of the table, the Tool Company got rid of an unwanted division and its costs, with the result that in the next 12 months, it would show a record income. Actually, Hughes Tool Company was the only completely satisfied entity of the lot. Mr. Hughes got the benefit of a tax saving of about $2 million, but in so doing he gave away a company subsequently worth billions.

By the time I had my first interview with Mr. Hughes, his plans for the Medical Institute were developing fairly rapidly. Florida had been decided on as a site and the beginnings of an organization had been set up in association with the University of Miami.

Negotiations on these concepts continued for a couple of years. As time went on Mr. Hughes became disillusioned with the notion of a hospital. In a telephone conversation with me, he recalled our initial meeting in which he stated that he wanted to leave his estate as the largest donation to a medical foundation that had ever been made. And he had said that this foundation should be wholly devoted to forward-looking research. In the present conversation he defined more of what his plans were. He believed that construction and operation of a great hospital would be a monument to him, but that was not what he wanted to have happen. He said a hospital was for current operations, and there were many people who could build hospitals and run them and do fine work. But their purpose was short term. What he wanted to finance was something looking into the future where young doctors with ideas would be supported and encouraged over a period of years if necessary, to bring about innovations that might otherwise be impossible to accomplish. Hughes was sure of what he did *not* want, but he was not quite certain what he *did* want in a medical research organization.

Disintegration of the Hughes Empire

During this period, several forces were at work.

First, under Dr. Verne Mason, the surgeon who had repaired Howard's hundred broken bones, a team of doctors was being assembled for the Medical Institute board. Dr. Mason was pressing Mr. Hughes for formal organizational support—i.e., operating money.

Second, the Aircraft Division of Hughes Tool was going forward by great leaps and bounds, specializing in aircraft radar and air-to-air missiles. The management and a group of first caliber scientists from all quarters of the country had been attracted by good salaries and attractive working conditions. This division grew into the $100 million annual sales class in a very short time.

The Tool Company didn't know what to do with this brilliant, uncontrollable and cash-hungry child. Many managers and scientists wanted direction and participation from Mr. Hughes. The division was chewing up capital for expansion, and booking start-up losses in great amounts. The Tool Company's other divisions, the oil tool and drilling areas, were immensely profitable but the profits were being chewed up by the requirements of the Aircraft Division. Finally, Hughes Aircraft was established and its assets assigned to the Hughes Medical Institute.

The Tool Company was in strong management hands that had been on the job for years. This group reported directly to Dietrich, who also had directed that business for years. Their profits were excellent, even though burdened to some extent by the losses of the Helicopter Group. But at the Tool Company, the management, though competent, was getting old. The relationship between Dietrich and Hughes was deteriorating. This entire situation was an ideal setting for so-called "palace politics"—and the politicians were at work. This was the situation I blithely—and somewhat blindly—stepped into on the morning of November 22, 1954.

The Challenges of a New Job

During my first two days on the job, I was exposed to all of the departments and executive personnel of Hughes Aircraft Company. There were overlapping areas of accounting responsibility and several sets of books for different purposes. But no one could give me a comprehensive financial statement. The internal fog was thicker than the weather outside, and it lasted longer.

Looking back, I realize that at the time I had the "rose-colored glasses" public view of Howard Hughes. I didn't understand the total intertwining of his diverse operations. They were out of control.

Years later Noah Dietrich told me that I was on trial for a period of three months after I was hired. Contract or no contract, Air Force or no Air Force, Mr. Hughes was determined to find the answer to the business. It was his business, he had founded it, and if this man couldn't run it, he would find another.

I must have passed the test, for three months later, in February 1955 Hughes held the first and only board of director's meeting for Hughes Aircraft Company since the original corporate organization.

At that meeting he accepted the resignation of my predecessor, William Jordan, recognized my appointment as vice president and general manager, elected me a director, formed an executive committee of Howard Hall and myself (I was chairman), adopted a resolution stating the limits of authority of the executive committee, and then adjourned the meeting. Mr. Hughes himself wrote the minutes on a yellow pad and gave the two sheets of paper to Mr. Hall, as secretary of the company.

I was not present at the meeting and did not learn of the existence of the executive committee for some time.

It did not occur to me then, perhaps not for years, that the Howard Hughes of 1954 was not the Howard Hughes of 1944. The earlier years were founded on the acquired habit of waiting out the opposition in order to get a better deal, and of brushing aside detail that did not concern his own immediate projects, thus compelling his executives to run their own shows. He neither criticized nor praised, but expected performance.

Needed decisions always came in time, albeit sometimes in the middle of the night and when the last possible gain had been made by the delay.

This well-established pattern of operations concealed the great changes in Mr. Hughes that came after the Beverly Hills crash.

By 1954, Mr. Hughes was out of touch with reality for increasing periods and had adopted a slovenly way of life, interrupted only by occasional emergence into reality. The very small group of people in the know never talked; a truly amazing situation. The first of the insiders to tire of the situation and go was Tom Slack, Hughes' personal lawyer. Finally, even Noah Dietrich, who wanted to take his boy on an African safari, persisted against Hughes' direct orders. He was fired and locked out of his office. But Tom and Noah never talked.

Government administrators, industry, the public, nor most of Hughes' top executives, ever knew about his addiction, even though his periods of lucidity came at longer and longer intervals. During his lucid intervals, Mr. Hughes was still very sharp.

That his empire disintegrated so slowly under these circumstances was a tribute to the fundamental soundness of the enterprises themselves, particularly Hughes Tool Company. The one enterprise that survived intact and prospered through the final 15 years of Hughes' life was the Howard Hughes Medical Institute and its supporting corporation, Hughes Aircraft Company.

When I was being considered for general manager of Hughes Aircraft, I was told that the reasons for the delays in arranging my job interview and in the signing of the employment contract were the habitual procrastination and secrecy with which Mr. Hughes conducted most of his personal and business life. Those occasions on which he appeared in public were carefully orchestrated for some particular purpose which he had in mind.

(I learned in later years that the reason for the delays in my interview was that Miss Henley was trying valiantly to get Mr. Hughes straightened out, dressed in a suit and tie—which he despised—to meet with me. She was concerned that if I saw him in his usual appearance, I would immediately conclude the negotiations.)

It did not cross my mind for years that these strange habits of his had become amplified and were a shield for his addiction to pain-killing drugs, the possession and supply of which had become his overriding concern. There must have been a couple of dozen people, some of whom I knew very well, who were aware of this terrible affliction, but they kept a wall of silence around Howard Hughes and never talked. Only by bits and pieces and inferences that could not be denied, did I enter that silent circle around a great, powerful, talented and merciful man, who was unable to stop the use of the malicious drugs that were destroying him. His only choice was either pain or drugs. He never really recovered from the effects of his last and worst airplane crash.

When Dr. Chaffin was called in during occasional crises in Hughes' health, Hughes would insist that drugs were not involved and that he could stop at any time.

The shift from the hospital morphine to Valium and Empirin A came about after his insistence that he had to leave the hospital and return to work. Thereafter, his formerly rather even temperament gradually disintegrated into erratic swings between alertness and torpor.

Hughes always had a great natural penchant for secrecy. He varied his automobiles from limousines with window shades to conceal the passengers, to old, beaten-up-appearing Chevrolets, which he used for local travel. He would frequently use such an unidentifiable vehicle to pick up a business appointment at some prearranged street corner in order to keep his purposes and business dealings secret.

The Perennial Tax Avoider

Hughes hated taxes and throughout his life went to great lengths to avoid or minimize his liability. His taking up residence in Las Vegas after WWII was primarily motivated by his desire to avoid California state income taxes. Hughes would spend dollars to avoid pennies in taxes as a matter of principle. His flight routes, for example, were laid out to permit refueling in states with lower fuel taxes.

Time was also of little importance to him. It was his common practice to phone employees at any hour of the day or night, on weekends, holidays or every day, if he wanted information or to utilize their services. He was slow to pay. This applied to professional people, doctors, lawyers, accountants and consultants. He did pay ultimately, but frequently stretched the patience of these people to its limit. He loved to trade. He never paid the asking price, but would negotiate. He could never be found for telephone calls, but he invited conferences on his airplanes and talked from the pilot seat. He would stall negotiations on any pretext, until he got prices and terms that satisfied his ego. Having virtually unlimited funds, a keen sense of values, and a willingness to take risks, whether physical, intellectual, financial, political, or legal, and being unafraid of business losses or confrontations, he held innumerable aces, both visible and concealed. He demanded instant obedience, but had unlimited patience with himself and won many a contest by just waiting.

He did not win all games and contests, but he lost very few.

Taking all of these characteristics into account, it is easy to see just how prodigious an operator he was. It is also less surprising that he managed to conceal for so long the comas and ailments that came upon him with increasing frequency. During his lucid intervals, he was keenly interested in technical matters and discussions, and tolerated a certain amount of business discussion.

In his later years, Howard loved old movies, because in the euphoria created by those pain-killing drugs, he could look at the old films and see his former girlfriends in their prime years. In the fantasy world he could relive former times.

When Mr. Hughes was "down," only his personal attendant and one security man from his regular staff were allowed to see him. Jack

Real was on call as was Dr. Chaffin when needed and sent for. But just before TWA and Hughes Tool Company were sold, the brokers demanded to see Hughes. They, along with attorney Davis, were ushered into one end of a room where Hughes was seated at the other end. Hughes consented and approved the sales of those companies, reserving to himself, however, the right to adjust by telephone the offering price of the shares up to the very last moment.

Flying Again Makes It Seem Like Old Times

The times between Hughes' comas and lucidity occurred at unpredictable periods; it kept his staff and associates, and even the outside world, in continuing uncertainty regarding his availability. During his last stay in London, he seemed to be a little more lively and aware of the condition of his life than he had been for some time. He evidenced an interest in flying again and Jack Real arranged for an aircraft to be specially positioned and fitted out for easy access. When the craft was ready, Hughes took the left hand seat (pilot) and Jack was co-pilot. During takeoff, Hughes came to life and was delighted with the hour they spent in the air.

There was hope this renewed interest could lead to better things, but unfortunately, Hughes had another accident. This time, he fell in his bathtub and broke a hip. That did it; the one last hope for him was gone. Dr. Chaffin was called in to pass on the surgery and the convalescence. He made a last try to interest Howard in giving up the drug habit.

Howard was adamant that the drugs did not affect him. He could give them up tomorrow morning. But since they alleviated his pain and facilitated his fantasies, he saw no reason to change. He did ask Dr. Chaffin to stay with him since his health was failing and he wanted the best advice. However, time was passing, and the six months of stay in England allowed by his entrance permit was nearly gone. The bugaboo of taxes had to be avoided, so Hughes and his entourage headed for the Bahamas again, this time to the Xanadu Hotel. There, isolated in luxurious surroundings on the top floor, he might just as well have been in a dungeon, because he insisted that all windows be shaded so that no one using binoculars could possibly see into his rooms.

His way of life did not change. There were business days and there were days (now more often than not) when he was in a coma. For years he had not laughed or smiled except during that one hour of flying in England. There was no fun in his life.

In the Bahamas, his staff began to urge Mr. Hughes to go to Acapulco, Mexico. When he did not seem to encourage the idea, it was made plain to him that the drug supply in the Bahamas was beginning to be difficult and they were concerned he would no longer be able to get the materials he needed. To Howard that was a compelling argument; he agreed to go to Acapulco.

The Final Days

Mr. Hughes arrived there in relatively poor health. Dr. Chaffin and his recommendations were more or less disregarded by the staff. Howard's attending physicians got in touch with a Mexican physician, but their combined efforts were ineffective. Soon it became apparent that Hughes could not survive much longer. Dr. Chaffin was finally permitted an examination. He observed a multiplicity of syringe punctures, accompanying inflammation, and even some needle shafts broken off and embedded in the tissue, where Hughes had injected himself, or had tried to do so.

The only hope was to remove Mr. Hughes at once to a major medical facility.

No exit permit had been asked of the government, because there was some likelihood that Hughes would not be permitted to leave Mexico. However, Jack Real succeeded in getting an airplane to the airport without attracting much notice. On the next evening, Hughes was smuggled onto the airplane, with Dr. Chaffin and Jack Real in attendance—and just in time. As they approached the runway, Mexicans, in government cars and with their pistols waving, came into view. Jack urged the pilots to take off in a hurry. There was some shooting but no hits, and they got into the air safely.

Hughes died during the short flight to Houston, Texas. His age was 70 years, four months. The saga of the great independent and talented character came to an end.

The drugs Empirin A and phenacetin had a particularly euphoric effect on him, but at the same time had a horrible and irreversible side-effect—his kidneys progressively shrank and lost much of their function. In the autopsy, Hughes' kidneys were found to have shrunk to one-tenth normal size, to the size of a walnut.

During the flight from the Bahamas to Acapulco, Hughes told Dr. Chaffin that he had wanted to go to the United States, but could never do so because he would spend the rest of his life in court. Nonetheless, his abilities as an entrepreneur and his wisdom in selecting growth areas for exploitation paid off. He was particularly proud of Hughes Aircraft and the Medical Institute, because those were entities he started himself. He was also satisfied that he was free of debt and able to call the shots without reference to any financial institution.

Any assessment of Howard Hughes must show a great positive balance. Unquestionably, he had faults, but his virtues outweighed them. To many of us in the multitudes, nature often seems to be unfair, but Howard Hughes deserved better than he got.

Howard's tragic addiction should not be criticized without appreciation of the circumstances. Howard's advanced experimental airplane, the Beverly Hills crash, and the ultimate pain not otherwise endurable: these are the factors that killed him.

After the death of Howard Hughes, the many pieces of his empire were gathered up under the leadership of William Rice Lummis, a cousin and great lawyer, who has done a masterly job of taking a leaderless aggregation of disparate assets and converting them into a great structure for the benefit of the legatees and the preservation of the memory of that once-remarkable man, Howard Hughes.

If not even Howard Hughes, with all of his talent, knowledge, courage, fortitude, and will power could survive or withstand the grip of addictive drugs, what chance does an ordinary mortal have, once captured? Little. It is far better never to start.

(Editor's note: This observation by Pat Hyland may have been one of the first times anyone said "Say No to drugs!")

HHMI, Hughes Tool and Hughes Aircraft; the Complications

As evidence of the close link between HHMI and the Aircraft Company, during my first days of service at Hughes, I was reminded of the fact that the Aircraft Company was owned by the Medical Institute and that it was obligated to pay the Institute about $3.5 million annual rent for the facilities and equipment with which it did business. This information was contained among many other briefings, some of which brought out matters that demanded immediate attention. However, as the immediate problems unfolded during the next weeks and months, the Medical Institute reminder was forgotten and only resurfaced one day when an accountant informed me that we might be delinquent in our next payment to the Medical Institute. I obtained copies of the documents relating to the transfer of the properties and also received a briefing on the composition of the facilities, working capital, etc.

One of the things that attracted me to the company in my original visit had been the fine machinery and electronic test equipment I had seen in the various shops and laboratories. I was more impressed with what I saw there than I had been in many other comparable laboratories throughout the country that I inspected on official government committee visits. Of course, I was under the impression this equipment belonged to the Hughes Aircraft Company. It did not! A part of the very best equipment belonged to the Air Force. All the other good equipment, it appeared, belonged to Hughes Tool and was therefore under lease. There was a considerable amount of rather ancient equipment in fair condition that appeared to belong to Hughes Aircraft since nobody else claimed it. It was not on the Aircraft company books since it apparently had been fully depreciated many years ago and was in the custody of the Aircraft Company because the Tool Company did not want it.

At age 57 it was certainly a new—and sometimes strange—adventure in what had become a lengthy career path.

Chapter VIII
The Early—and Revealing—Years at Hughes Aircraft

At 9:00 a.m. on November 22, 1954, I arrived at the front door of Hughes Aircraft Company prepared to go to work.

Leaving my new home that morning I was happy, confident and ready for what I knew to be the greatest challenge of my life. I had driven the road and cased all the turning points the previous Sunday afternoon. As a final landmark, I identified the Loyola University tower in the background of the Hughes buildings.

In the morning, the first 15 minutes of the expected 25-minute drive into this new environment were interesting and stimulating. I had planned to ride around the plant in order to fill in the time because I had left an hour early. However, the remaining 10 minutes I had planned on turned into a 45-minute nightmare, because fog—a dense London-like fog—covered the entire area in which the plant, the university and all surrounding reference points were located.

I crept along and made a right turn from the main highway. I passed one street and came to another where I should make a left turn, but I wasn't sure. After a series of twists and turns, I was hopelessly lost.

Finally, in desperation, I stopped at an intersection, got out and waited for another car to come along. I managed to stop it and asked the driver directions to the Hughes Aircraft plant. He said, "Follow me." We slowly proceeded and ultimately arrived at the entrance to the plant, right at nine o'clock. But, instead of a confident, happy leader, I was a perspiring, frustrated one—with barely enough composure left to thank my guide.

When I finally reached Building One (where my office was to be), I was met by a bright, young business school graduate, Ray

Neevel, who introduced himself as my administrative assistant. Ray introduced me to the receptionist, who gave me a badge. My office was without ornamentation and about the same size as the president's office at Bendix. I had hardly put down my hat, when Neevel hustled me off to the start of two long days of briefings, at 15-minute intervals. I was introduced to the remaining senior executives and department heads.

I was impressed with the briefings, with the orderly and efficient way in which the presentations were made, and with the remarkable products shown, marketing plans and operating practices. Financial summaries were disclosed and budgets presented. During one briefing the resident Air Force contracting officer confirmed the satisfaction of his office with the company's performance.

Camping Out

At the close of the second day, when I went home to my new and as yet unfurnished dwelling I opened a few cans and packages. I had a somewhat unsatisfactory supper. But nothing could dampen the exhilaration of spirit I had from those two introductory days.

Ray Neevel had provided me with a chair, a cot, a mattress, a couple of sheets, a pillow, and a blanket. I sat around and thought over what I had seen during those days, and identified a couple of anomolies that needed clearing up. I was not concerned about them, I just needed more explanation. I was tired from the strain of having to be on good behavior for two days. I went to bed early and slept well.

The next morning I went in with almost pleasurable excitement. Eager to get on with my new job, I drove to my parking space, walked in and was a little surprised when everybody seemed to come to attention as I smiled, walked by, said hello, nodded to the guard and went upstairs. I was to learn much later that this was not the way one important executive in this company had heretofore conducted himself either on coming to work or on leaving.

As I entered my office, my new secretary followed me in. This was the first time I'd had an opportunity to talk with her. I made a few introductory remarks about the weather, and voiced my pleasure at finding such a smoothly operating company. She surprised me by saying that my office was completely inadequate for one of my position. I mollified her by stating it was better than the one I had left in Detroit.

After a few weeks on the job, I became aware of the considerable pushing, shoving, and pressuring that had taken place among and between the staffs of the Tool Company and the Aircraft Company before my arrival. These struggles were concerned with such weighty matters as office assignments, parking spaces, and executive dining room privileges. This opening comment of my secretary was the first hint I got of this silly business.

The Challenges Ahead

For the first time, I sat down at my desk and started to put together the beginnings of an understanding of the job and of the priorities ahead of us. With me it has always been a truism that whether it be a hurricane at sea, an extremely rough aircraft flight, a severe business setback, or a difficult personal problem, it is necessary to play out the string to the best of one's ability. Surprisingly, the goal in the last 10 seconds, or the home run in the extra inning, has its counterpart in ordinary life. In this case, I uncovered problems that had existed for months and also uncovered means that led to their solution. I also discovered a group of people of uncommon competence, anxious for leadership and almost unanimously accepting me for the job. And there was certainly a job to do. As the requirements began to unfold with each passing day, it seemed that my entire life had been devoted to getting the education, skills, patience, and fortitude together with the decisiveness necessary for the trials ahead.

That third morning I told Ray Neevel I needed more information from three sectors. I wanted rebriefings from Ray Parkhurst of manufacturing; then from the Air Force contracting officer, and finally from Earl Hall, who appeared to be the chief accountant. The briefings were arranged and I departed for the offices of the three men. I always like to see the other fellow in his own office and not stand on the protocol of who should see whom first.

Before the morning had passed, my uncertainties were confirmed. From the briefings of the head of manufacturing and the government representative, it appeared there was a $180 million unfavorable balance between the books of Hughes Aircraft and those of the Air Force.

In a later rerun of the chief accountant's charts, it appeared there would be a $10 million shortage of cash within the next 17 days. These disclosures were upsetting indeed, but worse was the frustration when I was unable to discover why we were in such a predicament.

Financial Dilemmas

These two items were so serious I had to stop thinking about anything else until I could get the real facts. Should a government auditor discover the imbalance before we solved it, headlines would sprout all over the United States and perhaps around the world. Furthermore, unless cash could be found, there would be no pay day on December 15th—also headline material. I tried to get a statement from Earl Hall, but he insisted he was only the bookkeeper for the cash accounts. In fact, he was the cashier.

Hall stated that the corporate books were the responsibility of the "two Ms," i.e., two gentlemen, one of whom, William McGee, was a minion of the Tool Company, so placed that he could overlook and pass upon major commitments, expenditures, and receipts. The other, M2, was a senior professional, who had been loaned by a national firm of accountants for an indefinite period to ascertain the true condition of the company, reform the financial practices, and effect necessary personnel changes.

M2 had been given full powers and theoretically was responsible to the general manager, but actually reported to Noah Dietrich. In the course of the afternoon, I found that he had endeared himself to the people in the accounting department by putting them all through a psychological test, which in those days was a rather demeaning process. He had also determined that a new chart of accounts was necessary, and that all of their current activities were incorrect. Therefore, he had decreed that former practices should be abandoned and that the department would engage in the analysis and redistribution of all accounting activities, according to the new chart of accounts, which had not yet been fully established. I not only could not get an answer from M2 on any question I asked, but I was sure that neither he nor anyone else would be able to even give a valid answer under the circumstances.

I telephoned my old friend, Charlie Hummel, the comptroller of Bendix and asked him for their basic chart of accounts, which I knew well. It could be applied to Hughes Aircraft.

I demanded of M2 that he get together, as soon as possible, a statement of our condition. He replied that, due to the confusion in the department, the best he could do would be to put something together for the month of October. I unhappily told him that he had to start somewhere, even though the information would be two months old.

Finally, I sat down with Earl Hall, who explained the basis on which he was keeping the cash books. I satisfied myself that he was honest, competent and although nearly of retirement age, courageous in his answers. By the end of the week, I knew that we had to have $10 million, but I wasn't sure what we would do after that unless I could unscramble the books.

On Friday, I telephoned Noah Dietrich, stated that I urgently needed to see him and made a date for that same morning.

My First Exposure to Romaine Street

The driver took me to a fortress-like building at 7000 Romaine Street in Hollywood. The front door was locked. The driver went through some rigamarole, the lock clicked and we entered. He carefully shut the door.

With very little preamble, I told Noah the Hughes Aircraft books were a mess and it was going to take me a while to unscramble them. But, one thing I was certain about—we needed $20 million in order to carry out our obligations for the next month. I really only needed to borrow $10 million but I said $20.

Noah listened, smiled and said, "Well, the Tool Company had a hell of a month in October, and there is every reason to believe we'll have a great year. So it happens that for a while, I have $12 million that I don't know what to do with, and I will let you have that for three months."

Since I needed only $10 million, I agreed to take it, but insisted that the time be six months, because I didn't know how long it would take me to find out what the score was. He finally agreed.

At the time, I thought this transaction was too easy. Hughes Tool must be loaded for Dietrich to pull that much out of the hat on short notice. Now I'm positive he knew how much was needed at Hughes Aircraft, had known all along, but wanted to see how long it would take me to find it out and what I would do when I did.

The old fox might not have known anything about electronics, but I'm sure he knew where every dollar was.

During my second week, the avalanche commenced. When it was found I had neither horns nor tail, that I was reasonably well known in the high-tech world in which the company did business, that I was an honorary Doctor of Engineering with wide business experience, the mudslide of demands on my attention began. And there was plenty of mud, of all types and description!

In December 1954 year-end closings had to be prepared. Annual budgets were proposed and needed approval; factory and engineering space were in short supply; and a succession of wartime temporary buildings were being occupied near Los Angeles Airport. We were still losing engineers, managers and foremen at an undesirable rate, considering the projects on hand. But important suppliers were calling to express their pleasure at my appointment and to tell me what a fine purchasing department we had. I wondered about their angle. There were also get-acquainted parties and other distractions.

I had been through this sort of pressure before, but it had not been as concentrated nor sustained. There were enough good engineering, manufacturing and research people remaining to keep the plant going, so I first tried to clean up the accounting mess and stem the flood of resignations of pivotal people. My working day was 8:00 a.m. to 6:00 p.m., an hour for lunch and a nap. My wife and I adopted a rule of only two evenings out per week, leaving for home around 10:00 p.m. except on special occasions. Emphasis was on company-related activities; there was a great deal of getting acquainted to do.

The $180 Million Mystery

Much more than bad bookkeeping was involved in the mixed-up affairs of the company. Recall that in establishing Hughes Aircraft, nothing but goodwill was given to the Medical Institute to support its 75,000 shares of stock. All tangible assets used by the Aircraft Company belonged to the Air Force or to Hughes Tool. Although we had no tangible equipment of value, the Air Force contracting officer claimed we owed the government $180 million.

It took very little investigation to find we had only a small working account with the Bank of America, but no credit with any bank, insurance company, factoring agency or anybody else in the financial world.

That $180 million, it turned out, was the cumulative account of government-furnished plant, equipment and loaned test-bed aircraft we had used to develop, test and manufacture products for the government, plus work in process. Later I found that much of the equipment listed in that accounting, particularly the aircraft, had already been returned to the government. But future knowledge did not help me when that USAF officer was first pushing his claim. That hassle went on for months. The Contracting Office records were eventually brought up to date.

I discovered there were four individuals in the financial hierarchy of the company. First, there was the chief accountant, Earl Hall. Then there was M2. He had been placed in the job by Noah Dietrich but had not been able to find or generate reliable financial information from either existing or prior finance personnel. I concluded he knew little about financial management. Third was the plant "overseer," Jack Jerman, a competent manufacturing man who was an employee of Hughes Tool. He had responsibility for maintaining the plant, seeing to it that appropriate charges were made for services exchanged between the remaining Tool Company people and the Aircraft Company. He approved changes or use of property by the Aircraft Company under its rental agreement.

The fourth individual, William McGee, was also a Hughes Tool employee, but he had the additional responsibility of approving commitments, contracts and major expenditures of the Aircraft

Company. Bill reported such matters to Noah Dietrich in his capacity as managing director.

I told Earl Hall to continue to keep the cash books, verifying with some of his account specialists and the bank as to cash on hand and in prospect. I wanted to see what had to be done about the probable cash shortage. I felt fairly certain the situation was not quite as bad as had been painted. I phoned M2, asking him to come to my office with the latest statement. He finally arrived but explained the preceding September statement was not yet ready. I told him it was normal for statements to be available 10 days after the end of a month. He said the delay was caused by the changes required in accounting procedures because of the department's confused condition when he came aboard.

In reply to questions about length of time until I could have a statement, he was unable to be specific. He said it certainly could not be done in two weeks, but might be available in a month. I said another month would mean year end. I was beginning to see a pattern. I asked how the books were shaping up for year-end closing. He said the department would not be able to close for some time after the end of the year.

The meeting was unsatisfactory. I told him I wanted his best estimate of a summary financial statement in two weeks and a complete statement by month's end.

Then I went to see Jack Jerman. Jack was a capable man with a nice personality. He assured me of his desire to cooperate and said he recognized the difficult state of affairs at Hughes Aircraft. I left his office with the feeling we had a meeting of minds, that he would be fair and just to deal with. That proved to be true.

My next stop was with Bill McGee, the financial overseer. He was a conservative Scotchman, near retirement and in poor health. I found that his duties were purely reporting and did not include preventing or changing any of our activities. Apparently Mr. Dietrich was interested only in knowing of commitments or undertakings outside the normal scope of the business. I decided I could neglect Mr. McGee thereafter. I went to my office, knowing my problem was going to be with M2, the mysterious financial manager.

Defections Pose a Problem

I had to consider the engineering departures, which were becoming serious. Most departures were to Ramo/Wooldridge Corporation, which was building up rapidly under the drive from the Air Force to get its intercontinental ballistic missile into being. Fortunately, I knew both Si Ramo and Dean Wooldridge. I had worked with them extensively as well as with General Schriever, the Air Force boss charged with management of the project. I called General Schriever and Dean Wooldridge, asked them to lunch, and told them I wanted to talk about the relationship between the missile project, Ramo/Wooldridge and Hughes. We met a couple of days later.

We had worked together for several years on the same side of the fence and were comfortable with each other. I told them of the low morale at Hughes Aircraft and my fear that if there were continuing employee departures, we might not meet our commitments to the military services.

Dean Wooldridge countered that he doubted that, because we were loaded with one of the finest aggregations of engineers in the country. I told him he used the right verb and tense—that we *were* loaded.

General Schriever asked if I had any suggestions. I said I needed about a three months moratorium on any proselytizing or hiring of people from Hughes Aircraft Company by Ramo/Wooldridge. I told them that if, by three months, I hadn't been able to stabilize the situation, then the fault would be mine; there would be an open field.

Dean nodded and said, "Well, if that's what you want, I see no reason why we shouldn't try to cooperate and I'll agree to that now."

General Schriever, with a smile, in effect blessed both of us and we went on our ways.

Wooldridge kept his promise; within three months, confidence in the company returned and recruiting was "Even Steven." Occasionally they took one of ours, and once in a while we took one of theirs. From that day forward we remained competitors, associates, prime and subcontractors back and forth—and friends.

During the two-week wait for a financial summary from M2, there was plenty to do. Year-end closing of the business plus 1955 forecast and budgets loomed. I received figures and estimates from the factories and the engineering and sales departments. Nothing, of course, came from the finance department.

There appeared to be a planning operation—a one-man show conducted by Paul Collins. I was unable to find exactly for whom Mr. Collins worked, but he had a history of good forecasts and had recorded for many years results of the Aircraft Division. He had been able to forecast with an astonishingly high degree of accuracy. I was never quite able to find out where he got his information. He wasn't exactly evasive, but for all practical purposes, the only answer I got from him was: "Here and there." Shortly before the New Year, I asked if he could give me an idea of the probable results for 1955, the coming *full year.* He said he thought he could tell within two percent.

I protested that one cannot do that well for just a *month* ahead, to say nothing of a year. It's rare that one can forecast the coming month within 10 percent, I argued.

"Oh, yes we can." Collins proceeded to tell me the factory operated on a rigid schedule. If the schedule on the first day of the month was not met, they immediately went into overtime and delivered every day's scheduled production throughout the entire month, every day, every month.

I thanked him and complimented him on the job he was doing. After he left, I leaned back in my chair with a feeling of relief. I had been in enough factories and company divisions to know that even in repetitive quantity production, over an extended period of time such forecasts could be made only when there was a management reserve of money, material and production available to smooth out disturbances. My problem was to get the financials straightened out, because primary design, production and sales were probably completely satisfactory.

Solving the Procurement Mystery

I continued to be surprised by the number of suppliers and subcontractors who insisted on seeing me and giving high compliments as to the wisdom and efficiency of our purchasing department. This was out of character with my experience. I decided it needed attention.

I struck up conversations with people on bus rides and on airplane rides to Tucson, Arizona, where we operated a large plant owned by the Air Force. I spoke with people in our employee store. My informal survey told me we paid top prices on purchases, regardless of quantity, and, as a rule, we designed every item with slight deviations from standard sizes; high costs were coincident with the special item.

There was little evidence of kickbacks. Almost all of our problem stemmed from the fact that many of our engineers had never worked with any other industrial establishment. They weren't aware of availability of standard hardware and the discounts resulting from volume purchases and from combining similar requirements from several departments.

I was amused by the dodges employed by engineering supervisors to split up their buy orders into several smaller amounts in order not to make a single requirement appear to be excessive. I had done the same thing as a young engineer and had been suitably admonished by my superiors. I grouped several orders together and sent them back with a note: "Who are you kidding?" The word got around fast; the grapevine was extremely effective.

There was actually a suggestion that an association should be formed: "How to keep Hyland off of airplanes." It seemed I was getting too much information riding with suppliers. For quite awhile, I insisted on seeing all purchase orders for *nonproductive* material. Later this was expanded to include all material and orders of any kind.

A change in practice of our purchasing operation probably would have happened anyway because, unknown to me, a new purchasing director had been chosen. He took office about the same time I did. He had the talents and virtues necessary as head of purchasing in a large company. He ultimately left us and eventually became Assistant Secretary of Defense and later head of Teledyne Ryan, San Diego.

That's how I first met Barry Shillito.

Barry was just as interested in correcting our slovenly purchasing practices as I was. But to keep up morale, we had to work carefully and not throw our weight around too fast. We worked patiently.

Finding a Wealth of Top Talent

Also at about the time of my arrival, and unknown to me, a truly fine scientist, Dr. Andy Haeff, had been named vice president and director of Hughes Aircraft Research Laboratory. Organizationally, he was on the same level as the heads of Radar and Guided Missile Research and Development Divisions, and the Culver City and Tucson manufacturing divisions.

Budgets submitted for Radar, Missiles and Research were for the same amount of money, presumably in accordance with similar numbers of people in their organizations. The two manufacturing division budgets were largely for capital and overhead, with one exception: Tucson had a capital item of about $22 million for new machinery.

Ray Neevel warned me of the coming proposal from Tucson for a large amount of money for new machinery. He stated that in the past couple of years, similar budgets had been submitted and if refused, Bill Wooldridge, the Tucson plant manager, had always presented his resignation. Because he held a vital, income-producing job, the managing director always capitulated and gave him the requested amount.

I had visited Tucson shortly after my arrival and was impressed with the business-like and orderly operation. From what I had seen, the plant appeared to be working at about 75 percent of capacity. I could not imagine a request for new machinery unless there were substantial additions to the backlog. The Tucson plant and much of its tooling were U.S. Air Force property at the time.

I telephoned Bill Wooldridge and asked him to come to Los Angeles to justify the request for new machinery.

When he appeared, I asked for an explanation of his substantial requirement. He replied that in his judgment there would be new orders for missiles and new types of missiles, thus justifying added machinery.

But, no hard facts supported the requirement. One item was interesting: it appeared that in prior years requests for new capital for machinery increased by about 50 percent each year; this year was no exception. I concluded that he had caused my predecessors to back down. I finally told him the company was short of funds and that unless he could prove dire need with facts much more persuasive than those he had presented, I would have to turn down his request.

With that, Bill pulled an envelope out of his pocket and said, "Well, if that is your attitude, here is my resignation!"

I took the envelope, did not open it, looked at him and said, "Bill, take this envelope back and put it in your pocket. If you present it again, I shall accept it, and I don't think that is what you want."

Wooldridge looked at me, smiled and said, "Well, you can't blame me for trying."

From that point on, we got along very well for several years. He was personable, likeable and ambitious, but pushed his manner of operation as close to the edge as he dared. He had a fine sense of what he could get away with.

Confrontation With M2

I had been through almost every kind of technological and administrative confrontation and problem before, but usually only one or two at a time. I had never before experienced anything like the simultaneous streams of crises that came from every activity within this large technological business. A confrontation came with M2, the mysterious director of finance.

At the end of the two-week wait for his financial summary, he was not ready. So I leaned on him and told him I certainly expected him to have a complete statement by the end of the 30-day period. When that time arrived, I had to summon him again. When he appeared, a little late as usual, he had a pile of papers almost a foot high. He came in, laid them on my desk and said, "There's your statement."

I looked at the pile and at him with amazement and asked if he had a summary I could see.

He replied that I had wanted a statement and that it could not be summarized so he decided this was what I should have.

"You have decided this is what I should have?" I thought for a minute and then said, "I see. Let's take a walk down the corridor, because there is something I want to show you." We walked down the corridor to the steps and down to the guardpost and the receptionist.

I walked up to the guard and said, "Guard, never let this man into this plant again!"

I returned to my office and put in a call for Earl Hall, the cashier. When he came in, I showed him the stack of papers, told him what had gone on and that M2 would not be back. He said the equivalent of "Thank God for that." I told him to take the papers, unscramble them and get me an assessment of where we were as fast as he could, hopefully within a week.

The stories about the Bill Wooldridge confrontation and the summary firing of M2 quickly got around; there was a distinct rise in general morale, but no slowdown of problems.

The Christmas Turkey Trot

One problem had to do with distribution of Christmas turkeys, a custom in the company. A carload of turkeys was unloaded between a pair of buildings, so that each employee could receive a turkey at the end of the shift. But about two o'clock on Christmas Eve someone came to the office to announce that the weather forecast was for about three inches of rain, starting in the next hour. I went out, looked at an ominous black cloud, and that huge pile of boxed turkeys and thought of the shambles if the weather forecast proved correct. I got on the loudspeaker to tell all employees the plant was shut down immediately—and they should come get their turkeys.

That decision made a hit with employees; but the morning after the holiday, I was visited by the Air Force plant representative. He said we were not authorized to shut down the plant and he would not allow those two hours of lost work to be reimbursed by the Air Force. We wrangled over this issue for a couple of months, but it was finally satisfactorily settled by negotiators.

Incidentally, the rains did come, but not for two or three days. When it did, we were literally swamped. The storm drains in the hills between Santa Monica and Hollywood dumped rainwater into Ballona Creek, a stream adjacent to the Hughes Aircraft runway. The creek had tide gates. At high tide the gates were closed; any rainwater would accumulate in back of the gates. But with the tide gates open, the creek drained into nearby Santa Monica Bay. The day the rains came we had the worst of all worlds. High tide was in, the gates were closed, and the storm drain water backed up and flooded the runway and the lower floors of some plant buildings. When I came to work, the water was up to the car's floor boards; I barely made it to the parking lot. With its runway operation tower, the plant looked like a sinking aircraft carrier. Ultimately the tide receded and the field drained, but even nature seemed to want to contribute its share to our problems.

A Medical Mystery Unravels

Problems kept coming from all directions. But I was neither surprised nor concerned. One example, however, was interesting. About the middle of December, I had a sore throat and asked my secretary where to find the Medical Office.

The clinic was just opposite the entrance to the plant. I assumed it was part of the Hughes operation. There were three or four people waiting in a rather shabby room; I waited with them for one of the three doctors. I was one of the regular employees; I could see how the system worked.

When my turn came, I went into the doctor's office, greeting him as doctor so and so. When he asked what my trouble was, I told him I had a sore throat. He took a flashlight, told me to say "Ahhh," pressed a paddle on my tongue and then said that it looked a little inflamed. His instructions were to take a couple of aspirin every four hours and let nature take its course. He said, "That will be all."

My impression was not a good one. There seemed to be no special equipment around; the furnishings were worn; the doctor's smock was not clean. The clinic looked untidy, which was also the appearance of the building, inside and out.

I was surprised at this for even though Hughes Aircraft occupied several temporary buildings, including most at the Culver City site, the outsides were neatly painted. Some structures looked like big hangars, and several buildings were of cheap construction, but they were clean and tidy outside and immaculate on the inside. By the time I returned to the plant, more problems had arisen; I forgot about the appearance of the medical outfit.

Within a month however, I began to have a little stomach trouble. I went to the "clinic" to see the doctor; and happened to get the same one.

I told him I had an upset stomach that had been bothering me for the past two or three days.

His first question was, "What did you have for breakfast?"

I told him I had eaten my usual breakfast of pancakes and sausages.

He said, "That's your trouble. You've got to stop eating the pig." He said I should take a couple of aspirin four times a day and change my eating habits to eliminate the pig; the examination ended with, "That will be all."

This time I didn't forget the clinic. I found the clinic didn't have any doctors at all. One of the three, who called themselves doctors, had been a Navy pharmacist mate; another an orderly in an Army hospital; and the third was obscure as to background. I also discovered that their building was actually owned by Hughes Aircraft and although the facts were not clear, it appeared these clinicians occupied it without rent. They did not seem to have any patients other than from Hughes Aircraft, which they billed monthly for their services.

I discussed this with Howard Hall, our company attorney and co-director. We concluded that Hughes Aircraft now justified more formal medical services. Several months later, we established a medical unit with an experienced industrial physician, two nurses, a stenographer and provisions for keeping medical records. With this new unit established, we terminated the old clinic.

Reduction in Force Forced

I knew my stomach trouble was caused by the fact that I was in the process of closing down an important unit of the radar engineering operation. This meant transferring about a hundred people and terminating a hundred more. I had been through this experience several times before at Bendix and Radio Research Company, when it had been necessary to reduce our staffs because of low business. In each case, I lost my breakfast on the way to work, because it had involved letting people go who were competent and loyal. My stomach upset was to me a perfectly normal thing. I had hoped the "doctor" would give me a relaxant. Finally, with our reduction in force completed, I returned to normal.

The reason for the reduction had to do with establishment within the Radar Division in early 1955 of a diversification project aimed at the business computer field. There had been a broad technical and marketing study. Everything about the project looked extremely promising—except the finances. The first payoff could take place *at best* in three or four years. We were unable to fund the project in the face of current uncertainties, nonexistent credit, and existing customer pressures for performance on current engineering and manufacturing requirements.

In spite of my best efforts to explain this to the head of radar engineering and particularly the project manager of the computer group, I was unable to get their agreement that it was necessary to curtail the new venture. Finally I had to arbitrarily take the unfortunate action of placing a stop order on the project with a termination date of 30 days.

I requested a meeting be set up with the affected engineering section and department heads and the shop foreman to explain the action. Reluctantly the project manager arranged the meeting; two days later, he invited me to address the group. The project manager met me at the door of the building where the work was being conducted; I walked with him to meet the expected group of 20 or 30 at one of the larger offices. But when I walked in the door, it was into a large room with about 200 people standing up, waiting for me. Instead of section heads, every person of the entire computer group was in that room, all having stood there several minutes, and all knowing their work was to be discontinued—many of them to be separated. None of the faces I could see in the first few rows had anything but grim looks.

I was nonplused. The project manager showed me to a small box on which I could stand to address the group.

I had been set up! It was what Horatio Alger used to call "Do or Die." So the adrenaline started pumping, I "Did" and survived. I explained the situation carefully, step-by-step. I told them my regrets, complimented them on their performance and told them the decision was irrevocable.

I got off my soap box, nodded to two or three people around the project manager, walked to my car, and went back to my office. On that day, I think I saved the company—but I destroyed a great project that under other circumstances would have been a success; and I also dealt a disheartening blow to the beliefs and hopes of a fine group of people who would now be scattered to other activities.

I ultimately forgave the project leader for putting me on the spot. I knew too well that the role of a leader is neither always easy nor pleasant.

Wearing the Management Mantel More Comfortably

By the end of the winter of 1954-55 I began to have a fair understanding of my job, who I was working for and with, and the names of the major players.

I got on well with these people. My own satisfactory relationships were not, however, always duplicated by people down the line. Beginning with my secretary and administrative assistant, Hughes Aircraft Company was one entity and Hughes Tool Company was quite another. The people in those two organizations had been differing with each other ever since the Aircraft Division had been a financial burden to the Tool Company in the years before December 1953. The legal separation further exacerbated the situation as internal problems of each group spilled over on the other because their respective properties and privileges were in many respects poorly defined in the legal documents.

Following the announcement of my appointment as vice president and general manager, there was a real scramble by the *staffs* of the vice president and general manager of the Tool Company's Aircraft Division and the vice president and general manager of the Aircraft Company over three things:

1. Who would get the number one position in the parking area?
2. Who would get the mahogany and walnut offices at the south end of Building No. 1?
3. Who would have the right to the executive dining rooms?

Can you believe that? I knew nothing about this at first, and didn't learn of it until a couple of weeks after I joined the company. I understand the controversy over the parking lot was number one hot spot. The position of the Aircraft Company staff was that its 20:1 business and personnel superiority over the Tool Company justified taking all the front spaces. The Tool Company position was that the two vice presidents and general managers were of equal rank—and they should take half the executive spaces. Moreover, since their man was first on the job and really owned the whole thing, he should be given the No. 1 spot. Just before I arrived, it was finally settled. Actually there were two No. 1 spots—one on the right-hand side and one on the left-hand side. Some genius proposed the Tool Company take the space on the right-hand side and the Aircraft Company take the space on the left-hand side. A major decision.

The office situation was more complex. There were four executive offices at the south end of the building on the second floor. One, a corner suite, was occupied by General Ira Eaker, who had been the first of several retired U.S. Air Force generals hired by Hughes Aircraft and now a vice president without portfolio, but very important to company external affairs, including the military, and for his relationships with the Hughes main office.

The other corner office had been occupied by General Harold George, the former Hughes Aircraft general manager who left the company in late 1953 after the departure of Si Ramo and Dean Wooldridge. This office was vacant. The third office was occasionally occupied by Noah Dietrich in his capacity as managing director. Obviously that would not be changed. The remaining paneled office was occupied by Richard Dabney, who had been hired to head international affairs for Hughes Aircraft. Who had given him that office was not clear.

The next group of offices on each side of the hall were smaller, the equivalent of most executive offices at Bendix. I was allocated the one adjacent to Mr. Dabney, and Rea Hopper, vice president and general manager of the Tool Company Aircraft group, was allocated a similar one on the opposite side. My staff was furious; they thought I should have the vacant office on the southeast corner, formerly occupied by General George. But that was impossible because it would leave Mr. Hopper in an inferior location. The things people worry about!

Not knowing about all this furor, nor of the offices available, I was satisfied with the one allocated to me. It was at least as good as the one I had left, and I had too many other things to be concerned about in those early months.

The Aircraft Company prevailed on the dining room. Aircraft had more executives in the adjacent buildings; it made sense to give us the larger room. However, it was agreed that a corporate dining room for the Tool Company would be fixed up in the cafeteria building and there they would be provided with facilities similar to those in Building No. 1. Peace in our time!

All these things happened before I got on the job. But by the end of my third day, both my secretary and administrative assistant insisted I should occupy the corner office and Mr. Dabney should not be allowed to occupy the third one, although Mr. Dietrich certainly should have the right to the second one. However, I told them there were more important things to be considered first. Moreover, I thought it inappropriate that my first request to the main office would be about where I should sit.

These little squabbles need to be talked about. In a general sort of a way, I had been aware of executive perks and corporate protocol, but since my quarters had always seemed adequate, I paid no particular attention to niceties. I observed, however, that on occasion others created a fuss over their "rights." Also I had ascertained that on occasion visitors were impressed with office facilities.

Although my office turned out to be perfectly satisfactory, my staff and the senior people in the company felt I should have the corner office. In many ways they would bring it to my attention. After three or four months, Mr. Dietrich suggested I take the corner office; I agreed. It was a nice place to work but not any more efficient than the other quarters. Later, when Mr. Dietrich left the Hughes organization and Mr. Dabney our organization, the situation was finally resolved. From these incidents, however, I learned a couple of facts:

1. The staff of an executive is usually more concerned with his perks than the executive. Anything that increases stature or indicates importance also raises their stature and importance.

2. It is important the executive lives up to his office. People want to follow a leader; they want the leader to have the trappings of office and physical appearance of leadership so they can be proud of him. Also, except in dire circumstances, the leader can do no wrong. The mistakes are the fault of his associates or the failure of his people. But if the fault finally does pin itself on him, they turn against him almost instantly.

Hooray for Hollywood

A bright spot during Christmas week 1954 came on December 29th when I received a telegram from the National Bank of Commerce in Texas, stating that $12 million had been deposited to our account in the Bank of America in Los Angeles and was at our disposal. This came only a couple of days after I requested the money from Noah Dietrich and there it was.

Also during December, Noah gave a party in our honor at his home. Among the guests were Hollywood personalities, four or five Hughes Tool executives from Houston and a cross section of Los Angeles business and cultural community. The catering was by Pat DeCicco, not only a big time personality himself but also owner of Southern Cross Catering. For the first time, I learned Mr. Hughes owned RKO, which accounted for the movie folks there. In a fair-sized projection room, movies were shown throughout the evening. The Dietrich's imposing home included a ballroom with a roll-back ceiling. The weather was fine, the ceiling was retracted, and we had a little open-air ampitheater under the stars. It was a big time performance for me. This was the stuff I'd seen in movies as the life-style of important executives.

Another example was when I visited the Romaine Street main office of Hughes. Just as I arrived, Noah Dietrich was leaving. Out dashed a man who stood in the middle of the street and stopped traffic in one direction, followed by another, whom I recognized as a company chauffeur, to stop traffic in the opposite direction. They were followed by Dietrich's chauffeur, who came out running and got into a car. He drove to the door and Mr. Dietrich strolled out. Traffic in both directions was stopped until the Dietrich car moved out.

Air Force Tells It Like It Is

In January I went to see Harold Talbot, Secretary of the Air Force, and Roger Lewis, Under Secretary. Neither pulled any punches and properly regarded me as the instrument that had caused many of their troubles. In the Navy I had learned that when the captain of a ship takes over his new command, he takes over all of the leaky boilers, the inoperable radio, the fouled hull—the entire ship whatever its condition. For the first time I heard: "You guys at Hughes Aircraft think you're operating a country club. You are an arrogant and expensive luxury and you can't continue to get away with it."

Secretly, I agreed with them because I had twice visited Hughes Aircraft a couple of years before I went to work there. Both times my mission was as a member of the Guided Missile Committee. We were there to look over their facilities and progress on certain air-to-air missiles. We never did get in to see the generals in charge, nor Tex Thornton, Roy Ash, Si Ramo or Dean Wooldridge. Everywhere else we visited in the industry we were greeted by presidents, general managers and chief engineers. Not at Hughes.

At Hughes, we were treated courteously by a top radar engineer when we wanted to see a top missile engineer. We received an expert brush-off with almost no information. It was evident we were regarded as interlopers.

I knew I was in no position to brush off the two Air Force Secretaries; I minded my manners. I listened as they told me what we had to do. I said, "yes, sir" at appropriate intervals and when they rose, I rose too, and hastily made my departure. Later came letters which confirmed the conversation.

In general terms, they wanted a cap on engineering. They were particularly exercised over an account called Sustaining Engineering, which I had never heard of. The Service Secretaries wanted strong reassurances the company would meet its contractual commitments to the Air Force, and was not about to collapse, as the former head of Hughes Aircraft had predicted (or threatened) would happen. Finally, they wanted assurance that Hughes would deliver equipment responsive to the Air Force's version of its requirements and not Hughes' opinion of what the Air Force ought to have.

I left with absolutely no doubt I had heard them and would spare no effort on my part and the company's to satisfy their demands. Leaving Washington, I actually felt relieved. There had been no threat of default, nor of contract termination, nor Tucson plant takeover. I had been worked over before by experts and had survived and expected to survive this time.

Back at Culver City, I immediately looked into Sustaining Engineering. This account had been invented by Roy Wendahl and John Richardson, both of whom were in marketing. At that time Hughes Aircraft had a group of engineers with a capability not available elsewhere in the world. It was to the benefit of the Air Force to keep these engineers available. With only a few contracts, if one was terminated there was a period of time that elapsed before another could be found. It was financially impossible for us to carry engineers through these lean periods, waiting for another contract. This had been communicated to the Air Force and a special account, Sustaining Engineering, was set up to provide carry-over funds until new contracts were obtained. This was a sensible and valuable provision that allowed engineers to do pre-contract work, ultimately reducing contract time and costs.

But the account could easily be misused. In the confusion of accounting and administration in the preceding several months, it appeared such abuses might have occurred. Special controls were installed. An arbitrary and temporary limit of 5,000 engineering employees was established and a total employment limit for the company was set at 14,000. There was considerable wrangling over the distribution of these employees in various departments, but the limits held. At least we had a fair notion of the ultimate costs.

The Fire Hose Mystery is Solved

In my frequent walking around the plant, it seemed to me we were doing a great deal of digging of roads. I inquired and was told that from the beginning of our effort in radar and missiles, the company had grown rapidly. New buildings were required; these were reluctantly supplied by Mr. Hughes, who was afraid growth was too fast. In desperation management received permission to put up two warehouses which, it was stated, were required to house incoming materials. In order to assure the buildings would be used *only* for warehouses, Mr. Hughes stipulated that no water nor sewer lines should be connected to them. Only electricity could be furnished. But since the intent had been to use these buildings for additional engineering space, water, sewer and gas were required. To furnish these utilities, fire hoses had been laid underground. But fabric hoses only lasted about three months; there was almost continuous digging required to keep the buildings supplied with necessary services.

This satisfied another curiosity I had developed in my studies of procurement operations. I wondered why we used so many fire hoses. This was the answer.

The powers allocated to me at the February 1955 board meeting (when my probationary period had expired and Mr. Hughes was satisfied) were such that I had the right to install pipes with permission of our overseer in the Tool Company. He granted it. There was one last dig and then the streets were left untouched for years.

The Parameters of Mr. Hughes

At the February 1955 board meeting, Mr. Hughes set up an executive committee consisting of L.A. Hyland as chairman and Howard Hall as member. The committee was given all powers in the operation of the Hughes Aircraft Company except:

1. The name of the company could not be changed.
2. The executive committee could not authorize payment of dividends.
3. The executive committee was not empowered to take title to any real estate, but was empowered to take leases as might be necessary for corporate purposes.

We followed these instructions. The name of the company was never changed, nor any dividends paid. As regards real estate, we consulted Mr. Hughes.

On three occasions involving major plant acquisitions, we went directly to him. In each case, we received permission by telephone within three or four days to go ahead with the procurement and take title. But on several minor situations in the early years, involving $1 million or less, we requested approval and delays of several weeks occurred. Finally, a pattern evolved for these situations in which, if no approval was given within 30 days, we went ahead with the transaction. Over the years the length of time decreased and the maximum amount increased.

On only two occasions in my 22 years were approvals denied. On one, the refusal came because we wanted to buy some land owned by Hughes personally. He said he had bought that land for a purpose and that purpose did not include reselling it to the Aircraft Company. The other occasion concerned an investment where ultimate control was probably not possible. Mr. Hughes always wanted control, hence approval was denied.

Both of these were benchmarks which set limits on a delegation of otherwise enormous powers.

Another definite benchmark had to do with the implicit denial of further funds from Mr. Hughes or any agency owned by him for either bail-out of a bad situation or extension of our operations. Without outright denial or direct question, it was apparent the $12 million loan to the Aircraft Company from Hughes Tool had to be paid on time—and any further funds were out of the question. The umbilical cord had been cut. The child, already full grown, could nurse no longer and was on its own.

By February 1955, however, I was confident I knew the boundaries of our problems and what to do about them. Apparently the Air Force felt the same, because Secretary Talbot wrote a letter to Howard Hughes congratulating him on having turned the company around and that the Air Force was no longer going to apply any constraints on his operations.

I did not learn about that letter for several months and then only by the back door. During the 22 years I worked for Howard Hughes he never criticized me directly; he did so indirectly—and slightly—only once. Nor did he ever praise me except on one occasion a few days before the end of his life. I'm glad he didn't let me know of the Air Force letter; I might have slacked off a bit in my efforts.

Management Teamwork is a Challenge

A major element of the company's immediate problem was that more than a hundred of the top leadership of the company had resigned. Most of the technical management went with Si Ramo and Dean Wooldridge to form Ramo/Wooldridge Corporation. The business leadership of the company went with Tex Thornton and Roy Ash to Litton Industries where, by financial mastery and business acumen, they built a major corporation.

Some middle and junior management also departed. What was left was an adequate plant—and great numbers of talented people.

Throughout the company there were islands of groups having different missions. Without common leadership, these islands were individual protectorates with little assumption of corporate responsibility. The same trouble had existed at Bendix, except that the islands were much larger. There I had begun a cure by initiating engineering management meetings on an annual basis. Later I influenced corporate management to do the same with general management meetings. These meetings countered the morbid and self-defeating insularity that is latent and endemic in large organizations.

To combat this same disease at Hughes, I started with a general corporate management meeting at a hotel in Palm Springs, California. I began with the senior executives of the company plus Mr. Dietrich as an invited guest. Wives were included.

The participants included eight engineers, one lawyer and an accountant. Of the engineers, two were factory managers, one the sales manager and one the chief pilot. But there were no accountants or finance managers on the senior officer level. Hughes Aircraft had a reputation of being dominated by engineers, but I hadn't realized the degree.

Meetings were held Friday and Saturday mornings, with afternoons and Sunday devoted to recreation. The agenda was relatively simple: a report by each person on his products, problems, sales, profits and a look at his budgetary problems. Howard Hall talked briefly of our legal position. I talked of our goals for the year, our external reputation and the need for horizontal cooperation within the company. Dietrich talked about the overall Hughes operations and of his hopes for our success.

In my opinion the meeting was a disappointment. It appeared to me our executives were not particularly comfortable in each others' presence, nor were they particularly interested in each others' operations. Of the two nights there, we had dinner together one night with free choice the other night. There was no common entertainment for the free time.

But I felt the meeting was also extremely valuable. It indicated the seriousness of the problem. For, if senior executives were not comfortable with each other, then the situation down the line could be pretty sorry. Knowing that General Motors and Bendix had monthly meetings of an administration committee, including middle management as well as top management (I had been a member of the Bendix committee for many years), I decided to establish one for Hughes Aircraft. Realizing that engineers might not like the idea of a top committee associated fully with administrative matters, I decided to call it the Policy Board. Meetings were held with a regular agenda and each division or department head was called upon to report, with discussion following led by me when it seemed appropriate.

I determined who should be present at these meetings. My only limitation was the number of people the room could hold.

Actually, policy was not the primary purpose of the Policy Board. Its basic purpose was educational: a training ground for executives. It also facilitated establishment of common goals and just plain interpersonal familiarization. The prestige of participation was also involved and valued.

Walking the Shop a Way of Life

As a regular practice I visited our buildings and tried to take time each week to walk through one of the plants and observe operations in detail. People like to see the boss at their own location. I would show up occasionally on night shifts or on Sundays or holidays when some particular project was being worked on. Thus, bulletins and directives signed by me were not just an abstract piece of paper, they were messages from a human being.

The first priority in executive personnel was to find a comptroller to take over the accounting and financial operations of the company as a result of the departure of M2. We hit the jackpot. Alexander MacGillivray, who was able to come with us on short notice, had everything: competence, personality and drive. He got along well with Earl Hall (who was glad to be relieved of a part of his burdens) and was well received by other executives.

Next we had to find a vice president for administration. This took a little longer, but we were also fortunate in finding W.L. Hoffman, a man with broad experience, who had such a job with one of the big aircraft companies in another city, but who wanted to live in Los Angeles. So we began a corporate staff.

In the initial furor of briefings and financial problems, I forgot all about the employment office. It was not on the plant site, but about a half a mile away. The building was owned by Hughes Tool and was included in the lease of the plant. As a part of my get-acquainted routine, I visited it once or twice, became acquainted with the personnel manager and was satisfied we had a competent personnel group.

I was pleasantly surprised to find that the anxieties and disarray of upper management at Hughes Aircraft did not extend far down the line. Moreover, our problems loomed large, but the weapons industry was in a transition stage; even those firms that had been well managed were having problems with organization changes necessary to meet completely new product requirements. We were not alone.

After my non-proselytizing understanding with Dean Wooldridge expired, I was also pleasantly surprised to find that the quit rate of our engineers was only two percent a month; all other employees was only four percent. To those in older companies, particularly in the East and Midwest, these figures might seem high, but in the high-tech parts of the defense industry, they were actually surprisingly low. In fact, we were the lowest I knew of in the industry.

The personnel office informed me there was an Employees' Association with thousands of members. The Association had elected officers and was active in many areas, including various clubs for different activities in which employees had an interest. The Association offered scholarships, conducted occasional picnics, and staged well-attended mass meetings. Membership was encouraged from top to bottom. I was given an honorary membership and attended the next general meeting.

There was also a separate Management Club. It had been initiated by foremen in the manufacturing department. These men had been members of foremen's organizations in other companies and had affiliations with a National Association of Foremen. It was highly respected throughout industry. The national organization had delegates who supplied the necessary organizational literature for new groups. Our group, when organized, decided to call itself the Management Club of Hughes Aircraft Company.

Foremen and supervisors had always regarded themselves as members of management. The unions concurred in that and did not allow any of their members to come from the ranks of foremen or supervisors.

Initially, Management Club membership had been almost exclusively foremen from manufacturing, but in view of the broad implications of management, there was included now a sprinkling of administrative types as well as a few engineers.

A little questioning disclosed that finances of the Management Club were in rather shaky condition; the quality of speakers they could afford did not always encourage attendance at meetings, which always included dinner. I indicated to the club's executive committee a willingness to subsidize their activities for two purposes:

1. To provide suitable compensation for speakers of higher quality.
2. To encourage a soft-sell membership drive to get more administrative and engineering types to join.

The subsidy was accepted, and then was gradually decreased over the years as club officers responsibly required less help when membership rose and gross dues increased. Finally the day came when they proudly came to my office, said they were able to run on their own and thanked me for my cooperation.

Forty Years of Preparation for this Challenge

Overall, of the 13,000 employees at that time, only the top 100 or so had become disaffected and left as a body. Another 100 or two of lower rank left, but the overall loss was less than two percent of the total. In the new arena of high-technology weaponry, we were one of the top two or three firms. We needed only to reassign responsibilities at senior levels and define and publicize our company objectives so that all our people could pull together in the same direction.

My unorthodox education and rich experiences over the preceding 40 years were all in preparation for this opportunity.

Chapter IX
Hughes Aircraft, the Growth Years

Hughes Aircraft is a company of the new era. The old era ended in the 1940s; the new era began at the same time. Because defense weapons are always in the vanguard of technology, and because Hughes Aircraft was in the advanced weapon business, we were literally born into the new era.

In a short space of time, we were confronted with radar, nuclear energy, jet and rocket engines, supersonic flight, semiconductors and computers; a change factor of a millionfold in many technologies was applied in an incredibly brief interval compared with prior centuries. The profound effect of new technologies on the mores and structures of society has become increasingly apparent. Decades may elapse before industrialized nations reach a condition of stability—and centuries before the world as a whole adapts to this new era.

Within defense establishments there are some, including military leaders, associated industrial management and consultants, who are always alert to the potential of innovation. They quickly recognized the new forces, though they may not have quite grasped the significance. During the later years of World War II, limited deployment of new weapons had begun. The public and politicians, tired from years of war and its huge losses of capital, men and material opted for "push button war." Funds were liberally voted for new concepts, while orthodox weapons were starved.

Mass production of older weapons virtually ceased. Instead, funds were channeled into exotic weaponry. New laboratories were established—or enlarged—many under the aegis of leading universities. New test ranges were laid out and instrumented.

Newer companies, with more flexible and innovative management, with experience in aircraft engines, supersonic aerodynamics and rocketry—and with far-sighted ex-military men in management—were ideally positioned to contribute to the new era in weapons.

Hughes Tool's Aircraft Division fit well into this unprecedented situation. Mr. Hughes with his aircraft design experience, familiarity with engines and expertise as a pilot, his long-term interest in electronics, and his passion for innovation, would have been ideally suited to head such an enterprise.

But the Beverly Hills crash took him out of the picture. Before the crash he had authorized Dave Evans to bring together a cadre of individuals having great electronic talents. His own factory people supplied the mechanical interest and factory experience. Three experienced Air Force generals, who had retired, completed the core of the operation. (Editor's note: Generals George and Eaker are immediately identifiable; the third is unidentified.)

Unusually competent business executives were added as the business progressed. As the war with Korea got under way, the need for rockets and fire control systems was recognized and contracts with the Air Force were executed.

The successful completion in record time of those early contracts was a springboard for further and larger orders. The operation grew at an unbelievable rate in the early years of the '50s.

Proposals were made and contracts received for air-to-air short range guided missiles. These were the Air Force's entry into such missilery. Requests for bids came out shortly for what was called the "1954 Interceptor" equipment. This was to be the complete electronic package for a new type of airplane. The first of the breed was called the F-106. Hughes became the contractor for the first completely electronic flight and fire control package for a new aircraft. The so-called "1954 Interceptor" was to be the first to contain all of elements—computers, fire control, missile guidance and navigation for air defense in the new era.

This success story was interrupted by the controversy between Mr. Hughes and company leadership. It was never resolved; his top team left in a body in 1953. When I came to the company in 1954, it had sales of $200 million, about 18 months of orders on the books, was believed to be profitable and was loaded with talent—except at the top.

Looking Into the Future

On the last weekend in February 1955, I had two days without commitments. I sat before the fireplace at home to make an overall assay of the company. On financials, little had changed. Two glaring vacancies had been filled, but one or two more senior people had left. Many tangible problems remained, but in spite of apparent imperfections, I was strangely content.

Beyond the numbers, there had been progress:

First, employee uncertainty about the future was relieved, with a corresponding rebirth of enthusiasm.

Second, purpose and responsibility for the enterprise were being restored.

Third, the environment in which I had to work was unique; there was no SEC or other requirement that we wash our linen in public. I did not have to allocate blocks of time to placate irate shareowners or the media. Fourth, there was no interference from a board of outside directors with no knowledge of the business.

And fifth, no problem had turned up with which I had no prior experience. I felt competent to handle things, given a little time.

These observations certainly contrasted with perceptions I held in mid-December 1954. I was then quite aware the road ahead would be rocky and winding, requiring fortitude and a special empathy between all elements of this corporate system. Given a chance, the system would bring satisfaction and achievement. The situation was made to order for me. Although the ownership and ultimate control were amorphous, it was noninterfering. I had the confidence of my principals.

Company personnel were talented, loyal, enthusiastic and competent. They were not motivated solely by personal gain, but also by the opportunity to address the challenges of the new era. They were achievers. I believed I could mold the organization to appropriate and responsible goals and principles.

Clearly my job was to get the composition of employees arranged so that each individual could utilize his or her talents to the maximum, and so that smaller groups could act as do parts which go together into an assembly. Each piece is as important as any other, and all must work smoothly together as a system.

The lessons, conclusions, frustrations, mistakes and successes that comprised the experience which took me from the agricultural age through the industrial age and to the threshold of the space age was like a great tide—some good, some bad, and some that needed to be made part of a plan of action. In random order, here are some precepts I selected as action items:

✈ Although Hughes Aircraft had a monopoly position in air defense electronic systems, I regarded this as dangerous in the extreme. A monopoly position leads to overconfidence and complacency, which are the seeds of self-destruction. Also, a monopoly position leads to poor production efficiency and high prices. A sheltering umbrella is held over the competition. Eventually someone will successfully attack the monopoly position and will have been helped to do so by the vanquished. During its tenure, a monopoly has a duty to serve the market; it has to accept and continue business without choice when it might prefer to focus resources on other, potentially more profitable product lines.

✈ Although good decisions are invaluable in a profitable business, any decision is preferable to no decision or a long-delayed one.

✈ A general manager's function is to encourage the development and expression of informed opinion—not to win arguments or save face, but to find facts and to make judgments based thereon.

✈ General managers are in fact generalists. They cannot be wise on all things. They may give a stamp of approval to a decision, but must take account of the recommendations of specialists in arriving at the overall policy and plan.

✈ Decisions and control must be extended down the line to where information and knowledge exist. The temptation of a manager to hold on to all of his or her power must be overcome.

✈ Control at any level cannot be effective without control of the money, which must be passed down formally from level to level so that strict responsibility can be seen and maintained.

✈ Organization charts show centers of responsibility. Boxes or lines must not be thought to deny responsibility or foreclose cooperation.

✈ Military and industrial organizations have little in common. The need for each, and their differences, must be understood.

✈ Supervision at all levels is a part of management; supervisors must be indoctrinated and counseled with principles of management.

✈ The short-term, bottom line orientation of much current industrial management is a national tragedy. Too many big companies are harvesting today, single mindedly, without replanting for future harvest. We are exporting our production economy; the nation is taking itself down the same road to economic anemia already trod by Great Britain. Collapse of the United States is but a matter of time if domestic productivity is not revived, and in many fundamental sectors markedly improved.

✈ Entrenched bureaucrats at the middle level, whether in government or industry, are powerfully oriented to preservation of the status quo. While not individually vicious, these bureaucrats collectively are an immense impediment to progressive change. In industry, job rotation (strongly practiced in Japan) can defeat entrenchment and its evils. But in government, civil service presents formidable obstacles for which no solution is apparent.

✈ Almost without exception, top-level civil servants are dedicated, intelligent, hard-working, and motivated to serve the national and public interest.

✈ Patience and skill are required to introduce innovation or change into an organization. Success may require a number of individual small steps. The process is complete and a success only when the target organization proclaims the innovation or change to be its own idea.

✈ Writers and educators on management have rarely managed on senior levels and few of them have had the privilege and responsibility of trying to meet a payroll.

✈ The major defense issue of the democracies in the current era arises from a profound disparity among the natural time constants of events. We are attempting to address 50-year political and strategic issues with 20-year weapons programs administered by sincere officers who change jobs every three or four years and who operate under the guidance and scrutiny of a Congress which must get itself reelected every two years and which propounds a budget with a span of one year. The whole scene is analyzed, and therapies prescribed, by a media establishment whose span of attention is about six hours.

✈ Industrial management must see modern weapon systems through their lifetimes. The life cycle of an aircraft or missile family is basically long-term: 20 or 30 years. Proper industrial management commands a correspondingly long-term view.

✈ The cancellation or redirection of a weapon system program, for cause or without cause, with or without warning or recourse, is a fact of life.

✈ Despite assurances by the military to the contrary, off-the-shelf items in new weapons are rarely purchased. Innovation is therefore paramount.

✈ Despite assurances by the military to the contrary, performance-to-cost ratio is not nearly as important as performance alone in awarding procurements.

✈ Virtually unknown in industry and weaponry before the 1940s, doctors of science were prevailed upon to leave universities and government scientific laboratories, and even to come from other countries, during the great push for nuclear and missile development.

✈ Led by the new weapons technologies and the exploration of new operating environments, practitioners of high technology command new respect and much higher salaries than had previously been accorded the technical professions.

✈ Leadership is inherent, but not inherited. It has dimensions and may be trained. Because of scarcity, it has high value.

✈ Natural ability for achievement is also inherent but not inherited. It has dimensions and may be trained. Because of scarcity, it has high value.

✈ It is said only two works of humankind could be seen from the moon: the California aqueduct and the Great Wall of China. The aqueduct is beautiful and effective; the Great Wall was not effective and its objective beauty is a matter of personal preference. Only brute strength and fear were needed to make the Great Wall.

✈ Philosophy has not changed throughout the ages. The current fashion is for bigger, not for better or different. This has always been the current fashion.

✈ Writers about management tend to confine themselves to one facet of the subject matter. Perhaps they should be forgiven because they write about management in a narrow area and particularly do not write about general management, which has to take into account all of the foregoing items and much more. This comment goes for Peter, Deming, Parkinson, Drucker, and a host of others.

Motivation was last on the scheme of things I reviewed before the fireplace. I disagree with the view that money is the primary motivator. Money is important. It must provide a way of life that gives satisfaction and enjoyment to all members of the employee's family. A bonus in one form or another is primarily important for signaling that the employee is recognized by the company. In my observation, the magnitude of the bonus is less significant than the fact of the bonus as a motivator. For nearly 50 years, I have participated in or watched bonus plans and their effect on the general performance of people. To be on the bonus plan in any degree, no matter how small, is a mark of prestige that is valued at all times.

What then besides money is of great importance to employees?

✈ Adequate working quarters—nothing fancy, but suitable and to a degree which gives expression to the personality of each.

✈ Association with and stimulation by those with whom they work.

✈ Respect for and from their supervision and co-workers.

✈ Knowledge that they are masters of their own destiny to the extent that they have the delegations they need to do the job at hand. If problems arise, knowledge they can expect intelligent help and not criticism.

✈ Recognition of the need for and implementation of continuing education.

✈ Recognition for achievement and for leadership qualities.

All of these characteristics were in rich supply in the environment of Hughes Aircraft. The environment so necessary to the evolution of the new weaponry was evidenced by the magnitude of the technical operation; engineers and scientists in the thousands were available and were the largest single group in the company. This was a completely different order from that of Bendix, or even Hughes Tool, where engineering was a small fraction of the total personnel and expense.

There were perhaps only four or so comparable organizations in the entire country. We and they quickly outdistanced all others in the rapid advance of high-technology defense systems.

I am convinced most scientists, engineers, administrators, and others involved with the discovery of knowledge like to see the fruits of their work put to use. Without citing names, I have in mind a couple of large laboratories, well staffed and well budgeted, which are nevertheless ineffective because the staff do not see the sponsoring entity putting to use their results in products or services. So the staff busies itself on irrelevant investigations that are more akin to hobby recreation than creative contribution.

So Hughes was in the right business at the right time for what the country needed and wanted. I promptly made it known to our administrative people that they had to adapt themselves to the realities of the new era. I also made it clear that henceforth engineering salaries would be equal to or above those paid in the manufacturing or administrative operations. Protest against this policy was handled by explanations for the reasons thereof. If my reasons were not readily accepted, I followed up with a thinly-veiled suggestion that perhaps the protester might look elsewhere for a job.

As evidenced by contracts on hand, business goals of the company from 1955 were to devise and install on aircraft platforms, devices that could detect an enemy aircraft at a long distance, launch a missile towards that enemy, and have the missile seek out and destroy that enemy aircraft. Such a weapon system did *not* exist.

The concept was not new, but its implementation so far was primitive and workable only at short range. It was obvious a research and development organization with talents for innovation would be required. Engineering departments were considered an item of overhead and in modern accounting this was called (and was regarded as) "burden"— on the backs of the factory and marketers. In the weapons business, engineering had a somewhat larger recognition, but it was still only a small part of total employment.

The Organization of Hughes Aircraft

Hughes Aircraft, in light of its existing contracts and goals, had to be organized on grounds somewhat different from conventional practices in large companies.

Aircraft companies (those that made airplanes) were halfway between the old type manufacturing company and an organization now required to build aerial platforms for advanced electronic systems. Every aircraft company, large and small, was headed by an engineer. It was necessary that he understand technology, reliability, tests and risks. He should be a star salesman to his counterparts in the military establishment, who had to use the aircraft in a sometimes very unfriendly environment.

Reluctantly, most aircraft company heads came to appreciate their need for legal, accounting and administrative officials of wisdom and character. I, too, learned that the hard way. The composition of aerospace companies, particularly those in the missile and space business, differed vastly from those of other companies, even those in the chemical business. Engineering was no longer a small "burden" charge in the overall scheme of things, but was now a primary direct cost. Engineering and science represented more than 50 percent of both cost and employee count. Certainly this was true of Hughes Aircraft, as over the years, sales volume had increased 30 times, while number of employees increased only six times. Half of that factor of six was engineering.

On that February 1955 weekend, many of these facts were yet to be learned. But I was satisfied the proportions of employees were substantially correct for opportunities that lay ahead and available talent was superior.

Clearly, my job was to get this composition of employees arranged so that each individual could utilize maximum talents together with those of his neighbor; then smaller groups could create parts for an assembly. Assemblies go together into a product. Each piece is as important as any other piece, each assembly is as important as others, and all must work together as a system and a product.

Even the most complex mechanical, electrical, or chemical product is trivial compared to the complexity of a person. And that complexity increases as natural ability, experience and education of the individual increases. In no other gathering of human beings is there such an aggregation of individual complexities as in aerospace. The job of arranging large numbers of people into an effective and productive organization requires understanding, tolerance and mutual respect.

The lessons, conclusions, frustrations, mistakes and successes that took me from the agricultural age through the industrial age, to the threshold of the space age, was like a great tide. Some good and some bad.

A Look at TWA

In January 1955 Noah Dietrich and I were feeling each other out because of our mutual relationship with Howard Hughes. Noah was preoccupied with not only me and Hughes Aircraft, but also with TWA. The great airline was falling apart because Mr. Hughes in his drugged state, floating randomly between coma and reality, failed to recognize the onset of the Boeing 707 jet era and did not succeed in finding the right person to run TWA.

As if I didn't have enough to do at the Aircraft Company, Noah called me in to look at the airline to see what could be done to improve its situation. For this I made a trip to Kansas City, where I met with TWA's president, Ralph Damon, and a vice president.

They took me to the new overhaul facility installed in the outskirts of Kansas City. I watched them tear down, examine and refit engines. There was nothing wrong with the facility, nor was there anything wrong that I could see with management.

However, TWA's Lockheed Constellations were about a half-hour slower in cross-country flight than Douglas DC-7s. Moreover, TWA food at the time was awful. I had confirmed this on my trip there and had observed it before.

My hosts felt they would really lose out when 707s arrived with the promise of five-hour coast-to-coast flight time. They believed TWA would be at least two years late getting those planes. This together with steadily falling receipts, had them worried and unable to take corrective action.

I told them I was just an observer—and a more or less unwilling one at that—but I would see what I could do.

I unloaded all of this on Noah, who said the boss was trying to correct the 707 situation. It was a major financial hassle because of Mr. Hughes' habitual delay—this time taking action to get places in line for 707 delivery.

Noah also said he couldn't run the damn airline for them. If they had food trouble, they ought to fix it themselves. I told him that they didn't have the money.

Noah said they've got cash flow, if they would make right use of it. He said that's the job of any management. With that the conversation ended. At least it gave me a valuable hint on how *I* should act.

Seeking Independent Financial Support

Early in January I met Ben Fleming Sessel, vice president of Irving Trust Company in New York. Dietrich asked me to receive him, because he was a potential banker for both the Tool Company and Aircraft Company. He was a very nice gentleman who expressed a real interest in our Aircraft Company financial problems; he said he thought loans could be arranged.

A few days later I received a call from Keith Carver, a vice president of Bank of America. He was in charge of the Hughes Aircraft account for which B of A acted as depository; in addition, as an accommodation, B of A handled our checking account. Up to that time, no financing of any Hughes Aircraft had been arranged with Bank of America.

Mr. Carver, also a fine gentleman, indicated he and Mr. Sessel were considering working together to provide short term loans for Hughes Aircraft in the event such an accommodation was needed. He also stated the lead bank had not been agreed upon; they needed a much closer look at our books and prospects if such an arrangement was to be provided.

I was extremely interested in their visits. There was a possibility they might provide an answer to a serious problem that was developing.

Pressure was building for more space for both engineering and the factory. Orders for new equipment and repeat orders were coming in at a pace impossible to fulfill with the existing plant. We were already using a few 20-40,000 square feet buildings near L.A. airport, but were going to need a further large unit of space to meet commitments I saw ahead.

The company's books and records did not support my conclusion. But I had come to rely upon financial, sales, and product forecasts of Paul Collins, and personnel forecasts of Jim Feeney, the personnel director. The factory and engineering people passed in information in bits and pieces, but Collins put it together. In my limited exposure, I learned his forecasts were indeed extremely accurate. Feeney was equally helpful about personnel and their distribution, but it seemed to me he was a bit too far on the liberal side.

My First Hughes Expansion

I had scouts out for a week looking for additional space when a report came back that the old Nash automobile plant in El Segundo was available. It was sound structurally, but in awful condition inside. It was discouraging for anybody without a little imagination and knowledge of what it took to create a plant. I felt a million dollars could make a great difference. I was confident we could get it ready in a year, during which we could prepare for a quick move of the entire Culver City factory to the Nash plant. Building No. 6 at Culver City could be converted from a factory to an engineering department. Our space problem could be solved—for the present.

I talked it over with Howard Hall. I said the asking price was about $5 million, but I thought it could be bought for less. He said he was sure it could be; but we had to get Howard Hughes' permission. He questioned where we would get the money.

I went to see Keith Carver at B of A, asking what he could do about a loan for about $5 million. I brought with me a summary of our current business—1954 actual and 1955 estimated profit, sales forecasts and backlog. He was impressed and indicated something might be worked out. I made a date to see Dietrich at Romaine Street. He said the purchase was all right with him, but I had to talk directly with Mr. Hughes. He didn't seem optimistic, but I told him I would try it.

The next day I called Hughes; to my surprise, his office called back within an hour with instructions to go to a certain phone booth and await a call. Howard promptly called me there. I told him about our need for plant space, about availability of the Nash plant, the probable price, and plans for conversion and utilization of Building No. 6.

He said he would call me back—and hung up.

The abruptness did not seem to bode well. I had heard about Hughes the procrastinator and that it would be days, weeks, or maybe months, if ever, until I heard from him again on the subject. I had also been warned that when he got ready, he would probably call me in the middle of the night, instantly demanding a stream of data I would be hard put to give him without access to my office files.

To my utter amazement I received a call from his secretary the next day with instructions to go ahead with the acquisition. He had not inquired how I would get the money or even asked for further details. I'm sure he did some checking with Dietrich and other of his minions, whom I knew were in the plant. But he gave me permission to stew in my own juice. We put $100,000 down, said we would pay the balance in cash, and executed a contract to take possession subject only to clear title.

I cautioned our people against talking about the matter because I knew if the name Hughes ever got into the picture, the price would skyrocket and the escrow might be somehow broken. All arrangements were made by Howard Hall who I found was a master at secret acquisition.

The deal was quickly completed. Within a week after occupancy we were offered as much for 20 acres as we had paid for the whole deal.

In the meantime, I had really put the heat on Messrs. Ben Sessel and Carver for a $5 million loan. After a remarkably short time, the loan was granted. Only one hitch occurred in the negotiation: the bankers wanted to put a statement in the loan agreement that in the event I left the company, the loan would immediately mature and require payment.

Although it would seem to have been to my benefit, I refused to allow such a condition, stating the company could stand on its own merits; our condition was such as to make such a loan reasonable; and

I thought it was an insult to the people who had built up the company to put such a condition in the agreement. The stipulation was withdrawn; we were on our way.

Meanwhile, I had tried another approach, shopping around a bit to find a good architectural organization. More and more, the name Pereira and Luckman seemed to come to the top. So I invited them to submit a bid for revamping buildings and space at Culver City for possible enlargement or reconstruction. I decided to let them continue on that project, because I was sure we would need added space before our growth could be contained.

One of the first visitors I had after assuming office was a man named Del E. Webb, a top-ranked contractor. He had built a host of fine structures. He was part owner of the New York Yankees and president of the corporation that owned the Sahara Hotel in Las Vegas. I was impressed with his record and with the alterations and structures he had already put in place in Culver City. So I chose him to take charge of reworking the El Segundo plant and changes necessary to modify Building No. 6 to an engineering building. Subsequent events confirmed the competence of the Webb organization.

A little investigating revealed we had a young, overweight, pleasant young man in the building department of Hughes Aircraft who seemed to have done a good job of keeping the plant going in spite of some of the peculiar constraints of Mr. Hughes and the Tool Company ownership. At least he knew where all of the bodies were buried. So I decided to take a chance on him, because to put a new man on the job would guarantee confusion and this one might work out. And it did. Under that pleasant manner, Dick Sutton was a driver. He knew his business and acted as a perfect middleman between the Hughes and Webb people. Both jobs were done economically and within a reasonable amount of time.

Learning Firsthand About USAF Attitudes

I had technical committee meetings once a week; every Friday a meeting with the USAF plant representative; plus at least one Washington meeting a month with a DoD or Presidential advisory panel as well as one with the CIA advisory group. And at home, there were many parties, some involving big Hollywood names. The novelty soon wore off; the two nights a week limit and ten o'clock curfew became standard practice.

During this time I became better acquainted with our sales department, run by Roy Wendahl, a brilliant aeronautical engineer, who had worked for Howard Hughes on several aircraft, including the famed Flying Boat. He was not only technically sound, but also had a unique capability to work out contract terms such as progress payments and sustaining engineering payments.

At Wendahl's urging, I made a trip to Wright Field, the Air Force technical and contracting center. On this first meeting, our Hughes Aircraft field representative in Dayton introduced me to USAF program management. I reported our progress on various USAF contracts, our plans for new engineering projects, and our new plants for manufacturing and engineering. But problems surfaced in both radar and missiles. In no uncertain terms the USAF said we were a country club organization, were arrogant, and given to doing things our own way, regardless of Air Force requirements.

I had been warned about this kind of a reception, so I was not surprised. I didn't duck the issues but told them what I proposed to do. I noticed the group included a red-headed major who seemed to be point man. He knew in detail what was going on, including weaknesses and strengths. No doubt about it, he knew his business. I decided to keep an eye on him; he appeared to be the kind we could use at the company if he ever decided to leave the Air Force.

Fortunately, the Air Force group and the Hughes group were still speaking to each other at the conclusion of the meeting.

Returning from my visit, I decreed weekly meetings with the new Air Force plant representative so there would be no uncertainty for either of us about what was going on at the plant or in Washington or Dayton. The new plant representative, Colonel Ole Griffith, was an extraordinarily competent officer, experienced in contract administration. Our meetings were constructive, frank and productive.

During this period I had another luncheon meeting and several telephone calls with Noah Dietrich. We discussed Mr. Feeney, our personnel director.

TWA was having difficulties in its personnel department. Mr. Dietrich wanted to know if Mr. Feeney could be made available to them. Sensing it might be wise (from several points of view) to concur with this request, I nevertheless told Noah of Mr. Feeney's importance to Hughes Aircraft—and that he was one of the few people in the administrative department who was performing well.

Following these discussions and further conversations between Mr. Feeney, Mr. Dietrich and myself, it was agreed Mr. Feeney could go to TWA as personnel officer. My "cooperation" pleased Mr. Dietrich, pleased Mr. Feeney because of his promotion, and pleased me because of my uneasiness with the overly liberal views of Mr. Feeney. Everyone was delighted.

Discovering Our Social Conscience

Later, when Dr. Rabe from UCLA's Industrial Management School became our personnel chief, he provided me with an interesting bit of information.

I had been surprised at many telephone calls complimenting Hughes Aircraft on its generous and forward-looking policy of helping employees who were alcoholics. It did seem to me we certainly had our fair share, but in any company it's always surprising to find out how many people are alcoholics. Dr. Rabe's contribution was a statement that we made a specialty of hiring alcoholics so we could cure them. I *thought* our policy had been a bit too generous. We put a temporary ban on hiring alcoholics.

Twenty years later, we had a similar problem. Word came to the administrative office that several convicted murderers—who had served their sentences—were on our payroll. Again, I found we had a warm-hearted employment counselor, who made a specialty of trying to help parole officers. We changed that policy, too, because several of our women employees strenuously objected to working with paroled murderers.

In general, my philosophy has been that I did not care about the ethnic background of people—if they had the capabilities we were looking for. If they were clean, tidy, and interested in production, we wanted them. If they were talented, we loved them. We didn't care if they were prima donnas, provided they could sing in tune.

Management Under Siege at Hughes Aircraft

By early 1955, I had begun to get a handle on both the personalities and groupings of various elements of the technical and factory organizations. In prior years there had been no lack of organizational efforts. One office had to do with policies, procedures and work statements. Another was continuously studying needs, overlaps and special requirements of the administrative operation. There was not always a close association between the views of these two offices. But I soon understood where organizational problems had their inception.

There were three important factors contributing to the confusion that existed in Hughes Aircraft—and the basis of misunderstandings between Howard Hughes and his prior top management.

First, top officials and many at lower levels were retired military men. Some had great stature and recognition. Moreover, military life had placed its stamp on many in the organization, whose experience and training had been governed by the Articles of War or Articles of the Government of the Navy. There was no recognition either by them or Mr. Hughes that military organizations are basically quite different from industrial organizations.

The military operates under circumstances where the organization must function effectively under catastrophic conditions, when each post and level may be occupied by a person of limited experience and whose capability for doing that job may be minimal. In the military each official from top to bottom had not more than eight people reporting to him, and usually fewer. He often had a deputy. Responsibilities of each person were precisely defined by command instructions, work statements, or job descriptions. Consequently there were multi-levels. Almost every action required several approvals. Such an organization is effective in war or other catastrophe, but is much too bulky and slow for industrial operations.

Regardless of the type of organization the need for close supervision over relationships between major units and between executives heading each unit is of paramount importance. They must communicate, cooperate, and collaborate. The tidy boxes and subdivisions of an organization chart should delineate but not segregate the flow of information and purpose.

Second, interspersed above, below, or in between these military people had been a succession of civilian executives. Some had prior experience in unrelated work, but most were from small companies dealing with simpler products or from mature organizations with minimal demand for creativity or from academia with business administration degrees.

Third, although there was a competent lawyer and a good factory manager among the top people, the dominant force within the Management Committee (and the company at large) was a cadre of engineers—men of great talent who had progressed from universities to large laboratories or directly from academia to Hughes Aircraft. It's my recollection that none of them brought significant business experience nor did they have any empathy for either military people or business administrators. However, they developed a rapid grasp of affairs.

Turbulence resulting from boiling together these three disparate ingredients caused confusion and uncertainty over the years in the management of Hughes Aircraft. By the time I arrived, the situation had been simplified. The primary military players were gone or on the way; senior business administrators were nearly all gone and I helped the rest of them on their way. For the most part, only engineers, plus a fine senior accountant, a great lawyer and some excellent factory people were left. The objective Howard Hughes had given me was direct and simple: "Run your business to the satisfaction of the Air Force." There was no mention of profit, of stockholders, or of his own interest!

I accepted Mr. Hughes' instruction as the corporate objective, addressing the organizational vacuum: The acquisition of new people for comptroller, administration, and purchasing, plus already-competent people at several levels in those departments, quickly brought order out of chaos on the business side.

I propounded two important principles about organization charts: While they display tidy boxes with stated functions or duties with connecting lines to show paths of authority, the real facts of business life are quite different. Organization charts should be considered as depicting the *average centerline* of paths of authority and reporting. Paths widen or narrow, become rough or smooth and occasional temporary detours. It's the business of management to define the limits of these paths to keep their functions directed towards the goals of the company; to encourage innovative organizational thinking, but not neglect a reasonable extrapolation of current organizational arrangements. Organization is a continuing process.

Any attempt to set up and run a high technology industrial operation as a tightly-structured organization, comparable to an army in time of war, is foredoomed to failure. A field army is designed to operate in the midst of calamity, with parts subject to catastrophic elimination at any time. The field army organization is intended to achieve unity of action—to squelch individual innovation—so the army's full strength can be applied in accordance with the plan and orders of the commander.

In contrast, a high technology industrial organization should be designed and operated to encourage and benefit from the best thinking and cross fertilization of its members; to achieve good communication of thoughts, ideas, questions, answers, and results—up, down, and sideways. All parts are presumed to be present and functioning. The purpose of the organization is not to sustain operation in the midst of calamity, but to see and grasp opportunity. The head of the operation never dreams he has all the answers or that his forward plan is uniquely superb.

Businesses sometimes have the notion that if all the boxes on organization charts could be properly arranged and described, the business could run by itself.

Housekeeping duties and the necessity of getting acquainted throughout the corporation took the majority of my time during the first couple of months. But there was every indication that my real chore was to convert the team spirit of the complex engineering departments into mutually supporting teamwork—and to bring order into their relationships with the factory and marketing operations. In engineering much of the top three levels of management had departed. Strangely, on a technical talent and personality basis, the departure was hardly noticeable. The average age in engineering was about 32—a young organization—with a few topnotch men in their forties.

The Intricacies of Financial Allocations

In the company were three areas of operation: Radar, Guided Missiles and Research. Radar and Missiles each had its own factories, plus specialty operations in small buildings at other sites. Research had its own laboratory in a part of the primary Missile building, but it also had much more. The three department heads felt they should control equal amounts of money. In the case of Radar and Missiles it could be justified; but because the Research operation was much smaller, in order to keep the budgets in balance it became necessary to allocate unrelated functions to the control of the vice president for Research. Most of these functions were administrative or specialty products. They were a burden to the head of Research but put him in the right head-count category for the allocation of funds.

What had made the aggregation function in the past was sheer technical talent of the people and appeal of their innovations to the Air Force and Navy, who wanted the products of their ingenuity in the new era of weapons.

The military answer to this disparate organization is to allocate equal funds to each department with special segments separately provided for. In the Pentagon the result is fine, but uncoordinated service departments, with overlapping efforts and an almost total inability to communicate with each other in the field.

In industry, the need for coordination is usually recognized. There is a belief there should be one head of manufacturing, one chief engineer, one chief financial officer, and so on. The strong men in the operations compete for these jobs with tactics varying from gentlemanly to merciless. Fortunately within Hughes Aircraft the competition trended toward the gentlemanly side.

I felt our organization would have to be molded around individuals and arranged to fit programs and projects. For our many-faceted, high-tech operation, I felt there could be no chief engineer as such. There could ultimately be a coordinating engineer with an assistant. Provisionally, I concluded that department heads could be left alone, but departmental segments could either be left alone, redistributed, or set up as new departments.

The first easy step was to take all responsibilities, except for research, out of the control of the vice president for Research, reassigning those functions to the administrative department.

Early Organizational Structures

During these early months, I had been much impressed by the radar manufacturing operation under Ray Parkhurst, and by Ray's assistant, Harper Brubaker. I badly needed help in overseeing our entire manufacturing operations, not from the standpoint of "command" control but for coordination of all our factory operations and techniques, as well as inspection.

Furthermore, I wanted to put radar engineering and the radar factory under the same executive. In doing this, I did not want Ray Parkhurst, a vice president, to feel he had been demoted and would have to report to Bob Shank, the executive I had chosen to run the radar operation. The availability of a good factory man, Joe Ferderber, allowed me to promote Ray to be the company's manufacturing vice president with staff duties, Bob Shank to vice president of the Radar Division in charge of both engineering and manufacturing, and Harper Brubaker to be staff vice president for planning and programming.

The Radar Division contained a complete product operation. It took appropriate information from the Research Laboratory, did considerable applied research and continued development, engineering, manufacturing, quality control and delivery of a complete product. It had its own sales department and had allocated to it the necessary funds from its own contracts.

The product division avails itself of services from other departments such as field service and support, plant maintenance and repair, flight operations, corporate field offices and central office administrative services. These support services may be categorized as blessings from the central office; but when changes arrive they are often called other names, most having an earthy connotation.

Other product divisions, including the Missile Division, were organized much the same as Radar. Their identity had to do with special product engineering and sometimes manufacturing of identified specialties.

The Research Laboratory, on the other hand, had been relieved of its administrative functions; it was a separate unit with functions closely associated with advanced research usually appropriate to the requirements of various operating divisions.

But the Research Laboratory was also doing work parallel to, or at the request of, various governmental agencies. It had its own sales department; the deficit between the revenue from its sales and the cost of running the research operation was picked up by the central office and allocated as overhead to operating divisions.

The product division is the primary unit around which Hughes Aircraft is built. Supporting product divisions were service functions that included: corporate sales office; flight operations; quality control; field service and support; plant and equipment maintenance; and treasurer and comptroller, with attendant accounting and finance operations.

There were also smaller units, such as the legal department, including general counsel, and a tax department reporting to the treasurer. Another small unit, reporting to the law vice president, was the patent department, in a formative stage at this time.

In addition, two specialty operations were product, not systems, oriented. One, an offspring of the Radar Division, was devoted almost entirely to aircraft radio. Another offspring, specializing in ground radar, was growing rapidly.

An additional specialty product operation was the Semi-conductor Division. This operation started out making diodes and other semi-conductor products that were taking over many of the functions of smaller vacuum tubes. Monitored by both the Radar and Missile Divisions as well as the Research Laboratory, Semi-conductor, in fact, reported to the general manager as a growth operation.

This corporate structure was all in place and functioning within two years of my coming aboard. This fundamental organization with various name changes along the way, has remained virtually intact throughout the huge growth of Hughes Aircraft. There are, of course, more product divisions, more specialty units and a larger administrative operation, but the basic structure remains intact and functioning.

The next major need was to state the principles of management, establishing internal control of programs and projects so that product authority and corresponding funds authority could be delegated. Thus each subgroup had a responsibility to deliver its part of a project to meet cost, schedule and performance.

It had taken only two years to get a basic organizational structure in place, but another five was needed to refine program and project operation.

In Hughes Aircraft, each major product division was in essence a system operation. A radar set, for example, is a combination of many technologies—radio, electric, mechanical, hydraulic—all at the outer limit of knowledge. Within *each* of these disciplines a new order of achievement in strength, stability, packaging, stress and human factors requirements was demanded. Each of the arts and sciences had to be considered and molded into the characteristics of the aircraft, its pilot and crew.

Radar Division had several ongoing systems; each composed of subsystems created by programs and projects. Each program or project had to be organized and staffed according to requirements upon individual parts that together made up the whole.

Actually, the organization of subsystems within a system was usually more complex, requiring more detailed management than the organization of large units that made up the more obvious elements of the company. In order to establish a pyramid of systems, contributing programs and project managers, it required many meetings, an analysis of situations, training and the promulgation of instructions, not only within each division but across divisional lines. We had to discover how to do these things ourselves. There were no role models to copy. But we tried not to make the same mistake twice.

Refining the Corporate Organization

The reassignments of Shank, Parkhurst and Brubaker were the first moves in changing the corporate structure from a committee-controlled aggregation of independent departments to a line and staff organization. This form of organization had proven suitable for a large corporation, having demonstrated the nurturing of growth, control of multiple product lines and successful operation.

We even invented a method of distinguishing between line and staff on organization charts: line operations were always shown in red and staff operations in blue.

Establishment of line and staff organizations and appointment of the heads of the major divisions and functions was comparatively easy for me for two reasons. First, the departure of the top hundred executives and managers from Hughes in 1953 and 1954 was a blessing. Had they remained, and had I to sort out and realign that highly talented, competent, willful and experienced group of people, the job would have been impossible for me or even for a Solomon or Alexander. I knew and had worked with many of them. Some were my good friends. Their dissatisfaction had been with Mr. Hughes; they bore me no ill will and in fact helped me out on several occasions.

Second, the departing executives had built and hired well. However, in their running battle with Mr. Hughes, and with their having a new general manager every year, they had not been free to adopt, nor most probably were they even familiar with, the benefits of a suitable organization, clear objectives, basic management principles, or explicit lines of delegated authority and financial control, with tight accountability back up the line.

With the top boxes filled with competent people, the next and biggest job was fine-tuning the organization by the appointment of program and project managers within the divisions. The program manager has authority for an entire product from conception through proposal, negotiation, contract, development, manufacture, delivery, sales and field operations. In effect, he runs a business, sometimes a rather big business, all its own.

It was not the duty of the general manager to appoint the program managers; that was the task of division management. In turn, it was not the duty of division management to appoint the subordinate project managers.

At the end of the first three months, we had worked out the framework of a good organization, capable of growth. The essential elements were identified and we had allocated the time and created the atmosphere necessary for fine-tuning the organization by selection and training of the program and project managers. But it would take us a good three years to carry out the program adequately. It took time for the word to spread that a major function of executives is the discovery and training of program managers. We were staffed to conduct cost and method studies and apply the results. We were attending to quality assurance and forward planning.

Individual are the Key to Success

Individual talent was important. There might be only one individual in the entire company capable of completing a particular element, because the requirements might demand an educated, natural problem-solving instinct rarely available. To find such a person, pick them out and put them in the right place was an unusual requirement of not only personnel management, but individual, scientific and engineering screening.

Our requirement for special problem-solving skills arose because we were constantly doing things that had not been done before.

The result of these observations was that delegation of authority in Hughes Aircraft was particularly directed at finding and developing the unique, full capability of the *individual*, the root of all talent.

Each division and its components ultimately had a general organizational structure, built around the individual. There could be no standard approach, applicable throughout the company, for tackling various jobs. We devised appropriate organizations for each project and system division and their supporting units. We also developed a method for putting financial authority down the line where it was needed, in the appropriate amounts and with appropriate responsibilities.

There were occasions when we were examined by groups of military people, descending upon us on short notice, looking over our situation from top to bottom, expressing many dissatisfactions. One thing we found necessary was to match the organization coming in, man for man, with well-informed members of our team, to try to educate the inquisitors, showing them what was going on so they could interpret what they saw. It was this care that from time to time caused our guests to believe we were trying to mislead them. On one occasion a delegation tried to examine the methods in one place in one part of the company, then quickly get into a car and drive to another place to check on statements we'd made to see if such and so procedure was, in fact, the case. It was a circus.

To this day, the effective methods Hughes Aircraft employs to marshal the talents and drive of good people in doing technically advanced work are still not understood by some agencies of government.

The occasional charges being made now, 30 years later, are the same as those made in the '50s. We are recognized as having a great engineering organization—but not knowing how to run a business with high costs, loose management and inferior performance. But our costs are less than competitors' or we would die on the vine.

I'm reminded of Kelly Johnson's "Skunk Works" at Lockheed. This fabulous organization built, in complete secrecy, at least three remarkable aircraft: the F-80, the U-2 and the SR-71. The U-2 and the SR-71 have not been duplicated by anybody. (Editor's note: This written in the 1980s before revelation of the F-117 Stealth; and before it became Lockheed Advanced Development Company, under Johnson's successor, Ben Rich.)

The "Skunk Works" was unique within Lockheed Aircraft in that Johnson reported directly to Bob Gross, the chairman, and to the comptroller for accounting. This format was developed by Johnson as the only way to keep complete secrecy and to develop and produce a remarkable airplane on an economical basis in a short period of time without all the paraphernalia of approvals, interferences and paperwork that large organizations (both government and industrial) demand. Many contended that this type of organization, held up as a model of how to do it, could only be utilized on a single product.

The fact is Hughes Aircraft in its engineering organization utilized the "Skunk Works" theory with its own internal structure and accounting policies. It functioned well. The make-up of each segment depended upon the individual who managed it and the requirements of the particular job. That is why the divisions worked so well; they were built around individuals and their projects. Our cost was about 20 percent under a comparable "big company" paper structure.

It is interesting to note that the Army, Navy, Air Force and NASA each has its own accounting requirements, each unique to some degree. Setting up interpretive books was no great challenge. It was mandatory that we keep a set of books to satisfy our own financial requirements; these were extremely conservative. We could not afford to keep a separate and complete set of books for each government agency customer. Instead, each month we used our own books to adapt the manner of presentation so that it fitted the customer agency's requirements. Everyone was reasonably satisfied—although never completely.

Management Principles

The general pattern of our organization was now established and most of the leadership in place. Also most of the paper structure (now called protocol) had been examined and found wanting. We needed to establish new and more appropriate principles on which to run our business, to describe all parts of the organization and then to indoctrinate all the players on how to employ these sets of statements.

As a foundation, I had a collection of documents and lessons from experience. I had, over the years, picked up management, financial and personnel principles enunciated by such people as Alfred P. Sloan, John Rascob and Donaldson Brown of General Motors and James McDonnell of McDonnell Aircraft. I had the chart of accounts and the formats of monthly and annual financial statements from Bendix. In Detroit, I had asked a neighbor, a senior accountant with General Motors, to get me the documents teaching the principles of pricing and cost accounting. I had attended a session of the Aircraft Industries Association where James McDonnell gave a short lecture on *elan vital*, roughly translated as "vital force." I have never forgotten that speech and I wanted to incorporate its lessons into my statement of management principles for Hughes Aircraft Company. I also made use of certain maxims from the U.S. Navy Seaman's Manual and from the Horatio Alger stories I so much enjoyed as a youngster and even lessons remembered from my boyhood McGuffey's Reader.

I distilled the teachings from all these resources into eight principles that I thought were the core of good management. I gave a little talk on these eight principles at an informal meeting of Hughes Aircraft senior executives and advised the group that I proposed to use them. I urged each member of the group to do likewise. Eventually I put the eight principles into a little pamphlet which was widely distributed in the company.

The principles were given and received as guidelines, not as preachments, and have well served their purpose, in my opinion.

It should be noted that "profit" is last on the list or, if you are more accustomed to the current expression, profit is "the bottom line." That position is intentional and important, for while profit is a purpose in any industrial activity, it can only be achieved and sustained when all the other principles are first applied. The services to be rendered, and the resources of people and their tools to render them in a continuing manner, must first be defined and deployed. Profit can only be reached after the service is given. Talking about the bottom line first, and trying to conduct a business from the bottom up, are perhaps major contributing causes of the gradual deterioration of many once-great companies.

The Reality of the Hughes Aircraft Image

During this time, guided missiles, submarines, jet aircraft, nuclear warheads and computers—in fact the whole gamut of weaponry—were undergoing major changes. The demand for engineers and new production methods was enormous. That we were able to maintain and expand our workforce in the face of stepped-up competition in both industry and government laboratories was a tribute to the reputation of Hughes Aircraft Company.

But remember, in my first visit to Wright Field, my Air Force hosts, among other comments, categorized Hughes Aircraft as a "country club" and its staff as arrogant.

Actually, it would have been difficult to classify the Hughes facilities as a "country club." About a third of our staff was in temporary buildings. The two main engineering buildings could not have been classed as superior; one was a wooden hangar, the other a smaller metal hangar. Trailers were used as turnaround space for the factory. All this was managed from a wooden office building and a recently-added concrete structure. This motley aggregation of buildings hardly deserved the appellation "country club."

Similarly, the designation "arrogant" was the wrong word applied to the right attitude. Confusion arose because our engineers sometimes disagreed with the customer as to what was possible or practical, as distinguished from what was wanted. They would not encourage the customer to order the impossible, nor permit him to expect to get it.

I was among those who wanted performance to extend the state of the art, but not beyond available funding or within too short a delivery time. On two occasions I flatly refused to bid on weapon systems of questionable utility that would meaninglessly chew up an enormous amount of valuable engineering time, even though the contracts, if won, would have represented very profitable enterprises for the company. Then, as now, sound technical minds and their supporting organizations are a national resource, not to be wastefully deployed or misapplied.

Competence and integrity should not be misnamed arrogance.

A Period of Concentrated Growth

During the six year period from 1955 to 1960, we continued to grow in all directions. We were practicing new arts; there were no precedents or prior technology to call on. We had to discover it as we went along.

The main radar project was of considerable interest to me. While at Bendix, we had received the request for proposal from the Air Force for a completely new type of electronic equipment for what was called the 1954 Interceptor, a new type of aircraft. The requirements were way ahead of current state of the art. I was relieved when Hughes Aircraft was awarded the job in a close contest with Bendix.

Now here I was heading Hughes Aircraft; and the whole job was in our lap. Still respectful of the requirements, I nonetheless felt confident we had the talent and equipment to make the system.

Prior to the 1930s weapons were developed and manufactured on the basis of long-known principles. During and after World War II accelerating technology and rapidly advancing demands for performance by the military customer drove weapon system development into uncharted areas of technology. In the 1950s the industry and the military customer had not yet learned how to strike a balance among the desired, the practical, the possible and the cost effective. Mistakes were made on both sides. I learned a new formulation of Murphy's Law: If you are not positive you have the right answer, your best guess is probably wrong.

Initial specifications for the 1954 Interceptor were too far in front of the art. The time it would take to do the job was considerably more than was compatible with demands of the Air Force. To fill the gaps, there were two or three interim fire control systems. These were offshoots of preliminary work for the so-called MX-1179 electronic equipment, which was to be the name of the electronics for the 1959 Interceptor. There were even two interim aircraft. The project turned out to be larger and longer than anyone had originally anticipated.

Missile armaments for the various interim aircraft were separately contracted for. Our first contract was for a Falcon missile for mid-distance range, able to function not only during fair weather and clear skies, but also through smoke and clouds. It was competitive with Naval missiles such as the Sparrow (radar guided) and Sidewinder (heat-seeking), which after launch could pick up and follow thermal radiation from the target aircraft, particularly from engine exhaust. We felt the Falcon missile could be adapted to heat-seeking guidance; that was one reason we were anxious to acquire the Santa Barbara Research Center. It specialized in infrared technology.

Our fire control equipment had worked well as long as we were launching unguided rockets. We were ahead of the competition. But the guided missile was a much more difficult problem. Our progress was not sufficient to achieve hoped-for delivery dates.

At the same time the Navy at its Inyokern Laboratory in California had a remarkable young man named Dr. McLean who put together an infrared-seeking guided missile, dubbed "Sidewinder." It was a simple design. It was good only for relatively short distances in clear weather, but those distances were considerably greater than could be achieved by gunfire.

A "shootoff" was arranged between an aircraft carrying two Hughes Falcon missiles and another carrying two Navy Sidewinder missiles. I went to the test range for the shootoff. At Hughes we were hopeful, but rather doubtful of success on this occasion. The Air Force clearly recognized the probabilities; the Hughes missiles were to be fired first and the Sidewinders later. Although the Hughes missiles picked up the targets and launched satisfactorily, the seekers did not work properly. My heart sank.

The first Sidewinder was launched and destroyed the target; the second was not required. We went back to the drawing board. We continued with a series of tests, which, although showing improvement, were still not satisfactory. In the meantime, our missiles were in production; the production rate was increasing. Telephone checks with our Washington and Dayton offices indicated the Air Force was becoming extremely exercised about our performance. I decided we had to take radical action. So I telephoned our plant in Tucson to shut down production. By then, evening was coming on, but I had to inform the Air Force. I telephoned Dayton, found the project officer at a Christmas holiday party. I told him what had been done. I expected a blow up, but instead he said, "Thank God for that." He said, "We were going to have to make a decision pretty soon and it is very difficult to shut down a contractor and be faced with all kinds of charges for arbitrary action. Your action lets us off the hook and I want to tell you we'll help you all we can in getting a solution for this problem as early as possible."

That decision turned out to be one of the best in my career at Hughes Aircraft. It established a climate of integrity and responsibility which overcame any doubts our military customers might have of our objectives.

That was valuable, but other fallout came as well.

Impact of the Missile Decision

We had to do something about the Falcon; I learned by the grapevine that vigorous action was being undertaken in the Missile Division. The people involved planned to work through the New Year period. I decided to come in and observe. I wanted to see who was working with the troops. At the office at 9:00 one holiday morning, I went to the Missile Building, finding perhaps 100 people on the job.

The vice president of the Missile Division was not among them. However, his assistant, Allen Puckett, was there. (Dr. Puckett was also a member of the Guided Missile Committee of the Department of Defense—of which I was also a member.) I found him in a room surrounded by about a dozen top engineers. As a rule in those days, when I walked into a room at the company, I was the center of attention. But not that day. They were hard at it in unbelievable concentration. The man leading the discussion was a physicist and aeronautical scientist who had written one of the great papers on supersonic airflow, but who was not noted for achievement in electronics.

I could do no good there other than to give a silent blessing to the efforts. I wandered in and out of engineers' rooms, chatting with them about the problem. I managed to get a general description of the circuitry of the missile and the nature of the problems. True, I was 30 years away from my best years as an electronics engineer, but I still remembered a few "don't" rules in circuit design, particularly three that must never be included in any product. To my amazement, I found the design of the missile seeker had implemented all three of those "don't" circuits in the unit. I did not let on my feelings, but I went away with a sinking sensation we had a bear by the tail.

Work on our missile problem never let up. There was redesign, recircuiting, more tests. The new device began to take form. It was rapidly given captive air tests and, in cooperation with the Air Force, flight acceptance tests. After four months the Falcon D missile was approved for production. Somehow, under Dr. Puckett's leadership, needed remedies were found, incorporated and we were once again on our way.

During that period I had initially given orders that the workforce at Tucson be reduced. Several weeks later, I found out the order had not been carried out. I called the Tucson plant manager to ask why.

He stated he did not want to let the people go because it had taken much time to get production organized; he was afraid if he let people go he could not then get them back when the missile was fixed and thus could not maintain production schedules. I told him the cost of keeping those people over an unknown period would be astronomical; we could not handle that cost; and he should get busy at once to lay off the necessary people. A week later, he sent his deputy to tell me it was impossible to lay off any of those people without damaging future production. The plant manager, Roy Wendahl, had been on the job there for about a year. He was our former sales manager (and a very good one) and a truly great aeronautical engineer. But he had not before been in a broad management position. This appointment was intended to give him experience to develop his qualities as a manager.

However, no further delay could be brooked. I phoned Tucson and said, "Roy, this time I am not *asking* you to do something, I am *telling* you to do something. I want you to lay off every single individual who is working on that missile. I want you to lay off the supervision associated with it. I want you also to lay off administrative personnel and reduce administrative cost in the same proportion as the reduction in manufacturing personnel and I want all this done on pay day at the end of this week. I repeat: *this week.*" He said, "I think you're making a great mistake."

I said, "Well . . . it's my mistake and we'll talk it over after we see what happens."

The layoff lasted three months and three weeks. People were called back by degrees as the situation with the corrected product firmed up. A loss of millions of dollars was avoided. A company which was operating on a perilously small amount of capital could not have sustained that loss.

Layoff as production or orders go down is something any manager hates. Among those laid off, there are always friends. And among them always are those he knows cannot comfortably do without funds they would be paid on the job. But the move has to be made in order to maintain company solvency; to hopefully get back the man's job as soon as possible. No company can pay out funds it does not have. It is necessary to remain solvent today in order to generate or maintain jobs tomorrow.

Continuing Growth—and Need for Physical Expansion

One component division contributed a great deal to our financial viability. The Semi-conductor Division was going strong on the newest of the electronic components, a simple diode of great use in circuitry. The division had a good product in great demand at the time. Orders had been flooding in and we gave them every possible help in finding good process operators and in getting out production. During the nearly four months when our missile production was on hold, several million dollars was earned by that division. It literally carried the corporation during a trying period. When everything else in the company began to go well, however, the Semi-conductor Division got into trouble. Several years elapsed before it again became a big winner, although in the interval, it supplied us with invaluable products for other divisions.

During this often trying time, the rest of the company was growing. Ground System products were achieving excellent acceptance in the Navy. It became apparent we were going to need a new plant for that operation. Hughes Aircraft facilities at Culver City and the nearby airport site were already stretched to the limit. There were nearly 10,000 people employed there.

My past experience told me 10,000 people is the maximum that could be appropriately handled in one industrial location. With more than that, distances traveled to work by some become excessive, traffic is heavy, and communities in which the plant is located frequently regard the operation as more burdensome than desirable.

The Ground Systems branch of the Radar Division was overcrowding two buildings at the airport site. They had in hand orders and prospects that would demand 100,000 square feet of plant within a year, and more thereafter, if present prospects materialized. It seemed wise to find a plant site which could accommodate 200,000 square feet, have a minimum of 100 acres, be located in an area with an adequate supply of high grade employees, be adjacent to good roads and highways, have immediately available facilities for electricity, water, sewer, telephone and gas and be in a decent climate. Also desirable was a tolerable political history and a land price not in excess of $10,000 an acre.

Although a railroad siding within a mile would be desirable, it was not absolutely necessary; but availability of between 50,000 and 100,000 square feet at once in the vicinity was required because we had to accommodate Ground Systems' growth during the two years of plant construction.

Harper Brubaker had been the solidly performing assistant to Ray Parkhurst, the manufacturing vice president. He was chosen to head this enterprise and charged with finding a location for the new plant.

Within a month, he located 400 acres—ideal for a plant site. Since even more growth had taken place during that month's search, I decided to present the proposition to Mr. Hughes. A phone call was immediately returned. I told him the need (a minimum of 200,000 square feet), the land price ($9,000 per acre), the location (near Fullerton), and the overall cost estimate ($10-15 million).

He immediately seized upon the land price issue, stating it was too high; that we should be able to negotiate something better. He had no comment on any other factors; I assumed he would approve the project.

Corporate attorney Howard Hall and I made a date with the owners to try to get a better price on the land. In the short interval since our last meeting with them, an important event occurred that seemed to favor a price reduction. North American Aviation, which had a fairly large plant in Downey, California, not far from Fullerton, announced it was closing its Downey plant because of poor market conditions. Moreover, they had no estimate as to when or whether it would ever be reopened or sold. This would put several hundred people out of work and change the economic picture in that portion of Orange County.

Hall suggested we take a check with us for $1 million and see if we could get the owners to agree to a price of $6,500 per acre.

At our meeting we talked about the disturbing situation with respect to prices and employment in the area, which certainly would be materially affected by the recent North American developments. We indicated the price of $9,000 per acre was much too high; that when we presented the proposition to our board of directors, they told us to search elsewhere. I said we really didn't need that much land and could probably find a suitable piece in the same general area.

Mr. Hall stated we could make a firm offer for about $6,500 per acre; he was prepared to present a check for $1 million as earnest money to begin escrow. The owners asked for time to talk it over; in a surprisingly short time they returned and accepted the offer. We were in business.

We authorized Mr. Brubaker to lease for three years several buildings not far away from the new site. By the time we got the plant drawings and facility plans together and had work permits, the building had grown to 300,000 square feet. It is now the core building for a magnificent plant of more than 1 million square feet.

We informed Mr. Hughes that in our discussions with the land owners, we ascertained they would consider a cash offer of $7,500 per acre if we put up sufficient earnest money to back up the offer; we also committed to make an immediate settlement when escrow closed. He authorized us to go ahead. We concluded the deal, reporting that we had achieved a further reduction to $6,500 per acre. Hughes sent word he was pleased with our negotiations. Nothing further was said about any other part of the whole proposition; we proceeded.

Learning to Work With Mr. Hughes

The transactions for the El Segundo and Fullerton plants were invaluable experience for me; they showed that much of the talk about delays and uncertainties attributed to Mr. Hughes was not really true if information provided was appropriate, the need demonstrable, action immediate in response to his suggestions, and if long and short term considerations had been taken into account. I was convinced Mr. Hughes liked to tantalize by negotiation and procrastination where there was uncertainty or when a victim could or would put up with him. But he could move fast enough when it was important to do so.

I have worked with others not considered to be erratic, but who gave me more difficulties than I ever had with Howard Hughes. He only firmly overruled me twice in 22 years—once on the Louisiana development project and once on acquisition of factory land in Arizona.

Recalling an Old Lesson

One custom left over from prior management of which I thoroughly approved was a weekly seminar of about an hour in which authoritative speakers from various staffs and specialties of Hughes Aircraft gave talks, ranging from 20 minutes to perhaps an hour, on basics and current status of their specialties. About once a month, an outside speaker was invited to address the group of about 75-100 senior executives.

It was astonishing how this seminar series added to the education and competence of the body as a whole.

In my early time with the company, I was invited to a talk by one of our engineering vice presidents in which he was to forecast the trends of our business.

He outlined the rather remarkable progress made in the past few years and spoke about the curve of growth. He had placed us near the bottom of the curve just before it began to shoot upward at an accelerated pace. At the end of his talk, he left us at that point. He asked me to comment. I was sitting in the first row; I couldn't decline. But I found myself in a difficult predicament. If I followed the curve he had shown, in about a quarter of a century we would be responsible for a large hunk of the Gross National Product.

I didn't want to disagree publicly or drastically with the speaker's up-beat remarks. I got out of the predicament by stating that in my personal experience, just about the time I felt I had a situation under control, when everything looked good and the future secure, I always tried to turn around quickly to see where the next kick is coming from. That's exactly what happened at Hughes Aircraft.

At the time we had a strong position in night fighter and interceptor aircraft fire control equipment. For one airplane, the F-106, we even had almost the entire navigational and electronic equipment. It was also believed new bombers should have modern fire control equipment for the tail gunner to give them greater protection against improving fighters.

Several factors required that I make frequent trips to headquarters of the North American Air Defense Command (NORAD). Although our equipment was recognized as superior, we (and everybody else in the business) were still using vacuum tubes in many missile and aircraft circuits. These tubes had a short average time to failure. That contributed to problems. Moreover, NORAD generals were indoctrinating us on their needs. And we were striving to impress them with our dedication to solutions. This was in contrast with the company's reputation for arrogance some years before.

For the trips, I usually took along one or two engineers. On one occasion, in mid-1956 the engineer assigned was Dr. Allen Puckett. I later learned that his presence was a put-up job. He was to use the occasion of our being together to sell me on the approach the Missile Division wanted to adopt for a major new competition.

I knew we were going all out to bid for fire control equipment for a new aircraft, the F-108. The request for the proposal to supply the electronic equipment emphasized for economic reasons the desirability of using off-the-shelf equipment, but nevertheless asked for the best possible performance. We would be up against the stiffest competition, for both TRW and Westinghouse planned to propose, and both were competent. Preparation for such a proposal was a huge engineering task. It would involve, in addition, substantial groups of people from manufacturing, field service and support, and from aircraft test departments. We were looking at almost 20 years of business, because it takes that long for a modern fighter series to become obsolete. What was involved was a risk of many millions of dollars of our own money, despite the Air Force's assurance they would pay for the preparation of the proposal and for preliminary engineering of the first models. Subsequently, the magnitude of the contract could be upwards of $1 billion. It was big business. I had long since realized my own engineering expertise was worthless in this kind of a situation, but I felt we had the talent and know-how from recent fire control equipment and missiles we had put on Air Force and Navy aircraft.

Arriving at Denver, we had an hour wait before connecting with the aircraft from Denver to Colorado Springs. Puckett and I stood leaning on the fence that separated the airport building from the runway. He outlined the company's plans on the F-108 proposal. He said we had two choices. One, we had the most modern and up-to-date equipment available on an "off-the-shelf" basis. These fire control sets were being produced in quantity; we had the benefit of field experience; we knew our costs and could make some equipment improvement and still confidently be way under anything either of our competitors could possibly bid. The alternate choice was to ignore the stated Air Force preference for "off-the-shelf" equipment, but taking advantage of new engineering, proposing what we felt we could deliver within the specified time. This option would run the cost up and perhaps extend the time a little, but would give the Air Force better equipment and better mean time to failure.

The probability, however, was the competition would decide on this second alternative because they didn't have anything competitive with current equipment. Then he asked, "What course do you recommend?"

It did not take much thought for me to reply. I said, "I know all about the habit of the military asking for "off-the-shelf" equipment as the economical course to follow. Such statements are there for political reasons. What they really want is the newest, best performance, highest quality, longest mean time before failure, delivery matching the availability of the aircraft and a price that will give them a cost they can justify as reasonable at the time of the award. They know and we know the price will probably be raised from time to time by change orders as engineering and manufacturing changes are called for. That would be the way I would go on a philosophical basis. But Allen, you will have to decide which way to go on a practical basis."

He said, "That is the way I think we should go also."

Months later when proposals went in and the evaluation was made, we were awarded the contract. We felt our future was guaranteed in that division for the next 20 years. We also had success based on similar reasoning with self-defense fire control for the B-52. The future of the Radar Division, by far our largest operation, looked very good indeed.

Our backlog was up to $750 million, indicating we would certainly fill up the newly modified Building No. 6 with additional engineering.

Customers 1955-1960

The U.S. Army, Navy and Air Force were all important customers of Hughes Aircraft; however, the Department of Defense has a regulation that one service is assigned responsibility for any one plant or a whole company. Each service was jealous of its prerogatives and anxious for the assignment to the Hughes Aircraft Company. (The climate in California is quite enjoyable.) The company was assigned to the Air Force, which found itself in a somewhat embarrassing position. At various times three retired Air Force generals had been among the highest officials of the company. Of these, two had already left and had joined competitors.

Captains, majors, colonels, generals and civilian officials up to and including the Secretary of the Air Force were watching the actions of Hughes Aircraft and doing their best to monitor the management, for one purpose; namely, to preserve the performance and integrity of the company's products, which they needed. Air Force interests at company headquarters were in the charge of the Air Force plant representative, or AFPR. The AFPR had a staff of about 100 skilled civilian observers, many of whom had high positions in the civil service. In addition, there were one or two military officers.

Thirty years after the fact, I found that the red-headed major who impressed me so much on my first visit to Wright Field had been a special representative at our plant, nominally under the AFPR colonel, but actually under the direction of General Clarence "Bill" Irvine. He had been put there to keep the general informed of the situation during the critical year of 1954, when the company was run by a committee. The major left a week before I arrived; that was not a coincidence.

The Air Force went about its job of managing me and the Hughes Aircraft Company in a very professional way. They gave me a few weeks to get the feel of things and then I was worked over from the top down: from Secretary Talbott himself to his contract officer.

Somewhat later, General Eisenhower, the steady, conservative and wise President, took a leaf from Calvin Coolidge's book and clamped down hard on government spending policy. At one time, he went so far as to declare a moratorium on government payments to defense contractors for a period of three months. That threw the defense industry into a terrible tizzy; the screams and complaints were anguished indeed.

Responding, the Air Force convened a board of generals at Dayton; they invited chief executive officers of the large defense companies to appear before them and voice their predicaments and suggestions. About a dozen presidents and chairmen appeared before the board. From their appearance both before and after the sessions it was apparent the going had been rough. As a lowly vice president and general manager of a large and important, but controversial, company, I was the last to come before the board.

I could see the members were tired and distraught from their hard day; I smiled, said hello to General Irvine and General McKee (both of whom I knew well), and sat in the hot seat.

I think it was General McKee who sternly asked, "What are your problems, Mr. Hyland?"

I replied I had no problems.

My reply was greeted with astonishment. After a short pause, still smiling, I went on. "I can think of no other circumstance which would have made it possible for this country boy to walk into a bank and say that I want at least one hundred million dollars for a considerable period of time at the prime rate and get an immediate favorable response!" I added, "That line of credit will allow us to operate satisfactorily for a period of three months. I hope you will allow the interest costs as an item of expense. I have no further comments."

Nor did they. But it was apparent they appreciated the break from the continuous dirge of complaint and resentment that, until then, had been their day. When I left, we shook hands all around. The day had ended on the upbeat for them.

The hullabaloo over the payments moratorium was such that President Eisenhower withdrew it well before the three month period ended.

With our bank credit line established and Mr. MacGillivray's riding herd on financial matters, we were in good shape by mid-1958. True, we had no reserves, we didn't have much capital and no depreciation base. But many of our contracts were cost plus; we could keep our inventory down and our work in process under control, so our working capital requirements were minimal. These conditions allowed us to direct our attention to the principles that a customer is satisfied when the price is right, the performance is good and the delivery is on time. At the time, it was rare to satisfy these three conditions simultaneously. Knowledge had advanced to the point where new desires could be conceived and specified, but systems could not always be configured to realize those desires. Doing something that had never been done before was difficult for precisely that reason: it had never been done before.

In the decade of the 1950s, the defense business climate became cloudy, even turbulent, as new political and military appointees replaced the pioneers who had managed the introduction of high technology into weaponry and space exploration. Government procurement agencies became less tolerant and flexible. The contracting and negotiation process for high-technology systems began to resemble that for standardized systems. Soon this practice extended to product testing and colored the attitude of the users, so that the relationship between government agencies and contractors became somewhat strained. This was particularly true for the Hughes Aircraft Company, since its management problems in the early 1950s were superimposed on the general industry problem.

Obviously improved communication and understanding between our customers and ourselves was a paramount requirement. We indoctrinated all those directly associated with the customer to adopt a more diplomatic attitude and avoid technical and contractual confrontations entirely. Our field service and support organization under Ed Boykin, who was already aware of the requirement, redoubled its efforts.

Then another favorable event took place. John Winkel, the red-headed major whom I had spotted at Wright Field, resigned from the Air Force and we hired him immediately. John was particularly well versed in the need for communication and understanding and agreed to be our special representative in the field, to go to all the testing and using agencies to assure better communication and understanding both ways. He did that and continued thereafter to do a great job for both the company and its customers. Fortunately, our products were top grade. With suitable training and understanding, the users were well pleased with their operation. And that has continued to this day.

Learning the Business of Business

There are many books on management; each has a valuable place in the literature of business. Those I have read or sampled treat the specifics relating to economics, quality and competence with authority, but are limited in their breadth about the general management of an enterprise of almost any size. For example, C. F. Phillips, W. Edward Deming, and C. Northcote Parkinson make great contributions to the art of management in well-defined areas. Peter Drucker, however, comments in a broad way about a large business from an academic point of view, admiring "bigness" for its own sake in its relations with the body politic.

Business schools seem to concentrate on economics and the bottom line, with minors in marketing, organization and personnel, taught by specialists in those areas, with occasional exposure of the students to successful senior managers. Here there is a problem. The executive and student cultures do not communicate well; they speak different languages using the same words. The translation has to be learned by exposure. In my experience as guest speaker at business schools on more than a dozen occasions over the years, I have concluded (by analyzing questions I was asked) that students did not "hear" some of what I know I said. I came to believe students should have more exposure than they were getting to working executives willing to discuss the specifics of their work, problems and methods.

It is a rare big company where the basics of cause and effect in the business are close enough together to be understood automatically by nearly all employees, unfiltered by organizational, political or procedural mazes. Communication is important. To some extent, leadership and communication can be taught; one function of a business school ought to be such teaching.

These skills cannot be learned by a career of subordination, uninterrupted by periods of responsibility. Progressive increase in leadership responsibilities should be a standard career path feature, interspersed with staff and deputy functions to broaden scope along the way. Occasional assignments involving cultural and community affairs, trade, or government associations should be part of managerial development, but should not interfere with professional performance and hence with career progress. Somewhere in mid-career it becomes apparent that even with a 1000-hour day, the time would still be insufficient to engage in the full range of worthwhile activities that loom ahead.

Incidentally, I regard the proper function of any manager or supervisor to be guided by a conditioned response to authority. Managers must sense what the higher authority wants and expects and conduct themselves accordingly, without explicit direction, in almost all circumstances. I knew, for example, that Vincent Bendix did not want to be bothered with details on the operations I headed for him. He wanted me to manage, keeping him informed of those aspects of interest to him and important to his image of himself and his company. I was confident Mr. Hughes, also, did not want to be troubled with information or consultations irrelevant to his grand design. He would and did master all details on matters that concerned him.

I initially regarded it as necessary to speak with Noah Dietrich about any commitments above one million dollars (equivalent to six or seven million in 1986). That threshold was gradually raised as Dietrich and I became familiar with each other's patterns of thought. After the "consultation threshold" had reached several million dollars (and particularly after the departure of Mr. Dietrich in 1957) I developed the practice of attaching to financial briefs submitted for approval a notice stating that unless I heard to the contrary within a month, I would assume approval of the proposed commitment and take action accordingly. That method of operation continued until the death of Mr. Hughes in 1976.

Some Matters of Productivity and Morale

Prior Hughes Aircraft management had left behind some very constructive accomplishments. One was use of, and accommodation for, the handicapped. In this area the company was a leader in the country. Former management had also done an excellent recruiting job, both in presenting company policies to deans, professors and students at universities and in selecting talented applicants. A third residual benefit of past stewardship was a remarkable educational program, both in-house programs and collaborative studies and advanced degree programs with colleges and universities. These were continued and acknowledged with grateful thanks to the initiators.

Two interesting and stimulating suggestions came from outside the company. The first, called "Value Engineering," was defined as an organized means for evaluating procedures, designs and practices with the view to improving performance and reducing cost. We were the first company to adopt the idea enthusiastically and to organize to make them effective.

The other suggestion, "Zero Defects," came via the government; it was a means for quality and performance improvement with recognition and awards based on achieving the objective. The results were gratifying and the state of mind and sense of individual and collective responsibility induced were a tribute to the people who generated the idea.

There were supercilious supervisors and managers who looked contemptuously on these ideas as gimmicks. Sure they're gimmicks, but so are many ideas that captivate the attention and interest of human beings. One of the finest "gimmicks" I knew was used in one of our factories in 1960. An assembly line had been set up for a computer used on the first Polaris submarines. At the time, this computer was said to be the most powerful digital computer in existence. The line workers were all women. One of them got the idea that those working on a remarkable new product of such value in the defense of our country ought to have a distinctive uniform to show their patriotism and appreciation for being trusted with such a job. A red, white and blue blouse was designed and proudly worn by the line workers. Production was never higher; quality never better.

Hughes was proud of them, too. The next time Vice Admiral W.F. Raborn, the Navy Polaris project chief, was in the area we invited him to visit our El Segundo factory and the Polaris assembly line. The admiral, a very expressive person, was delighted. He congratulated everyone in sight and told the story at every level, including Congress. It was a fine example of American spirit and the desire of people to rally round an indentifiable project with an attainable objective.

Where Was the Next Kick Coming From?

I should have quickly turned around to see where the next kick was coming from. Hints of things to come were offered even in 1955 when we had a visit from Brigadier General Bill Irvine. I should have paid more attention.

I believe General Irvine came to see for himself in 1955 the present status of Hughes Aircraft and to find out where we thought we were going. I did not know it at the time—nor could I confirm it later—but it is not at all unlikely Irvine was making an assessment for Howard Hughes and Noah Dietrich on how things looked at the company after a couple of months of my service.

At the end of his visit, he seemed well satisfied with what he had seen and heard. He said he was pleased during the short session we had in my office at the end of his rounds.

But then he also said, "I hope you know, as you should, that your company is on very uncertain ground in the future. The Administration is trying to hold down defense expenditures and is determined to put the new, big, intercontinental ballistic missiles in the forefront of new weapons."

I was, of course, well aware of this policy. In fact, I was active on high level defense and intelligence advisory boards that wrote the recommendations on which the policy was founded. But I had to tell General Irvine we were in no condition to move one single engineer or spend one development dollar for a new, big project at the present time. I emphasized it would take every effort we could muster to complete our commitments to the Air Force. We were counting on the new F-108 interceptor and searching for other uses of our fire control and missiles, perhaps on bombers for defense against interceptors.

Irvine replied, "I commend your dedication to the interceptor program, but I warn you that any money for anything but big missiles may become mighty scarce in the not-too-distant future."

The F-108 interceptor and the bomber defense programs—major programs to us—were ultimately canceled.

Chapter X
Hughes Aircraft, Pursuing New Directions

During the period 1954 to 1960, profits rose as we began to benefit from sustained production without intervening long periods of development. Prospects looked good. During this same period, in addition to my duties with the company, I still maintained memberships on technical committees in the Department of Defense, the President's Scientific Advisory Committee and the Central Intelligence Agency. This allowed me to be helpful and information obtained helped me keep abreast of the rapidly changing military equipment picture in the United States and throughout the world.

Our company was riding a wave into the future. We were in the vanguard of air defense, which for some years had been a primary concern of our government.

There was however another and even larger wave building—the warfare of offense. It had started at Peenemunde in Germany with V1 and V2 missiles. It was now growing rapidly in the United States with intercontinental as well as intermediate range missiles with atomic warheads.

Intelligence indicated the USSR was also concentrating on these weapons; it was necessary that the United States put comparable development and deployment on top of its priority list. The cost involved in doing so, however, would be enormous. These huge self-propelled long-range and electronically-guided bombs represented the ultimate in push-button warfare. They captured the imagination of the public, Congress, the military and even the President. But something else had to give. That something was the next generation of manned bombers and air defense fighters—which was where we came in, or went out, depending upon one's point of view.

I knew this kick was coming, I just didn't know when. General Irvine by now had made two visits to Culver City to point out the probability the emphasis in Air Force procurement would shift to guided missiles.

Unfortunately, we were helpless because we had neither engineering nor plant available to undertake anything major beyond commitments in hand. Nor did we have funds to finance further operations in addition to present commitments.

The Shoe Drops

The inevitable happened. The sudden kick, which I had forecast, came in a visit from the colonel in charge of the F-108 program. He appeared in my office one October morning in 1959 to deliver the bad news that the F-108 would be canceled forthwith, all work stopped and negotiations begun for contract termination. I asked the Colonel how much time we had to act and he said, "Action must be taken today. The actions taken will be considered next week when I come out to arrange the termination conditions."

Shortly after similar notice was given of the termination of the bomber fire control radar. Though we were well aware of its possibility, the actuality came as a severe shock.

I called the principal department heads, the personnel department and the division vice presidents to break the news. I told them to go through their personnel lists and make immediate layoffs of all concerned factory people except those working on two sample units plus two or three essential liaison engineers. I said the primary engineering people for development tasks should be retained. Also comparable reductions should be made in overhead and administrative personnel, considering reduced operations. I also called on the vice presidents of the radar and missile factories to come up with definitive plans of action.

There was no time to cry over spilled milk. I brooked no debate over what we should do about layoffs. But we adhered to the letter of the law respecting proper notices to employees.

Working through this situation was strictly up to me. There was no need nor any hope in appealing to Howard Hughes. Actually, this was going to increase our profit margin on paper because the cost of much work in process—a charge against current assets—would be converted to real assets and contribute to profit. We were bound to have a good profit year. All elements of cost buildup of getting into production on the F-108 would be eliminated.

Moreover, in our hasty growth there were some personnel who had been tolerated but were not the most effective employees. This enabled us to remove the inefficient, underqualified and job jumpers.

The main decision, however, was what to do about retention of the truly great radar for the F-108? It was a full step beyond the MX-1179 unit, involved solid state technology and other new concepts, particularly associated with extended range, target detection and identification and display. But another element of this decision was the best utilization of our funds as well as the best size and scope of the company.

I had been associated—either as victim, witness or participant—in similar situations in the past. Never, however, had I participated in top decisions about action to be taken. In my opinion, most of these prior decisions had been bad, made primarily on a short-term capital conservation basis without regard to the longer-term future of the agency or company. I had heard many director's statements —made during times of profitable operations—that research appropriations should be continued under all conditions and advertising continued regardless of business conditions; both were necessary for the health of a continuing business. Nevertheless, when business conditions changed and profits suffered, among the first things reduced were research and development and advertising.

Immediate Damage Control Action Required

I decided our course of action required two things:

1. Continue development of radar, although at a much slower pace. With both the Navy and Air Force as potential customers, one was quite likely to need this class of equipment in the not-too-distant future.

2. Immediately set up a blue ribbon team to determine a product or product line to fill in the enormous gap caused by the nearly complete reduction in air defense expenditures.

Also, I told the comptroller to hold termination fees in a reserve category, because they would be needed to finance these two objectives.

The following five years were low profit years. We sharpened our already-effective controls and speeded up utilization of our money, actually turning it over as many as 100 times a year, twice a week! We established drops around the country where funds paid in by either military or civilian customers would go immediately and then transferred the same day to our main bank account.

We were "slow pay" during our financial stringency. We would pay smaller suppliers on time because we knew they needed their money. But we made "big guy" suppliers wait, because we knew they could afford it. It helped us to have use of their money for an extra 60 days or so. Incidentally, the vigor of complaining about slow pay is usually exactly the reverse of need. "Big guy" suppliers have staff and methods to turn on the heat to collect receivables. But smaller firms seemed to have more pride. They seemed to feel it self demeaning to ask for payments due. We paid them on time. As a consequence of these actions we managed to finance our two-part program, make changes necessary and still squeeze out a little continuing profit.

As an aside, this performance might not have been possible had the company been publicly owned. With a host of financial and media analysts searching for stories and soft spots, our predicament could have been shouted from the rooftops. But we were always regarded as a triple A credit risk and assumed to be loaded with money. Instead we were loaded with good people, sound policies and a long-term view. We had a company president (Howard Hughes) who had always operated similarly. He had not been consulted, nor did he want to be, about these matters.

The results of these decisions came slowly. During the termination process, the Air Force decided to continue development of our radar, which seemed to have much promise, at their own expense. Our decision had been justified. Second, the work of the blue ribbon team in deciding upon product lines proceeded slowly but thoroughly. I attended early meetings and was initially disappointed. The team had looked at many diverse products in electronics, but had not yet begun to pinpoint specific targets. Finally recommendations came in.

There were two product lines that needed attention—good candidates for engineering and manufacturing abilities we had in the company. The first was tactical air equipment. In all the years of concentration on air defense and now on ballistic missiles, the tactical air operations side of the Air Force had been literally starved. It was now becoming vocal, finding listeners in Department of Defense and Congress. Tactical air was going to want fire control and missile attack armaments. With our advanced radar and missiles we could be given prime consideration. This ultimately proved true.

The second area exploited was a unique classification of space. With President Kennedy's announcement of a program to land a man on the moon, a great deal of money and effort would be directed there. We decided the "man on the moon" project had relatively limited life, requiring equipment that did not fit well into the pattern of Hughes Aircraft.

There were bound to be many uses of, and multiple programs for, unmanned spacecraft. The team recommended we concentrate there. History records it as a wise decision.

Today's Hughes Aircraft business is largely a result of decisions made at that time. What satisfies me most, however, is the fact that the product research and development concept—as an element of what it takes to pull a technology-oriented company out of the doldrums—has proved correct. This concept is true for other classes of business as demonstrated by the negative results of those that have *not* done the R&D work necessary to keep them in the economic mainstream. In the United States, one can cite the steel industry and railroads, for example.

Bomb Threat Defied

The 1950s brought another special problem to defense establishments: the beginnings of bomb threats against weapons manufacturers and student uprisings against the Korean War. There were perhaps a dozen bomb threats at Hughes Aircraft. Many establishments shut down operations while searches were made by security police. A halt at Hughes could mean as much as a half day of lost production, which we could ill afford.

At our first warning after I took over, I went on the loudspeaker to all plants to state that most of these warnings were hoaxes; that we had an obligation to continue our work for the defense establishment; that our officials, including myself, would walk the plants and take the same risks as all of our people; and that we would *not* shut down, thus accommodating the terrorists. Our plan proved effective. There was never an explosion; the threats stopped.

The Beginnings of New Business Ventures

An opportunity arose in 1955 to test a belief founded in my Radio Research Company in the 1930s and reinforced in the '40s and early '50s. It had to do with two kinds of components—vacuum tubes and semi-conductors—essential parts of equipment we manufactured.

Most equipment for specialized weapon system functions required vacuum tubes having unique characteristics. To get these tubes we had to go with hat in hand to tube makers to persuade them we might provide a small but continuing market and that it would be profitable to make tubes for us. We had to show them the purpose of the equipment and circuits to be employed; that meant giving away valuable information we had created at some expense. Also an element of competitive advantage had to be given away.

It took some years for me to sell the concept of a specialty tube division in Bendix. And it cost a little money to set up the operation. But it was a going concern at the time I left Bendix.

I was delighted to find Hughes already had a Semi-conductor Division, but no vacuum tube operation. The original promoter and scientist who had set up the Hughes Semi-conductor Division had left the company. The division he created had good people, but none of the caliber of the originator.

The division's new product developments were not particularly successful; we were unable to provide them with adequate facilities or to find leadership for them to be competitive. Soon they began to lose money, but I was determined to keep the division going in the business of designing specialty semi-conductors, required in our Radar and Missile divisions. We were only able to find these items outside at high cost, coupled with disclosure of circuits—or not at all.

Eventually, when we had available funds, a small new factory in Newport Beach, California, became available at an attractive price. Our people decided it would provide a suitable building for our Semi-conductor operation with considerable potential for growth. Accordingly, we acquired it, arranged financing, and moved the operation from the temporary building in Los Angeles to Newport Beach.

The decision to move Semi-conductors to Newport Beach brought to a head management and engineering dissatisfactions on both sides. I think the division manager and chief engineer on one side, and I on the other, parted company reluctantly. They did well for themselves thereafter; and after their resignations we did poorly for some years.

After acquiring the plant, alterations had to be made. I left this job to the assistant general manager, Bill Wooldridge, a competent industrial engineer and a good manager at Tucson. The operation was not of major importance. Because of other problems, I did not pay enough attention to it. However, rumblings began to creep in about reconstruction of the plant. I decided to look for myself. The day before New Years at the end of 1958 I went to the plant. It was a shambles. Walls had been torn out, bricks lying around, and wires hanging all over the place. The stories I heard from Bill were that work was progressing slowly because of architectural delays, but completion was only a matter of a couple of weeks.

I was furious. I felt like firing those with the assignment right on the spot, but we were in a critical situation at the time. I assigned one of our plant engineers to bring order out of the mess at Newport Beach.

Reconstruction was finally completed at a cost about double the original estimate. I now know the delays and confusion had been part of a deliberate plan to discredit me—and have me removed from my job as general manager. Bill Wooldridge had written a letter to Mr. Hughes describing my incompetence, using the mess at Newport Beach as a prime example, and reciting other delinquencies.

I heard about this letter because I had inner circle sources at

Romaine Street. Finding out about the letter, I allowed the man to resign.

Mr. Hughes never paid attention to such letters from any source. Years later I learned he trusted me implicitly and would hear of no criticism. He evidently dismissed my brief adventure with the development project in Louisiana as a momentary aberration, never to be repeated.

Even in its new quarters, the Semi-conductor Division continued to be a problem and a loser for several years. Managers and engineers came and went, but the division did a creditable job of supplying specialty solid state devices for our bigger divisions.

Nevertheless, our system divisions were not satisfied with the amount of production and engineering available at Semi-conductor. They were critical of money spent to keep the division alive. They pointed out that the same money, used elsewhere in the company, could pay off in better performance.

I persisted in its support; the division finally came to life when it was part of a major organization in which several of smaller units were combined into the Industrial Electronics Group. Not only did it do a good job on semi-conductors, but spawned other profitable operations.

A similar circumstance took place with vacuum tubes. We did not have a vacuum tube producing unit, but we had a promising tube project in the Research Laboratory. The Laboratory had worked on a new technology called a traveling wave tube.

A small company in the Los Angeles area produced specialized vacuum tubes. Their quality was good, but they had a hard time keeping abreast of customer requirements because they did not have enough cash flow to keep up with rapid advances in technology. The company made inquiries concerning our interest in an acquisition. We found they had good management, led by a first class engineer and his associates. They had enough equipment to get us going in specialty vacuum tubes and recommendations for improvements that made sense. The price was not out of reason, so in 1959 we made the acquisition.

As usual the unit initially was a loser, but still a producer. Like most small specialty units, in ours or any other business, its accounting practices (particularly those associated with depreciation, and those requiring distinction between use of fixed and working capital) made it almost a certainty the operation would lose money. The accounting help we gave them, the addition of the traveling wave tube, and other specialized requirements, produced a more rapid changeover to profitable operations.

The businessman leader of the company, Jim Sutherland, proved a valuable acquisition as well; he, with the rest of his organization, filled a definite requirement as a supplier of transmitter vacuum tubes.

The succession of traveling wave tubes from that division proved an invaluable asset; they are utilized in almost every satellite—and were the deciding factor in the award of several systems.

As I write of these examples of the value of research and development in making a technology business grow and be profitable, I do not want to give the impression that I was key to that success. The plain fact is that the experience I had gained over 30 years had given me valuable insight into how to utilize research and development and a grasp of its tremendous value in any technical enterprise. I had been a manager in a small business and in large corporate organizations. I had experienced the creation and loss of an enterprise where I made all the mistakes on my own, with my own money, and ultimately had to sell out.

The real key at Hughes Aircraft was an aggregation of scientific, engineering, and manufacturing talent that had been brought together by others. These people needed only the benefits of experience of how to help these talents fit together and work well as a team. My real job was to create and sustain an environment where these talented people could do their work, both individually and collectively.

Focusing on the Major Problems

Locally, I had accepted a post on the Los Angeles Harbor Commission at the invitation of the mayor. I was active in United Way activities. Three giants on the California scene—Willard Keith, Asa Call and Ernest Loebekke—gave me friendship and introductions to community affairs. Public relations was not a priority problem. There were, however, two other serious areas that *did* need attention:

finance and customer relations, both at a critical stage and demanding almost all of my attention.

The finance problem was peculiar. We seemed to have unlimited credit with suppliers and substantial technical acceptance by our military customers. Moreover, the $12 million loan from the Tool Company had eased my immediate needs in the face of other troubles. Mr. Dietrich had told me not only about the squeeze on TWA but had also reiterated the facts of Mr. Hughes's overextensions at banks and insurance companies, including cancellation of an account at Mellon Bank in Pittsburgh. In short, the public image of the Hughes empire was fine; its private image in the finance world was one of question.

The Middle Years at Hughes Aircraft

By the late '50s affairs of the Aircraft Company were in reasonably good order. The business was put on a reasonable track.

Then came the big cancellations. Military emphasis changed from air defense to intercontinental and intermediate range ballistic missiles. However, active research enabled us to develop and substitute new product lines. We were on a smooth and rising course thereafter.

From the outset it had been my practice to send Mr. Dietrich regular financial summaries of operations. I kept sending those statements to Mr. Hughes' staff even after Mr. Dietrich left. Whether Mr. Hughes ever saw those statements, I shall never know. I did realize though, beginning in the mid-'60s, that my telephone conversations with Hughes took place at ever-longer intervals. As intervals grew longer, the frequency of visits or calls increased from people whom I knew to be associated with either legal firms, the Tool Company or the Romaine office. From time to time, my assistance was sought by some of these people on matters relating to government requests for information or testimony to support the needs of some Hughes interest for government permits or approval. In some cases, I was able to get hearings and decisions through channels different from those they used.

Hughes Aircraft was enjoying profitable operations and national recognition, but some other Hughes interests were proving troublesome. The association among various principals became adversarial, except for two individuals. One became my line of communications of last resort to Mr. Hughes—Jack Real, a most capable aeronautical engineer.

From the Aircraft Company's standpoint, the horizon was clear and bright, except for the cloud in the direction of the Medical Institute. But even that adversary was kept under restraint. I knew Mr. Hughes was sole trustee of the Institute as well as president of Hughes Aircraft and sole stockholder of Hughes Tool Company. As long as that relationship existed and I had my direct line of communication to Hughes, I felt tolerably comfortable, though not secure.

As the financial position of Hughes Aircraft improved and its earnings increased, the interest of the many agencies kept pace. The Internal Revenue Service was interested because of the tax situation on the gift of the Aircraft Company to the Medical Institute; and because the status of the rental of Tool Company property to the Institute. The leaseback to the Aircraft Company had never been settled. Tax law had changed, resulting in changes for IRS' and Hughes' positions. Department of Defense and individual service officers annually battled with the company over high rent payments to the Institute. They also fought over the $9,000 paid by the Institute to the Tool Company in return for intangible assets transferred from the Tool Company to the Institute at the time of its establishment.

There were insistent, sporadic attempts to get added membership on the Hughes Aircraft executive committee. One approach was by an executive committee purported to have been named by Howard Hughes to handle affairs of the Medical Institute. The signature to that bylaw change was later challenged; as was a later handwritten insertion of two or three words intended to strengthen the bylaw. This bylaw was later thrown out by the court. However, for a long time, members of the Institute's questionable executive committee exercised a great deal of power over the Institute and, in some respects, over financial contributions to the Institute by Hughes Aircraft. When it appeared a few times that an appointment might be made by this group to the Hughes Aircraft executive committee, the suggestion was summarily rejected after a call by way of my "private line" to Mr. Hughes.

HHMI and the Tax Implications

In the 1965 era, the Internal Revenue Service had become restless; it looked as though it might have its Jacksonville, Florida office make a decision, demanding tax payments on endowment of the Medical Institute by stock of the Aircraft Company. I was called to Washington a couple of times to meet with Seymour Mintz and two associates.

For the next few years, almost until acquisition of the company by General Motors, the tax situation for foundations was one of the foremost concerns of the Medical Institute.

In 1966, we at Aircraft began to study the matter carefully and by agreement with the Medical Institute, raised our annual contribution to $3,600,000. With the advent of final tax legislation in 1969, we determined to comply with the tax requirement for a public medical foundation and increased our annual contribution to $4,000,000. From 1968 to '72 or '73 we tried to put dividends from Aircraft to the Medical Institute on a rational business basis. We surveyed dividend payments of other companies in a comparable business and paid dividends equal to about the same percentage of earnings as other companies. We hoped this decision would meet with approval of both the Medical Institute and the Internal Revenue Service. Contributions to HHMI were raised to $16 million per year in 1976, with further increases in following years.

Although amounts we paid did *not* meet minimum requirements for distribution by a company owned by a public foundation, we felt, because of growing needs for buildings, machinery, equipment, working capital and personnel arising from our rapidly growing business with the Department of Defense, we could satisfy the IRS, HHMI, and our needs.

However, near the end of each year the Medical Institute, for what they always described as critical needs, demanded additional payments, frequently above $10 million. We reluctantly complied, although we could ascertain no reason or evidence to justify their needing the sums of money involved. Their demands unquestionably penalized the

Aircraft Company since our earnings were our only source of funds to finance growth.

No one at HHMI seemed to understand that in a growing business such as ours, the usual practice of raising funds to finance growth would be to go to financial markets for a stock or bond issue. This privilege was denied to us because:

1. Mr. Hughes, although sole trustee of the Medical Institute, was fully extended financially and in no position to subscribe to a stock or bond issue. And Mr. Hughes could not endorse a sale of shares or debt to others, who would then become his financial partners.
2. The agreement between Hughes Tool (100 percent owned by Mr. Hughes) and Hughes Aircraft, set up at the time of the gift of the latter company to HHMI, expressly stipulated there should be no business transactions between the two companies. (Although that rule was bent on a couple of occasions.)
3. As I have noted before, I had once made an attempt to obtain for Aircraft by purchase, lease, or gift, some land belonging to Mr. Hughes we could have used. That request had been emphatically denied.

It was apparent to me Mr. Hughes intended the Aircraft Company to be self-reliant and self-sufficient. We had to husband every dollar we could earn or borrow to finance growth. That realization meant we could contribute to the Medical Institute only that amount that would satisfy their minimum requirements. Our assessment of those requirements placed them at a level less than the Institute received from our rental payments.

However, we were accustomed to financial brinkmanship. We learned to keep inventories down, to promptly write off losses, to make collections on time, and never kid ourselves about the value of the work in process, or to rely on the good fairy to get us out of trouble. That we were able to get through this period of growth, adverse tax legislation, and Institute demands was due to management principles we had had to practice during the first 15 years to get an insolvent corporation converted to a financially sound business.

The Perspective of Years

All of this might have been frustrating and bothersome to a chief executive of a large and growing company. However, at that time, I was 68 years old. I had spent 45 years in a series of intriguing environments: first the Army and Navy, where a certain amount of rumors are the order of the day; then at the Naval Research Laboratory where I began to be part of the secrecy atmosphere many new projects demand; then at Bendix, working for Vincent Bendix, whose style resembled that of Hughes in many ways (the prime difference between the two men was that Hughes was tall and thin and Bendix was short and fat); and now at Hughes Aircraft.

The Bendix experience taught me about life in a big corporation, not only from a business standpoint, but also from observing first-hand the intrapersonal activities, rumor mills and ceremonial rain dances, backbiting, the great opportunities provided by business structures to achieve or fail, and, of course, the deadly risks of competitive life at all levels.

Further, I had the advantage of having lived for 25 years with the advice given me by Oscar Ewing, of the New York law firm of Hughes, Hubbard and Ewing. That firm was general counsel for the Bendix Corporation. I came to know Oscar Ewing in the course of business because I spent several years in the Bendix New York office where important antitrust defenses were being developed.

Later, when I became a member of the top side at Bendix, I witnessed the cutthroat antics of several top executives. They seemed to get greater satisfaction from cutting up each other than they did from cutting up competitors. So one day at Bendix, when I was particularly concerned, I called Mr. Ewing to suggest we have lunch. I told him I was concerned about the attitude of some senior executives of our company. They seemed to spend more time harassing and trying to undercut other Bendix executives than they did attending to the business of the corporation. I wondered if that was the way affairs were always conducted in big corporations.

Mr. Ewing grinned. "Well, I can't answer that question directly, but I think I can help you out a little bit, Pat. You are now in the big leagues. You are at the same level with and competing with other people who are just as bright as you are or more so, they are just as competent as you are or more so, they are just as greedy as you are or more so, and they are just as ambitious as you are or more so. They play hardball, and in the big leagues you have to play hardball. Now you have a choice, you can go back to the minor leagues, where you can be a pretty big frog in a much smaller puddle; the games will not be as tough, but the rewards will not be as great. So really you have a choice."

That cleared up a lot of things for me. I learned how to play hardball and play it well. I played to win, but to me that meant playing *on* and *with* the team, not trying to improve my own position at the expense of others. I also learned to recognize probing, positioning and maneuvering constantly taking place in what is often called "palace politics." Consequently, in later years as the business of Hughes Aircraft improved and was noticed by all kinds of agencies, legitimate or otherwise, I was able to walk through the mine field with security and confidence, but always aware of the palace politics associated with any enterprise.

The Forces Were at Work

I became aware, too, that avaricious forces were coalescing in efforts to get control of all or part of the various Hughes properties.

With Howard Hughes in full possession of his faculties, as he was at least occasionally, such conniving forces were about as effective as a bunch of toy plastic robots going against a battleship.

But after the Beverly Hills XF-11 crash and Howard's reconstruction, it gradually became apparent the magic touch was gone. An erratic force of ever-changing strength and vague direction replaced enthusiasm. Caution became negligence and indecision. An impish sense of humor vanished. Loyal personal relationships were degraded by petty demands. The concentration that had previously resolved so many problems withered when the goals were dissolved by drugs. Bad luck, bad judgment and indecision began to have the inevitable result—breakup of the conglomerate.

The first to go was RKO, then came the delayed jet airliner order, compelling sale of TWA. It was during the TWA hassle that the relationships of long standing between Hughes and Noah Dietrich unraveled. Finally Hughes fired Dietrich and confiscated all office papers. Mr. Dietrich was never replaced. The contributions of his skill and loyalty were withdrawn at the very time the need for them was becoming most apparent.

With the departure of Noah Dietrich, the conglomerate was a ship with no captain, or more accurately, no navigator. Then a new whim entered. Hughes, bedeviled by failing health and drug addiction, tormented by lawsuits, and suspicious of some of his executives, decided to change a temporary residence in Las Vegas into a permanent occupation.

He and his immediate staff took the ninth floor of the Desert Inn, a set of suites normally occupied by high rollers, the people to whom casino operators cater. But Hughes did not frequent the casino; he was asked to leave the Desert Inn to make room for high rollers. He declined; the Inn became insistent. Hughes retaliated by buying it. Thus began another phase of his life and career: a series of acquisitions of other hotel-casinos in Las Vegas. Soon, Howard Hughes became the largest owner of hotel-casinos in the area, but in so doing he again accumulated enormous debt.

The appearance of Howard Hughes as an active presence on the Las Vegas scene was welcomed by the gambling-management fraternity, the Las Vegas municipality and the State of Nevada as putting a stamp of class on the area. Hughes was a world figure; he still carried the image of a great achiever. But he nonetheless had to deal with his mountainous debt.

The Tool Company had been a consistent producer of handsome profits, but Howard Hughes had no love for the company. Hughes-watchers have opined that he felt no love for Hughes Tool because it was not something he, himself, had acquired or built.

Thus, a group of lawyers and executives did not have a difficult time convincing him the sale of the Tool Company was necessary in order to pay off some of the accumulated debts. With the sale of the Tool Company, the last of the Big Four had been disposed of. Three had been sold and one given away. What remained was relatively small Hughes Helicopter, a brewery, and a small airline (all losers at the time) plus the hotels, Nevada land, and Hughes Communications.

This latter was a small organization skilled in putting together radio networks for sports events and similar attractions of widespread audience appeal.

Shifting power struggles among lawyers and executives were controlled by Hughes in his few lucid moments. He allowed no interference with the Hughes Aircraft, but took no particular interest in the Helicopter Company or the Medical Institute.

As palace politics surrounding Mr. Hughes escalated to internecine warfare, the tactic of real or imagined threats to his drug supply-line was used and was responsible for many of Mr. Hughes' moves. These began with his undercover departure from Las Vegas to Miami, and from there to Nassau in the Bahamas. From there, Hughes was taken to Vancouver, British Columbia, and from there to London, England, where Hughes had an interval of comparative well-being interrupted by a fall which damaged his hip and forced discontinuance of his one remaining personal enjoyment: occasionally flying his own airplane.

From London, he went to Managua, Nicaragua, but was chased from there by an earthquake. He had a few intervals of well-being in Managua, too, and as has been well-reported elsewhere, he was successful in important discussions with representatives of the State of Nevada, sent there to see him concerning his hotel operations. From Nicaragua Hughes returned for a time to the Bahamas, and from there left on his sad final move to Mexico. Within a few days of his arrival in Mexico he was finally relieved of his pain and chemical dependencies.

Howard Hughes left no will, although he had tried many times to make one.

Mr. Hughes' financial confidant, Lee Murrin, later told me of Hughes' many efforts to make a will, all of which were aborted by Hughes' loss of concentration stemming from drug addiction.

Hughes' final attempt to make his will took place in early July in the late 1960s. He ordered his entire administrative staff at Romaine Street to be available at any time, regardless of weekends, holidays or hours. He stated that he was determined to make a will. He quickly decided upon several provisions of "boiler plate" and routine items of such a will. He informed Mr. Murrin that, to these approved paragraphs, would be added a few benefactions; then the terms for liquidation of his assets, investment of capital in behalf of the Medical Institute, and instructions for administration of the Howard Hughes Medical Institute.

Hughes became interested in a study to forecast the economic future of the nation in order that he might plan the best long-term investments to benefit the Medical Institute. This study so much interested him that he delayed further work on the will. The group of people assembled to work on the will became restless and endeavored to persuade Hughes to resume progress. But as days wore on, his addictions deflected his concentration and needed decisions and directions were not forthcoming. One by one the members of the group resumed the routine of their jobs and the rhythm of their former daily lives. The work on the will was never resumed, and the document never completed.

Howard Hughes hated taxes, but because he left no will, his estate went largely to the State of California, the State of Texas, and the government of the United States. What remained went to relatives by court order. However, the tax loss benefit gift of Hughes Aircraft stock to the Howard Hughes Medical Institute has gone from a zero value gift to many billions of dollars and will more than carry out the youthful plans of the benefactor.

Redirections

During the late 1950s and early 1960s, there were a series of decisions that established the form and enlarged the product base and physical facilities of Hughes Aircraft.

Concurrently, the military was reoriented to develop and deploy guided missiles as well as nuclear and electronic potency into the defense establishment. Turbojet engines, computers and rockets affected military and civilian life. Communications were elevated to a higher order of capacity and convenience than ever before dreamed of by the use of semi-conductors. Yet, before these changes could be assimilated, the space age was upon us with satellites, space exploration vehicles and moon landings.

NASA was quickly formed, becoming another major customer for our products. The stated purpose of the founding legislation was to separate the non-military use of space, which was to be the domain of NASA, from the military uses, which was to be the domain of the Department of Defense. This ridiculous concept would cost us dearly in the future, but was promoted solely for the purpose of demonstrating our peaceful ideals to an international audience.

Hughes Aircraft chose not to participate in the man-in-space program, but instead to take part in the unmanned space programs. The Air Force requested our participation in a mid-range ballistic missile program. We agreed and received a contract that was later canceled when the Air Force withdrew from that field.

During that same time period, we decided to bid on the electronics for the Navy's F-14 advanced fighter. The proposal request called for long distance radar to detect and measure the range to the targets. It also specified a missile of great range plus fire control ability to handle several missiles flying against different targets at the same time—even at these extreme ranges. We knew, and the Navy knew, that this weapon system could not possibly be built with then-existing technology. There was another bidder who also knew that, but whose factory was empty and who was going to have to gamble that he could meet specifications. We also knew we were looking at 20 years of potential business and a possible empty factory ourselves if we didn't undertake this risk.

We had one major advantage. The radar we had originally proposed for the USAF F-108 fighter, and had continued with some Air Force assistance on a development basis, was almost good enough to meet Navy requirement. It could be upgraded. We were confident radar would not present a major problem.

The missile was a much more difficult proposition because nothing like it had ever before been seriously contemplated. It presented an almost impossible task. We had to create a design to meet requirements that were beyond the state of the art and to quote a price on the completed article even though we did not know what it was going to look like.

Prior to the 1950s, weapon systems (i.e. bombers, artillery, massed armor, infantry) were analogous to the duck hunter's shotgun, firing many projectiles in the statistical expectation that eventually one of them would hit the target. The Hughes Aircraft contribution was the addition of in-flight guidance, which amounted to conversion of the weapon system from a ring-and-bead shot gun to a stabilized scope-sight rifle.

The oil was burned through many midnights in preparing the proposal for this extraordinary weapon system. The combination of that nearly-sufficient radar (which we felt we knew how to upgrade) and our credibility on missiles (where we had well-known past successes in both command-controlled and automatic seeker types) netted out to a demonstration of overall systems capability which won the contract for us. A few years later several of us proudly stood on the observer station above the flight deck of the *USS Kitty Hawk*, and watched a Grumman F-14 aircraft, with Hughes armament system aboard, take off and land on that magnificent ship.

An Army project came along for a relatively small missile to be used against tanks. Fired from a launcher on a jeep or a tripod on the ground, guidance was to be from a sort of telescope on the launcher from which a trooper would track the target. The missile would fly down that line of sight guided by signals sent by way of two fine wires, which unwound from spools at the rear of the missile. The range was to be more than a mile and a half; the warhead was to be able to pierce tank armor.

Through intelligence reports I heard that the French and Germans had tried to develop such missiles. Their efforts had proven to be unsuccessful and were abandoned by both countries. I was skeptical of the wisdom of bidding on such a project, which seemed to me to promise great difficulties just winding spools of wire to permit unwinding at extremely high flight speeds. It also seemed unlikely that a man, using a scope sight connected to the launcher, could accurately track a moving tank at long distance. All this performance was demanded at a price quite low.

However, several of our engineers were convinced the job could be done. I reluctantly agreed to spend company money to launch the development.

It turned out I was correct about price. The weapon cost more than the Army hoped. But our people created a design; initial experiments showed great promise. Accordingly, we bid on the program at a price which was considerably more than the Army projection. The combination of our promised performance and realistic price seemed satisfactory and more acceptable to the Army than the offers of the competition. We won the job. The customer was also pleased we had financed a few important experiments before and during the proposal effort, to guide our thinking.

The unwinding process of the guide wire proved to be only one of several obstacles to be overcome in development of this anti-tank missile, but in due time we evolved to a good design, though at a cost still above the Army's hopes. That little missile, called TOW, is a complete success.

The Army insisted we supply another contractor with our designs and knowledge, and to help this competitor into production as a second source. However, we managed to withstand the competition and have actually produced more than 250,000 of these wire-guided missiles. They work well in the field; they're much liked by the troops. (Editor's Note: By the early 1990s Hughes had produced more than 600,000 TOW missiles.)

During the 1960s we became a supplier of weapon systems that, in the 1980s, are on aircraft for the Navy and Air Force, are anti-tank missiles for the Army, and are equipment for nuclear-powered submarines and submarine-launched strategic missiles.

Space: The Next Challenge

By the late '50s, the space pot was boiling. The Army, Navy and Air Force each had missile range, rocket engine, space frame, guidance, aerodynamics, and warhead projects.

Hughes Aircraft was closely associated with ongoing work on long-range missiles, both through our memberships in several senior government committees, and because we had smaller missiles in test at the big Alamogordo and White Sands ranges in New Mexico. I had visited these ranges earlier as a task for the DoD Guided Missiles committee.

The Hughes space group was in continuing touch with NASA and knew of its plans for various satellites. This information, together with our knowledge on progress being made by other firms, prepared us for the requests for proposal from NASA.

Three NASA requests for proposal were issued. We bid on two.

The first was for a moon orbiter. The second was for a moon lander, which, although more difficult, still seemed within our capability. We chose to bid on the project, named Surveyor. The third was for a mid-height communication satellite, called Saint. Saint would be a large and costly project; it was for communications we thought might be one of the important satellite uses. We bid, but a GE/Bendix combination was successful bidder.

Independent of NASA, but with their permission, Bell Laboratory and Western Electric were building a satellite system called Telstar with many of the same characteristics as Saint. Both systems required ground stations with antenna dishes that would rotate to keep pace with the motion of the satellite around the earth.

Ground stations were constructed for each system. Telstar had imposing structures. The Saint team put one ground station near New York City and another on a ship to be positioned near Dakar, Senegal, Africa. Both systems ultimately demonstrated successful transmission of test signals, consisting of Presidential messages, but little else. That little was at very high cost. Yet, at one time Western Electric had a series of Telstars on an assembly line. AT&T was thinking of going operational with the mid-altitude Telstar bid.

Reaching for the Moon

We were fortunate not to be successful bidder for Saint. Otherwise, we might not have been able to go ahead with Surveyor or another project that was to come along a little later. As it was, Surveyor kept our space group not only busy but overworked. We had a target, time and price arrangement on something we were to build that had to work in an uncertain environment from the moment it left the launching pad and passed through several different conditions of gravity, temperature, space debris and orbit to reach and land on the moon. There we were unsure of the character and composition of the landing area and its angle of inclination.

We soon found we not only had a bear by the tail, but several bears pulling in different directions at the same time. The contract was cost-plus fixed fee. The fee remained more or less fixed, but costs ultimately more than doubled. The Jet Propulsion Laboratory at Pasadena was manager for the whole program, including launch vehicle as well as the lander. JPL understood the problems, was helpful, and was both fair and firm in its criticism and guidance.

NASA headquarters management was something else. They were under the gun from Congress; they did not hesitate to pass on Congressional projectiles. The controller, publicity people, technicians and business advisors from NASA headquarters took us over the jumps, using me as a focal point of their criticism. My prior experience as a government engineer, advisor and major government contractor prepared me well for the onslaught our company was subjected to in the process of doing the Surveyor job.

One official of another company on loan to NASA to help in their administration department was particularly offensive in his criticism of me, Hughes Aircraft, our technical capability (about which he knew nothing), our accounting policies and responsibility in the expenditure of taxpayer dollars. He really got my internal goat, but I steadfastly held my temper, put on my most responsive demeanor and promised to continue to live up to our agreements. I also promised myself to call him up immediately on our first successful moon landing.

Some months later I did. By then he had returned to his company, then in financial difficulties. I alluded to that fact—among others—in my comments to him. At the conclusion of my remarks, he replied with a few words about my legitimacy. I felt the score was even, so I hung up.

The Adventure of Contracts for High Tech

Let me offer personal comments on the business of contracting with the government for development and production of high technology items. In signing, the successful bidder is betting a significant portion of his firm's assets—sometimes literally the whole company—that his people will come up with inventions needed to meet specifications the customer has stated.

In the '50s and '60s, there was a more or less gentleman's understanding that contractors who worked diligently and intelligently to meet requirements would not be penalized for justifiable over cost or late delivery on cost-plus fixed-fee contracts, but the fee would not be increased unless mutually agreed upon changes in the statement of work had been made.

In the early years of NASA operations, administration of contracts was a more abrasive process because of limited experience of the people involved on the NASA side in military-type equipment procurement. Their expertise was in other directions.

The acrimonious debate on Surveyor changes, delays in delivery and mounting costs, continued until minutes before landing of the first Surveyor. Dr. Puckett, then assistant general manager, conducted price negotiations because I had to be at Jet Propulsion Laboratory as a special guest to watch the final stages of the Surveyor flight. Just minutes before touchdown, a final fee figure was agreed upon that proved satisfactory to both parties. In the meantime, I was sweating it out in the visitor's gallery over the control room at JPL.

I was truly frightened; the event put our future in the space business on balance. This first flight unit had been literally tested to death. It was worn out; we were not sure it would hold together through the vibrations, course changes, star sight corrections and thrust reversals, let alone a landing bounce in the low gravity of the moon. Yet every critical maneuver during the 250,000 mile voyage to the moon was flawlessly carried out. Touchdown was announced by telemetered signals. The wait commenced while instruments on board Surveyor were activated. After a seemingly endless wait of only a few minutes, a picture began to form on a monitor. The camera was initially directed at one leg and foot of the tripod frame. It showed them clearly, with the foot making a couple of inches penetration into moon dust. The shouting and applause in the audience and the control room released all tension. Surveyor was a success!

Creation of the Laser

One decision point on a basic customer issue was research on lasers. Studies at MIT, Bell Telephone Laboratories and elsewhere had concluded that the MASER (Microwave Amplification by Stimulated Emission of Radiation) phenomenon, whereby energy could be stored and released at microwave frequencies, should occur at the frequencies of light. Years of effort by brilliant investigators had not proved the theory.

The director of Hughes Aircraft Research Laboratory came to my office one day to tell me there was a bright young man at the Laboratory, Dr. Theodore Maiman, who believed he could prove the optical MASER—or laser—theory. Time and money would be required for staff, equipment and materials. The Laboratory director opined that the solution of the laser problem would be a great scientific achievement, even though it might not have any immediate practical use.

As he talked, I recalled the time when, as a young man with no particular qualifications, I created a couple of inventions that turned out to be important.

At the same time I thought of another young man who, in my Bendix days, had come to my New York office to present a proposal on which he had already made a patent application. He had no money to pursue the idea, an accelerometer based on a gyro. I neither knew enough, nor was I curious enough, to really understand the principle. In my eminence as an executive engineer, I turned down the man's proposal, just as a Navy bureaucrat had turned me away years before.

What the young man offered was the principle for a gyro compass—and other important aircraft instruments. Within five years, I knew the magnitude and stupidity of my decision.

In the meantime, I knew also what a dedicated young man can do by extrapolating present technology with a fresh vision into the future, not hindered by problems of the past. So I agreed to go forward with the laser project, asking for an occasional progress report.

Months later, Harley Iams, the division chief to whom the inventor reported, called and said, "Dr. Maiman has solved the laser riddle and repeatedly demonstrated the performance to his colleagues."

Mr. Iams asked for permission to make the announcement in a scientific publication. I agreed, provided that a fully-witnessed disclosure was made, dated the day of the first witnessed performance then followed as quickly as possible by a patent application. A patent was granted, the laser was introduced to the world, and thousands of uses have been subsequently proved.

Great laboratories do not inventions nor innovations make. They provide facilities and a suitable environment, but it is *people* who make the inventions. Judgments on inventions should be rendered by a peer who understands the work—not by a position occupant who does not. My view is that innovation comes from recognition of a need by a talent with the tools and motivation to observe or address it.

Syncom: What It's Meant to World Communications

During the past 100 years, several European scientists speculated about the possibility of satellites hovering over a single spot above the Earth by moving in orbit with the same angular velocity as the Earth. After hearing of the great work of Professor Goddard in America and of what German engineers did at Peenemunde, the scientific storyteller, Arthur Clark, speculated that three such satellites positioned at points equally spaced around the earth could provide global communications.

Following Russia's launching of Sputnik, the American military made frantic efforts to catch up by utilizing long-range missile engines as boosters for satellites. When a political hue and cry resulted from Sputnik's launch—as it had with introduction of the atomic bomb—Congressional policy concluded that national interest would be best served by taking control of atomic weapons away from the military and placing them under a separate Atomic Energy Commission.

Similarly, when Congress decided space activities should be divided between military control for space weapons and NASA for control of non-military uses of space, NASA set up several projects on space communications. Within a year, NASA invited bids on specifications for the Saint project, a system involving mid-altitude satellites and rotatable ground stations.

As noted previously, Hughes Aircraft was an unsuccessful bidder. We had spent a great deal of money working up our proposal; we were terribly disappointed by the failure to win. A large amount of valuable engineering time and millions of dollars of our own funds had been invested, backing our decision to go into the space age. With our limited capital, we would have to study very carefully any future ideas before committing funds.

Within this unfavorable environment two young engineers came to my office one morning in late 1959 to ask for a hearing on a proposition for a communication satellite.

Although my door was always open, it was usually entered by senior people with problems, or with proposals only mildly beyond existing state of the art—and within a believable company budget.

These two engineers admitted their offer fitted neither limitation, nor had their superiors approved of their proposal. Nevertheless, they felt their ideas were sound and potentially very profitable, so they sought and received permission to make their views known directly to me.

They had come to propose that Hughes Aircraft develop, build, launch and operate a communication satellite that would hover in a geographically stationary orbit at enormous altitude, held there by the centrifugal force of its 24-hour orbit. It would accomplish the vision of Arthur Clark.

Dr. Harold Rosen, who put together the elements of the basic system, and Dr. Donald Williams, whose mathematical computations determined the exact forces, orbits, times and control commands, collaborated in a step-by-step explanation.

A satellite would be launched into space by using three booster stages. The first would be the big Atlas missile engine and structure; the second would use a new and only partially-developed hydrogen engine and the third stage would need a completely new solid-fuel engine to be developed to our specifications. The launching had to take place from a point near the equator and be pointed East so that rotation of the earth would help the satellite get into position. On the way to its 22,300 mile-high orbit, the satellite would capture light from a certain star, Canopus, which would thereafter be its positional point of reference. The device would then be precessed to put its axis tangent to the desired final orbit and an engine be fired to increase speed and make the orbit a circle in space. Puffs of control gas would then drift the satellite to the desired longitude. Gradually the satellite would be precessed a further quarter-turn, to align its spin axis with that of the earth—all under fine guidance from the ground controllers—as it reached its final, precise, planned position.

They described radio frequencies to be used—one from ground to satellite, the other from satellite to ground.

The selection of a launch site was critically important because it had to provide the efficiency of an equatorial orbit and the safety of more than 1,000 miles from the launching site down-range to any inhabited land. From sites available, Christmas Island was chosen.

Admitting that the cost of the operation would run into many millions of dollars, they pointed out that a simple satellite with only a few channels of radio could produce revenues of $65 million a year, constituting a very profitable commercial venture.

Their presentation complete, the two engineer scientists stood on either side of the big easel on which they had drawn diagrams of various stages of the new system. They looked at me with expectant faces.

In a precious few seconds, I had to decide how to handle the situation. It was clear to me that at the time the company was in no position to undertake a new, large and unanticipated investment.

Rosen and Williams had outlined a complete system, had pointed out unknowns to be overcome and had admitted bold assumptions, which they were confident could be fulfilled. They did *not* understate probable costs, but delicately implied that it was my job to take care of that detail. They had chosen the launching area because of technical and safety reasons without regard for political and logistic considerations.

I felt Rosen and Williams had already survived several technical reviews more penetrating than any I could think of. My best chance of retaining their respect and enthusiasm, but declining to pursue their project, would be by setting forth the logistical, political and financial barriers I foresaw. I explained that the Christmas Islands belonged to Great Britain and the British were normally very reluctant to have another nation control pieces of their territory. It seemed to me political negotiations between the U.S. Department of State and the British Foreign Office could last a long time with no guarantee of approval. Furthermore, I said there were no true harbors at any of this group of islands, the remains of extinct volcanoes, rising steeply out of the sea. Landing heavy equipment and a constant stream of personnel and their supplies would present continuing problems.

I then told them the Hughes Aircraft image of financial stability, built up over the past 10 years, had become shaky owing to a shift away from manned interceptors. Our earnings had dipped. And although our backlog was building again, we were a long way from having the reserves, both in orders and capital, needed to maintain our present work force. I admitted that our future looked bright, but that we were operating with our resources strained to the limit. For the present, we simply could take no further risks.

I well remember how my mind was troubled during my response to Rosen and Williams. Everything I said to them was true, but was I looking for solutions or for problems? The famous line of Dr. Samuel Johnson kept coming to mind: *"Nothing will ever be attempted if all possible objections must first be overcome."* What they had proposed was too much for me to assimilate and endorse on short notice. I clung to my negative posture and wondered if time would ultimately gain me the insight to do the right thing.

After an hour of discussion, Rosen and Williams reluctantly agreed we should not proceed with the proposal at this time.

Later I discussed the matter with Dr. Puckett. He knew both men well and was convinced of their value to the company, but we were in agreement the project was pretty "far out" for consideration at that time.

A month went by. Then one morning Don Williams came to my office. He was no super salesman so I smiled to myself when he got right down to business: "Mr. Hyland, here is a certified check for $10,000. You told us the company was strapped for money. There are many of us in the engineering department who are certain the synchronous orbit satellite project is worthy of their investment and have agreed to put up their money with mine to help finance the project. This check is for my participation."

That Don Williams, a quiet and unassuming man, came to see me was indeed a tribute to his belief in the project. His willingness to risk his job against any opposition or his savings and reputation were strong arguments.

I had been faced with many challenges in a lifetime of civilian and military service, but never one quite like this. I was sure the word was already out amongst our thousands of engineers that Don was putting up his money to match his mouth and there would be keen interest in finding out what my answer would be.

In those days the very talented were scarce, moving from job to job based on performance, fortitude and imagination of upper management.

Taking the check from my desk, I looked at it and handed it back to Don. I told him this was a very serious matter and I appreciated the opportunity to review it again, because Dr. Puckett and I had been thinking about it during the past month. Then I told him I felt that before we could make a decision, it would be necessary to find another launching place, perhaps within the continental United States, even though it might involve more second or third stage total energy and perhaps a couple of course changes.

I also explained that the attitude of NASA in supplying a booster assembly or allowing one to be built by another company was something that had to be negotiated.

As to financing, I suggested we might find research money in either the military or NASA; we would examine that situation also.

I agreed the company would look into launching costs and the probability of success as well as into the availability of financing; while he looked into alternative launching sites and in-flight course changes. I added I thought we could have an answer in a couple of weeks, he seemed satisfied.

We shook hands on the agreement.

I immediately got together with Allen Puckett. We agreed the geosynchronous orbit communication satellite project was something that had to be looked at seriously, not only for the morale of our engineers (who were lifting us out of the tragic consequences of the F-108 fire control cancellation) but also because of the clear potential that might result from a communication satellite. Other communication satellite projects then under contract were in some kind of performance trouble. Nevertheless, progress was being made.

At Hughes, through the work of Rosen, Williams and a few of

their immediate colleagues, a step-by-step concept for achieving a valuable military tool as well as a means to address a huge commercial market was in hand. Our imaginations were inspired, attitudes changed and we began to find solutions to problems of a few months before.

Dr. Puckett went to Washington to talk with John Rubel, deputy director of Defense Research and Engineering and to Dr. Bob Seamans, deputy director of NASA, both top engineers in top jobs. They evidenced more than a little interest, which was all we needed.

I called in our comptroller and reexamined our research and development budgets. By our next Policy Board meeting, Puckett and I had agreed the project merited support; we could find $2 million, which over a two-year period would bring us far enough to make a formal presentation to the two government agencies that had shown interest.

Actually we were able to get government support in much less time because of increasing difficulties with the low and medium altitude satellite projects, particularly Saint.

Our work during the interval presented us with several surprises. Although we'd been in the missile business for several years, we found that neither it nor our prior aircraft experience was much help on the Surveyor program or other space projects. The enormous vibration encountered in rocket liftoff, stresses resulting from the extreme temperature differentials of 300-400 degrees Fahrenheit below zero on one side and superheat from the sun on the other side, had to be overcome. The extremely light weight and long life (seven to ten years) expected of a communication satellite required a level of design care, material selection, fabrication quality, testing and redundancy unheard of in any other devices. After launch, the repairman could never be called.

Our contract with NASA, funded 50 percent by DoD's Research and Development Agency, provided funds for two satellites to be launched beginning in 1963. The contract award started a scientific controversy about the utility of such a device if it were successfully placed in orbit. The time delay for a signal leaving the earth, going the 22,300 miles to the satellite, then returning to earth another 22,300 miles for a total of 44,600 miles, would cause a delay in transmission of voice of about a quarter of a second. It was argued that this delay, in combination with delays common to long distance lines on the ground, would present an intolerable break interval between talking and listening. We could and did simulate this condition experimentally by tests that artificially introduced such delays and found them to be of no consequence whatsoever in practice. However this did not silence critics. One physicist continued to predict the futility of such satellites.

When launch time arrived we were advised by the space group it would take approximately 18,000 seconds (five hours) from launch to positioning in the correct orbit, after which there would be the process of gradually (a day or two) bringing the satellite to the correct position over the operational spot on the earth, where it would remain under control of the ground unit.

Telemetered signals from the satellite on the way up indicated that all maneuvers took place on schedule. Our hopes grew that this concept of a useful space venture would be successful.

Time passed slowly indeed. But as the end approached, our people began to count up to the 18,000 seconds: seventeen thousand nine fifty five, fifty six, fifty seven, until ninety five, ninety six, ninety seven, ninety eight, ninety nine. Suddenly signals stopped.

We couldn't believe it.

One second to go and failure. It was hard to take, but at the end of two days of searching, we accepted the fact our first unit had failed.

Then began the search for the reason. We checked and rechecked tests and units for the second satellite launch. During these tests we found to our chagrin that one little high pressure, titanium, spherical bottle containing the positioning gas, which had proved to be completely reliable at ordinary pressures, developed a bad leak in the frigid vacuum of space. There were other charged bottles on hand. On the first two we tried, the same accident occurred.

Don Williams asked for use of our largest computer for an indeterminate time. He sat at the console for several days until he had his calculations and the results. If his calculations were correct, the satellite could be found by a high power telescope locked into position, so that stars would show up as long streaks on film, while the satellite would appear as a very short streak.

Consultation with astronomers indicated an observatory at Johannesburg, South Africa, would be suitable on certain days when the satellite would pass over that spot. We found that observatories are scheduled years in advance and it is virtually impossible to break into these schedules; however, by urgent pleas, we got permission to take photographs at Johannesburg. It was truly a shot in the dark and chances for success seemed infinitesimally small. But when the film plate was developed, lo and behold, there amidst the mass of long streaks was one tiny little streak: our satellite bathed in sunlight at its enormous altitude.

The gas leak from that little bottle was confirmed as the seed of the trouble. The bottle was redesigned to be immune to temperature shock.

That Rosen and Williams so accurately determined the fault, the amount of the gas leak and its effect on the vehicle's drift through space during so long a time, was more than a good guess. It was a miracle of analysis and synthesis—assisted perhaps by a few lucky assumptions.

Furthermore, we now knew unquestionably the accuracy of the satellite controls and the performance of the boosters. It was with more confidence than ever that we readied the second satellite for launch. This flight gave us an opportunity to check the telemetered information at every point against calculations and to further refine the course and look in more detail for potential problems.

In the meantime, critics were no longer questioning the likelihood for successful positioning, but were even louder in their predictions that the delay in transmission up and down would seriously interfere with acceptable conversations.

Knowing the answer would come from a successful launch and positioning in orbit, we relied on our simulated data and knew we could prove a satisfactory performance of the communication equipment.

Launch day finally came. Again we waited expectantly through the five hours until orbit had been established. This time the telemetering did not stop and perfect contact was maintained with the satellite, both during positioning in space and for several years thereafter.

Test conversations established the validity of our projections about excellent performance and absence of perceptible delay in conversation from person to person. It was interesting that performance was equally good from a neighbor across the street or two persons conversing over 8,000 miles.

The public was aware we had had a degree of success, but only when President Kennedy communicated to the Premier of Senegal by way of a ship carrying Bendix equipment stationed in Dakar was it demonstrated to radio and television reporters our synchronous orbit satellite experiment was a complete success.

Space: Where Do We Go From Here?

That success brought us a number of questions. Within the company we met to assess our position with respect to satellite communications. We could see three fields of action:

First, the satellite itself.

Second, ground stations for control of satellites and to terminate up-links and down-links.

Third, ground antennas associated with cable TV to provide commercial broadcast service.

We elected to participate in all three.

In the first category, we would go it alone. And in numbers two and three, we would look for partners.

Other companies interested in space ventures and communications were examining their interest and positions. For example, Western Electric almost at once terminated its efforts to build mid-altitude satellites and the very complicated ground stations associated with them. Some time later, AT&T, parent of Western Electric, reluctantly made a decision to buy satellites and satellite time for use in their Long Lines and International departments.

These were exciting times. It appeared the world was on the threshold of the first breach of established communications (both physical and, more recently, electrical) in more than 400 years.

Centuries ago, Sir Francis Drake sailed around the world, planting the English flag on islands, promontories and alongside waterways that would become the modes of world commerce. In the era of sailing ships, these were resupply points for fresh water and food. Then in later times these were ports for restocking of coal as well as water and food. Still later, these points were intermediate terminals for submarine cables of telephone and telegraph. Great Britain became the filter through which much of the world's government and commercial communication traffic had to pass. With competent decoding, the British knew well what was happening and (perhaps more important) what was going to happen throughout much of the world.

Suddenly the prospect arose of bypassing a huge, entrenched and enormously costly infrastructure using synchronous orbit satellite repeaters. The howls of pain and protest were a wonder to hear. The established long-distance carriers, various ministries of post and telegraph around the world, for once sang in unison: the synchronous orbit communication satellite *cannot and must not* be permitted.

Other companies took contracts from the United States military for low-altitude or mid-altitude satellites, all of which proved of little value for communications. Several decided to enter the synchronous satellite business by developing, over the long term, the expertise necessary to do the job. It was a long, hard road for them, as it had been for us. But after some years, four companies have succeeded in giving us strong competition, although for all there are patent infringements to be settled.

NASA as an Impediment

Before any government money entered the picture, we had made invention disclosures regarding synchronous orbit communication satellites to patent authorities at home and abroad and had reduced our inventions to practice.

NASA fought issuance of these patents every step of the way, but finally the courts decided in Hughes' favor and now additional litigation is necessary in order to establish the amount of damages.

Successful demonstration of the geosynchronous orbit satellite unleashed a host of competitive, political and administrative problems, both domestic and foreign. Although technology for satellites, their ground control and transmitter-receivers was now available, as were necessary ground networks—and even though financial opportunities were evident—years elapsed before we were able to launch the first commercial communication satellite, called "Early Bird." It was quickly overloaded with traffic and became the harbinger of the greatest revolution in communications since the beginnings of the telegraph and telephone.

Chalk up another one for research and development and the environment in which it can flourish.

From the Hughes Aircraft viewpoint, it was tragic that the United States government soon decided that a firm could not both build and operate commercial communication satellites. Commercial satellite operations were presently vested in COMSAT Corporation which did, we shall generously say, a poor job utilizing its literally golden opportunity.

Harold Rosen and Don Williams, who bucked the Establishment in invention and perfection of the geosynchronous satellite, were rightfully accorded acclaim. Rosen, though unassuming, gracefully acknowledged the tribute of admirers and associates. Don Williams, however, seemed unable to adjust to his new posture in the public eye. On one occasion when I presented him at an awards dinner by the local Junior Chamber of Commerce, he was visibly embarrassed and distressed by the applause.

One day when Dr. Puckett and I were at a space meeting in San Diego, we received an urgent telephone call. We were informed Don Williams, the mathematical genius, had shot himself.

He had wanted no acclaim or publicity. He only wanted tranquility and to be left alone with his math analyses and computations.

The people in his life, including me, had not understood that. I and others, had lacked the perception and sensitivity to recognize his dilemma. We failed to nurture the great gifts Don Williams possessed.

High Tech, Space Exploration Become Targets

Finally in the 1980s the law of averages hit the technology industries. A series of spectacular failures in space programs—particularly the loss of the shuttle Challenger and its entire crew before a television viewing audience of millions—was a focal point. The subsequent failure of the two remaining production boosters added to it and grounded the entire United States space program. These United States failures were followed internationally by the reactor explosion and partial core meltdown at Chernobyl, USSR and the failure of a European Arianespace launcher.

The Chernobyl disaster resulted from the conduct of an undisciplined experiment. The operating crew defeated the reactor's safety systems and backup safety systems in total breach of written instructions and prior training. The reactor core overheated, causing an explosion of superheated steam. The high temperature ignited blocks of graphite that interlaced the core. There was no available flood of inert gas to starve the fire. Burning graphite and reactor fuel together generated terrific heat, sufficient to vaporize a number of radioactive species in the core and allow them to billow into the atmosphere.

(In contrast to standard United States practice, the Chernobyl reactor was not enclosed by a containment structure.)

In the first half of 1986, United States and international nuclear and space domains were presented to the world as shocking spectacles.

The sorry performance of the United States space-launching organization was continued into 1987 when a satellite launch was attempted during a thunderstorm. The vehicle was struck and destroyed by lightning. There can be no extenuation of that inexplicable launch decision. It must be remembered that the people who originally made these new forces possible also knew how to contain them. If however, that knowledge is distorted by political expediency, unrealistic budgets, misinformation, public relations errors, procurement policies that do not value experience and is further immersed in inflexible schedule demands, then the benefits and promise of these new achievements will not be realized.

The nation was able to assemble a team of bright, skilled young people to perform the Apollo program. After the final lunar landing and safe return, the question was: "What do we do now?" The response was essentially silence. NASA was oriented almost completely to the space shuttle. Most of those Apollo teams dispersed. NASA found itself with a different lead crew, not the tiger Apollo team. The record of results matches the change.

Such is the degradation that happens to a big organization that goes on for years without a significant performance challenge and without inspirational leadership to focus attention, effort and enthusiasm. The same sort of thing (I'm tempted to say atrophy) is apparent in older, benevolent foundations of this country.

These same degradations and false economies are now intruding into United States civil aeronautics operations. The number of air-to-air near collisions or actual accidents has been rising each year. Of the technically-able nations of the world, the United States has the least sophisticated, least up-to-date system for air traffic control. Funds for modernization have not been listed in federal budgets on the grounds that the observed accident rate is acceptable to the public. The authorities decline to plan for avoidance of tragedy and instead await tragedies as a signal for action.

The real customers for technical systems are the nation's operating services, whether military, weather, communication, navigation or public utility—not the intervening bureaucracy. That fact seems to be forgotten all too frequently by both the bureaucracy and the public.

The several launcher disasters emphasize the hazards in complex, high energy systems in early stages of their development. In mid-1986, the free world found itself in these ridiculous positions:

1. The only available launcher at that time, outside of the Soviet Union, was in China.
2. With the unexpected short lives of two of its satellites, the United States had only one weather and one intelligence satellite in operational use.

Satellites are now important factors in both military and civilian life. Their management can no longer be entrusted to a government agency with an appointed head with undefined tenure and all other jobs protected by civil service. That situation is guaranteed to produce obsolescence and stifle talent, all at high cost. If this arrangement must continue, it should be governed from above. At the very least, there should be a commission, composed of representatives from science, industry, politics, communications, space medicine and the general society. From this board, a chairman and a vice chairman should be elected; one of them preeminent in technology, the other in administrative affairs. This commission would oversee the affairs and operations of operating government agencies in the same way a board of directors oversees the continuing operations of a company.

Communications Satellite Saga

In our company we were seemingly in a unique position with the geosynchronous satellite. But despite the fact we and our people invented the satellite and put up the money to prove the initial concepts, we were not allowed rights of ownership of patents, nor were we allowed to participate in use of the satellites (until recently for a quite different reason). We were required to compete for the right to manufacture and sell the satellite, although for some time this was academic because nobody else knew how. Leadership can only be maintained by leading. I stated that COMSAT (Communication Satellite Corporation), despite its virtual monopoly situation, was unfortunate in many of its business decisions and technical applications. COMSAT had to be sold and is now part of a communication company.

Another glaring example of leadership taken away is that of American Telephone and Telegraph. After being pecked at by government agencies for almost its entire life, AT&T was finally forced to divest itself of vital corporate associations and technical rights. The greatest business and public organization in the world was broken up by court decree and government persecution and prosecution. The consequence of this victory of government is that the cost of phone service to individual and corporate users has doubled, service has deteriorated and great technical and research and development organizations have been partially destroyed.

COMSAT (as a government-created monopoly), in association with the Federal Communication Commission, allocated spaces around the equator at which communication satellites could be placed. There was a mandatory separation of several degrees in order to avoid interference between radio waves from nearby satellites. Other considerations were that there were a limited number of ideal satellite locations for providing intercommunication between continents as well as across large land spaces and sprawling populations such as the USSR, China, Canada, Australia and the USA.

Finally it was decided that all usable locations had been allocated and therefore no additional satellites were needed or could be utilized. Our company, in its command of satellite techniques, found that the monopoly powers had neglected two particular spots that could be used for additional satellites. By then the deteriorated position of COMSAT and increasing powers of the Federal Communication Commission resulted in the commission granting those two spaces to Hughes. Now we were in the user business. We built two satellites and looked forward to a rosy future of rental income. That rosy glow soon disappeared. The Shuttle disaster of January 1986, coupled with two satellite engine failures, put the whole space program on hold until problems could be identified and remedies applied.

The Shuttle disaster was particularly bothersome because of prior decisions by NASA requiring future satellites to be launched into orbit from the Shuttle instead of by individual boosters. In order to assure this, NASA officials canceled work on new boosters and discontinued production lines on old boosters. The delay for the next Shuttle launch was 20 months. In the meantime the remaining quantities of Atlas and Thor boosters, used for launching satellites, began to dwindle. Soon the government gave total priority on use of these boosters to military purposes. That left commercial, weather and earth resources satellites without boosters.

A further difficulty now is with insurance. Satellite failures resulted in high losses to insurance carriers. These, coupled with several oil tanker losses and other commercial disasters, have made carriers either disenchanted with satellite insurance or forced to demand impossibly high premiums.

Hughes has tried to interest Chinese, French and Japanese space agencies in launching our satellites but without success (Editor's note: when this was written in the 1980s this was the case; subsequent efforts have generated international interest). The hitherto vaunted American "can do" capacity for organization and production has fallen flat on its face in the space era. But as in most earthly affairs, it is darkest before the dawn. The situation is critical enough that it is bound to turn around soon. We *can* recapture the zest, inspiration and satisfaction of those early years in space that have been so stunted by bureaucracy.

But at the current rate of progress, we shall need several years to get the program in full swing and to replace tired old leadership and confused bureaucracy with more vigorous, courageous and talented young people.

Chapter XI
Hyland's "Other" Jobs

During more than three decades—from the end of World War II to the mid-1970s—I had two "lives" running in parallel. First, of course, was my professional association; second was my participation on a series of long-lasting and *ad hoc* committees, variously serving the Federal Administration, the Department of Defense, National Aeronautics and Space Administration and the Central Intelligence Agency.

"Conflict of interest" taboos in United States law required that I carefully keep a wall between my two professions. Most of my committee colleagues coped with the same dual life. Both Bendix and Hughes donated my time and expenses without charge to the government. I devoted portions of my own time such as vacations, weekends or evenings and some expenses, also without charge to the government.

The motive for the companies and myself was to contribute to the nation during that quarter-century of transition in which weapons increased in range and lethality by factors of a hundred to over a million, a circumstance without parallel in history. That circumstance dictated a change in strategy from continental to global dimensions.

Leadership was supplied by a comparatively small number of people, perhaps as few as a couple of hundred. They came mostly from companies, colleges and the military services, where each continued to carry on normal full loads of work. These people were in the top rank of their own fields of interest and occupation, but they were all novices in the problems they faced in this transition era. It was new ground: nuclear energy, rockets, jet engines, missiles, semiconductors, supersonics, computers, satellites, inertial guidance and more.

My government committee work began because I was curious about the Navy's Bureau of Aeronautics post-WWII investigation of rocket propelled missiles similar to German V-1s and V-2s at the Applied Physics Laboratory of Johns Hopkins University.

I visited the lab and was most interested in their research. Ever since that initial visit I've been closely associated with some facet of missile activities.

Because of Bendix work for the Applied Physics Laboratory, I came to the attention of Carl Kellerman, then executive secretary of the development board that served the Department of Defense. Mr. Kellerman had me appointed to the first of a string of high-level government committees. Through these committees I had the opportunity to be involved with monitoring the entire United States missile program as well as in the transition from World War II-style of combat—from TNT bombs, artillery and foot soldiers—to so-called "push-button warfare."

Initially, I considered these committee memberships an honor or act of recognition as well as a public duty. But I soon came to feel there was a third and equally important aspect: it was a profound and broadening experience. I met and worked with excellent people and wrestled with new technical, public and strategic issues. This education by immersion made me, and surely others, a better generalist and manager.

The "Roots" of My Government Service

In 1947 I was invited to become a member of the Guided Missile Committee of the newly-established Department of Defense Research and Development Board.

That committee, with its control of research and development funds, was the first and most important organization to carry out the mandate of the public for "push-button warfare." The military members, one from each service, had flag rank. The civilian members were from industry and universities. During the first two or three meetings, I just sat at the committee table and listened, keeping a low profile. An admiral or general were rarely within the vision of a former enlisted man. I was equally impressed that the civilian members were top technical people from industry or academia, including deans, department chairmen or presidents of universities.

While showing due deference and respect to these august personalities, I remember a certain feeling I had from time to time in these early meetings. I was executive engineer of a major firm; from that lofty perch I judged that some of my high-level colleagues, both in and out of uniform, were a bit out of touch with the latest technology. In later years, when I became a high-level personality myself, beset with hordes of simultaneous pressures from all directions, I better appreciated and respected what those colleagues of earlier years had accomplished. I regret that I learned that lesson so slowly.

The Postwar Guided Missile Committee

Early meetings of the Guided Missile Committee were primarily occupied by bitter wrangling between a Navy vice admiral and an Army major general with the Air Force general occasionally breaking in to protect his service's interest. The controversies were over distribution of funds; the Navy had been given the largest allocation, the Air Force next and the Army at the bottom.

To my surprise, I found I could make a contribution to the work of the committee. None of the flag officers knew anything about missiles and very little about technology other than that represented in conventional military or naval equipment.

About $150 million and various former wartime facilities were at our disposal, ample for programs at that time. The Secretary of Defense and President Truman were adamant, to say nothing of Congress, however, about holding the line on expenditures. In the postwar period, there was a drive to lower the federal budget and get the huge debt from the war under control.

The Secretary of Defense, Louis Johnson, a fine West Virginia lawyer with neither military nor technical expertise, saw no political advantage in building and maintaining great test ranges for guided missiles that did not exist. The Secretary directed that the Guided Missile Committee survey all guided missile ranges in order to select one range for continued use and terminate activities at all others.

This order hit the Guided Missile Committee like a thunderbolt.

Recalling the success of the German V-1 and V-2 missiles, which almost brought England to its knees and aware of encouraging progress the United States was making, it seemed incomprehensible that such a directive could be given. Nevertheless, the order had been given; it was necessary to gather evidence, make a thorough study and report. The consensus was that a committee of two civilians should do the job. Because of my technical and industrial background, I was named chairman. The other member was Dr. C.C. Furnas.

We were briefed by the Navy on a small range at Johnsville, Pennsylvania and by the National Advisory Committee for Aeronautics about its small range in Virginia.

The major briefing concerned a 10,000 mile range from a base to be established at Cape Canaveral, Florida and extending in a Southeasterly direction over Ascension Island and ending south of the Cape of Good Hope below Africa. The presentation was made by the Air Force. It happened I knew about Cape Canaveral, having visited there in connection with blind landing operations during the latter years of World War II. I agreed with its suitability. It was ideal for testing long range missiles.

The Air Force briefing included proposed instrumentation facilities at Ascension Island and showing that the flight path was entirely over international waters. The Army supported the presentation, stating that a group of German scientists and missile experts had been brought from Peenemunde. We had the benefit of their work on V-2 missiles, a true ballistic type expected to have extended range.

The Air Force said range planning and equipment acquisition required time comparable to that for missile development and should be commenced immediately. We were impressed with the USAF briefing and also with information on the potential threat predicted by the Army because the Russians had captured over half of the experts at Peenemunde and had taken train loads of equipment to Russia. Intelligence information indicated that priority attention was being given this new weaponry by the Soviets.

We believed a visit to all projected missile ranges was necessary. However, Dr. Furnas said his work schedule could not accommodate time for such visits. However, I had already arranged to take a three-week vacation. Dr. Furnas volunteered that an analytical report on my visits, plus documentation from the briefings, should be adequate for our final report.

The Air Force provided a B-25 aircraft and assumed responsibility for logistics and arrangements for visits. The itinerary included the Air Force range at Alamogordo, New Mexico, the Army range at White Sands, New Mexico, the Navy medium and short distance range at Inyokern, California and the Navy long range facility at Point Mugu, California. Discussions with the Navy at Inyokern and Point Mugu made it clear that Navy medium and long range missiles would be launched from submarines; hence requirements for missile design and launch were completely different from land-based missiles.

Parenthetically I must say this was pretty heady stuff for a former Army artillery sergeant and Navy chief radioman. That euphoria lasted for perhaps an hour. Then I recognized the magnitude of my responsibility. The United States progress in missiles and atomic bombs since the end of World War II had been remarkable. That the Russians had made similar progress was probable. The threat of atomic bombs, carried by missiles having a range of a few hundred and later even a few thousand miles, was frightening indeed. It was my job to look, listen, evaluate, probe, gather every scrap of evidence and bring back documentation and objective opinions which we could fairly present to the Guided Missile Committee and through them to the Secretary of Defense. He needed a report from which he could determine policy and funding required for the protection of our national interests.

There was every evidence of cooperation, interest and high morale at all stops. When I returned to Washington, Dr. Furnas and I met for two days before the full committee was scheduled to convene. We were in complete agreement.

When the Guided Missile Committee convened, it was evident from the unusually large number of civilian and military personnel in attendance that many in the Defense Department were concerned about the demand to close ranges which they judged to be necessary for development of important new weapons. Chairman Dr. Clark B. Millikan of Cal Tech ultimately stated the meeting would be open for presentation of the Range Planning Committee and any subsequent discussion. I presented our report, outlining the situation at each of the five locations under consideration. After summarizing the sites, programs, projects, facilities, equipment, staff and logistics of each, I presented these recommendations to the full committee:

1. Range facilities in place were adequate for the present level of missile tests;
2. Within a year, range facilities then available would be inadequate for scheduled tests;
3. The rate of progress against plans was excellent; forecasting was on a sound, reasonable basis;
4. Competition between the Army and Air Force for range control exists at high levels, but cooperation at working levels on ranges is notable. Both Alamogordo and White Sands are needed, and though individual service requirements are different, they can be handled by working level cooperation.
5. The Navy installation at Inyokern is utilized for other than missile purposes; some instrumentation, materials and logistics are available for missile use. That portion presently funded which is used for short range infrared guided missiles is particularly well organized, has great potential and funding at current and forecast rates is appropriate;
6. The long Pacific over-water range being planned and installed by the Navy at Point Mugu for all classes of missiles for Naval aircraft, surface, and sub-surface ships, has appropriate yard and dock facilities nearby. The number and kind of launchers and environmental conditions to be encountered make it necessary to have these test facilities. Missile launches from ship decks and from submerged missile submarines, present issues different from those of ground and air launches. The vital importance of medium to long range missiles and the pioneering effort involved, justify the complementary approaches which superficially appear to overlap at Point Mugu and Cape Canaveral; both ranges are clearly needed;
7. Cape Canaveral is ideal for a range to test USAF missiles for long ranges. White Sands is similarly desirable for Army land-based medium ranges;

8. It is the conclusion of the subcommittee that present test range funding is barely adequate, that work is being carried on by competent, dedicated personnel with economy in their research, development and field operations; and with frugality in personnel housing and family accommodations;

9. We therefore recommend no changes in current operations or proposed fundings.

After discussion, Chairman Millikan called for a vote; the Guided Missile Committee adopted a resolution, confirming the findings of the subcommittee and approving forwarding those findings be sent to the Secretary of Defense.

Candor May Not Be the Best Policy

Within a few days Dr. Millikan called, stating that Secretary Johnson was infuriated by our report, had rejected it and had appointed a representative from his office to investigate the situation promptly. He was to present his report to the Guided Missile Committee, which would carry out his original instructions. The Secretary invited the committee to approve the plan for reductions at the next regular meeting.

At that meeting about three weeks later the investigator, a personable young physicist, presented his report. The meeting room was literally jammed with observers. There was standing room only, with dead silence as the meeting was opened. All realized that decisions to be reached that day might involve the security of the nation. Dr. Millikan called the meeting to order with a statement that, in view of the importance of the subject, we would devote the meeting entirely to the matter of missile test range planning. He invited the special investigator to report.

In his discourse, the investigator stated he had been directed by the Secretary of Defense to recommend a course of action which would allow all ranges except one to be closed with as little interference with the missile program's efficiency as possible. He did not state he had made any visits to the ranges nor had read the report of the subcommittee. He was articulate, but his remarks had little substance, included no technical factors, but did consider redundantly the

Secretary's directive and necessities for a reduced budget. At about the fifth repetition of this thesis, I became upset and seriously concerned we were getting a bureaucratic brush off that presented a real danger to this vital missile program.

I rose from my chair and said, "Mr. Chairman. I must state from what I have heard and now continue to expect, that this investigator has no qualifications for the task he has been assigned. That, as a matter of fact, he could not tell the difference between a guided missile and a backhouse."

For a short interval there was silence. Then observers and a couple of the Guided Missile Committee literally roared with laughter. They began to clap hands in a scene I had never before or since seen at any meeting or hearing I have attended.

When the furor died down a bit, Dr. Millikan rapped on the table, frowned at the committee and said, "I believe it is the intent of this committee that the investigator's report shall be rejected and that the report of the subcommittee shall be resubmitted to the Secretary of Defense. And I will entertain a motion to that effect."

The procedure was carried out and the meeting adjourned. I expected there would be hell to pay. But to my amazement neither Chairman Millikan nor I learned of any acknowledgment, recognition nor action on our report. There was no indication from any service that any funding change had taken place. It was as if the whole matter had never happened.

Our regular meeting was convened a month later in a normal environment—with one exception. On the wall behind the chairman were two large white plaques. On one was an outline of a large, streamlined shape with the wording, "This is a Guided Missile!" On the other was an outline of an old-fashioned outdoor toilet, with the wording, "This is a Backhouse!"

A Change of Administration Means a Change of Policy

This arrangement lasted until the election of President Dwight D. Eisenhower. He, of course, appointed a new Secretary of Defense who in turn appointed Dr. Don Quarles as Under Secretary in charge, among other things, of the Research and Development Board. Dr.

Quarles was a top-rank scientist-engineer. Prior to this appointment he had been president of Bell Telephone Laboratories. He was superbly qualified for the job—except in one very important government area: He didn't know the secret of real power.

Quarles' first lesson came from his experience with the Research and Development Board—of which the Guided Missile Committee was part. He had enormous respect for the civilian members of the board but was surprised to find they were burdened with not only technical but financial matters as well. He was accustomed to acting promptly; he ordered that the R&D Board be relieved of responsibility for financial matters. The result was apparent at the next meeting of the Guided Missile Committee. Where generals and admirals had previously been the military representatives, new appointees were present. They were captains and lieutenants. The function of the board was now advisory and no longer directive. Secretary Quarles, however, learned quickly and soon had personal control of all technical expenditures.

Secretary Quarles later invited me and a senior General Electric engineer and top jet engine expert, Neil Burgess, to be a committee of two to determine the need for, progress of and budget for the Air Force's Tullahoma, Tennessee, supersonic wind tunnel and its collateral facilities. It was intended to be capable of full-scale tests of engines and of some aircraft at high altitudes.

Tullahoma was truly a monster project. Electric power required placed an enormous load on the Tennessee Valley Authority; full power tests would have to be scheduled between midnight and five a.m. to avoid interference with power for homes and industry.

The assignment initially required monthly visits and then quarterly checks for a couple of years. Our committee of two approved plans and progress of this great project, which proceeded to completion without either military or political questioning.

Korean War Changes Ground (or Air) Rules

With the onset of the Korean War, Congress, in a burst of patriotism, hurriedly made large appropriations in support of the "police action" in Korea. Specifically, funding for the guided missile program was doubled and appropriate action ordered by the Secretary of Defense. Competition between the United States military services for missile funds became so severe (particularly long-range missiles) that President Truman had to intervene. He appointed K.T. Keller, former chairman of Chrysler Corporation, to become, literally, the missile czar, giving him complete authority for financial and technical decisions.

The services started wrangling amongst themselves on amounts to be allocated to each. Recognizing there was only one way to cut this Gordian knot the committee agreed to divide funds equally. We addressed the committee's work towards accelerating range instrumentation and logistics, reducing time between range experiments and appropriate utilization of results. During this period the Navy developed the Sidewinder missile, that turned out to be one of the most effective aerial weapons of the era.

The appointment of Keller was fortunate, particularly since his crony, Dr. Robert R. McMath, was not only a notable astronomer but also board chairman of his family business. Thereafter a working arrangement was made in which the Guided Missile Committee supplied a considerable amount of expertise; Dr. McMath, the astronomer, acted as liaison and head of a small elite group from the military side; Keller provided the muscle.

It became apparent, however, that dominance of the military in this wartime atmosphere made expenditure control by a civilian research and development committee almost impossible.

Beginnings of the U.S. ICBM

Meanwhile, the Air Force had appointed a high-level committee of its own, initially called the Inter-Continental Ballistic Committee, but later known as the von Neumann Committee because of the eminence of its chairman, John von Neumann.

With establishment of the new Air Force Research and Development policy under Trevor Gardner, Under Secretary of the Air Force, and my appointment to the von Neumann committee, I resigned from the Guided Missile Committee of the Department of Defense.

The Air Force committee consisted of renowned scientists and aeronautical engineers. I was the "odd man out" who was neither a scientist nor aeronautical engineer.

Mr. Gardner told me privately he wanted me on that Air Force committee because of my performance on the DoD Guided Missile Committee. Moreover, he said the Air Force needed advice from experienced, pragmatic engineers of demonstrated capability.

Of those on the committee, I already knew Dr. Millikan of Cal Tech and Dr. Puckett. I had worked with Charles Lindbergh in 1927 when he was considering a small radio for his Atlantic flight. But the balance I had never met.

At the first meeting of the committee, we were introduced to the celebrated Dr. John von Neumann. He outlined the initial purposes of the committee, then emphasized the need to select for further production one of three existing Inter-Continental missile projects. He also said it appeared the funds to pursue the project were such that only *one* of the Air Force candidates could be considered.

He appointed three separate committees. The first would look at the Northrop Snark and be chaired by Dr. Millikan. The second would be chaired by Pat Hyland and would check out the North American Navajo. The third would examine the General Dynamics Atlas and be chaired by Dr. von Neumann himself. He said the studies should be conducted within three days. The committee would then reconvene with each chairman reporting.

Fortunately, I knew a good deal about the North American Navajo, though I doubted anyone on the committee knew that.

Counseling North American About the Frontiers of Space

My exposure to that program went back a few years. Immediately after World War II, North American Aviation, chaired by "Dutch" Kindelberger, was in the same predicament as all of us. Within a couple of days our entire government business had, for all practical purposes, been canceled. We were scrambling for something to do. At North American they had nothing else on their string but military airplanes.

In desperation, Kindelberger went to see Ernie Breech. He had been appointed chairman of Bendix only a short time before, but still had his office in the General Motors' building. Dutch felt that GM should help solve his problem because they owned about 23 percent of North American, giving them practical control. Breech told Kindelberger there was nothing GM could offer because the corporation was going to be busy for the foreseeable future converting back to automobile production. Breech also explained that he felt none of GM's aviation interests fitted North American requirements. However, he did say there was an engineer at Bendix named Pat Hyland who knew something about missiles; since the public was interested in push-button warfare, Pat might have some suggestions.

Breech sent for me; and I met with "Dutch" Kindelberger. In effect I told him: There wasn't much in the aircraft business that looked promising, but there were real opportunities in the missile business. Among other things, I mentioned that missile programs were amply financed, not the case with other projects in defense. Four or five companies were interested in designing missile fuselages, but since not very much was known about space, except by the Germans, everybody was currently working along the same lines. I told him the real opportunity was in missile engines. He could step in with the kind of know-how and drive North American had always shown, achieving something in the missile engine business.

Dutch shook his head. "But we don't know anything about engines."

"Neither does anybody else in this country," I assured him. "Up until the last day of the war, Pratt & Whitney was in full-scale production, using all of their engineering and manufacturing resources to deliver piston engines to the Navy and Air Force. Now Pratt & Whitney, along with Curtiss-Wright, is scratching and clawing to get into the aircraft jet engine business. General Electric is interested in jet engines, but all of their know-how has been focused on steam turbine production."

I said GE did have some German know-how and was trying to make a copy of the V-2 rockets, but I'd heard they were not doing very well. I understood Westinghouse had no particular interest in the jet engine or missile engine business. In sum, I told him I believed there was an opportunity to develop a large engine for guided missiles and to start almost level with everybody else in the United States.

"In my opinion," I added, "German technology is just as available to North American as to any other producer."

Kindelberger decided his company should get into intercontinental ballistic missiles with big rocket engines. He hired several German engineers as consultants; with characteristic Kindelberger energy, he went after business in a big way. He found a ready customer in the Air Force.

North American's progress was phenomenal. They set up a missile engine office and test station at the foot of the Santa Susanna hills in Canoga Park, California and commenced engineering for a new launching concept. They would piggy-back the missile on a large carrier airplane for the initial part of the flight. It would take the missile up to 30-40,000 feet and give it enough forward velocity to help the missile continue its onward flight to the target with only an onboard engine. It eliminated the need for a larger powerplant that would have been required to get the missile off the ground.

A few months later, as part of my position on the Guided Missile Committee, I spent several days at North American viewing their first approach to the rocket engine. I checked out beginning construction at their Downey plant, visited Canoga Park and inspected their test site in the Santa Susanna hills.

When our subcommittee was assigned the North American Navajo project, I brought in several North American engineers to describe their project. Addressing topics the subcommittee needed to understand, we soon had a grasp of progress and were impressed by parts of it.

When the full committee reconvened, I explained that our subcommittee felt the North American's piggy-back missile launch approach might be both costly and unsatisfactory. It would require development of not only the missile structure, but also of a new type of aircraft.

I reported that progress made by North American in their conception of the rocket engine, of aerodynamics involved in the nozzle structure and of overall understanding of what it would take to do the job, was impressive. Regardless of which structure was selected for the missile fuselage, we thought North American's engine would be necessary. I said the Army-backed GE approach seemed to be going nowhere and there was no other avenue for development of an appropriate engine.

A Decision on the First U.S. ICBM

Dr. von Neumann gave his report on General Dynamics' Atlas program. His analysis was quiet, effective, thorough and to the point. His presentation showed an enormous command of logic and language. In masterly fashion, he dissected both Millikan's and my remarks and concluded the Atlas approach seemed by far to have the best prospect for early success, but agreed with me on utilization of the North American rocket engine. Finally, he presented the whole proposition for the committee's consideration. Most committee members were being introduced to this kind of team operation for the first time. There was considerable discussion for the rest of that day. We reconvened the following day to determine a plan for further conduct of the committee and to create instructions for the Air Force and contractors.

Under John von Neumann's direction and guidance, the committee came up with a very presentable report. It formed the foundation of what was to be a successful Air Force program. After Dr. von Neumann's premature death, the committee once again became the Inter-Continental Ballistic Missile Committee but his stamp on it and its work will last forever.

Soon a Colonel Ben Schriever was placed in charge of Air Force activities in the Inter-continental Missile field and brought together an astonishingly capable staff to assist him.

Existing aircraft, engine and radio control experience was of little use in a completely new technical era. Only the little known Dr. Robert Goddard of Worcester Polytechnic in Massachusetts had performed embryonic work on the first American rocket in a field not far from his college. Dr. Goddard was revered in rockets. The Germans had gotten their main ideas for the liquid-fueled rocket technology from Goddard's work. It enabled them to come up with V-2 engines.

For the American long-range ballistic missile, exotic fuels at high pressure were required to supply the flame to produce gases that flowed from the combustion chamber through the nozzle. Guidance, accomplished by gyros, required new orders of accuracy. At every turn there seemed to be new and hitherto unsolved problems.

Needed: A Coordinating Agency

Early on it became apparent there was no agency available to manage the whole system. A new organization had to be created to supervise and integrate design work on contributing tasks and ultimately to oversee production. No existing industrial organizations could undertake such an assignment. It was necessary to enlist hundreds of the best talents in our country—an extraordinary group of scientists and engineers from industry, university and military environments—into a single organization. It could be put together only by offering salaries and working conditions attractive enough to detach excellent people from secure positions. Such people came high.

Strangely enough, the beginnings of such an organization already existed. In the early 1950s the remarkable, but turbulent, Hughes Aircraft organization had begun to disintegrate at the top. The two leading engineers, Simon Ramo and Dean Wooldridge, along with nearly 100 other employees, left Hughes Aircraft in a body after a final unsatisfactory meeting with Howard Hughes. This group set itself up as an organization with headquarters in what had been a small barber shop. They were well-known and respected by the Air Force because of their achievements in advanced technical systems at Hughes Aircraft. They needed affiliation with a major, non-competing company as their sponsor while they sought work for their new company.

At the informal suggestion of USAF, Ramo and Wooldridge contacted Thompson Products Corporation of Cleveland, Ohio. That organization was headed by a very unusual individual, Fred Crawford, who had great competence, imagination and vision. After hearing their story, Crawford offered them a proposition that Ramo and Wooldridge accepted. They were in business.

Initially the company was called Ramo-Wooldridge. It later became Thompson, Ramo, Wooldridge. It is now the huge TRW Corporation.

Within the von Neumann committee there were in depth discussions about how the big missile operation could be conducted. Serious consideration had to be given to backing the Ramo/Wooldridge Corporation as system integrators and manager.

General James H. Doolittle, an important consultant to the Air Force, was brought in to meet with Schriever, Gardner, me and a couple of Gardner's aides. With the public in a flurry of postwar buying, most big companies were in the burgeoning production of consumer products. None were willing to make the necessary arrangements for big missile work.

Ramo and Wooldridge had done an outstanding job at Hughes Aircraft. They seemed willing to undertake the new missile operation, providing the Air Force would furnish the initial administrative support.

Near the end of the meeting I pointed out that we were endorsing a major innovation in the American industrial process. We were going to set up an organization of the utmost competence necessary to accomplish this job. But looking ahead, I could also see that in 5 or 10 years—when new technology had spread throughout the industry and this same competence became more widespread—we would have introduced a capable and experienced competitor that would be a continuing problem for all of us. But I, for one, was willing to take that risk because I saw no other way in which the Inter-Continental Ballistic Missile program could be accomplished.

There were nods of approval; without a formal vote the committee agreed we should back Ramo/Wooldridge, a decision that proved to be one of the best ever made.

My forecast has also been realized because today TRW is a force to be reckoned with in many sectors of the United States industrial system.

CIA Committee Activities

One afternoon at Bendix, I had an unexpected visitor from Washington. Dr. H. Marshall Chadwell quickly got down to business: President Truman had wanted the matter of Inter-Continental ballistic missiles examined by the intelligence community; so, he asked the Interdepartmental Intelligence Committee to prepare a report. That committee, consisting of 28 individuals from the 28 different intelligence activities in government, was presided over by an Army lieutenant general who appointed a subcommittee to do the actual investigation and draft a report.

Dr. Chadwell, the subcommittee member from the CIA, was dissatisfied with the composition of his subcommittee, even questioning his own ability to handle usefully such an assignment. He had received permission from the CIA director to establish a group of senior scientists to act as his advisors and be available to the Interdepartmental Intelligence Committee at the time of the report. He asked that I chair the group and choose the members. I was flabbergasted. However, he insisted that the scientific, military and business communities had agreed on the choice and that I should regard it as a vote of confidence.

I finally said I would take on the job. To my surprise, the first four persons I approached agreed to serve: Dr. Robert McMath, astronomer and mathematician; Dr. George Kistiakowski, Harvard professor of chemistry; Dr. Francis Clauser, an explosives consultant and one of scientist twins (his brother, Milton, was professor of aeronautics at the California Institute of Technology); and Dr. Chadwell himself.

When the Interdepartmental Intelligence Committee convened, the chairman introduced our group as having scientific competence in the field and proposed we comment after the report had been delivered. We listened with interest to an articulate introduction; as the presentation continued, our interest changed to questioning, then to doubt, then to disbelief. We were hearing an uninformed amateur's version of the American missile program represented to be what the Soviets were doing and what the Americans would have to defend against. There was no hint of understanding that the strategic requirements of each country were radically different. I watched our group's increasing anger, disgust and even amazement. The faces of the Interdepartmental Intelligence Committee members, by contrast, exhibited interest, acceptance, even admiration.

At the end of the presentation, the general praised the report as being the finest the committee had ever listened to and asked for comments. Practically all those on the Interdepartmental Committee confirmed the general's words; it was a regular love feast of admiration and satisfaction.

The general finally turned to us and stated in a somewhat

condescending way: "I should now like to call on the advisory committee for what comments they may have to make on this fine report."

As chairman, I commented: "General, this is a very serious situation we are facing. The threat posed by Inter-Continental missiles is something that never before has even been imagined and it must now be recognized. The President must be properly advised as to the gravity of the situation. Therefore, I am going to be blunt. I have never in my life listened to such a bunch of crap as that just delivered by the subcommittee and by the various members of the committee. I go farther and say that as I look around this table, I see lawyers, accountants, administrators and bureau chiefs. Everything but engineers and scientists who can appropriately grasp the technical facts of this situation. The report you have been given is not only worthless, it is misleading. You dare not issue such a report to the President of the United States. I'm not looking for a job, but if you want an appropriate estimate of the dangers, the threats and the promises associated with Inter-Continental ballistic missiles, our group will write the report for you."

The mouths of the committee members on the other side of the table hung open in disbelief. The general said, "I see." Then, "I think we may now excuse the members of our scientific advisory group."

We went directly to the office of the CIA director. The agency's representative on the subcommittee reviewed what we had done. After a moment the director smiled and said, "I think you should go ahead with the report."

We went to work. Although we'd cooled off a little, we were firm in our conviction that we had to write a full, technically correct, militarily sound assessment of the picture. About the time we finished, we learned the Interdepartmental Committee had accepted our offer. We delivered the report, the committee approved it a few days later and, after crossing a few t's and dotting a few i's, sent it to the President. It is apparent that it exercised considerable influence on subsequent United States policies.

I think the dedication and competence of the Interdepartmental Intelligence Committee officials is proven by their action in this situation. They recognized the weakness of their position when it was pointed out and saw their responsibility to take appropriate action. It speaks well for the country that we did what we did and they did what they did.

I remained chairman of that committee for the next 20 years, resigning only when I could no longer make informed judgments on the technology involved. The committee averaged five or six civilian members and one member each from the top level of the Army, Navy and Air Force. Our mission was expanded from time to time and included not only ICBMs but other items of strategic importance such as strategic aircraft, ground radar, ground-to-air missiles, intermediate range missiles, atomic bombs, reentry vehicles and space. As time progressed and the technology increased, we achieved and sustained a good understanding of the Soviet and Chinese strategic weapon programs. We were impressed by the rapid progress of the Chinese both in bomb technology and in long-range missiles to deliver them. They did very well in preparing to defend themselves.

The President's Scientific Advisory Committee

On several occasions I was urged to become a member of the President's Scientific Advisory Committee, PSAC. Finally, after looking at the legislation on conflict of interest, I asked for an opinion from the Department of Justice as to the propriety of such an appointment. After a month or so I received a seven-page document saying my appointment would be permissible. I was, however, bothered by the last sentence of the last paragraph. It said that while the appointment was apparently satisfactory, the Department could give no assurance that no difficulties would arise under future circumstances. What did that mean? I decided to forego the PSAC appointment.

I did participate in several panels—involving space and Inter-Continental ballistic missiles—set up with a PSAC member as chairman. For example, the Titan missile, the largest of our Inter-Continental missiles and backbone of our deterrent capability, was beginning to evolve into final configuration. There was, however, disagreement about fuel for the first stage. It was critical because one combination of fuels, albeit more efficient, should only be loaded at the last minute. Another fuel combination—somewhat less efficient for propulsion—could be put into first stage tanks and remain there permanently, providing an immediate readiness for action.

Somehow, the disagreement got beyond usual channels within the Air Force and had not been resolved by the missile czar. It had gone past the Joint Chiefs of Staff and came into the hands of the President.

There were not only the military people involved, but also contractors who had muscle. The President decided the matter should go to his Science Advisory Committee for resolution; he charged Dr. Killian with achieving a solution. Dr. Killian chose me as arbitrator in this controversy. In his book about those critical years, Dr. Killian explained in one paragraph why he chose me for the job. He stated, "Hyland was not only a great engineer but also a master of the expletive." In other words, those personal attributes that had been responsible for my trouble in Bendix were now going to be utilized to resolve an important national issue.

Time was of the essence; I requested a detailed briefing from each side and included military, civilian and contractor personnel.

The performance deficiency of the permanent fuel was not sufficient to interfere with practical launching of the missile itself. But we found situations where time required to put fuel in the missile could be longer than the time of flight of an enemy missile to this country. It was clearly apparent we had to decide in favor of permanent fuel.

That decision was communicated to President Truman through Dr. Killian; the President settled the controversy once and for all.

CIA and the U-2 Mission

Another special assignment came much later. Eisenhower had succeeded Truman; then been succeeded by Kennedy. Early in his Administration, President Kennedy proposed that within ten years the United States land men on the moon and return them safely. This was one answer to the shock of the USSR's Sputnik orbit. Americans were horrified by Sputnik. In a crash program the Army Redstone Arsenal in a few months was able to launch the first United States satellite, a small spent rocket case.

The United States soon announced the Project Mercury "Man in

Space" program. But the Russians were first to orbit a manned capsule. There was a mad rush to reorganize NASA to carry out Mercury. Then, to further weld the national will and pride to a major goal, President Kennedy announced the Lunar manned landing program, Apollo. These were splendid responses to the Russian achievements—but they did not explain how and why the United States had lost the space initiative to the Russians in the first place.

Although the story is relatively simple, it has never been properly explained to the American public.

We had actually been too successful with our Inter-continental missile program. Our guidance equipment was so accurate that instead of building huge rocket boosters to heave large warheads into space, we were able to do the same military job with much smaller warheads; hence smaller boosters were designed with increased effectiveness on target. These smaller (less costly) boosters resulted in much less nuclear fallout; thus were less damaging to the population in the northern hemisphere. The upshot is that the United States initially did not need—did not have—boosters capable of putting heavy payloads into orbit.

Realization of the Russians' plan, however, was slow to come. Almost from my first association with the Central Intelligence Agency, our efforts were devoted to trying to determine what the Russians were doing about nuclear warfare. We were, of course, taking advantage of work the Germans had done in making rocket boosters; we assumed the Russians were doing the same. The considered belief of the United States scientific community, however, was that the Russians would be somewhat behind our progress on atomic energy. That was *not* an appropriate conclusion. Very little information came from secret agents because the Russian work was being conducted in guarded areas isolated from the rest of the country. We turned to U-2 photography.

The U-2 observation aircraft program was financed by the Central Intelligence Agency. The aircraft were built under the supervision of the great Kelly Johnson of Lockheed and Richard Bissel of the CIA.

The Russians had radars of extraordinary capability. As U-2 flights progressed, we found their radar coverage progressing as well. As a flight proceeded farther and farther into the Soviet Union, radar information on its progress was handed from station to station.

Fortunately, the Russians did not yet have a ground-to-air missile that could reach the U-2's altitude. As our photographic coverage and quality increased, we were able to get somewhat of an idea of USSR progress on booster development by observing the scale of assembly buildings and launch facilities at their Tyuratam development facility.

Permission from the President to make overflights of Russia was becoming harder to get. President Eisenhower, who appeared to have a fond hope of winning a Nobel Peace Prize, was limiting all United States actions that might be considered provocative or stimulating international disapproval.

As rumors of Russian progress continued, authorization to make an overflight of the northern Russian area was delayed longer and longer. Finally, approval was granted. The wait for suitable weather was the only obstacle.

The day finally came when the U-2 Russian mission was launched. Unfortunately, it was too late. When the aircraft was well inside the USSR and headed towards the reconnaissance target, a guided ground-to-air missile was launched. It exploded near the aircraft, damaging it, but not destroying it. When it crashed, the aircraft and pilot, Gary Powers, were captured. The American intelligence effort was a complete failure. Of course, there was not only national frustration but international disapproval of what had taken place.

Scattered Intelligence Gathering

Our intelligence estimate, put together from scattered bits of information, rumors and educated guesses, was given to authorities. We reported that at Ploecetz the Russians had built a large military installation with between 10 and 20 huge missiles in place, along with support people and equipment needed to launch missiles. We did not doubt the missiles could carry large-yield nuclear warheads.

Much later we found our estimate was correct. In the meantime, American missile development efforts were increased.

But of much more concern to the American public, the Russians, using their much larger booster, were able first to launch Sputnik on its round-the-world orbit and later to launch a capsule with a man in it to circle the globe.

The decision was made that our goals in space would be divided between military objectives under existing Department of Defense structure and a new space administration built around the former National Advisory Committee for Aeronautics, NACA.

A search was made for leadership of this new space organization. Vice President Lyndon Johnson was charged with responsibility for this national search. I was among the first candidates he interviewed. He urged me directly and indirectly to take the job. In the course of two long telephone conversations I thanked him for his consideration but told him I was not the man for the job.

I explained that he already had in Dr. Hugh Dryden of NACA the best *technical* leader in the country. But additionally, the new administrator needed to be a skilled politician of great intellectual capability. He would need a tough hide to withstand criticism, especially during the early years of unspectacular performance while costly development was underway. The administrator must also be able to accept the recommendations of the technical visionaries who had convinced John Kennedy of the high probability for success.

The man chosen, James Webb, a North Carolina lawyer, was ideal for the job. The combination of Webb and Dr. Dryden was exactly the right leadership for the task in this rapidly expanding technological world.

The dedication, enthusiasm and pragmatic vision they were able to bring, together with the best elements of technology, industry, politics and people, provided a functional, economical achievement of the objective.

An Opportunity Inside the Government

After a few months on the Air Force's Tullahoma supersonic wind tunnel assignment, Secretary Quarles asked me to lunch at the Pentagon. We dined in a room adjacent to the office of the Secretary of Defense. After lunch he and the Secretary urged me to take the job of director of the Research and Development Board. I told them I did not feel competent; the job required the highest political, technical and management experience plus special educational qualifications.

They pointed out that I had unusual qualifications, adequate education because of my active Army and Navy experience, a commendable performance record at the Naval Research Laboratory and demonstrated industrial management success. I was flattered, but told them my family obligations and limited finances made it impossible for me to accept.

I left feeling uplifted, hardly believing that such an offer might have been made by such an eminent man as Secretary Quarles.

Government Committees Changed My Life

My association with the Guided Missile Committee of the Research and Development Board had marked an important turning point in my life. Although prior to then I had had a series of interesting work assignments, covering a lot of geography that had provided me with experience in several new industries, I was nevertheless bound by a need to support my family, satisfy my superiors or customers and maintain a professional scope limited to immediate and future requirements.

My years with the Guided Missile Committee changed that. My span of interest expanded greatly, including concern for matters of national and even international impact. I was exposed to some of the best minds—political, military, technical, industrial, educational and social—in the country.

Concurrent with my participation on the von Neumann Committee, I was appointed to the Scientific Advisory Committee (later called the Hyland Committee) of the Central Intelligence Agency; then to a Space and Missiles Panel of the President's Science Advisory Committee in June of 1948. I declined membership on the Advisory Committee because I was running out of time and did not care for the pertinent legislation.

Another government assignment was given me at the suggestion of Dr. Jerome Wiesner, then Provost of MIT and chairman of the President's Scientific Advisory Committee. He asked me to become a member of a group of five to examine the Apollo and "first Man in Space" programs. In the '50s, I agreed to be a member of the

Advisory Committee of the Argonne National Laboratory of the Atomic Energy Commission. To aid my usefulness on that job I was offered a course lasting about a month given to government executives at the Oak Ridge National Laboratory.

My exposure to, and participation in, the pioneering stages of exotic systems was a further chapter in my unorthodox education.

The "Man in Space" Adventure—from the Ground

Great minds tried to assess the probable difficulties awaiting manned flight into the stratosphere. Most recognized that the unknown usually contains the unpredictable.

The launching site at Cape Canaveral near Melbourne, Florida, was selected as base for the United States space program because it was already partially equipped with everything needed except the launcher itself; a contract for the launcher had been let. Overall administrative and design was to be in Houston. Specifications on the Mercury spacecraft were prepared and bids received from aircraft contractors.

The capsule project was awarded to McDonnell Aircraft Company, St. Louis, which was unusually well qualified. It had a long history of design and production of high performance military aircraft, recent experience with a solution, after painful failures, of a serious fighter plane tail flutter problem, and had been chosen by Johns Hopkins Laboratory to do structural design and ramjet booster for the large Talos missile.

As the Mercury capsule program was nearing completion, final preparations for a manned flight were in progress when President Kennedy called in Dr. Jerome Wiesner, then his Science Advisor, and asked him to form a committee to examine the readiness of the project and to assay the probability of mission success.

The President told Dr. Wiesner that every precaution must be taken that the mission not fail; he was, however, aware of the risk. He stated that the reputation of the United States *vis-a-vis* Russia would receive a humiliating blow if our first attempt failed.

Dr. Wiesner appointed a committee of five. Four were members of the President's Science Advisory Committee, among whom were an eminent biologist, a prominent medical doctor and a couple of physicists. The chairman was Dr. Edward E. David, a renowned physicist of Princeton University. I was the fifth appointee.

Dr. Wiesner, no stranger to large and difficult technical projects, knew the Mercury Advisory Committee had to have great scientific stature. But he also wanted one pragmatic engineer with them. At our initial meeting, he outlined what the President wanted and why, noted the various centers we should visit, wished us well and hoped for a prompt report. On the way out, he walked with me and said, "Pat, I want you to know that you have a great responsibility in this matter."

For our initiation into the project we assembled at Langley Research Center in Virginia, one of the older National Advisory Committee for Aeronautics centers. We were thoroughly briefed by Langley officials on the philosophy of the Mercury project, the centers where work was progressing, a likely timetable and some of the more esoteric problems that had arisen in the past several months.

We visited Cape Canaveral and the launching site, which as I recall, was either the original or a copy of the Atlas launching structure. I had been there once before when the Air Force was in the middle of the Atlas program. Since those early days, the launching operation was regarded as routine.

Our primary interest was safety of the astronaut. If there was a failure on the launching stand, or in the first 200-300 feet, or at 1,000 feet, or 100 miles, what could he do? The answers given were prompt and satisfactory. It was evident the launch people had gone far beyond our simplistic questions in their studies as to risks involved and how they could be handled to ensure safety of the astronauts under any conditions.

Along the way I had become impressed with the performance of my fellow committee members. They were not bothered by unfamiliarity with the technology of this project. They wanted more information about things they did not know about rather than those things they were familiar with. They asked questions about little things that brought answers surprising to all of us. For this task Wiesner had chosen well.

From Canaveral we went to Houston. We met Dr. Bob Gilruth, project manager, and the remarkable Chris Craft, both of whom participated in our briefing. Dr. Gilruth was knowledgeable, soft spoken and his pleasant manner disguised an ethical and hard-nosed competence. A third and important man we met was the medical director, Dr. Berry, responsible for the health, both mental and physical, of the astronauts. He was a pioneer in this new space specialty; his wisdom and carefully thought-out procedures, combined with a natural liking for people, established a pattern since followed in all subsequent American man-in-space operations.

Each of the astronauts briefed us on important aspects of the proposed flights. They were good speakers, radiated confidence, enthusiasm and readiness. As they spoke, I formed my own opinion about the most likely candidate for first flight. I put Glenn as the one most likely to make the first flight for the 800-mile penetration of the stratosphere and Shepard the one to make the first orbital flight. I had the order reversed. Shepard made the first flight and Glenn the first orbital flight.

Our final visit was to McDonnell Aircraft at St. Louis. We were met by James McDonnell, chairman and president (Editor's note: the famed "Mr. Mac" who ruled over his company empire). He conducted us through his plant where F-4 fighters were in production. There was a long production line; the big facility was busy, orderly and radiated good management.

Under the guidance of the Mercury project manager we saw the test pond and tall crane from which the capsule had been dropped with the same speed it would have when the parachuted spacecraft dropped onto the ocean. We saw the "different" shape of the capsule and were assured that aerodynamic tests and the initial monkey-crewed flight had demonstrated it to be aerodynamically sound for reentry into the atmosphere. Approximately conical, it reentered the atmosphere with the blunt end first. Energy, converted into heat by a shock wave over the blunt end, was continued until the capsule was slowed down enough for parachutes to be opened, permitting descent to the ocean surface.

As we returned to Washington, I felt many of our uncertainties had been resolved. I could find no soft spots in any briefings, equipment, or people—a remarkable situation for such a complex project. The committee convened one day ahead of our date with Dr. Wiesner. We reviewed the presentations, inspections and questions at each center and, in particular, the risks and probabilities that had been discussed with the astronauts. They were all experienced flight personnel.

I knew McDonnell had been through a painfully difficult time in solving a tail flutter problem on the original Navy F-101, prototype of the F-4. That experience had made them extremely sensitive to safety. It was a sensitivity McDonnell carried over to the Mercury project.

Almost without debate, we came to the conclusion that risks to be expected in the first two Mercury flights were about the same as could be expected on the first flight of any new, high performance aircraft. In spite of efforts to anticipate everything, unknowns would surely crop up. But we thought it unlikely that a problem of serious magnitude would arise. The training, extended practice with the equipment, availability of adequate reaction time and the remarkable ability of the flight director, Chris Craft, to select and integrate from many subdirectors gave us assurance that any unforeseen incident would be capably resolved.

Dr. David decided we would make a simple statement to Dr. Wiesner:

1. The committee is of the opinion that the risks associated with the planned first two flights are no greater than the risks associated with the first flights of any new high performance aircraft.
2. The probability for success is the same as that for the first flights of any new high performance aircraft.

But Dr. David brought up the *third* question from President Kennedy: "What would be the probable cost of the project to land a man safely on the moon and have him returned to earth?"

The committee turned to me. I had wrestled with that question, as we moved from center to center. I had arrived at an answer; a few simple factors led up to it. I said this topic, surprisingly enough, frequently came up for engineers estimating new jobs. Past experiences, gossip and conversations about a myriad of other, even unrelated activities such as digging subway tunnels, drilling for oil, constructing dirigibles, ships, buildings and dams— all were integrated and defined in terms of time, manpower and material. The experienced engineer often could come up with a figure within 10 percent of a cost laboriously calculated, item-by-item, by cost estimators.

A step-by-step analysis was impossible on this project. The only things we could tie to were the objective and time specified by President Kennedy. I said the total cost of a large new, high-performance airplane from its conception to the first satisfactory flight was on the order of $2-3 billion with a time of five to ten years. I said this project was going to cost ten times as much—at the very least. Consequently, in my opinion, the best estimate I could come up with was that the cost should be not less than $35 billion nor more than $50 billion.

None of the others would hazard a guess; I certainly didn't blame them. I was not too sure of my answer, but I couldn't think of a better one. Neither could the committee. They decided to go along with that estimate.

We met the next day with Dr. Wiesner. Dr. David presented our conclusions and how we had reached them. Dr. Wiesner asked for comments from the members, then reiterated our answers to the three questions asked. He thanked us and we were dissolved.

The 800-mile suborbital flight with Commander Shepard and the orbital flight with Colonel Glenn were completely successful. It is also notable that when all costs were added up as accurately as possible a couple of years after the final Apollo flight, the total was $36 billion.

Chapter XII
Hughes Aircraft, the Transition

Inventions, projects and innovations were but highlights—not only of Hughes Aircraft—but also of thousands of engineers, scientists and inventors who created during these exciting years. They brought the transition from the smokestack age to whatever this new period will be called in the future.

While important, interesting big-ticket items were carried on at Hughes Aircraft, there were also hundreds of other projects or contracts underway, nearly all involving some aspect of new high technology. To manage them, keep them in focus, do product development and fabrication and keep accountability (not only for corporate purposes) but also for the four sets of requirements from major governmental departments, was a chore for the whole company.

In these formative years of high-tech weapon systems, products were not only complex, but nearly always involved frequent change orders even after production began. In fact our largest product line was change orders—and how to handle them.

The weapon system manager must deal with frequent interruptions, precipitated by change orders, involving engineering as well as factory delays, and often pricing changes. Then customer approvals must be obtained—adding further major delays. Unsympathetic generals and congressmen often get upset.

But as Harry Truman said, "If you can't stand the heat, get out of the kitchen."

Weapon system managers have asbestos skins and iron stomachs, soft hearts and high sensitivity to customer requirements. The customer—in the air, in or on the ocean, or in the field—has to use the equipment. Both supplier and user groups *do* try to do their best for the defense of the United States, to preserve its freedoms and promote its search for peace. However, sometimes in setting individual and company objectives, we forget the special fiduciary relationship defense contractors have with the nation; nor is that responsibility always well understood by those who take office to defend the nation. All too frequently, under the whips of competition and political necessity, the government and the contractor become adversaries rather than co-workers.

An occasional reminder of that shared responsibility could help keep the record straight.

It is tragic reality that, from time to time on one side of the table or the other, a dishonest person is driven by greed to defraud the system. I personally believe that eventually they are all found out; and that overall the system functions well. It is unfortunate that these few rotten apples debase the reputations of all players, most of whom are honest and patriotic.

It is also a tragic reality that in developed free-world nations, news is a business, thriving on bad news. With often-spotlighted military and space-system procurement, some news media tend to focus on those few rotten apples and dwell but little on the great majority of supplier and customer people doing their jobs honestly and well. The continuing result is an unwarranted suspicion and condemnation by the public and politicians of all government suppliers and their customers—what has now derisively been mistakenly called the "military/industrial complex."

Hughes Aircraft, Howard Hughes and HHMI

Until early 1986, Hughes Aircraft had, in addition to its responsibility to its government customers, another fiduciary relationship—being the sole asset of the Howard Hughes Medical Institute, a public charitable trust dedicated to research for public health.

That Hughes Aircraft was owned by HHMI, with its lofty philanthropic goals, was well known to company officials and all workers. Periodic reports were issued by the Institute; on occasion seminars were given by HHMI to our management. Unquestionably, people in the company were proud of the affiliation, including the fact their company was supporting such an Institution. When the sale of

Hughes Aircraft to General Motors (at a price of more than $5 billion) was made, there was a great satisfaction evident among employees at all levels that the future of HHMI was assured; that the long-time ambition of Howard Hughes to have made the largest charitable donation in history had been realized.

I had had only minimal exposure to the Medical Institute when I first became general manager of Hughes Aircraft. However, I had hardly settled into my new job when Mr. Dietrich called to say the Governor of Florida would be in my office the following morning regarding land for the Medical Institute. I knew nothing about the Institute except the amount of the rental we paid. I asked Dietrich what it was all about and what I should do. He gave me limited information, saying my chief job was to keep the Governor happy, fill in his time until Dietrich could get an opinion from Howard Hughes on the project.

Governor Collins arrived the following morning. I received him in our board rooms. I had a sheet showing our annual sales volume—$200 million at that time with a backlog of $300 million. I told him we were the sole asset of the Medical Institute and explained that our prospects for growth were excellent.

A senior engineer gave the Governor a product briefing, including an interesting movie of Hughes equipment in operation on aircraft.

After lunch I showed him around our Culver City facility.

Although the Governor expressed polite interest in and admiration for our products and manufacturing processes, as the afternoon progressed, it became apparent we were not the primary object of his visit.

While Governor Collins climbed into an airplane, I went to a telephone to call Dietrich. I said I was running out of ammunition; the Governor insisted on going to the Hughes Romaine Street office. He expected to meet Mr. Hughes.

Dietrich reluctantly made a date to see him the following morning. It was Dietrich's task to let the Governor down easy, to retain his affirmative attitude. But the Governor was *not* going to see Mr. Hughes. It would have been totally out of character for Howard to meet with the Governor before his plans were firm. At that time, long-range goals and strategy of HHMI were in complete flux.

At that meeting, Dietrich, who knew little about the Medical Institute except for legal, tax and financial details, gave the Governor a colorful account of Hughes, his charitable inclinations, his preoccupation with the Tool Company and TWA, and the amount of time Mr. Hughes was taking with the antitrust complication, requiring his frequent attention in New York.

Mr. Dietrich, a master at dissimulation, was also very perceptive in assessing both the effect of his explanations and the Governor's remaining patience. He had Nadine Henley, secretary for Mr. Hughes, come into his office on signal. He introduced her as coordinator of Medical Institute affairs and able to report on the progress of the plan. With that, Dietrich excused himself, stating he was late for another extremely important meeting. He left the Governor in the capable hands of Miss Henley.

She talked about the proposed research hospital and meetings with the Internal Revenue Service about allowability as a tax deduction of stock of Hughes Aircraft to the Medical Institute. Miss Henley asserted this dispute was the sole reason for the delay in activating the Medical Institute. She was sure the matter of land for this great project would be settled to the Governor's satisfaction as soon as legal hurdles were cleared.

Miss Henley discovered the Governor was planning to take a flight back to Florida in the early afternoon the next day. She suggested he should again visit with me at Hughes Aircraft for further financial details. (Those tax matters had not been permanently settled 30 years later when I retired.)

The next morning I explained to Governor Collins I had been through a similar exasperating experience endeavoring to negotiate with Mr. Hughes, but it resulted in subsequent satisfactory action.

He was partly mollified, commenting that major benefactors habitually tie many strings to large gifts, always have tax problems, and that extreme patience on the part of a politician is required to complete a bequest. When he left after lunch I was as thankful to see him go as I'm sure he was to get away.

New Application for Medical Research

Several months later Mr. Dietrich requested I attend a meeting at the Beverly Wilshire Hotel. When I arrived, there were half a dozen men in the room. I had met only one, Raymond Cook, before. Mr. Cook was counsel for the Medical Institute. The others were counsel for Hughes Tool from Texas, tax counsel from Washington, D.C., and personal counsel for Mr. Hughes. I was the odd man.

It was never quite clear what we were there for, but implications were the meeting was to review the overall Hughes position with the Internal Revenue Service. The assumption was that Dietrich, or perhaps Hughes himself, would attend the meeting and give direction to the proceedings. This never happened; we sat around the room, making small talk until even that ran out. Since I was not being paid on an hourly basis, I decided there was no need to stay. I shook hands all around and left.

However, the grapevine was beginning to work; little bits of information filtered down from Romaine Street. The company chauffeur assigned to me had worked for Noah Dietrich and my predecessor. He knew chauffeurs at the Hughes office; they knew whom they drove around. By listening, I soon had a good idea of what was going on in the Medical Institute.

By the end of 1954, four people had been assigned: William Rankin, assistant to the controller for the Tool Company's Aircraft Division, had been given additional duties with respect to the Medical Institute. Nadine Henley had been charged with liaison between Rankin, Dietrich and Howard Hughes, in addition to her duties as personal secretary to Mr. Hughes. Kenneth Wright had been hired as manager of an office established at the University of Miami, Florida. Finally, Raymond Cook remained as special counsel.

At about the time I was employed, the doctors' plan for a research hospital had been presented to Howard Hughes. To their disgust, he rejected the whole idea. He said it was not his purpose to have a research hospital with all the pressures for admissions from people all over the world. That could interrupt the orderly research required in a scientific approach to the cause and cure of specific diseases. He further stated he wanted specific categories of diseases designated as ones to be examined by HHMI. He indicated that association with established research hospitals would be necessary, but he would not allow assumption of any obligation to manage nor finance these hospitals.

It was several years before I heard anything further about the Medical Institute. Regular rental payments were made to the Romaine office of the Hughes interests. On rare occasions I talked with Howard Hughes, but the Medical Institute came up only once after my first meeting with him.

Renewal of the HHMI-HAC relationship came with an invitation to attend a dinner of the Institute's Medical Advisory Board at the Bel Air Hotel, Beverly Hills. When I arrived, I was greeted by Miss Henley, who seemed to be master of ceremonies. She introduced me to the six doctors who comprised the Advisory Board. At the conclusion of dinner, Miss Henley arose, gave a greeting to us from Mr. Hughes and said it was a momentous occasion to have us gathered together for the first time. She called on me for a few remarks. (Shades of Noah Dietrich's tactics!)

Without preparation, I expressed appreciation for the privilege of being associated with such a promising enterprise—and my wish for its success.

Following me, Dr. George Thorn was asked by Miss Henley to respond. I believe he was chairman of the Advisory Board. Dr. Thorn was followed by another doctor who stated he hoped substantial financing in his area of interest would be forthcoming. Miss Henley adjourned the meeting. I went home.

There were other dinners over the '60s. At one I was introduced to the new board member, Dr. McIntyre from a medical center in Houston. The dinners were pleasant and always chaired by Miss Henley, an accomplished hostess.

Later on I received an invitation to come to the Medical Center in Houston, where Dr. McIntyre, medical chief, would host a series of briefings by heads of various activities conducted by the combined hospitals.

I accepted the invitation because I was beginning to wonder what was going on in the medical world to which we were contributing—and which would call upon us for yet more support.

The visit was impressive. A group of several hospitals in Houston, including from Baylor and Southern Methodist universities, had banded together into a Medical Center rivaling anything in the world. Dr. Michael DeBakey, the noted heart surgeon, was leader of the heart clinic. We did not hear him, but several doctors of similar stature from other hospitals and clinics gave briefings on a half dozen specialties. One of the presentations was by Dr. Thomas Caskey, who was introduced as a Hughes fellow, noted for his contribution to genetic research.

Following lunch, we visited an operating theater. I witnessed a heart bypass operation performed by Dr. Cooley, the great (but controversial) associate of Dr. DeBakey. We looked on the operation through a viewing glass directly over the operating table, watching the unhurried procedure and deft teamwork.

In a few hours, I received from authorities a new understanding of what medical progress and need were all about. It gave me a new dimension to the foresight of Howard Hughes and to the purpose for which proceeds from our work at Hughes Aircraft would be used in the future for the general benefit of humanity. I realized some of this information should be conveyed to management of Hughes Aircraft.

Within weeks I arranged for Dr. McIntyre to address the combined management clubs of the company. We had a full house of nearly 1,000 people at the Beverly Hilton Hotel. Dr. McIntyre did a magnificent job of explaining the Medical Institute's deep and substantial program.

Doctors Thorn and Caskey provided subsequent informative reports. There was an uplifting interest from our people in the variety and importance of the work the Institute was supporting with funds from profits of the company. Although an occasional scientific paper was presented by HHMI investigators, there were few basic enough to be newsworthy; their work was not widely known to the public. The unfortunate addiction of Mr. Hughes to pain-killing drugs had made him a recluse; it had changed his personality to such an extent that his previous occasional excursions into startling publicity (good or bad) no longer occurred to relieve curiosity.

My preoccupation with running a large, high tech company, combined with my membership on several government committees left me with little time to be curious about the affairs of a dormant stockholder with whom my main contact was a very intelligent and businesslike lady.

From time to time a new face would pop up. Among the first was Raymond Cook, counsel for the Medical Institute. Once or twice I was called to Washington to help Seymour Mintz and his assistants on tax matters relating either to the Medical Institute or TWA. These meetings were strangely interesting; they were one-way streets. They wanted something from me (actually, information of little consequence) but gave no information in return.

One interesting, warm friendship began early during this period. Lee Murrin invited my wife and me to have dinner with him and his wife at an old-fashioned Hollywood restaurant; the food was excellent, the conversation stimulating. He was an Irishman and assumed I was also. He went to early Mass every day of his life, was a devout Catholic and an honorable gentleman. He rigidly separated his personal life from his business life—managing the personal funds of Howard Hughes, who trusted him completely.

Over the years our friendship ripened. Since our common link was Howard Hughes, we usually had plenty to talk about. Murrin loved to hear about the progress of the Aircraft Company in what he called our "Blue Sky" operation. Once when I complained that I was not sure Mr. Hughes was getting some information I was sending to him, Mr. Murrin volunteered that he had access to him if it was important. I told him I appreciated the offer and would feel more comfortable in the future, knowing such a channel was available.

Some years elapsed before I needed Lee Murrin's help. But as the Aircraft Company grew and prospered, a struggle for power began around Howard Hughes.

Palace Politics

When Dietrich was fired by Howard Hughes he was never replaced. At first there was floundering. But with strong management in the companies, the only uncertainty was in the central office. It was now without a dominant, day-to-day, executive to hold together the diverse activities of Mr. Hughes.

Certain activities had been conducted by a young former FBI agent. Particularly in certain delicate areas, he had performed well. In a relatively short time, Hughes allocated many of the former Dietrich functions, aside from the many companies, to this man, Robert Maheu. For several years he was near, but not quite at, the top of the Hughes interests. My relationships with Bob Maheu were always cordial since he had no responsibility for, or interest in, Hughes Aircraft. Nevertheless our paths frequently crossed; he kept his word and, as far as I was able to learn, protected the interests of Mr. Hughes.

Another group was Hughes' personal attendants. Several traveled with him and, on a schedule, divided their time between a communication center at Romaine Street in Hollywood and whatever part of the world Hughes himself was occupying at the time. Major domo of this group was William Gay, through whom all correspondence and telephone calls to the Hughes headquarters were handled.

Several files traveled with Mr. Hughes. Many calls, regardless of where they were initiated, passed through the battery of recording machines at the Romaine Street office. Unusual precautions were taken to prevent bugging of phone lines. Through most of the '60s Hughes still took the precaution, on occasion, to take an old Chevrolet, find a couple of nearby, but separate pay telephones, and put a call in for me from one. He would instruct me to call him at the second pay phone—from another pay phone of my own designation—so we might have a conversation about which his "boys" would have no knowledge.

The "boys" were frequently sent on errands and were carriers of instructions to Lee Murrin, who despised most of these pretentious functionaries. But two of them were friendly and confided in him. They were his means by which I could get a message to Mr. Hughes.

Also within that close-knit group which controlled communications were the two doctors who attended Mr. Hughes. At least one of them was near him at all times.

This group was another power source competing for attention.

In 1957, when Hughes was under the gun on an anti-trust suit, he approached a firm of lawyers in New York. The firm found that it could not take his case because of a possible conflict of interest. However, a senior partner, Chester Davis, resigned from the firm and handled the anti-trust matters. It was Davis who selected that independent Texas lawyer of eminence in the constitutional law: Professor Wright. He appeared before the U.S. Supreme Court and obtained a favorable judgment in the anti-trust case.

From that successful base, Mr. Davis parlayed his influence until he became legal counsel to the Medical Institute soon after Raymond Cook, his predecessor, died in an automobile crash.

So the players in the power game were: Nadine Henley; the group headed by Bill Gay; Raymond Holliday of Hughes Tool; Raymond Cook and his successor, Chester Davis; and Robert Maheu.

Each of these players was at times in the ascendancy, sometimes more than once. They reminded me of a horse race, where one horse had the early speed and was out in front, and then the lead changed, passing back and forth during the entire race.

I was an interested observer—not a participant—of this race. My main interest was to preserve the independence of our company management. It was threatened several times before the death of Mr. Hughes.

On each occasion, I was able to get word to Mr. Hughes, who squelched the interloper. We maintained our integrity.

A Questionable Opportunity for Advancement

Shortly after the successful moon landing of our Surveyor spacecraft, I was in Las Vegas. Bob Maheu informed me Howard Hughes had decided to put me in charge of all of his holdings.

I was flattered; my first reaction was one of delight. Then reason set in. I contemplated the duties that would have to be carried out. They would include politics at all levels, from getting a sewer permit to promotion of a Presidential candidate; financial affairs, including coping with the SEC, to negotiating indentures attached to hundreds of millions in loans; and unending vigilance to monitor maneuvers by heads of giant Hughes enterprises. These considerations crossed my mind; I realized I had neither the personality, nor the span of interest, to carry on such activities.

I loved my job at Hughes Aircraft—my association with the bright young minds, expanding areas of exploration, and the reality we were literally shooting for the moon and beyond. These arenas were where my competence and interests lay. I wondered what in the world I could do to avoid this new responsibility without antagonizing Mr. Hughes. I needn't have worried. My sins caught up with me.

In my desire to diversify the business base of the Aircraft Company, I had considered participation in major rehabilitation of an area of New Orleans, Louisiana. I got involved with courts, lawyers, bankers, real estate agents and insurance people. The project soon expanded to include other parts of Louisiana. In one of these ventures, I actually put up $300,000 on behalf of Hughes Aircraft as earnest money for a major acquisition. Before negotiations were completed, however, I became concerned about the location of those funds. By devious means I found they had been transferred to a relative of one of the operators.

Ray Cook had visited a bank on behalf of Hughes Tool; a bank executive told him about our New Orleans adventure. That did it, for he also found out about the possibility of my becoming top dog.

While I was still wondering what to do about avoiding the top responsibility for Howard Hughes—and getting out of the New Orleans mess without being fired from the Aircraft Company—I learned by the grapevine there was a plan for referring this whole matter to Mr. Hughes as a lethal demonstration of my incompetence.

It seemed to me my only hope was to get to Hughes first with my version of what I had been trying to do. I spent a weekend composing a letter which in two pages described the Louisiana venture and asked for approval. I sent the letter to Mr. Hughes, through one of my special channels, marked urgent and confidential. Fortunately, my letter got to Hughes first; he sent back word I was to discontinue the project immediately.

That was all I ever heard about it from Hughes. But a year later, during another visit to Las Vegas, Bob Maheu showed me a handwritten letter he had received from Mr. Hughes, stating that since he could no longer rely on the judgment of Pat Hyland, he wanted Mr. Maheu to take care of another project. I could make all kinds of rationalizations for my actions, but the plain fact of the matter was that I had been a damn fool. The incident, however, removed me from consideration for the big job, much to my satisfaction.

Strangely, it in no way affected my continuing relationship with Howard Hughes. He had made bigger busts himself; I had offset it with other strongly positive things.

Jack Real is a Key Player

Then there was my first meeting with Jack Real. He was vice president of Lockheed Aircraft Company and had a reputation as the one man with whom Hughes liked to discuss aeronautical matters. Jack also arranged for air transportation of Hughes from one part of the world to another in his frequent travels. Jack Real was enormously respected, both in the military services and in aviation as a whole. He could arrange for aircraft and landing rights, quickly and secretly, almost anywhere.

Bob Gross, chairman of Lockheed, valued Howard Hughes as a friend and extremely good customer. He allowed Jack Real, who was important to Lockheed as a designer of airplanes, to take leave at any time, at the request of Hughes. Sometimes these periods of absence extended for several months.

Jack Real and I became fast friends and mutual admirers. He became my second channel to Hughes, one that served me well on at least two occasions. Jack differed in one important respect from others who had access to Howard Hughes: He was not trying to get control of the Hughes estate. His only desire was to befriend and protect Howard Hughes to the best of his ability.

The Transition Begins

In 1962 I reached official retirement age of 65. As is true for most Americans, I had always regarded age 65 as the milestone defining the beginning of old age and the disinclination to work. For years my plans had been made on this assumption. I had tentatively committed for activity on behalf of an educational institution and had arranged for improvements to our horse ranch near Lancaster, California, to be undertaken.

The plan, however, could not be carried out. Although Howard Hughes had always replied promptly to my requests for a major decision, the necessary 30 days notice about my retirement elapsed without acknowledgment, nor was I ever able to get any word, directly or indirectly about my retirement. I later learned he knew of the matter. And though he had long since given up the notion I was too old for the job, he just could not make up his mind what to do. This uncertainty did not bother me at all; certain personal objectives I had set for my retirement had not yet been achieved.

1. To have the company on a sound financial basis. (It was still a couple of years away in 1962.)
2. To have research, development and production going ahead on a broad spectrum of product lines. (Also still several years away.)
3. To be succeeded by an assistant general manager who had been in that office for at least three years; he in turn to have had a successor in training for his job. (Achieving this goal now required three more years.)
4. To have gradually disestablished myself from from various board committee chairmanships, a series of steps calling for internal stability and no surprises.
5. To show my successor to customers and Hughes estate litigants as being well known for his competence, experience, physical fitness and emotional stability.
6. To have all this take place during a period when there was an extended standoff, or better yet a settlement, of litigation of various HHMI and Hughes estate affairs, so that my successor could focus on the health of the business and not be concerned about "palace political infighting."

In 1962 I was in no hurry to leave. I was healthy, I did not feel old, I loved my job, I thought I was doing something useful for the company and the country and (since our daughter was in high school) I did not want to move our home.

For years I had been selecting, upgrading and training executives for the upper positions in the company. And in the '70s there were four men, progressively separated from each other by approximately five years, in line to succeed me. I was almost smug with satisfaction over my foresight and success in readying people for the top job. As so often happens though, "the best laid plans. . . . " The oldest, Roy Wendahl, took early retirement. The third in line, John Richardson, died of cancer. Number four, Bill Eicher, had a heart attack which laid him low for a year (although he survived). Only the second oldest, Allen Puckett, lasted the course and successively became assistant general manager, general manager, president, and subsequently chairman of Hughes Aircraft.

Foresight paid off. It pays to have backups.

Leadership in major corporations is a paramount requirement. However, no leader can possibly fulfill all requirements for all jobs. A successful leader in one job can be a disaster in another. No leader is a complete chameleon, enabling him to adapt into all kinds of business under all kinds of circumstances. Not even Churchill, selected by his countrymen to change certain defeat into glorious victory, could satisfy his electorate once peace had been achieved. A leader may have great accomplishments and experience, but those who select him must feel an instinctive satisfaction with his personality as well.

I am familiar with leadership in the history of Hughes Aircraft—from its formation in December 1953, to its acquisition by General Motors in 1986. Almost every problem a corporation can face was experienced by Hughes Aircraft during that period. Operating in areas where its products were of the most advanced technology, it was foremost in capturing good people as well as contracts.

Still in Charge

In the late 1970s, I had recovered from the upset of my prior succession plans. I was chairman and chief executive. Dr. Puckett was president and effectively chief operating officer. The number three man, John H. Richardson III, was executive vice president.

The three of us had been colleagues for more than 20 years. Puckett and Richardson had progressed through the ranks to the top. At that time, they had been in their assignments for more than three years.

One landmark day in spring 1978 the three of us were in my office. We had just finished discussing an intricate and troubling issue. I looked at them and in a flash recognized the time had come when all my objectives had been realized as completely as is ever possible in this moving world. Although I loved my job, I knew it was time to start letting go.

This was no instant decision, but rather the finality of many years of planning for this moment. After a brief moment of hesitation, I announced my plan for retirement.

Allen and Johnny were startled. Our relationship had been a happy and satisfactory one—and very productive. When asked if I was giving up my position as chief executive officer, I answered, "Yes." I then told them Allen should take over as chairman and John as president. I would continue as the chairman of an executive committee and some other committees, but would relinquish those posts one by one until I finally resigned from the board.

Although this plan of action was carried out step by step, its timing was more or less determined by tensions in the affairs of the Howard Hughes estate and the Medical Institute.

Superficially, this gradual change in management was a non-event. All agencies consulted quickly agreed. There was a small announcement in the *Hughesnews* on the bottom of the first page. Newspapers and national weeklies reported the changes with a small paragraph; *Business Week* said: "L. A. Hyland, chairman of Hughes Aircraft Company has announced his retirement. He is probably the most underpaid chief executive in the United States."

I probably could have stated the case a little better. I was perhaps underpaid in money, but from the achievements of the company and its preservation from inroads of opportunists after Howard Hughes' death, the rewards in satisfaction were rich indeed.

Increasing Hughes' Reclusion

Howard Hughes became more reclusive with each passing year after the 1957 dismissal of Noah Dietrich. The competition among people around him progressively intensified, each trying to take over the empire and run it as the departed Dietrich had run it. They played musical chairs through the 1960s and into the 1970s. There were many combinations, recombinations, and individual attempts to gain control. There were some partial victories and partial retreats, but no big winner during Mr. Hughes' lifetime.

The Hughes TWA interest was sold to pay the huge loans taken out for 707 jet transports and their engines. The Culver City land and plant had been put up as collateral for other loans; the interest on these loans ate into the earnings of Hughes Tool, through which the loans had been negotiated.

Howard Hughes was owner and president of the Hughes Tool Company and trustee of the Medical Institute up to the time of his death. Raymond Holliday was vice president and CEO of Hughes Tool and a member of the executive committee of the Medical Institute; Chester Davis and William Gay were the other two members of the HHMI executive committee.

This executive committee had been established by a handwritten change to the by-laws of the Institute, which also vested full trustee powers in that committee. (In later litigation, this alteration of the Institute by-laws was overturned. The Court ruled the change in the by-laws to be a forgery.)

Mr. Holliday wanted the Hughes estate to sell the shares of the Tool Company to the public, ostensibly to raise funds to pay off accumulated debt and stem the continual bleeding of the Tool Company for service of debt generated by the Nevada hotel operation and other losing Hughes operations. A side feature of such sale would be withdrawal of Howard Hughes as president, paving the way for Mr. Holliday to assume that office.

Messrs. Gay and Davis joined forces with Mr. Holliday to prevail upon Howard Hughes to sell the Tool Company. When that was accomplished, Holliday resigned from the Medical Institute executive committee, leaving Gay and Davis in sole control. In turn, Holliday was top man in the Tool Company.

Nadine Henley, for decades private secretary to Mr. Hughes, and who had kept alive the favorable public image of Hughes and of the Medical Institute, was named HHMI Secretary.

As time passed, the interest of this group of three in the relationship between Aircraft and the Medical Institute steadily increased.

This increasing interest on the part of Gay, Davis, and Henley was definitely tied to the condition of Mr. Hughes. Since leaving Los Angeles, he had been on a hegira that included Las Vegas, Boston, Montreal, Vancouver, El Salvador, the Bahamas and London. My contacts evolved from two personal visits to phone calls that were occasional, then infrequent, and then rare. His health, to my certain knowledge, was going downhill. In my opinion, the reason was unquestionably drugs, which were changing a brilliant and independent mind, and a body with great physical stamina, into an addicted slave in physical shambles.

In 1971, with five years still to live, the end for Mr. Hughes was clearly in sight. Most of the time he was in a coma that could be broken into by only a few people who knew how to arouse his interest. Various important business decisions were presented to him during his moments of lucidity. At such times he would enjoy technical talk with Jack Real and watch old films.

Concurrently, assumptions and assertions of the Medical Institute executive committee grew larger. Miss Henley was unhappy that her position of secretary of the executive committee had not proved equivalent to full membership, but the two remaining members dared not suggest any changes or additions. They took a different view, however, with the executive committee and board of directors of Hughes Aircraft. Although we treated them with courtesy and prompt compliance to their inquiries, the HHMI executive committee wanted a direct connection—and their own man—on the Hughes Aircraft Board of Directors and on its executive committee.

Pressure to make an appointment was strong and continuing. On at least two occasions I was on the brink of agreement, but managed to stave off action until my ally, who had access to Howard Hughes, obtained orders to me and HHMI forbidding such change. Howard had to walk a fine line. He needed the strength of Davis and Gay for access to his medicines and to arrange his camping places. But he could not risk their becoming too powerful within his empire. He succeeded in preserving the standoff among the executives of his various properties throughout his lifetime.

The HHMI executive committee had other concerns more demanding of their attention than Hughes Aircraft. They were somewhat involved in legal aspects and operations of five hotels acquired by Hughes, along with a regional airline (ultimately known as Hughes Airwest). All these were losing money, as was Hughes Helicopter Company—all that remained after the sale of Hughes Tool. Then there was the continuing vain attempt by Mr. Hughes to stop atomic bomb testing at Frenchman's Flats, not too far away in Nevada.

More importantly, Bob Maheu was beginning to emerge as the probable chief executive of Howard Hughes' affairs. The people around Mr. Hughes who monitored all communications to and from him became convinced of this intention. One of "the boys" (in his cups) made that known to Maheu with additional information that they would get him, the same way they got Hyland. And they succeeded. Shortly thereafter, Hughes did a disappearing act from Las Vegas (and never again returned). Maheu, who had been chief of the Hughes Nevada operations, was fired. Lawsuits began between Maheu and Hughes, from which Maheu won a judgment not yet paid because of appeals (Editor's note: True when this was written, but since resolved).

Affairs between HHMI and Hughes Aircraft remained at the same level of distrust, with occasional crossing of paths and one more attempt, also squelched, to place a man on our board. All of this was but the calm before the storm—in fact, two storms.

First was the new tax law of 1976 and second was the death of Mr. Hughes. In both cases however, we had been forewarned: on the tax law by the preliminary hearings; and on the death of Mr. Hughes by the rapid deterioration of his health.

The Tax Impact on Aircraft and HHMI

For more than 20 years the Internal Revenue Service, Howard Hughes, Hughes Tool, Howard Hughes Medical Institute, and Hughes Aircraft had been at loggerheads about tax consequences of the gift of the Hughes Aircraft to HHMI. Among other involvements, I had been subpoenaed for a hearing before a Congressional committee studying foundation taxation.

At that hearing, I watched the committee chairman and Congressional members tear apart A&P Foundation trustees for their ineffective management of the great grocery chain. After lunch, the chairman gently handled a beautiful lady who was a chief heir of the tremendous Irvine (California) estate. Without calling me to testify the committee adjourned. I went home happier and wiser about political views on large estates. However, I posed questions to our special counsel:

First, assuming Hughes would die without a will, and that HHMI had doubtful (but undisclosed) powers, and the residence of Hughes would be in question, how should Hughes Aircraft conduct itself in order to preserve its business, protect the interest of its stockholder (the Howard Hughes Medical Institute), and remain aloof from the avalanche of litigation affecting heirs and trustees and the clamorings of federal and state taxing authorities? What actions should we take now, before the passing of Mr. Hughes?

Second, what immediate actions should we take upon the death of Mr. Hughes?

Third, in the light of recent legislation favoring acquisition of companies by their employees, what might be the rights, opportunities and advantages, including the use of pension and savings funds for such purposes? Many mergers and acquisitions that are today so fashionable in American industry are funded by the application of employee pension and savings funds. Such manipulation of employee interests for the benefit of the stockholder can, in selected circumstances, be entirely legal. In the case of Hughes Aircraft, such manipulation was not an acceptable alternative.

Fourth, what would be the tax consequences if pending legislation was successful and either or both public and private medical foundations were redefined?

While no positive conclusions were reached, we did recognize the end of the halcyon days of operating a company without the burden of SEC reporting, without presentations to financial analysts, and without washing our linen before the avid eyes of the media, reaching for anything to grab public attention.

This exposure, and conversely its avoidance, is neither all good nor all bad. It may inhibit but not prevent actions by a management against the public interest. It also does not completely protect stockholders. But the requirement for public information about the affairs of large corporations is designed to help keep officials on their toes. It also helps both employees and stockholders know something about the corporations they work for or own, and provides regulatory agencies with information filtered and dissected by public experts so that intelligent decisions may be reached.

The executive and staff time, effort, and funds consumed by these disclosure functions are a major expense burden. Here is an example: a manufacturer of high-tech, classified, military equipment, must submit five pages of data per employee per month to one or another office of government. For 10,000 employees, that would be a hundred reams of reports every month.

It is foolish to expect that the risk of exposure for malfeasance is sufficient to ensure faithful service by a government or industry executive. Nor can such performance be commanded and enforced. Any system of accounting checks and balances, built to detect and thwart improper financial manipulations, can be bypassed by the sufficiently skilled and motivated operator.

Business must operate on an assumption of the good faith and honesty of most people. And most people are faithful and honest. There is a high premium on locating the best and on providing an organization wherein they can thrive and be straight. Equally there is a high premium on finding and disposing of those unable to resist temptations. That task is a major function of boards of directors and management reporting to them.

Preparing to "Go Public"

We in Aircraft needed to prepare for public operation and for appropriate accountability to whatever stockholders or owners survived the litigious days we could see ahead.

Since formation of Hughes Aircraft in December 1953, the chief executive officer and president had been Howard Hughes, who operated almost entirely in absentia. Also, as sole trustee of the Medical Institute, he had control over the stock of the Aircraft

Company. In the meantime, Aircraft had grown. Had it been a publicly-owned firm publishing its annual financial performance data, the company would have been high on the list of the *Fortune 500.* Hughes Aircraft was notable not only for its size but also for its respected position among the foremost high-tech companies.

In the early 1970s, we in management of the company recognized the passing of Mr. Hughes was inevitable. Correspondingly, our being a public company with requirements for financial disclosure, was also inevitable at some near future time. In response to this reality, we gradually adopted the reporting protocols of a public company in our quarterly reports to the Hughes Romaine Street office and to the Medical Institute. We worked up annual figures, with notes, into a complete form I believe could have been published. We did not publish those data nor initially did we furnish annual reports to Romaine Street or HHMI offices. We looked carefully at the compilations ourselves, though, making good use of them.

The Decline of Mr. Hughes

During two visits to the Bahamas in the early 1970s, I became increasingly concerned about the health and longevity of Mr. Hughes.

In London, the combination of his broken pelvis, the nearing expiration of his visa in Great Britain, and his concern about his drug supply affected his morale; he had decided to leave London and return to the Bahamas.

The departure was to take place well within the time limit on his papers and without any of the usual cloak and dagger secrecy. A deHavilland executive aircraft was leased. Mr. Hughes, Dr. Chaffin, and Jack Real headed for the Xanadu Hotel on the Great Bahama Island. The flight was without incident, but Mr. Hughes seemed to be in a sort of hopeless semi-coma from which he occasionally broke forth from an inner stirring to make a comment. One was of particular interest. Asking for Dr. Chaffin, he said, "I want to go back to the United States, but I can't because I would spend the rest of my life in court."

He was literally a man without a country.

Mr. Kelly, Howard's chief of security, and a couple of attendants had gone ahead to get the top floor of the Xanadu Hotel ready. Everything had to be sterilized to avoid any possibility of bacterial infection. Windows had to be shaded against the possibility of viewers using telescopes. Projectors were installed for old movies Hughes loved. All elevators to the penthouse floor, except one, were blocked. Only once was this sanctuary entered by an unexpected foreign object.

It occurred to me Howard Hughes had no idea of the number and variety of satellites that Hughes Aircraft had launched into space. Accordingly, I prepared an exhibit that would show a replica of each of the many satellites we had launched. These were mounted inside a Plexiglas case that could be carried through the door of our executive aircraft. A booklet was prepared with an illustration to show the position of each satellite in the case and a short explanation of the purpose of each unit. Our model makers and illustrators outdid themselves in the preparation of this exhibit. I was delighted with the completed assembly.

I telephoned Jack Real to discuss the exhibit and found he was in accord with the idea. He suggested I let him know when the aircraft would leave so he could make the appropriate arrangements for our landing in Freeport. A couple of days ahead of time when I phoned Jack Real he said he would call back when everything was ready. When he did, he said the cloak and dagger department was organized and I was to do exactly what he now told me in a set of instructions. First, I was to prepare a cloth cover for the case. Next, I was to be met by a customs agent as we debarked. This agent would take me to a closed room where the customs official would examine the exhibit. I was to leave the exhibit at that time and go with an immigration official for clearance into the country, after which I would be met by a driver who would take me to a hotel. Jack would call me sometime later in the evening.

When our aircraft landed on schedule, we were met by customs and immigration. I was hustled off to be examined and never saw the exhibit again.

Jack told me what happened thereafter. The exhibit was held in a special customs room and cleared as a museum piece on which no duty was required. It was well after dark before a van drove up and

Jack and a trusted friend loaded the case into it. Arriving at the hotel, Jack was met by two waiting porters and when the way was clear they loaded the exhibit into the elevator.

Hughes usually went to sleep in the early evening. This particular evening had been chosen because the attendant on duty was the only one Jack trusted to leave the exhibit undisturbed and ready for Mr. Hughes when he woke up. Together they carefully placed the exhibit alongside Hughes' bed. They took off the cloth cover and arranged the descriptive pamphlet to be within reach. Jack left and waited downstairs in his room.

According to the attendant, when Hughes woke up and saw this unexpected display close to his bed, his first reaction was: "What the hell is this?"

The attendant replied, "Mr. Real told me to tell you this is a satellite display prepared by Hughes Aircraft Company. The book tells you what it's all about."

Mr. Hughes read the pamphlet from cover to cover, identifying each satellite and what it would do. He read it again, giving it almost undivided attention for the next two days. Real said he became a satellite expert in those two days. He also said there was no question but that Hughes was really pleased.

As usual, there was no acknowledgment from Hughes that anything had ever happened. When Jack told me Hughes was pleased it seemed to provide an opportunity for me to write a short note to him about the continuing attempts of his Medical Institute executive committee to add a director or some kind of an official to Hughes Aircraft. I believed we needed no such help and, in particular, disapproved of the individual HHMI had in mind.

Jack agreed this time might be right for a written approach to Mr. Hughes, but stated the note had to be short, written on legal-size yellow paper with lines, and that the writing had to use letters two lines tall, and be written with ink. I just managed to get it all on one page and signed it "Pat." There was never an acknowledgment by Hughes of either the exhibit or the letter. It must be said, however, that there was never another attempt during his lifetime to impose any changes in the management of Hughes Aircraft.

Making Preparations for Post-Howard Hughes Days

By the time I returned to Los Angeles, I had determined a course of action. We had to get our house in order in all respects and prepare for the inevitable heavy weather I could foresee.

Fortunately, our top management was in place, but without suitable titles; they would have to remain that way until Mr. Hughes died. I was vice president and general manager of Hughes Aircraft, Dr. Puckett was executive vice president and assistant general manager, and Mr. Richardson was senior vice president and generally in charge of operations. Because of the insistence of the government agencies, one of us had to be designated as chief executive officer—a title I thought completely unnecessary, but I designated myself for that job. I also recognized there would have to be a man in the office in charge regardless of where the other two were at the moment.

Our business had grown rapidly so it was not unusual for one of us to be overseas, another in Washington or one of the other government agency centers in the United States, while the third was at Culver City. Therefore, to satisfy the executive situation, I created what I called an Executive Office, of which Mr. Richardson, Dr. Puckett and I were the three members. This was not an executive committee, it was an Executive Office—there was no distinction between us with respect to the capacity to act. In general we agreed that seniority would remain as before, but that when only one was present, he had complete and unquestioned authority.

The three of us had complete rapport and faith in each other. The arrangement worked very well and stood up under the rigors of doing normal business in what turned out to be heavy weather.

Upon advice of our counsel, we added another director to our board as a first step in readying a permanent arrangement. Next, we looked at minute books, financial practices, and any other internal matters that might be spread before the public, any court or government agency. Little change was required, except perhaps for cosmetic purposes, because for many years we had adopted the "gold standard" in order to ensure that in no case were we overlooking losses or obligations accounting standards would require.

We made certain our new organizational concept of the Executive

Office would be followed in practice so it would not be regarded as a hollow cosmetic principle. Approvals, appearances, perks, and compensation were glued to rules we had established for ourselves—so our actions and reactions became instinctive and the otherwise unusual became the normal mode of administration.

This Executive Office arrangement proved happy and effective. We could cover the centers in Washington, New York, London, and Zurich as well as mind the store constantly from headquarters in Culver City. Decisive action was always quickly available. Our own operating divisions received high-level visits, and on formal occasions, one or two or all of us would be on the podium so it became the custom to look upon us as a unit. We communicated with the press strictly through our public relations office since our attitude towards "leakers" throughout Hughes organizations was well known.

Of course the grapevine and the news media both informed our company personnel of what was going on in the world, but we always appeared confident and in control, never publicly discussing any problems other than regular business.

Organization changes were announced only after thorough consideration and then one step at any one time. A patient introduction over a week or two can almost always go unnoticed, while if it were all accomplished in a single day there might be employee irritation. All of us, even though we understand the need for change, nevertheless involuntarily oppose it when it happens.

The Death of Mr. Hughes

The death of Howard Hughes, a once remarkable man, on April 5, 1976, received front page coverage all over the world and especially in Texas, California, and Nevada. The situation was made to order for raiders, speculators, impostors, and of course the Internal Revenue Service and palace politicians.

It was of critical interest to 40,000 employees of Hughes Aircraft who, while recognizing the inevitability of the event, were also aware that hazards arise in changes of ownership or control.

On the day following Mr. Hughes' death, as chairman of the executive committee, with the consent of Howard Hall, the other director, I convened a meeting of the board of directors. At that meeting the board elected William Shaw, senior member of the company's legal staff to be a director, filling the vacancy created by the death of Mr. Hughes. The board also designated L. A. Hyland as chief executive officer. This action was required of companies who had contracts with the Department of Defense, and made formal the *de facto* arrangement made earlier.

Another meeting of the board was convened April 29, 1976. At this meeting, I was elected president and chief executive officer of the company. Allen Puckett was elected executive vice president and John Richardson was elected senior vice president.

At a meeting of the board August 18, 1976, the board decided to expand its membership from three to six and thereafter elected Allen Puckett, John Richardson and Richard Alden to the board. Howard Hall, who had previously retired from active duty in the company, was designated an outside director along with Mr. Alden, the outside counsel. These actions in April and August, all taken in accordance with the charter and bylaws, completed the changes in executive officers and the board of directors made necessary by the death of Mr. Hughes. They were also guided by our carefully-prepared business and legal opinions in support of our duties to the company and its stockholder.

During this same time, the Executive Committee of the Medical Institute, as well as officials of other Howard Hughes holdings, were busy trying to find a will, to determine their own legal positions, uncover the secret enterprises and contain innumerable public, private and government inquiries that kept flowing in.

None of these uncertainties, however, came from us. Our house was in order. The little flurry among company employees died down as our actions, which contained no surprises, were announced. Since we did not know to whom we had to report we waited for some sign of interest or authority.

It was early September before I received a call from Miss Henley. She said Mr. Davis was anxious to set up a meeting to discuss possible new appointees for our board of directors.

I replied there was no need for such a meeting since the Hughes Aircraft board of directors had been holding regular meetings, all vacancies for officers and directors had been filled and that business was being conducted as usual.

Over the years, in all the meetings and telephone discussions I had with Miss Henley, she was calm, collected, and articulate, with an unusually large vocabulary.

This time, in reply to my statement, she actually stuttered, could not find the right words, and hung up.

Subsequently, at the invitation of Mr. Davis, a meeting was held at the Century Plaza Hotel, attended by Messrs. Davis and Gay, representing the Medical Institute, and Puckett, Alden and me, acting for Hughes Aircraft.

Mr. Davis announced that the purpose of the meeting was to explore the relationship between the stockholder and the corporation. In his usual wordy fashion, he took quite a little time describing the rights of the trustees as custodians of the Medical Institute, with just hints of the powers they could exercise.

As spokesman for the Aircraft Company, I agreed with the stated fiduciary responsibilities of legally-appointed trustees, provided they represented an interest not invalidated by a will.

I also asserted it was incumbent upon the Aircraft Company to take a neutral position until legal rights of company ownership had been clearly established. I also stated we had ample funds and counsel to properly support our position in any state or court having jurisdiction.

Mr. Davis replied in a much lower voice, using fewer words, indicating that he understood our position. He suggested we meet a few weeks hence to review the situation. We shook hands all around and left with mutual felicitations.

We felt we had won round one, thanks to our preparation and prompt action.

Immediately after the death of Mr. Hughes, Mr. Davis and Mr. Gay had initiated an intensive search for any will that might have been made by Mr. Hughes at any time in his life. Many safety deposit box keys turned up, presumably owned by Hughes or his associates, but with no identification as to bank or security house issuing the keys. All possible leads were checked and rechecked. New wills or claims began to appear and had to be examined.

There were several relatives of Mr. Hughes who were potential heirs. The closest was an aunt, residing in Texas. Her son, William Rice Lummis, cousin of Howard Hughes, was a senior partner in the Houston law firm of Andres, Kurth, Campbell & Jones.

A second meeting was arranged by Mr. Davis. Either through HHMI or other estate activities of Mr. Hughes, Messrs. Gay and Davis now occupied the opulent executive suite at the Century Plaza Hotel that had formerly been leased by Hughes Tool. The same group met there, in the spirit of good fellowship on both sides.

Nothing of significance was brought up. Mr. Davis noted that the new tax bill might have important implications for both the Aircraft Company and the Medical Institute. The Aircraft delegates agreed, stating every effort would be made to determine the right basis for compliance. (Actually, we had already concluded from our in-house legal studies that we would live with the provisions of a public foundation, but would have difficulty meeting the requirements to be placed on a private foundation.)

Deeply involved in new legal and business problems of the Hughes estate and in the worldwide search for something relating to a possible will, Davis and Gay were busy. There was no change in the situation between the two groups for several months.

During that time, a new face appeared with the appointment by a federal judge of William R. Lummis as administrator and conservator of the Hughes estate. When first introduced to him, I noticed the astonishing similarity of his appearance to Howard Hughes. He proved to be remarkably capable as administrator and conservator. He could grasp, analyze and unravel complex issues and other matters relating to the Hughes situations. Then, one by one, he could delete, change, settle and regroup matters from all of the various elements into manageable units. He was competent, patient, thorough, had a sense of humor and a sense of purpose to protect, defend and carry out the purposes of his cousin.

To do this work, he had to leave his beloved Houston and take up residence in Las Vegas, where he was nearly inundated for several years in the activities associated with his new duties. Once, at our request, he visited Hughes Aircraft and its various establishments around the city of Los Angeles. At the end of a day, he paid us a high compliment. When asked what he thought of what he'd seen during the day, he said his foremost impression was that it was a company where the people really liked to come to work in the morning.

That answer, in the light of the healthy condition of our balance sheet, constituted a high tribute indeed. He vigorously asserted the interests of Hughes heirs in the ownership of the stock of Hughes Aircraft, and in the right of the two-man executive committee to have control of the Medical Institute. However, he assented to the court decision confirming ownership of Aircraft Company stock by the Medical Institute. Mr. Lummis reconstituted the Institute's board of trustees to include several distinguished public nominees in addition to Bill Gay, who by then was the only remaining member of the former executive committee of the Institute. Mr. Lummis was also confirmed by the court in his membership on the board of trustees of HHMI.

One day during a visit to him on another matter, and just as I was about to leave, Mr. Lummis asked how I had made out on the employee ownership matter. I grinned and replied, "You know very well how we made out. We were clobbered."

That was the actual result. But in the welter of litigation, claims, and counter claims on other issues and matters surrounding the Hughes estate and name, we had to make the try, though we knew our case was minimal. We were not surprised at the court's decision.

In all the lawyer-oriented turmoil, Hughes Aircraft was neither defendant nor plaintiff of any related litigation. Its officers and employees received but a handful of subpoenas to supply data or testimony for outside cases. To be sure, Aircraft was by then a strong company, respectably profitable, growing and highly valuable. The sharks circled about us hoping to find a route to lunge in and devour us. But our preparations during the last years of Hughes' life, and the prompt actions we took after he died, were effective barriers to outside interference.

The Howard Hughes Memorial Award

Another comment is in order. As a tribute to his cousin, in 1978 Mr. Lummis established the Howard Hughes Medal for leadership in aviation. The trophy is a beautiful sculpture, on the base of which is engraved the names of the annual recipients. The first two recipients were John K. Northrop and General James H. Doolittle.

At the annual award dinner for 1980, a very impressive affair, Mr. Lummis personally presented me with the third Howard Hughes Medal. (Editor's note: subsequent recipients of the Hughes medallion include Chuck Yeager, Robert Six, Clarence "Kelly" Johnson, Ed Heinemann, Barry Goldwater, Sr., Pete Conrad, Allan Paulson, Ben Rich, Clifton A. Moore—and Jack Real!)

Our paths cross less frequently nowadays and I notice Will Lummis spends progressively less time in Las Vegas, now that the affairs of the great estate have changed from confusion to order.

The stock of Hughes Aircraft Company was sold by the Medical Institute to General Motors Corporation, a transaction that served the best interests of all of the parties involved. General Motors and Hughes Aircraft each has a need for the talents and experience of the other.

As for the Medical Institute, the orphan duckling, initially regarded only as a tax deduction by legal and financial advisors, it has bloomed into a swan for which was laid the most beautiful cluster of golden eggs in foundation history. (Editor's note: HHMI was located in Miami, Florida; its headquarters in 1993 are in Bethesda, Maryland.)

(The court decision regarding ownership of the stock of Hughes Aircraft Company was finally made in April 1984. Among other things it threw out the handwritten insert to the HHMI bylaws. Thus this decision negated the power that had been exercised by the former trustees. The court appointed a distinguished Board of Trustees to run the Medical Institute. Dr. George Thorn, HHMI's second medical director, first appointed in the early 1950s, was named chairman of the Board of Trustees in 1984.)

The importance of these actions by the court cannot be overemphasized. Ownership of the multi-billion dollar Hughes Aircraft Company was allotted to the Medical Institute, and the authority and composition of the Institute's board of trustees were established. The claims of all others were directly or implicitly denied and the uncertainties of prior years were resolved.

The death of Hughes marked the end of an era for Hughes Aircraft (and many others). Prior to that we had lived under the umbrella of his personal image. In the early years of my association, Hughes Aircraft desperately needed that image, implying a financial competence we did not have. But performance and integrity as evidenced by our products in service, gave us recognition in the field of technology, and allowed for a liberal interpretation of our financial adequacy.

The name of Howard Hughes was magic throughout the world. He fitted well into the precepts established by P. T. Barnum, the great circus entrepreneur, who once stated that it makes no difference whether publicity is good or bad, just so you get it—and we got it indeed. There were times when we felt it was hurting, but the net result was always favorable.

From time to time in the defense business as leadership changes were made in the various administrative, congressional and military areas, there would arise (again) charges that defense contractors were slow in delivery, high in cost and inadequate in quality.

Many agencies believe each time they are discovering these deficiencies for the first time, but actually the practice of "viewing with alarm" goes far back in history. Sir Francis Bacon, in the early 1600s, wrote that the Admiralty, which buys the ships, complains that the cost is too high, the delivery too slow, and the quality is low. I expect we can look forward to the same charges at five- or ten-year intervals in the future.

Our problem with this situation was the automatic publicity value of singling out Hughes Aircraft as the very first to be examined in many of these inspection enterprises. These examinations were carried on with diligence and increasing intensity as findings became public and then one legislative committee or agency after another would climb aboard the bandwagon to grab a share of the publicity. After a few of the larger companies were reviewed, the process gradually wound down as the public and the agency were satiated for the time being.

Actually the process is necessary to keep everyone on their toes, both in government and the contractors. But each of these exercises leaves behind a series of new costly and frustrating directives, regulations and practices. It is my considered opinion that the current burden of paperwork in a complex government contract consumes at least 30 percent of the funds necessary to carry out the work. The flow of paper is enormous; it cannot possibly be digested by either contractors or government agencies concerned.

New Products in a Healthy Company

During the period of infighting among Hughes litigants, the Aircraft Company expanded rapidly in new dimensions. Some of our older products were maturing and being replaced by others, with increasing emphasis on national defense. Additionally, we were getting substantial new business in the heretofore neglected (by us) field of equipment for tactical aircraft, both for the Navy and Air Force. Another new product line, chosen for development back in 1960, was systems for deployment into outer space. We were becoming an extremely important supplier of space systems, not only exploratory vehicles, but also commercial and utilitarian vehicles such as communication, geophysical, and meteorological satellites. The acquisition of three small companies also gave Hughes Aircraft important new product lines:

✈ The Santa Barbara Research Center (SBRC) made infrared and multi-spectral detectors and scanners widely used on weather and earth-resources satellites. SBRC also makes night vision equipment.

✈ The Vacuum Tube Products Company, which became Vacuum Tube Products Division, produced radar and oscilloscope display tubes and storage-display tubes and commercial laser cloth cutters. Portions of this operation were split off and combined with microwave amplifier technology from Hughes Research Laboratories, to create a business which has thrived as the Microwave Tube Division.

✈ A specialty castings company became the kernel of the Hughes Connector Division.

A truly major product family evolved from internal company activities within the Hughes Radar Group. These are the electro-optical technologies and products used in aircraft fire control equipment and later in space operations. They have led to development of a product group which now has a $1 billion a year business.

Another activity was inspired by a conversation with an old friend who had retired as senior scientist at the Naval Research Laboratory.

He pointed out the limited number of suppliers of sonar equipment in the important field of underwater detection and guidance and suggested we might be well advised to get into this field. From my days with the Underwater Sound Division of the Naval Research Laboratory, I recognized the validity of his reasoning. I prevailed upon our Ground Systems Group in Fullerton, California, to consider underwater systems. Their first step was construction of a huge wooden water tank and employment of two or three underwater sound engineers. The company assigned a couple of top-rate systems engineers to the team and with a small staff and a big tank, we entered the sonar business. We ultimately made substantial contributions to the Navy undersea warfare business.

Simultaneously we were invited to apply our aircraft fire control skills to the new submarines being developed. This work ultimately resulted in an important association with *Polaris* and subsequent nuclear submarine programs and a further acquaintance with the undersea warfare operations of the Navy.

We were invited to participate as a subcontractor in a new Navy torpedo program. I worried about that opportunity.

The Challenges of a New Product Line

The decision to take on a new product line involves consideration of technology, competition, market to be served, fabrication, funding and a host of other topics. Even in a small operation it is difficult for one person to know enough about each of these requirements to make a correct decision. And succeed. But as a company grows larger, and more products with larger stakes are involved, it is unlikely any one person can have appropriate familiarity with all these requirements. The person at the top has come up through the ranks usually with one basic specialty. He (or she) fancies himself as competent to make a judgment on all issues regarding that specialty.

But in the high-tech game, advances are so rapid that even a five year absence from the "drawing board" almost destroys the value of any judgment developed in the past. Nevertheless, an amazing number of executives make unassisted judgments about product selection, sometimes reaping disastrous results. The use of experts from within or consultants from without the organization is not a sign of weakness or incompetence, but on the contrary, is proof of comprehension.

The standard torpedo in the U.S. Navy in World War I and for sometime thereafter was the Whitehead torpedo. It had an ingenious steam driven propulsion system and relied on a gyroscope to maintain a course towards the target to which it was aimed. It carried enough explosives to blow an enormous hole in the side of any ship and a relatively simple detonator to ignite the explosive upon contact with the ship. These torpedoes were manufactured in Naval factories and were adequate for the slow moving ships and submarines of the World War II era. Their successors, however, intended for use against deep-running, fast submarines and fast surface ships, were very unsatisfactory.

For two decades the Navy wrestled with inferior designs and problematic production. Finally, breaking away from traditional suppliers, the Navy approached two companies with no prior torpedo experience in an effort to inject the same kind of innovation and high technology into torpedoes as was being used in guided missiles. One of the companies, with Navy approval, invited Hughes Aircraft to provide the guidance and control for an extremely powerful multipurpose torpedo.

In the course of my government technical committee experience, I was well aware of the technical headaches and economic loss of torpedo suppliers and had made known my view that no one in his right mind would enter the torpedo business. Consequently, I was astonished one day when the group executive and chief engineer of our Ground Systems Group came to my office with a proposal that they would like to enter the torpedo business as a component contractor. They addressed the technology, manufacturing issues, competition, size and stability of the market, plus the opportunity to broaden our association with a fast growing part of the Navy. They also presented calculations of the appropriate long-term funding, conservative projections of time for design, testing and startup; and also argued with conviction that our part of this new torpedo was well within the expertise of their group and the company.

They had done their homework.

While they were supporting their story with graphs and illustrations,

I realized my knowledge of weapons was obsolete. My function was not to be the expert, but rather to comprehend the summation of the whole, assist the generality of their plans and conclusions, and compare this opportunity with that of other areas to be considered over the next 20 years—from inception to final product delivery.

After all, these men were not dreamers. They had demonstrated by experience, accomplishment, and profitability that they had a solid base for this business proposition.

Prompt review by senior officials, assessments that the risk was well within the tolerance we had accepted for other ventures, and it was within the scope of our abilities, led to approval of the proposal. Within a couple of years, the Navy confirmed our judgment by appointing us as a prime contractor to take the responsibility for the entire torpedo project.

I emphasize that the function of men in the so-called "ivory tower" is not that of final authority on the various elements involved in such a project. But by integration of experience, imagination, responsibility, faith, assessment of people, plus a sixth sense characteristic of leadership, they make choices upon which the health of their company depends.

Thus, my oft-stated prejudice against the torpedo business was overcome by a willingness to listen, a mind open to reason, confidence in innovation, and a profound respect for the organization.

A Metamorphosis at Hughes Aircraft

During the decade following 1976, employment of Hughes Aircraft doubled. It is well to remember that the best measure of size is number of employees since the effects of deflation and inflation are eliminated. Note also that the job of acquiring people and facilities to expand a high technology business from 40,000 to 80,000 people is a vast undertaking.

In the financial area, despite the heavy use of leasing and securing of advance payments from customers, the company went from a no debt position to nearly $1 billion of debt to provide working and fixed capital for expanded operations. Facilities and finances were, however, a minor problem compared with the essential and difficult job of finding and hiring thousands of scientists, engineers, and technicians of the quality and experience needed for high technology research, development and manufacturing.

The financial risk was minimized because many of our products could not be supplied by anybody else on earth. The hazard was assumed because the uncertainties surrounding legal ownership of the Hughes Aircraft prevented the issuance of any form of security.

Allen Puckett, who succeeded me as president and then chairman of the board, guided the corporation during the years of its greatest expansion and logistic exposure. He did a masterful job in the complex negotiations which took place when the board of trustees of the Medical Institute decided to sell Hughes Aircraft to comply with the law as regards excessive concentration of the assets of philanthropic foundations. HHMI initiated an auction of the company and had four bidders.

The successful one, General Motors, paid $5.2 billion for the company I had resurrected from the brink of insolvency 30 years before. At that, General Motors got a bargain. The technical, manufacturing, product and marketing attributes of the two companies complemented each other beautifully and managements of the two companies were completely compatible. Just what did General Motors get for its major investment? At the time of the acquisition Hughes Aircraft had six major product groups and one international group that took care of the worldwide distribution of the products of the other groups. Each of the product groups comprised about 12,000 people and accounted for about $1 billion of sales per year. Each was a complete business in itself with all responsibilities, varieties of personnel and markets to match. These groups were assisted and guided by a central organization that exercised coordinating functions supervised by specialist vice presidents.

The basic businesses of Hughes Aircraft and General Motors are different. Hughes products can be characterized by its satellites, most of which we invented; prices are around $100,000,000 each, with quantities around a dozen a year. Primarily General Motors' products are automobiles, manufactured in the millions per year, with prices averaging $10,000 each. (Editor's note: at the time this was written.)

Hughes' markets are mostly governments; General Motors' markets are the people as a whole.

In the highly competitive markets of the world's leading nations, these two diversified producers in combination will be an example of the type of organization needed in America to do business with the entire world.

To casual observers it seemed the mighty Goliath had overvalued the skills and innovations of little David. To the initiate, however, the decisive factor in the equation is that thousands of engineers, scientists, technicians, fabricators, marketers and administrators understand and are stimulated and encouraged by this association. A technology transfer—fallout, if you will—between high technology products for government and the consumer sector will be a positive dividend of this acquisition.

The addition of Hughes and Electronic Data Systems (EDS) to the GM organization at this time regained for General Motors the essential balance in the entire corporate network so remarkably achieved over a half century ago by the combination of Alfred Sloan in administration, "Boss" Kettering in engineering, Alfred Bradley in finance and William K. Knudsen in manufacturing.

Changing of the Guard

My withdrawal from active executive management of Hughes Aircraft was completed in 1980. However, my successors welcomed my continued occasional presence on the scene to take part in committees of the board and to act as a sounding board for their operating and long-range plans.

Not everything undertaken after 1980 worked out as projected by new top management. How do I confront that reality and comment upon events without looking like a Monday morning quarterback, a wizard of 20/20 hindsight?

Biased by frugal habits associated with financing earlier company growth, I was reluctant to endorse the rapidly increasing use of bank credit, deferred taxes, and long-term leases as the means of financing accelerating growth in the '80s. With my 1929 syndrome, I was chary of long-term commitments financed by short-term bank loans.

Consequences vary from heroic to disastrous; history shows the latter usually prevails.

In our case, in my judgment, two other important factors loomed. First were the enormous, stable contributions made by our engineers, scientists and factory people across the spectrum of defense and space electronics. Their performance seemed to assure a long-range, profitable business. The second factor, however, was the risk inherent in dependence upon large government contracts. Political volatility could be initiated by events ranging from the trivial to the momentous and trigger large reactions within governments and companies and the people of both. Continuity of interest, enthusiasm and responsibility on our part would be required to maintain assurance in the mind of the ultimate user that he is relying on the very best technology and industry can provide. The rate of our sales growth was at its peak at this time, as was profitability. A range of new products was getting into production and delivery. Studies of our backlog, our product life, cycles, research and facilities needs, and schedules of fixed and current capital all showed we were headed into a financial region beyond the purpose and function of ordinary short-term bank loans.

The three-person Executive Office, which had functioned well preceding and following the death of Mr. Hughes, had been reduced to two by my retirement, though I retained a temporary association as chairman of three board committees—Executive, Finance, and Audit and Compensation. The board remained intact with only exchanges of title: I was a member; Dr. Puckett became chairman.

In the first year, this arrangement functioned well. But with continued rapid growth, combined with ownership uncertainty requiring careful attention, there was ever-increasing demand for executive time. Our facilities-building and leasing program, which involved hundreds of millions of dollars, was beginning to show cost overruns and schedule problems. Rifts began to develop between the Executive Committee of the board and the Executive Office, but were patched over for a time. I finally resigned from my board seat since my old-fashioned caution could never be reconciled with the younger entrepreneurial viewpoint I had fostered in Dr. Puckett—and which he now had every right to exercise.

The Puckett/Richardson team kept the giant corporation of uncertain ownership, solvent customers and talented people under finely balanced control. Then the unthinkable happened. John Richardson, the charismatic, talented and athletic president of the company was found to have an incurable cancer. He died within a short time. John Richardson left behind a legacy of achievement, humanity and integrity that will continue to influence the company.

Months elapsed before a replacement was selected. Dr. Puckett was for a time the sole corporate officer with top executive status. During the interim, however, it was considered necessary to rescind the board action establishing the Executive Office. Dr. Puckett retained his position as chairman of the board and chief executive officer.

Trade associations, outside directorships and political considerations competed for Chairman Puckett's time. Defense, space and the company's satellite ventures clamored for attention as new and heretofore unknown problems in these areas developed. The business in hand was large; new growth dictated that the company was constructing, occupying or equipping facilities with consequent high start-up costs and inevitable confusion. These situations demanded experienced decision making.

The delay in filling top executive vacancies exacerbated the situation: It side-tracked the appropriate delegations of authority, resulting in a bottleneck at the highest level in the decision process; moreover, the slow selection of the people to fill the two or three open executive positions was an unsettling factor amongst the candidates. This extended several levels below. Speculation, rumors and frustrations were rife; they took the fine edge off morale so necessary for highest motivation.

Synergism became cooperation; cooperation became adherence to procedures and enthusiasm was beginning to wear away as individuals or groups began to adopt attitudes normal in a bureaucracy. There was more attention to form, rather less to substance. Trappings became more important than efficiency.

It is axiomatic that there can be no indictment without an intention to do wrong. Here there was certainly no such intention. Among the events requiring executive attention were the increasing demands of the Medical Institute (after the decision of the court certifying to its ownership of Hughes Aircraft). It soon became apparent the new board of trustees of HHMI wanted to sell or exchange all or part of its holdings of Hughes Aircraft stock to a qualified buyer. We had anticipated such a move, but its reality caused stirrings up and down our lines. We considered the rigmaroles imposed on public corporations by the SEC and other dedicated public officialdom in their mission to protect the interests of stock and bond holders.

With this prospect in mind, the management of Hughes Aircraft redoubled its efforts to prepare the affairs of the corporation and its operating units for the intense scrutiny we would doubtless be exposed to in the near future.

The temporary changes in the board of directors which took place immediately after the death of Mr. Hughes and which were further changed in response contingencies during the next four or five years, tended to take on a new shape in the early '80s.

The little executive committees prior to 1976 and the small board of directors thereafter allowed for first-hand discussion among top executives of past performance, present operations and future planning. Communications, delegation and decisions were thorough and prompt. The smaller boards were well suited for running the business when public ownership was not an issue. The new board was suitable to handle the sale, merger, legal, tax and financial problems that were just ahead.

There was an interim board which included a couple of outsider directors. The important function served by this short-lived group was to reelect the chairman, appoint the former controller as president and to designate the former outside counsel as an employee and elect him to be vice chairman of the board. The two latter appointments were a surprise indeed! Heretofore, corporation top management had been of an engineering bias; now it was apparent legal, accounting and finance were the look of the future.

The Changing World Social Structure

Hughes Aircraft was not alone in this changing scene. Beginning with the astonishing technical developments increasingly used in World War II, which spread by way of military, industrial and public acceptance during the next quarter century, scientists and engineers pioneered the route into the new territory of technology. Students thronged to take technical courses and became the darlings for which industry paid high salaries.

A milestone was reached in the successful moon landings. There were breathtaking accomplishments in other widely diverse areas as well.

Such a peak cannot be long maintained nor even absorbed by society. Inevitably, the letdown took place, even in such seemingly solid and revered entities as NASA, the Presidency and the student bodies of the great universities. Business administration and law are now the favorite subjects and the ones that attract the best pay upon graduation.

We reached a peak at Hughes Aircraft in the early '80s when the rate of growth was at its highest and demands upon all levels and departments of management were strained to the utmost. And, of course, at that time Murphy's Law went into effect. When the company most needed their attention, the three senior management officials became completely occupied with negotiations of the stock sale to General Motors and provisions for the continuation of the company.

General Motors, the Medical Institute, Will Lummis (both in his capacity as chairman of Summa Corporation and as a director of the Medical Institute) and Hughes management did a superb job, not only in negotiating price and terms, but also in providing for preservation of Hughes management and for introduction of an enlightened control of Hughes Aircraft by General Motors.

Unfortunately, Congressional furor and probes into the now infamous costs of a hammer and toilet seat that seemed to epitomize the "military/industrial complex" made it particularly difficult for us.

Hughes Aircraft had simultaneous demand for attention from three sectors: running the ongoing business; coping with government and media probing of procurement practices; and the concurrent examinations, negotiations and publicity associated with merger of our company with General Motors. Moreover, in addition to the three interested parties—General Motors, Hughes Aircraft and Howard

Hughes Medical Institute—there was impact on the subject from Summa Corporation, the Hughes estate and government interest, all big-time importance. In addition to direct staffs of these interested parties, there were also big name industrial and financial advisors—at handsome fees.

Security analysts and journalists had a field day in their speculation about prices, purposes and problems among competing bidders for Hughes Aircraft in what was billed as the second largest merger in business history.

Unfortunately, General Motors bore the brunt of most critical media comments. They were depicted as being the voracious buyer that was going to splinter Hughes Aircraft for its own benefit; alternatively they would inject their own management throughout the company; or worse—the same unhappy marriage would take place as with H. Ross Perot and his Electronic Data Systems Company.

Actually, the exact opposite was the fact, as is not unusual with fast, superficial exposure of media to complex corporate affairs with only short-term public interest.

The new board included an equal number of Hughes and GM officials. A General Motors' executive vice president, Don Atwood, was assigned to coordinate the new electronic company comprising Hughes Aircraft, Delco Electronics and Electronic Data Systems.

Don Atwood was an ideal choice for that job. Earlier he had been employed at the Stark Draper Laboratory of the Massachusetts Institute of Technology. I knew the laboratory well and knew Dr. Draper never tolerated any but the very best on his staff.

The General Motors' administrative rule of retirement at age 65 concurred with that established at Hughes Aircraft. In our case, however, the rule had not been enforced with respect to senior executives for the past two or three years because of possible merger complications. With most uncertainties removed, a gradual compliance with the rule became effective. My initial concerns about a merger with GM were quieted as I became better acquainted with GM management. During the long period between the administrations of Alfred Sloan and Roger Smith, there had been growth in volume and profits, but also a growth in complacency and bureaucracy. Those factors, too, had grown up within Hughes Aircraft, though to a smaller degree. The managements of both companies were in the process of correcting these conditions.

The automobile business, with its seasonal manufacturing, sales schedules and quarterly financial reports, is an entirely different business from that of Hughes with its long-term commitments and occasional extraordinary expenses based on the ever-changing military and space environment. Unquestionably these facts worried many Hughes people. But with early fears overcome by visits of top rank GM executives and the disposition they evidenced to leave the company to manage its own affairs, our people settled down to do just that, including the appropriate correction to our bureaucracy and readjustments needed to satisfy the Department of Defense.

Epilogue

The principal reason for documenting this lengthy tome on my career is to pass along to current and future generations what I learned over a period of more than 80 years that ranged from a youthful entrepreneur through Army and Navy service, as well as by personal experience, together with exposure to two giants of industry responsible for creating major corporations.

If nothing else comes of this effort, I hope the message of hope when I went out on my own—"For all I knew about business I might as well have been raised in a convent"—comes through to each of you thinking about striking out on *your* own.

As I near the end of my life, I look back with considerable satisfaction on the lessons I've learned. But, I feel a strong obligation to chronicle those lessons and that lifetime. I hope I have done so in the pages of this book.

The experience I gained has given me valuable insight into how to utilize research and development and to grasp its tremendous value in any technical enterprise. I have been a manager both in large corporate organizations and in a small business. My experience includes the creation and loss of an enterprise where I made mistakes on my own, with my own money, and ultimately had to sell out.

The achievement of synergism among groups, and management by principle, or in fact the installation of any management element, is not a one-shot product, but must be firmly and continually promoted and carefully enforced. This activity involves time and patience and an understanding of the fact that, adult or child, we do not like to be told that something is good for us, but rather we like to feel that we do something because it is our own idea. It frequently is, but in most cases it is latent, even very latent.

I hope this book has been fun . . . . an adventure . . . . and that it was your own idea to read it.

Good luck in the years ahead.

(Editor's Note: Pat Hyland joined Hughes Aircraft in 1954 as vice president and general manager; became its president in 1976 following the death of Howard Hughes; retired from his active management role in 1980; remained on the Board of Directors; was named Chairman Emeritus in 1984. Mr. Hyland died November 24, 1989. Continuing his commitment are his wife, Muriel, and daughter, Ginger. This work has been dedicated to them.

In its detailed obituary November 26, 1989, the *New York Times* headline read: *L.A. Hyland, Radar Pioneer, 92; Howard Hughes's Top Executive.)*

Index

A

B

C

D

E

F

G

H

I

J

K

L

M

N

O

P

Q

R

S

T

U

V

W

X

Y

Z